INSIGHT GUIDES

East African WILDLIFE

Discovery CHANNEL

APA PUBLICATIONS
Part of the Langenscheidt Publishing Group

INSIGHT GUIDE
EaST aFRICan
WILDLIFE

Editorial

Managing Editor
Clare Griffiths
Editorial Director
Brian Bell

Distribution

UK & Ireland
GeoCenter International Ltd
The Viables Centre, Harrow Way
Basingstoke, Hants RG22 4BJ
Fax: (44) 1256 817988

United States
Langenscheidt Publishers, Inc.
36–36 33rd Street 4th Floor
Long Island City, NY 11106
Fax: 1 (718) 784 0640

Canada
Thomas Allen & Son Ltd
390 Steelcase Road East
Markham, Ontario L3R 1G2
Fax: (1) 905 475 6747

Australia
Universal Publishers
1 Waterloo Road
Macquarie Park, NSW 2113
Fax: (61) 2 9888 9074

New Zealand
Hema Maps New Zealand Ltd (HNZ)
Unit D, 24 Ra ORA Drive
East Tamaki, Auckland
Fax: (64) 9 273 6479

Worldwide
Apa Publications GmbH & Co.
Verlag KG (Singapore branch)
38 Joo Koon Road, Singapore 628990
Tel: (65) 6865 1600. Fax: (65) 6861 6438

Printing

Insight Print Services (Pte) Ltd
38 Joo Koon Road, Singapore 628990
Tel: (65) 6865 1600. Fax: (65) 6861 6438

©2006 Apa Publications GmbH & Co.
Verlag KG (Singapore branch)
All Rights Reserved

First Edition 1989.
Third Edition 2003. Updated 2006

CONTACTING THE EDITORS
We would appreciate it if readers
would alert us to errors or out-
dated information by writing to:
Insight Guides, P.O. Box 7910,
London SE1 1WE, England.
Fax: (44) 20 7403 0290.
insight@apaguide.co.uk

www.insightguides.com

ABOUT THIS BOOK

This guidebook combines the interests and enthusiasms of two of the world's best-known infor-mation providers: Insight Guides, whose titles have set the standard for visual travel guides since 1970, and Discovery Channel, the world's premier source of non-fiction televi-sion programming.

The editors of Insight Guides pro-vide both practical advice and general understanding about a des-tination's history, culture, institu-tions and people. Discovery Channel and its website, www.discovery.com, help millions of viewers explore their world from the comfort of their own home and encourage them to ex-plore it first hand.

Insight Guide: East African Wildlife is structured to convey an under-standing of the region and its wildlife as well as to guide readers through its sights and activities:

◆ The **Features** section, indicated by a yellow bar at the top of each page, covers the history of safari and profiles the region's wildlife in a series of informative essays.

◆ The main **Places** section, indi-cated by a blue bar, is a complete guide to all the sights and areas worth visiting. Places of special interest are coordinated by number with the maps.

◆ The **Travel Tips** listings section, with an orange bar, provides a handy point of reference for information on travel, national parks, safari lodges, shops, restaurants and more.

The contributors

This edition was edited by **Clare Griffiths** at Insight Guides' London

Map Legend

—— ·· —	International Boundary
————	Province Boundary
⊖	Border Crossing
·—·—	National Park/Reserve
————	Ferry Route
✈ ✈	Airport: International/Regional
🚌	Bus Station
❶	Tourist Information
✉	Post Office
✝ ✝	Church/Ruins
✝	Monastery
☾	Mosque
✡	Synagogue
🏰	Castle/Ruins
⌂	Mansion/Stately home
∴	Archaeological Site
∩	Cave
⚊	Statue/Monument
★	Place of Interest
▪	Safari Lodge
△	Tented Camp

The main places of interest in the Places section are coordinated by number with a full-colour map (e.g. ❶), and a symbol at the top of every right-hand page tells you where to find the map.

and updated the feature essays on wildlife. Pike and his Kenya team also contributed to the Kenya Places and Travel Tips sections.

Philip Briggs, a travel writer based in Johannesburg, South Africa, has travelled widely across Africa. The author of 10 travel guides to African destinations, including South Africa, Tanzania, Uganda, Kenya, Ethiopia, Malawi, Mozambique, Ghana and Senegal, Briggs contributes regularly to a number of leading wildlife periodicals in South Africa and the UK.

As a major contributor to this guide, Briggs wrote the chapters on Uganda, Ethiopia and Rwanda and contributed to the chapters on Tanzania. He also assembled a new Travel Tips section and acted as an invaluable editorial consultant throughout. Briggs has also worked on *Insight Guide: Tanzania and Zanzibar,* and *Discovery Travel Adventures: African Safari.*

Contributors whose work has been retained from the previous edition of this guide include: **Karl Ammann, Deborah Appleton, Dr Harvey Croze, Dr Daniel Stiles, Peter Darvey, James Ashe, Sir Michael Blundell, Mary Anne Fitzgerald, Dudley Chignall** and **Iain Allan.**

Many of the striking images in this book are the work of renowned wildlife photographer **Ariadne Van Zandbergen**. Other noted photographers whose work appears here include **Karl Ammann, David Keith Jones** and **Tony Church**. **Sylvia Suddes** proofread the text and **Penny Phenix** indexed it. This edition of the guide was updated by Philip Briggs and supervised in-house by **Richard Carmichael**.

office. It was based upon the first edition, managed by **Geoffrey Eu**.

This book distills the very best safari experiences to be found in East Africa. Although it is aimed at those planning to go on a safari, it also discusses some major environmental and conservation issues. Because of difficulty of access for travellers or political instability, not all game reserves and national parks in the region are covered. But those explored encompass East Africa's extraordinary wealth of wildlife and variety of eco-systems.

Jeffery Pike, a London-based journalist and photographer, has travelled extensively in Africa since 1984. The editor of *Insight Guide: Kenya* and a contributor to *Insight Guide: Tanzania and Zanzibar,* he wrote the chapter on invertebrates

INSIGHT GUIDE
EastAfrican WILDLIFE

CONTENTS

Maps

Introduction

History

Features

A reticulated giraffe makes its way across a dirt road in the Meru National Park, Kenya.

Travel Tips

◆ **Full Travel Tips index is on page 321**

Places

AN ENCHANTED WORLD

East Africa is the last great refuge of wildlife forced

from the rest of the planet by human incursions

To go on safari is to enter an enchanted world. As Beryl Markham wrote in her wonderful evocation of 1930s Kenya, *West with the Night*: "Africa is mystic; it is wild; it is a sweltering inferno; it is a photographer's paradise; a hunter's Valhalla, an escapist's Utopia. It is what you will and it withstands all interpretations." Africa is very addictive. Few people visit only once. Most are drawn back again and again, venturing further into remote tangled corners, searching for the peace that comes only from immersion in the natural world.

While the animals are undoubtedly magnificent, there is much more to safari. It is important to leave behind your preconceptions and your fears of the unknown and look beyond the headlines to see the entire world of the African bush, down to its smallest insect inhabitants. Many of the plants you will see, from the humble wildflower to the pendulous fruit of the sausage tree, have medicinal properties only now beginning to be fully understood.

This book distills the very best experiences to be found in the East African bush, drawing a vivid portrait of its wonderful wildlife and the extraordinarily varied ecosystems that it inhabits. It is difficult to choose which national parks and game reserves to visit. Some fine reserves are unfortunately out of bounds as a result of the political turmoil that all too frequently ravages this part of the world. Others are so difficult to reach that only the most dedicated and resourceful traveller will make the journey.

Those that are covered in this book encompass mountains, rainforests, wetlands, woodlands, grasslands and even the underwater world. They represent an extraordinary wealth of wildlife, from the wildebeest herds of the Serengeti to the gentle mountain gorillas of Uganda. Most of the parks offer birdwatchers several hundred species to choose from in an aerial extravaganza unheard of in the Northern Hemisphere.

East Africa will inspire passions – some dark, some euphoric. It is subtle, complex, anguished, exotic, startlingly beautiful and waiting to be discovered. ❏

PRECEDING PAGES: mountain gorillas live in groups under a mature or silverback male; a pride takes a drink at a waterhole; hippos floating in a pool; close-up of the striking bateleur eagle.

LEFT: a young cheetah rests in the long grass during the heat of the day before starting to hunt in the late afternoon.

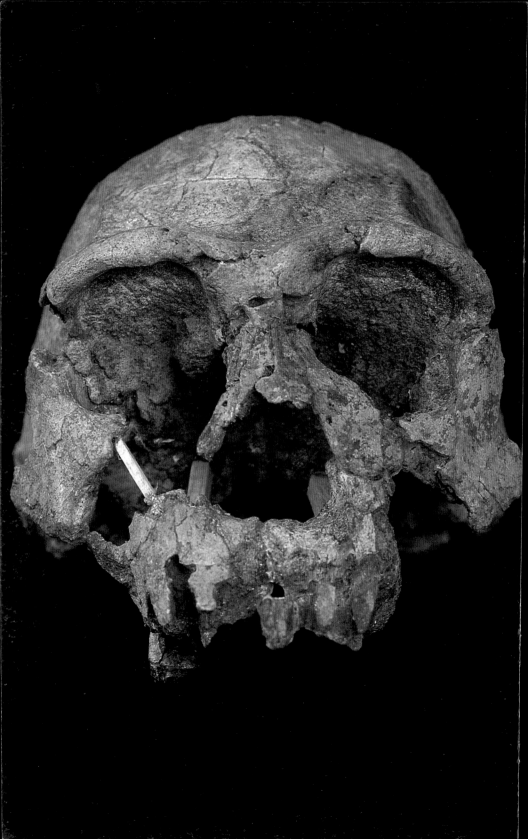

ORIGINS OF MAN

East Africa has yielded spectacular archaeological finds which suggest that the region was the first home of human beings

East Africa has provided more evidence of the physical and cultural evolution of Early Man than any other region on earth. But the story of the search for the "missing link" and the evolution of humankind is as much a question of differing opinions and personalities as it is of science.

The Great Rift Valley stretching from southern Turkey, through Israel and the Red Sea, and down the length of Ethiopia, Kenya and Tanzania into Mozambique contains a wealth of fossil remains. This huge, uneven trough in the earth has acted as a geological museum to collect, preserve and display the remains of animals and plants which lived, evolved or became extinct over the past several million years.

A long series of lakes exists on the floor of the rift. These lakes fluctuate in size over time, sometimes disappearing completely. Bones of animals which died nearby were covered first by water, then by silt, a process that preserved them as fossils. After a lake dries up, or its shoreline recedes, soil erosion may expose the fossilized bones which can then be discovered by curious *Homo sapiens* – modern man.

Bone hunters

The first curious *Homo sapien* to look for human remains in East Africa was L.S.B. Leakey, sometimes called the father of East African archaeology. Louis Leakey was born in Kenya to an English missionary family. He intended to follow in his father's footsteps as a missionary, but after a rugby accident in 1926 he was sent to "rest" on a dinosaur fossil expedition to Tanganyika with the British Museum.

Over the next 45 years he conducted archaeological and palaeontological research into virtually every period between the Miocene, some 25 million years ago, up to the Later Stone Age only a few centuries past. Leakey's ideas about

the evolution of early mankind influence theories up to the present day. After Leakey's death in 1972, his wife Mary and their son Richard continued to support his most controversial belief: that the genus *Homo* had very ancient origins, contemporary with or even preceding the genus most experts accepted as our right-

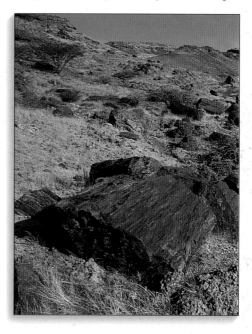

ful ancestor, *Australopithecus*. Most debates during the 1960s and 1970s about early human evolution centred on this belief.

The most important site worked by the Leakeys was Olduvai Gorge in northern Tanzania. It was discovered in 1913 by a German, Hans Reck, who was chasing a butterfly across the Serengeti plains. The Leakeys explored Olduvai from 1931 to 1959 without discovering a human fossil of any importance.

Then in 1959, Mary found the skull and jaws of a primitive hominid which was eventually classified as *Australopithecus boisei*, a species that became extinct about a million years ago. At the time of discovery this large-toothed

LEFT: skull ER 3733, found beside Lake Turkana and later identified as *Homo erectus*.
RIGHT: petrified wood in Sibiloi National Park dates back over 20 million years.

"Nutcracker Man" created a great sensation which led the National Geographic Society in the US to fund the Leakeys' research. In subsequent years many other hominid fossils were discovered at Olduvai, ranging in age from 1.85 million years to only a few thousand years old. But rather than solving the evolutionary puzzle each new fossil created more confusion as researchers interpreted the size, shape and markings of the skull parts, teeth and limb bones in different ways.

The most controversial find was one identified as *Homo habilis* by Louis Leakey. He believed it to be the maker of the oldest stone tools. It lived some 1.8 to 1.6 million years ago at the same time as another small form called *Australopithecus africanus*, first discovered in limestone caves in South Africa. If his interpretation were correct, it meant there were two forms of *Australopithecus*, one large and one small, living alongside the genus *Homo*. This was difficult for many to accept. Leakey defended his *Homo* by claiming that it had a larger brain than *A. africanus*.

Controversial bones

Most scientists agree that a type of forest ape of the *dryopithecine* family was the ancestor of

HIGH LIFE IN THE HIGHLANDS

East Africa has an impressive wealth of archaeological sites, from the oldest in the world, at Hadar, Omo and west Lake Turkana, all dating to more than 2 million years ago, up to Swahili coastal ruins of towns only a few centuries old.

In Kenya at Koobi Fora, on the shores of Lake Turkana, there is an interesting museum, a campsite and simple *bandas* (self-catering huts) which can be booked through the National Museum of Kenya in Nairobi, which also has a very interesting display on human evolution and archaeology.

In Tanzania visitors can explore a small museum and several of the sites at Olduvai Gorge excavated by Mary and Louis Leakey. There is also a small museum at Laetoli, south of the gorge.

Tourists can visit Melka Kunture in Ethiopia where there are several sites of the Oldowan (pebble tools) and Acheulean (hand-axe) cultures dating to several hundred thousand years ago. It is not practicable to try to visit Hadar or Omo. Finds from all these sites can be viewed in the National Museum of Ethiopia in Addis Ababa.

There are no excavation-site museums in Uganda, Rwanda, Burundi or the Democratic Republic of Congo, but archaeological research is going on in these countries. Interested travellers should enquire at local museums.

the first hominid. The first definite hominids begin to appear about 4 million years ago. A very early hominid can be recognised by bones which indicate that it stood erect and walked habitually on two legs. Further identifying traits are dental features such as small canines and a parabolic-shaped jaw, and a bigger brain in relation to the face and body than those of other apes.

The earliest evidence of upright walking comes from the Awash Valley in northern Ethiopia. The best-known find here was made in 1975 at Hadar in the Afar Triangle of Ethiopia by a team led by Donald Johanson. In

hominds dating back 3.7 million years found by Mary Leakey at Laetoli near Olduvai showed similarities to Johanson's Hadar fossils and seemed to vindicate Louis Leakey's theory. Then in 1979 Johanson published a paper with Tim White which announced an entirely new species of homind, *Australopithecus afarensis*, named after the Afar Triangle.

In 1968 Richard Leakey began a research project on the east side of Lake Rudolph (now Lake Turkana), in collaboration with the late Glynn Isaac of UCB. Many significant fossils and stone-tool sites were found around Koobi Fora, but in 1972 the most spectacular skull of

1974 the team found a 3-million-year old fossil skeleton which was 40 percent complete: it was named "Lucy" after a Beatles song popular in the camp. In 1975 the remains of 13 individuals dating back 3.5 million years were recovered. Johanson sparked a heated controversy with the Leakey camp when he changed his mind about what these and other fossils from Hadar represented.

He had originally agreed with Mary and Richard Leakey that some of the fossil hominds were of the genus *Homo*. Later discoveries of

LEFT: a prehistoric turtle unearthed at Koobi Fora.
ABOVE: Louis and Mary Leakey inspect a dig.

all was discovered and named KNM-ER 1470 (Kenya National Museum-East Rudolf). A photograph of this skull made the covers of *Time* and *National Geographic* and the front pages of newspapers around the world. It caused a sensation because it was then thought to be 2.9 million years old, and with its large brain it was undisputably a *Homo*.

Richard assigned KNM-ER 1470 to the species *habilis* created by his father. This seemed to settle the debate about an early *Homo*, and some distinguished opponents of the idea even conceded defeat. But then questions began to appear about the accuracy of KNM-ER 1470's age. Some scientists condemned as faulty the dating methodology, called potassium/argon, practised by Richard Leakey's team.

The potassium/argon method was used to date fossils of ancient pigs and elephants found in different layers of rock at east Turkana. Similar specimens had already been discovered and securely dated by a team working in the nearby Omo Valley in southern Ethiopia. Although stages of animal evolution were contemporary in each sample, neither team could agree on the age of the rock deposits: the east Turkana dates were consistently found to be older than those at Omo.

This uncertainty over the accuracy of potassium/argon dating meant Leakey's theory of an early *Homo* was again in dispute. The argument was still raging when Johanson withdrew his support of the existence of an early *Homo* at Hadar and Laetoli. To settle the matter, further rock samples from east Turkana were sent to be dated at UCB using a different technique from the potassium/argon method. The UCB dates were a million years younger.

In 1980, after fighting the evidence for more than five years, Richard Leakey finally conceded that KNM-ER 1470 was not 2.9 million, but rather closer to 1.8 or 1.9 million years old. This fitted well with the dates of *Homo*

habilis at Olduvai, but now there were only the disputed Hadar and Laetoli fossils to support an early *Homo*.

More species on the scene

After this golden decade of hominid fossil discovery, things stayed relatively quiet until 1984. Richard Leakey and his team, which included his wife Meave and his longtime co-worker Alan Walker, had now moved to the western shores of Lake Turkana. At a site called Nariokotome, their "Hominid Gang", a group of veteran fossil hunters recruited from the local population, found small pieces of a hominid skull. This find turned out to be part of the most complete *Homo erectus* skeleton ever discovered. The skeleton was dubbed Turkana Boy, for he was only 11 or 12 when he died. A most remarkable feature was his height: if he had reached adulthood, he would have grown to 1.8 metres (nearly 6 ft) tall. The fossil remains were dated at 1.6 million years old – very old for an *erectus*.

Meanwhile, Johanson's team, unable to work in Ethiopia because of the civil war, had moved to Olduvai Gorge, where Richard Leakey's mother Mary had stopped digging. They found a 1.85-million-year-old hominid and attributed it to *habilis*. However, this fossil re-ignited the *habilis* debate, for it was small and primitive. How could Johanson's OH 62, as it was catalogued, a primitive *Homo* less than 1.2 metres (4 ft) tall, have evolved into a 1.8-metre *Homo erectus* in a time span of only 200,000 years?

The solution was to split *Homo habilis* into three species. The Olduvai specimens, including the primitive-looking OH 62, continued to be designated *Homo habilis*. Richard Leakey's famous skull from Koobi Fora, KNM-ER 1470, together with some of the Turkana finds and also STW 53, a skull from Sterkfontein, South Africa, were reclassified as *Homo rudolfensis*. The rest of the Turkana finds, including Turkana Boy (officially KNM-WT 15000) were placed in *Homo ergaster*. But that did not solve all the conundrums: it is still unclear how these species interrelated.

To add to the confusion, in 1985 Alan Walker, Richard Leakey's co-worker, discovered a robust skull that belonged to an Australopithecine. It was 2.5 million years old. At first the Turkana team placed the skull in

Australopithecus boisei, but its appearance differed from *boisei* – and it was half a million years older than the oldest *boisei* ever found. So two years later they decided it belonged to a new species. Years before, the Omo team had found pieces of a badly crushed robust skull about 2.6 million years old, which they named *Paraustralopithecus aethiopicus*. Because the skull was so fragmentary nobody really paid any attention to the new species. Since Alan Walker's new skull, KNM-WT 17000, was from a similar period, it was placed in this species, which was renamed *Australopithecus aethiopicus*.

Recent years

In 1995, yet another two new hominid species were found. First Tim White, longtime associate of Donald Johanson, now back in Ethiopia, found the remains of a 4.4-million-year-old hominid which he classified as *Australopithecus ramidus*. But he later realised this hominid was different from the Australopithecines, so coined the genus *Ardipithecus* or "ground ape". Still very little is known about *Ardipithecus*, and some even doubt whether it is a hominid.

In the same year the Turkana team, led by Meave Leakey, found a 4-million-year-old hominid which they dubbed *Australopithecus anamensis*. This hominid was more primitive than *afarensis*, and about half a million years older, but fossil evidence is still so sparse that it is difficult to determine where exactly the species belongs on our family tree.

Future shocks?

With so many species found in East Africa, it seems tempting to assume our ancestors evolved there and then spread to other places such as South Africa. But in 1996 scientists discovered how difficult it is to make such predictions when you don't have all the fossils. For in that year a joint French-American team working in Koro Toro, Chad, 1,500 miles from our supposed Eden, found the fossil remains of an *Australopithecus* dated at 3.5 million years old – which makes it contemporary with *Australopithecus afarensis*. Although the fossils do resemble those of *afarensis,* their discoverer,

LEFT: the skull of the undisputed ancestor of *Homo sapiens* or modern man.
RIGHT: Richard Leakey made some major finds.

Frenchman Michel Brunet, placed them in a new species: *Australopithecus bahrelghazali*.

Yet another species was discovered in 1999 in Ethiopia, where an international team of researchers found the 2½-million-year-old remains of what they called *Australopithecus garhi*. *Garhi* means "surprise" in the local language and certainly no one had expected to find another hominid species in this timeframe. The team also found evidence of tool-making in the vicinity, which would make *garhi* the earliest tool-making *Australopithecus*.

In 2001, it was announced that the Ethiopian Rift Valley had yielded another fossil of shat-

tering significance: the jawbone and other parts of a 5.8-million-year-old hominid unearthed by an Ethiopian graduate student, Yohannis Haile Selassie, and assigned to the genus *Ardipithecus*. Almost certainly the so-called missing link between hominids and their apelike ancestors, this new finding, in an area that was densely forested six million years ago, undermines the theory that our ancestors first started to walk upright as an adaptation to a savannah environment.

But one constant in all recent theories regarding the evolution of mankind is that the key events were enacted in and around the East African Rift Valley. ❑

THE HISTORY OF SAFARI

The relationship between white men and African wildlife began as a battle of wits, with the odds heavily loaded on the side of the "White Hunter"

According to Theodore Roosevelt, "There are no words that can tell the hidden spirit of the wilderness, that can reveal its mystery, its melancholy and its charm." That nostalgic passage in the former US president's book *African Game Trails* refers to one of the first commercial hunting safaris.

In 1909 Roosevelt came to Kenya on an expedition to collect natural-history specimens for museums in the United States. Accompanied by two legendary professional hunters, Frederick Selous and Philip Percival, as well as some 600 porters, Roosevelt spent several months in the bush satisfying scientific curiosity and outraging some of the earliest conservation consciences by bagging over 500 animals and sending their skins back home.

Celebrity safaris

Roosevelt's caravan set off from the Norfolk Hotel, which still stands in Nairobi and is possibly the finest lodging the city has to offer. Otherwise, safaris and Kenyan tourism have changed a lot since those early years when setting off on foot across the African plains meant taking your life into your hands.

Edward, Prince of Wales, went on a shooting safari about the same time as Roosevelt and helped to popularise the concept of paying to hunt in Africa by fascinating his friends with tales of shooting rhinos, elephants and lions at close range.

Farmers and ranchers were quick to see the potential and many did seasonal work, as some still do today, taking wealthy men and women from the United States and Britain big game hunting. In the 1950s, the dilettante aspect of the sport faded and hunting blossomed into a commercial enterprise, the forerunner of today's tourist industry.

Then, in 1977, hunting in Kenya was banned by the late President Jomo Kenyatta, who stated

LEFT: an early 20th-century illustration satirises the White Hunter.
RIGHT: hunting plains game.

that this would help to stop poaching. Some hunters went to Tanzania where they still hunt today; others tried their hand, with less success, in Sudan and the Central African Republic. Many more reluctantly packed their guns away, sent their trackers home to their farms in the bush and looked for other jobs. The late 1970s

marked the end of a golden era of hunting that spanned well over a century. The men who took clients out in search of trophies were risking their lives as much for pleasure as for profit.

Sporting spirit

Hunting symbolised the code by which European explorers, farmers and settlers lived. The sport was conducted along lines as carefully marked out as the rules of a gentleman's London club. Apart from the exhilaration of testing vitality under dangerous conditions, there was the mystical communion with nature that culminated in the chase. Often an intimacy developed between hunter and hunted that, in the hunter's mind at least, was endowed with feelings of respect.

Some hunters turned killing elephants into a simple commercial business, selling the ivory at a pound a pound in Mombasa or Dar es Salaam. But some clients who hunted regularly would walk for miles, for weeks, without firing a single shot. For them the sport was in the chase and the trophy told all. When the wily old bull whose tusks weighed 45 kg (100 lb) each evaded them, they chose to walk away empty-handed.

> **HARD TO SPOT**
>
> Of the "Big Five" the leopard is the most elusive. Leopards are customarily shot from a hide overlooking bait – usually a zebra hung from a tree.

thick grass, ears twitching to catch the snap of a broken twig as the hunter approaches. Then they erupt from the shadows in an explosion of fury, head bent and very little else exposed to the poised gun.

It is hardly surprising that many hunters and, on rare occasions, clients too have been gored or mauled not only by elephant, leopard and buffalo but also by lion and rhino. Most survived their misadventures but there were those who did not. Vivienne de Watteville, then 24, and her father Bernard set out from Nairobi

The elephant was just one of the "Big Five": lion, leopard, buffalo and rhino completed the quintet of the most highly sought-after targets, reflecting the skill it took to track them, the risk involved in confronting them and the quality of the trophy retrieved from a successful kill.

For many hunters, buffalos were the most awesome animals. The thick boss of horn that curls over their head, a three-inch thick hide and overlapping rib cage makes them the Sherman tank of the animal world. Every professional hunter knows that buffalos are possibly the most difficult animals to down with one clean shot. If wounded, the tables are turned, for buffalos ambush their prey, lying up in the

in 1923 on an expedition to collect specimens for Berne Museum. While shooting his 19th lion, Bernard de Watteville was mauled. He managed to thrust the muzzle of his rifle under its jaw and kill it. But the claws contracted in his body as *rigor mortis* set in. He had to tear them painfully out one by one before he could push the huge body off him. He walked two hours back to camp, bleeding profusely. His daughter washed and dressed the deep cuts, but his stoic performance was in vain. He died later that night. The redoubtable Vivienne continued the safari, using the bushlore she had learned from her father to complete the collection for the museum.

Freedom

But above all, the attraction of safari life was the unparallelled freedom it allowed. "England is too small. Much too small. I shall go to Africa. I need space," declared Denys Finch Hatton before sailing to Mombasa in 1911.

Until World War II, the writ of the government did not reliably extend very far beyond the towns. Once in the bush, a professional hunter could dispense justice, advice and medicine by virtue of the fact that he happened to be there. Neither was it likely, as hunters roamed from country to country, that anyone would question their actions – as long as they adhered to an unwritten gentleman's code embodied in an ill-defined notion of honour.

as they do today and wallowed in hot water poured into collapsible canvas baths. Their trips sometimes took months and necessitated a long, snaking line of porters.

Everything that was needed was carried on a man's head. The baggage would be considered excessive by today's standards. On a hunting trip in 1891 to what is now Zimbabwe, Lord Randolph Churchill took with him a piano as well as a red and gold wheelchair for the gout-afflicted Lobengula, King of Mashonaland.

TAKING A TRIP

The Swahili word *safari* ("journey") is derived from the Arabic *safariya,* which means "voyage". Even today, a businessman making his rounds of a company's branches will say he is going on safari.

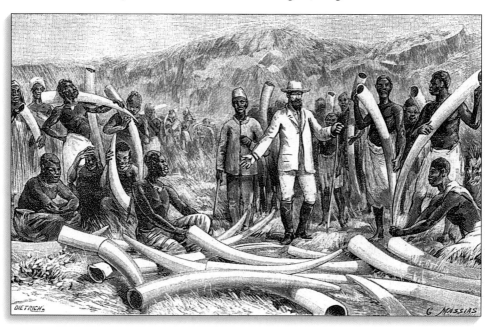

In the early days hunters travelled with their clients, as everyone did, on foot. There was little to differentiate a commercial safari from any other except for the extra larding of gunbearers, trackers and skinners. Clients slept in tents just

LEFT: an 18th-century illustration showing the killing of a rhino, one of the famed "Big Five".
ABOVE: showing off a collection of much-prized tusks.

The commercialisation of the sport was sired partially by the British imperative to empire build and partially by the Kenyan settlers' desire to pad out their bank accounts. By the time Teddy Roosevelt arrived in Nairobi in 1909, it was a libidinous frontier town that squatted on a swamp. Spear-carrying Maasai warriors mingled in the dusty streets with the restless younger generation of the British aristocacy. Ten years earlier, Nairobi had been the railhead for the Uganda Railway, where workers rested before tackling the inhospitable Kikuyu Escarpment.

The hunters of these years had either won their spurs hunting for ivory, as Frederick Selous had done, or they were farmers who moonlighted when the crops failed, or they simply wanted to earn more money and have some fun while doing it. There were the Cole brothers, Galbraith and Berkeley, brothers-in-law to Lord Delamare, Karen Blixen's husband Baron Bror von Blixen, and her lover Denys Finch Hatton.

The tortured relationship between the two lovers was aggravated further by Finch Hatton's habit of disappearing into the bush for months at a time. Karen Blixen was particularly peeved when both her husband and her lover took the Prince of Wales shooting, leaving her behind to mind the coffee farm.

Lord Cranworth's entrepreneurial spirit extended even further. He was a founding figure in Newland & Tarlton, the first safari outfitter. By 1914 it was the largest employer in Kenya, a point which angered colonial bureaucrats. They blamed Lord Cranworth and his partners for the labour shortage. The porters were paid the equivalent of US$4.50 a month.

Poor communications meant that publicity hardly existed except by word of mouth. It took eight weeks for a letter to reach Britain so safaris were arranged at least a year in advance.

Hunting safaris gained their elitist reputation as a pastime for the rich and famous thanks to

LICENCE TO KILL

Hunting is still legal in Tanzania, subject to very tight regulations. It is permitted only in specified areas (including, paradoxically, part of the Selous Game Reserve) and only between the months of July and December. Visitors seeking to bag a trophy must be accompanied by a professional hunter, and must buy a licence for each species they pursue. It is possible to hunt all of the Big Five except the seriously endangered rhino. Big-game hunting is still a pastime for the rich: the Tanzanian Government collects hefty fees for permits and licences – and the company that guides the hunter may charge up to US$1,000 per person per day.

clients such as the Duke and Duchess of Connaught. He was attended by an equerry; she was looked after by a lady-in-waiting. Seven-course dinners ended with savouries such as giraffe marrow on toast.

White hunters

The term "white hunter" was coined by Lord Delamare. He employed two men to control the wildlife on his ranch, an Ethiopian and a professional hunter called Alan Black. To avoid confusion, he referred to Black as "the white hunter". The term remained in use until well after Kenya and Tanzania gained independence from Britain in the 1960s.

The introduction of vehicles in the 1920s changed both the pace and the ethics of hunting. Clients travelled to campsites in wooden box-body Fords that rolled through mud and sand on spoked wheels. There were no windows but canvas blinds could be rolled down when it rained.

Motorised transport encouraged some to shoot from the car, a practise that outraged the hunters. Denys Finch Hatton and others lobbied against instances such as the slaughter of 323 lions by two Americans. Eventually, the game department in Kenya ruled that no one could shoot within 200 metres (220 yards) of a vehicle.

the stony ground of his ranch near Machakos and charged £10 to shoot a lion while on the train going to Nairobi. Wanting a proper education for his children, he chose a Bristol boarding school because it was so near a zoo the lions could be heard roaring at night.

Percival taught Ernest Hemingway his bushlore in the 1930s and '40s. The author was not always as fine a shot as he would have liked to be but he made up for this in the lyrical passages of his novels set in Africa and at the mess table in the evenings. Philip Percival kept his ego under control by appealing to his wife Pauline to "throw a drink into the beast and he'll quiet down."

Philip Percival, considered the finest sportsman of that period, defined the rise and decline of hunting with his own career. He came to Kenya in 1905 to join his brother Blainey, who later headed a fledgling game department. He took Teddy Roosevelt on safari and after World War I went into partnership with Bror von Blixen. Old photos show him in the hunting outfit that was *de rigueur* for both sexes – a wide-brimmed Terai hat with a double thickness of felt against sunstroke, breeches, puttees and boots. He chased lion on horseback over

After World War II, Hollywood finally discovered Africa. America exported its fiery emotions and inflatable budgets into the bush to dramatise the literature of Hemingway, Haggard and others. In the vanguard was *The Macomber Affair*, filmed in Kenya in 1946.

The film's production company became the first clients of Donald Ker and Syd Downey, who celebrated the defeat of the Germans by creating Ker & Downey. It was to become the largest safari company in East Africa. Their theatrical tradition lives on. In 1985 Ker & Downey mounted a gigantic field operation that put 340 people under canvas for the making of *Out of Africa*. ❑

LEFT: loading tusks at Mombasa, *circa* 1920.
ABOVE: a motorised safari in the 1930s.

WILDLIFE AND AFRICAN CULTURE

*The delicate balance between the East African people and wildlife, maintained
by traditional values and ways of life, is now in a precarious state*

Wildlife and the peoples of East Africa have had an intimate relationship since time immemorial. Wild animals and birds of the plains and mountains have always played an integral part in African culture and, more recently, in African economies. There is no other place on earth where humans still live in such close proximity to so many free-roaming animals, which is both a curse and blessing for the governments and people concerned.

African attitudes towards wildlife vary depending on tribal history and current local situations. These cultural dispositions are important as they will ultimately determine the future survival of wildlife. But East Africa encompasses many different cultural groups, which results in many predilections. To simplify things, present-day African attitudes can be classified according to profession. The oldest profession is hunter-gatherer, followed by agriculturalist and livestock pastoralist and finally, modern urban man.

Hunter-gatherers

Between 2 million and 5,000 years ago, all East Africans were hunter-gatherers. Wild plants and animals, in that order, were the basis of all life. Humankind was one small cog in the ecological nature machine, operating in small bands and graduating from the technology of wood and stone to metal only a few centuries ago. Controlled fire was the most influential factor affecting wildlife and environment, though the extent of its effect is still being debated. Some say that the great grass plains of Kenya and Tanzania, which today provide the necessary habitat for masses of wildlife, are a result of burning, first by hunters and then by pastoralists.

Not surprisingly, hunter-gatherers have a very positive attitude towards wildlife since their lives depend upon it. There are no peoples left in East Africa who are solely hunter-gatherers, though groups still exist who were

LEFT: a Samburu warrior, wearing traditional ivory earplugs.
RIGHT: hunting the lion.

until recently and who still retain many of the cultural aspects, including occasional illegal hunts. Wildlife is not, and never was, threatened by these people. Animals were never killed indiscriminately en masse as they are by poachers today. Traditional hunters killed for a reason, whether it was for food, ritual, or some-

thing to sell. Each species represented a unique value in a cosmology interlinking natural and spiritual worlds. To kill an animal without reason was to violate all that was held sacred, and would surely result in later retribution for the killer from the spirits.

Hunter-gatherer society was originally classless and life was simple and mobile. Then 5,000 years ago domestic livestock and cultivated crops were brought south from Ethiopia and the Nile Valley by new groups of people. It is thought that these hunter-gatherers – like the modern-day Bushmen of southern Africa and Hadza of north-central Tanzania – spoke a click-based language of the Khoisan linguistic group. The first immigrants spoke southern Cushite languages from Ethiopia and southern Nilotic languages indigenous to the Nile. Over the centuries many different groups came from the north speaking eastern Cushitic and southern and eastern Nilotic languages and about 1,500 years ago Bantu speakers appeared from the west. The result today is a complex mixture of many languages with ancient Semitic language-speakers still widespread in Ethiopia.

The true hunters

Hunter-gatherers now became subservient to the better-organised immigrants. Over time a

which refers to a people. Two former hunting groups live in the Lamu district of Kenya, the Aweer (Boni) and the Dhalo. These groups, especially the Wata, were, until the 1960s, famous longbow elephant hunters. Some of the Wata had bows that exceeded the famous English longbows in drawing power.

Other hunting groups in Kenya are the Okiek and Dorobo, associated with Kalenjin and Maasai. They are culturally a very mixed bag: the same people switch cultural identities to suit the situation. They are generally highland people who trap and spear animals rather than use bows and arrows. Honey-gathering is also

caste relationship evolved in many parts of East Africa, with hunters occupying the lowest rung, along with potters, ironsmiths and tanners. In Ethiopia today the hunting caste is called Wata and similar peoples in the south are the Manjo and Funa. With the changing political situation in Ethiopia and diminishing wildlife, these people are being slowly absorbed by the dominant groups with whom they live. Wata also exist in north and east Kenya where they traditionally lived in symbiosis with the Oromo and Somali pastoralist groups. They traded wildlife products and labour for protection, milk and use of land. In Kenya they are called variously Sanye or Ariangulo, often with the Bantu prefix Wa,

important. The Dorobo and Maasai extend into Tanzania, though Kenya is their main home.

In Tanzania there are also three small remnant hunting groups who today have taken up farming. These are southern Cushitic Iraqw, and the Sandawe and Hazda, whose language contains elements of the Bushmen clicks. The Hazda live around Lake Eyasi and some of them still hunt and gather, against government wishes.

Uganda, Rwanda and Burundi still have low-caste hunting groups called Twa or Batwa, the Bantu equivalent of the Cushitic Wata and Nilotic Okiek/Dorobo. Hunting is no longer practised in Rwanda and Burundi, due to the high-density population which is eliminating wildlife. A notable exception is in Rwanda's volcanic mountains, home to the mountain gorilla. Gorillas and monkeys were traditionally an important source of meat for the Batwa, and for some of the surrounding Bantu agriculturalists. But in the mid-20th century gorillas became more important for the money paid by foreign zoos and stuffed-animal collectors. In spite of anti-poaching legislation, mountain gorillas were in danger of extinction by the early 1980s. Conservation

LAKESIDE LIVING

Kenya's smallest ethnic group are fishermen – the 3,500-strong El-Molo, who live on the shores of Lake Turkana and eke out a subsistence living by fishing from doum-palm rafts. Their staple diet is fish, crocodile and turtle meat.

Mbuti hunt with both nets and bows and arrows and are proficient trappers. Nowadays, they still hunt for forest elephant – as much for its meat as for the small tusks – but their infrequent kills are not a threat to elephant survival.

All these hunting groups have, or had until recently, strong cultural beliefs and practices involving wildlife. Wild animals and birds were important in ceremonies such as initiation, marriage and prayer. They were used in divination and

organisations, local government support and the pioneering work of the late Dr Dian Fossey have all contributed to reduce gorilla poaching dramatically. The main strategy is to familiarise gorillas with humans: when these animals can be used as a tourist attraction, the resulting revenue and daily human presence help to discourage poachers.

The last hunting group in East Africa is the famous Mbuti pygmies of the Ituri Forest in the Democratic Republic of the Congo. The

LEFT: tribal people with ostrich feathers.
ABOVE: headdress of bird carcasses, worn after circumcision ceremony.

prophecy, for medicine, clothing and, of course, food. Without wildlife these cultures would have no meaning and could not exist.

Pastoralists

The herding peoples of East Africa also tend to have a benign attitude towards most wildlife species. Unlike their European or American counterparts, African livestock herders accept the right of animals other than cattle, sheep and goats to share land and water resources. Many pastoralist peoples even recognise the buffalo, eland and some other species as honorary cattle. Most other animals, especially birds and fish, are not regarded as fit for human consumption.

Many pastoralist groups have established a hierarchy for animals. The Borana of southern Ethiopia and Kenya, for example, have their own "Big Four" – lion, elephant, rhino and buffalo. To kill an animal single-handedly for the first time is cause for celebration in the community and the person becomes a "man". Each subsequent kill increases the man's reputation. Similarly, Maasai *moran* (warriors) organise formal lion hunts in which one *morani* tries to spear to death a cornered lion. Success means great prestige for the killer. Other wild, hoofed animals occupy a middle-caste position: they are not fit to eat, but neither are they despised.

to traders coming from the coast. Herds were rebuilt with the resulting income, and even today Borana and Gabra can point to cattle that are descendants of those bought with ivory.

Wildlife is important to pastoralists both culturally and economically. Birds and feathers are particularly significant in ritual and dress. Maasai and Samburu boys, for example, make stuffed bird crowns to wear after circumcision, and ostrich feathers are worn in ceremonial headdresses by many different peoples.

The camel pastoralists

Three-quarters of Kenya is inhabited by pas-

In normal times pastoralists did little hunting, since livestock was expected to satisfy all needs. It was a loss of prestige to have to resort to wild animals for subsistence. Associated hunter-gatherers were supposed to be the only ones to defile themselves in hunting activities, which were regarded in most cases as ritually impure. In abnormal times however, following drought, animal epidemics or raids, when livestock numbers were greatly reduced, pastoralists had to revert to hunting and gathering for survival. Elephant and rhino were practically wiped out in Ethiopia and northern Kenya following a series of natural disasters in the late 1880s, as pastoralists sold tusks and rhino horn

toralists. The Somali are in the northeast and east, as are the Borana, who also extend down the Kenya coast and hinterland as the Orma group. In the north, to the east of Lake Turkana, one finds the Gabra and Rendille camel pastoralists, and to the south are the Maasai-related Samburu. West of Lake Turkana are the Turkana people and south of them live the Pokot; the semi-sedentary Njemps live south of Lake Baringo. Raiding and cattle rustling still occur, and the introduction of modern firearms at some raids has created serious problems for governments trying to control poaching.

The major pastoralist groups in Uganda are the Karamajong in the northeast, related to the

Turkana of northwest Kenya, and the Bantu Ankole in the south. The latter are famous for their long-horn cattle.

Burundi and Rwanda are occupied by the Rundi and the Banyarwanda respectively. In Burundi, the Tutsi (or Watutsi) and Hima are upper-caste groups associated with livestock. The Tutsi also are present as a minority in Rwanda. The Hutu are a majority caste in Rwanda and a minority in Burundi. They are higher caste than the Batwa but fall below the Tutsi and Hima. This has caused considerable social strife, culminating in the catastrophic civil war in Rwanda in 1994, in which a genocidal campaign inspired by the Hutu government killed 800,000 Tutsis.

(There are two theories to explain the social and physical differences between the three main caste groups of Rwanda, Burundi and southern Uganda. The first suggests that Batwa hunters, generally short and dark, are descendants of the original inhabitants; Hutu are descended from Bantu agriculturalist immigrants; and the tall Tutsi and Hima are the descendants of later immigrant pastoralists of Cushitic or Nilotic stock who, because of their warlike nature, came to dominate the hunters and farmers. The second theory hypothesises that castes developed long ago among a homogenous people and that selective marriage resulted in the three different physical types.)

In Tanzania the main pastoral peoples are the Maasai in the north, with most other groups practising mixed agro-pastoralism and living sedentary lives.

The farmers

If hunter-gatherering and pastoralism were the only economies practised in East Africa, wildlife would be sure of a secure future. But farmers have very different attitudes to the sympathetic depiction of animals and birds in folk tales. An all-out war has been raging for centuries over control of the land – and the farmer is winning. Animals and birds that attack crops are his greatest enemy.

The first agricultural peoples to reduce wildlife populations to controllable limits were the Amharic- and Tigrinya-speakers living in highly structured states in highland Ethiopia.

LEFT: tending camels in Turkana.
RIGHT: crossing the dusty plains of Amboseli.

Over a period of 2,000 years, high-density population, deforestation and use of weapons by formal armies from the 19th century onwards resulted in the annihilation of wildlife. Internal and overseas trade stimulated localised extinction of desired species. The rise of state systems in Uganda among the Baganda, Banyore, Batoro and other Bantu peoples had a similar effect, though with lower population densities wildlife survived in large numbers in various parts of the country. But in the 1970s, social strife and the breakdown of effective government resulted in the slaughter of thousands of elephants and other animals.

Without appropriate habitats, wildlife cannot survive. Only a few small mountain areas still contain wildlife in Rwanda, one of the most densely settled areas in Africa. In neighbouring Burundi, the native animal population is virtually non-existent.

Encouraging attempts are now being made by indigenous clubs and conservation organisations to create awareness and respect for wildlife. But without traditional cultural values and with the increase in population and poverty, the future for wildlife in East Africa is in a precarious state. Tourism is one of the strongest forces working towards conserving the magnificent natural heritage of this part of the world. ❑

A VAST AND VARIED LAND

East Africa has every habitat imaginable, from savanna, woodland and rainforest
to the highest mountain peaks via semi-arid zones to lakes, river and swamps

Visitors to East Africa should realise at the outset that the environment is not fragile – an adjective frequently used to encourage people to support environment- and conservation-related activities. Better adjectives would be harsh, unpredictable, fundamentally impoverished, or resilient. In fact, most evolution and species development in the region has occurred under tough conditions that have been the rule since the Pleistocene era, some 2 million years ago. If the environment were truly fragile, as in the delicate chemical balance of a coastal marine ecosystem or a conservative climax forest, then it would hardly have survived in more or less the same form for such a long time. Most African plants and animals are remarkably hardy, adaptable and able to survive despite what we persist in doing to them.

The African environment is governed by a handful of ecological laws which appear at first glance almost simple in their concept. There is a finite amount of minerals and elements on the earth, just as there is a more or less finite, but of course smaller amount in an ecosystem. (An ecosystem is the collection of plants and animals in a particular region, together with the soil storehouse of materials that create the building blocks of those plants and animals.)

The energy that brings otherwise inert materials to life is provided by the sun, which is essential for the first food production – photosynthesis. Plants mobilise the nutrients in the soil together with the constituents of water to produce simple sugars which form the beginning of all terrestrial food chains. Herbivores eat plants, carnivores eat herbivores, and at one stage or another, decomposers, from bacteria to dung beetles, eat them all. So the basic materials are returned to the soil to be picked up by plants and sent through the ecosystem again in this sun-driven, water-lubricated carousel of life.

LEFT: rivers are essential for many animals' daily bathing routines
RIGHT: rainfall is at its highest in Kilimanjaro's forest.

Limited jungles

Popular attention to the Africa described by authors such as Karen Blixen, Elspeth Huxley, Beryl Markham or Doris Lessing has finally dispelled the Edgar Rice Burroughs image of Tarzan's equatorial jungle stretching from the Atlantic to the Indian Ocean. In fact, evergreen

forest covers only a small part of the continent: in East Africa it is confined to belts around major mountains such as the Virunga volcanoes in Rwanda, the Ruwenzoris in Uganda, Mt Kilimanjaro in Tanzania and Mt Kenya.

Ground-water forests occur where there is enough water seeping out of springs, such as at the base of the escarpment above Lake Manyara; riverine forests exist along major perennial water courses, along with remnant patches of low-lying coastal forest. Although tree species differ, the pattern is more or less the same: dense, layered canopies, trees up to 70 metres (230 ft) and a relatively thin undergrowth due to the shade of the dominant trees.

To enter a forest from the surrounding grassland is like escaping inside on a hot summer day. The light dims, the temperature drops, the wind drops, and one can almost feel the additional moisture in the soil and the air which the forest, by its very presence, retains.

The sweeping plains

Most of East Africa is covered in grassland, several different types of which are recognised by ecologists and described in terms of their physiognomy. Open grassland is the backdrop, such as the long-grass plains of the Serengeti covered with red oat grass *(Setaria* and *Th-*

beyond. Dwarf shrub grasslands are found on desert fringes, hill thickets, coastal thickets, swamps, and the like.

The "seasons"

The climate, which consists of average and actual precipitation and temperature, is a critical factor limiting the form and abundance of life in any ecosystem. It is important to recognise the difference between an annual average rainfall and the actual pattern of delivery. The Serengeti in Tanzania and Ireland have roughly the same amount of water falling on their territories each year. In Ireland, the rainfall is

emeda). Add scattered shrubs, such as the patches of "toothbrush" bush *(Salvadora)* in Queen Elizabeth National Park in Uganda, and one has bushed-grassland. Replace the bushes with widely spaced, flat-topped acacias and spiny desert dates *(Balanites)*, and the scene is wooded grassland.

If trees and shrubs occur in roughly equal numbers, it's described, not surprisingly, as wooded and bushed grassland, like the Acacia-Commiphora region of Tsavo East in Kenya, which stretches to the north and east. If trees are more numerous, with their canopies almost touching, it is woodland, such as the vast Brachystegia woodlands in southern Tanzania and

spread almost constantly throughout the year. In the Serengeti it rains in two peaks – April and November, when powerful storms hurl down more rain than the soil can possibly absorb. Water runs down the slopes, boils down the watercourses, swells the great rivers and plunges eventually into one of the Rift Valley lakes or the Indian Ocean.

In the long rains, usually April to May, there may be some constantly rainy days. But more characteristically, rainfall is discontinuous. Both plants and animals have to be adaptive, mobile or both. "Adaptive" implies the ability to breed quickly when there is sufficient moisture. "Mobile" means having the ability to be carried, such as a seed clinging to a paw, or to migrate, demonstrated by the wildebeest in their 1,000-km (600-mile) trek around the Serengeti, to places where the chances of reproduction and survival are better. Only trees and tortoises in East Africa stay in one place, and both do their best to make sure their progeny have the chance to get out of the neighbourhood if necessary.

FOREST ABUNDANCE

Rainforests support more animal species than any other ecosystem on land. But mammals – apart from monkeys and other primates – are usually few and far between.

In regions where annual rainfall exceeds 1,200mm (47 inches) – such as western Uganda and the Democratic Republic of the

fact, it has led to the evolution of a chlorophyll type slightly different from that of temperate latitudes. The sun, which provides the power to generate the ecosystems, takes its toll: nearly 80 percent of rainfall evaporates back into the atmosphere.

East Africa's geology

Much of East Africa looks unfinished: the gash of the Great Rift Valley which cuts through the country from the Red Sea to Zimbabwe has rugged step faults which drop, for example, from the

Congo – the seasons tend to merge, with no distinct rainy season, and forest vegetation tends to dominate. The other important atmosphere-related characteristic – generally of concern only if you are visiting East Africa's beaches – is the intensity of the sun. Incoming solar radiation is particularly strong at the equator and when combined with the relatively high altitudes of much of East Africa (Nairobi, for example, stands at 1,500 metres/4,920 ft above sea level) the light is intense indeed. In

LEFT: the Virunga volcanoes mark the border between Rwanda and the Democratic Republic of Congo.
ABOVE: Uganda has many magnificant lakes.

Ngong Hills 2,100 metres (6,900 ft) outside Nairobi, to the steaming soda of Lake Magadi at 610 metres (2,000 ft). There are active or recently extinct volcanoes – Virunga in Rwanda, Ol-Doinyo Lengai in Tanzania, Shetani and Teleki's in Kenya. Whole hill ranges are remnants of volcanic activities over recent geological eras, such as the Ruwenzoris in Uganda and the Chyulu Hills in Kenya.

All of these are associated with the restless state of the earth's crust at the edge of the two tectonic plates which make up either edge of the Rift. In East Africa the two plates are slowly pulling apart (unlike southern California where two plates are pushing together).

The relatively recent activity means that many of the soils of East Africa contain a high content of ash delivered from nearby volcanoes – for example, the southern Serengeti from the Ngorongoro highlands; the Nairobi National Park and adjacent Athi-Kapiti plains from the Aberdares and Mt Kenya, and others. Recent lava flows are common and look like black treacle poured over the landscape. Older lava-flows boulder are exposed as escarpments and great granitic boulders as picturesque *kopjes* (or inselbergs) from the age-old and continual erosion of the land surface.

Much of the variety of plant and animal life

relative numbers of species and the reproductive success of those less tolerant to dry periods. For example, Kenya's exceptionally heavy rains in 1997–8, caused in part by the meteorological phenomenon known as El Niño, were followed by a severe drought in 1999–2000: perennial grasses all but disappeared in favour of the more opportunistic annuals that re-seed each year.

When the rains returned at the end of 2000 the balance shifted back in favour of the perennials. (The drought also had catastrophic effects on agriculture, drastically reducing cereal-crop yields and decimating livestock.

in East Africa is due to the variation in elevation, from sea level to 6,000 metres (19,700 ft). This produces a range of temperature and humidity with extremes similar to both southern Florida and the Alps. Altitude produces impenetrable barriers to some species: baobabs are never found above 1,000 metres (3,280 ft); rock hyraxes rarely below 500 metres (1,640 ft).

Periodic drought

For thousands of years Africa has been subjected to short-term fluctuations in the rains. Annual failures of the rains happen at least once every 10 years and some decades are drier than others. The effect is temporarily to change the

The widespread food shortages that ensued triggered a massive international relief operation.)

Animal populations, too, respond to such fluctuations. In dry periods, reproductive success is suppressed by a failure to ovulate or for the foetus to implant. This is related to the mother's nutritional state which is lowered because of the reduced nutrition offered by plants in drier periods. The impact is relatively greater on herbivores than carnivores since lions can live quite well off skinny wildebeest, but wildebeest cannot survive on dust. When the rains return and the vegetation is verdant, then herbivore populations, even elephants, are able to rebuild their numbers very quickly.

Bush fires

Long before modern man, who loves lighting fires, African ecosystems were subjected to sporadic burning from natural causes such as lightning strikes. This is evidenced by the fact that many trees and shrubs are "fire-adapted", that is, they can not only withstand burning, but actually flourish or use the fire signal to produce flowers and seeds. Fire keeps many of the grasslands of East Africa intact: if they were not burned periodically, by whatever means, they would start to develop towards bushland.

Modern herders and park wardens take advantage of this fact and deliberately set the grass alight each year. This both clears the regenerating shrubs and ensures that new grass can catch the next available rainfall unencumbered by stands of rank hay. Burning is best done early, before the standing crop of dry grass accumulates into a fuel dump that will destroy trees and soils alike when burnt.

In the annual burning, some animals win and some lose. Tortoises are often roasted in their shells; snakes and small mammals usually cannot outrun a fire fanned by a strong wind. Birds of prey and egrets have a feast at the leading edge of the fire and later, the local herbivores, both wild and domestic, will have an unencumbered sward of fresh green grass.

Wildlife makes its mark

Animal signs are everywhere. Some are subtle and fleeting, like the nests of birds and insects; others are etched into the ecosystem, such as mighty termite mounds or the animal trails that criss-cross major wildlife areas. Elephant trails have been followed by human engineers when executing a road cut up a difficult escarpment, and others have been recorded by cartographers who mistook the trails for all-terrain vehicle roads on aerial photographs.

In general, the major herbivores make their mark on the vegetation, and therefore the look of an area, more than the carnivores. Grass along large rivers is kept short by hippos grazing at night. Feeding giraffes hedge the smaller acacia trees and create a browsing table which is more dense than if the shrub were not browsed. By their feeding actions giraffes stimulate the plants to produce more foliage.

LEFT: spectacular soil erosion in Ethiopia.
RIGHT: volcanic rock formations in northern Kenya.

Most large herbivores, such as buffalo and elephant, are fond of taking mud and dust baths to cool themselves and help rid the skin of parasites. This habit creates pits of activity around the ecosystem, spots which are temporarily clear of vegetation, but rich in the nutrients of the animals that visit them. When the wallow falls out of favour, the vegetation that recolonises the spot is particularly lush.

Man's role

In modern times the greatest modifier of natural systems is undeniably man. His activities have effects at varying levels of intensity: he

can remove materials and put them more or less back, as in subsistence agriculture; he can remove materials and export them to other ecosystems, as in commercial agriculture or mining; or he can just make use of the space for dwelling or commerce and manufacturing, as in villages, urban complexes or industrial parks. Each of these has a different level of energy requirement and differing degrees of physical impact on the look of the land.

Man continues to cut down forests, plough up the soil and kill or displace wild animals, just as he has always done over the past few millennia. Some modification is beneficial and non-destructive, such as early burning of grasslands, replacing some – not all – of the forest with tea or coffee plantations, or shifting cultivation with a cycle long enough to allow the cleared land to recover in an undisturbed fallow. Other forms of modification leave a lasting and denatured mark: forest clearing on steep slopes, the dumping of industrial wastes into waterways or the overexploitation of a vulnerable species, as in the poaching of elephants for their ivory.

In the longer term, there is now no doubt that global warming will have its effect on the East

> ### GRASS GUZZLERS
>
> One small animal species has a great impact on the appearance of the savanna. Harvester termites, which live underground and feed at night, devour more grass than all the wildebeest and other large herbivores added together.

African climate and environment. The accumulation of largely man-produced gases in the upper atmosphere (the so-called "greenhouse gases" – carbon dioxide, methane, ozone and others) will over the next three or four decades alter all major temperature and moisture regimes around the world.

Indications are that the centre of continents in the region of the equator will get hotter and drier. East Africa, however, may become on average wetter and warmer. Most of the models suggest that the sea level will almost certainly rise a metre or two, although history and better data may well prove these models to be wrong or inaccurate. Such changes will alter the shape

of natural ecosystems both in terms of plant and animal species as well as physiognomy.

Soil erosion

The loss of soil from the land under the indigenous farmer's plough or the hooves of the pastoralist's cattle is a favourite bugbear of well-meaning conservationists. The solution most often put forward is to teach the natives how to farm properly or to demand that the herds be reduced in number.

But a layer of silt at the bottom of the Indian Ocean off the East African coast proves that soil erosion has been occurring at varying rates over the past 25 millennia. The real reason for soil loss today is that over this last, relatively dry, geological period in the region, soil has not been made. Erosion tends to be cyclical. Vegetation thins out over a couple of very dry years; soils are sluiced away in the following excessively "good" rains; vegetation re-establishes itself during the rains, and the rate of soil loss slows down.

Conservation consciousness

Land-management strategies must be practicable in the African setting, useful to African people and linked to their society and economy. Wise conservation schemes must involve local people, not just by informing them what is going on, but by making them a direct part of the conservation process. At the simplest level this means getting some of the wildlife-generated revenue, such as game-park fees, back to the landowners who bear the cost of having wildlife graze on their land.

We are only just beginning to learn that conservation attempts work best when they are woven into the desires and aspirations of those they purport to help. But now that we accept that the environment, in all its manifestations, is not the exclusive trophy of the West, perhaps developing countries will become more involved in helping to conserve the region that is, after all, the home of all mankind. ❏

LEFT: bizarre volcanic rock formations in northern Kenya.
RIGHT: a waterfall in Nyungwe Forest, Rwanda, an important area of biodiversity.

Facing Extinction

Standing on the vast grasslands of the Serengeti, surrounded by thousands of lowing wildebeest, it may be hard to understand how any African animal could be endangered. In fact, thousands of African species face extinction, and human beings are the principal cause. The list of endangered species is too long to enumerate, but even a cursory examination of some of the best-known examples illustrates both the extent of the problem and some measures that are being employed to stem the decline. Both the white and

black rhinoceros are critically endangered, with fewer than 10 and 5,000 left in the wild respectively. The largest population in East Africa (about 400) is in Kenya, though Tanzania's Ngorongoro Crater affords the best opportunity for daytime sightings.

The black rhino was hunted heavily for sport throughout much of the 20th century, and its horn has long been considered a potent tonic in Asian medicine. But its most precipitous decline started in the 1970s, when rhinoceros-horn handles became the vogue for Yemeni daggers. Images of rhino carcasses with their horns hacked off became a staple in the press. In many preserves, game scouts briefly capture rhinos and cut off their horns as a preventive measure. In some circumstances, rhinos are also moved into areas where they can be easily protected by scouts and wardens.

Chimpanzees and gorillas

Chimpanzees share the rhino's plight. Chimps are highly valued for medical research, since they share most of our genome. Poachers usually obtain young animals for the medical trade by killing their mothers, a double tragedy. The implacable destruction of their forest habitat by loggers and farmers has also contributed to the decline of chimpanzees, as has the insatiable appetite for "bush meat". There are thought to be fewer than 200,000 chimps living in the wild, many in some of Africa's poorest countries, where the temptation to poach wildlife is particularly acute. In response to the crisis, an international organisation known as the Committee for the Conservation and Care of Chimpanzees is producing action plans for every country in the chimp's range to facilitate preservation work.

Gorillas are also in serious trouble. While the two species of lowland gorilla number about 126,000, the mountain gorilla is on the brink of extinction; only about 630 animals survive in the rugged mountains at the borders of Rwanda, the Democratic Republic of the Congo, and Uganda. The forest habitat of these gentle giants is shrinking rapidly in response to agricultural demands, and they are often killed in snares by hunters and poachers. The situation has been exacerbated by years of horrific warfare in the Congo and Rwanda and by terrorist attacks in Uganda. For a while, rangers could not patrol the mountain gorilla sanctuaries, and poaching increased. However, the Rwandan and Ugandan governments, and communities living around three protected areas in Virunga National Park, are committed to protecting the gorillas, which can bring in much-needed tourist money.

Highland wolves and painted dogs

Extinction also threatens the Ethiopian wolf, a wild canid reviled by herdsmen for livestock predation. It's an unfair accusation: this shy predator feeds mainly on small rodents, especially the giant mole-rat. The wolf also competes for food with domestic dogs and cross-breeds with them. Such hybridisation could eventually wipe out the wolf as a true, distinct species: there may be as few as 400 pure Ethiopian wolves alive today. Scientists are now monitoring wolf populations and eliminating hybrids, and have set up a captive breeding programme. Efforts are also under way to bolster funding and regulation enforcement at the Ethiopian national parks in which they are found. Another endangered canid is the African wild-dog, also known as the painted wolf. No more than 5,000 of these beautiful, piebald predators are left in all Africa. The only substantial wild-dog population in East Africa is in southern Tanzania. Kenya and Ethiopia have small populations, but it is not clear whether these are viable in the long term. Like the Ethiopian wolf, this wide-ranging hunter is heavily persecuted by farmers whenever it leaves the game parks; it was even routinely shot inside the reserves as late as the 1970s. Wild dogs are good hunters, but they suffer when they have to com-

signs to warn motorists of their presence, and education campaigns to encourage greater tolerance by farmers.

The problem of poaching

There is one threat that affects virtually all of Africa's larger wildlife species: poaching. It is also particularly resistant to a solution, given the utter poverty afflicting most of the continent. A wild animal represents meat for a protein-starved family, and may also be a convenient source of profit. If Africa's wildlife is to survive well in the 21st century, poaching must be addressed. Most experts favour a holistic approach. Education programmes

pete with larger, more aggressive predators such as lions. They are also less than adept at dealing with traffic, and many end up as road kill. But the biggest threat facing them is disease from domestic animals. Wild dogs have little natural resistance to the diseases routinely shrugged off by domestic dogs. The close social behaviour of wild dogs assures that a malady will spread rapidly once an infectious agent enters a pack.

Aggressive measures are under way to protect and augment wild-dog populations, including captive breeding and reintroduction programmes, road

LEFT: the white rhino is almost extinct through poaching.
ABOVE: the mountain gorilla is on the endangered list.

help, but they must be accompanied by economic incentives so that wildlife becomes more valuable alive than dead. For many areas, ecotourism holds the greatest hope.

Game farming is also gaining favour. Here, certain game species are "farmed" and harvested in natural habitats. This mode of agriculture protects habitat for a wide array of animals in addition to the commercially valuable species, and allows locals to have their wildlife and eat it too. Efforts are under way, too, to establish corridors between reserves, providing the opportunity to resurrect some of the great game migrations. Such corridors will reduce the periodic culling needed in some parks to reduce overpopulation by particularly fecund species. ❑

OBSERVING WILDLIFE

*Time in the bush is more rewarding if you know about wildlife-watching
techniques, animal behaviour, their habits and conservation issues*

Africa's game parks are not zoos. Though animals in some parks are habituated to the presence of humans, you'll need both dedication and a little luck to score a sighting of many species. As with most endeavours, wildlife-watching requires a certain set of skills and some crucial equipment.

First, the gear. At the top of the list should be a good pair of binoculars – the best you can afford. Choose 7x to 10x magnification; anything more powerful will wobble when you attempt to hold them steady. Go for large-object lenses (the fat ends farthest from your eyes), as these admit more light and give a clearer picture. A pair with roof prisms rather than porro-prisms is likely to be lighter and less cumbersome. Spend your money on a reputable make with high-quality optics, avoid fancy gimmicks such as zoom or antishake features, and don't forget the option of buying a good second-hand pair.

Pack your binoculars securely in your luggage to avoid damage, but keep them around your neck, uncased, when in the field. Wildlife often comes and goes in a flash, and you need to be ready when an animal reveals itself.

Practise with your binoculars before leaving home, so you can bring them up to your eyes and focus on target objects at varying distances with minimal difficulty. If you find it comfortable, shorten the strap so that the binoculars hang just below your chin – nearer your eyes. Old Africa hands always look at the game, never the binoculars; they stay sighted on their quarry, bringing the binoculars up and "inserting" them between the animal and their eyes.

What to wear

Spotting wildlife is only half the challenge; the other half is making sure it doesn't spot you. Khaki, grey, or olive-green fabrics are good choices. Avoid white or light colours, which signal your presence to game like a beacon. Long-sleeved shirts are best, as sleeves can be turned up or down depending on temperature. It's nice to have shirts with breast pockets for pens, notebooks and sundries. Shorts or long trousers? That's strictly a matter of preference. Long trousers can get a little sticky on a hot

afternoon, but they protect against insects and sunburn. Take a light jacket or sweater even during high summer. Pre-dawn mornings can be bitterly cold on the veldt.

Choose desert boots or other light, rugged footwear. Even four-wheel-drive vehicles get bogged down in sand or mud once in a while. You may have to get out and push or walk back to your lodge.

Perhaps most important, wear a hat. The sun can kill, or at least make you miserable. Baseball caps are best in open vehicles, where bush hats may be blown off. But when the sun is beating down and you're trekking through the veldt, only a broad-brimmed hat will provide

LEFT: hot-air balloon safaris can be taken across the Maasai Mara or the Serengeti national parks.
RIGHT: subdued clothing is best for safari.

adequate protection. Also bring polarised sunglasses, lip balm and a reliable insect repellent. Use a 30-SPF sunscreen all the time.

Photography

Though cameras are *de rigueur*, it's also a good idea to bring a notebook and – if you're of an artistic bent – a sketchbook. Journal entries will greatly augment the pictorial record, and provide an account of the trip that can be enjoyed for years. Compact cameras are gaining in popularity on safari, but they

FULL OF BEANS

When photographing from a safari vehicle, you can avoid camera-shake with a bean bag – a small "pillow" filled with beans or sand. Rest it on the roof of the vehicle and mould the lens into it.

when used in a vehicle. A monopod is a practical compromise; a door frame, tree or rock is better than nothing. For obvious reasons, shooting from the back of a horse or camel is generally unsatisfactory. Most safari pictures are taken from the roof-hatch of a vehicle, but shooting everything from above can create stereotyped images. Shooting from a lower angle out of a side window frequently results in more striking and dramatic pictures. Always take more – much more – film than you think

should be equipped with built-in telephoto lenses. Because wildlife photography invariably entails telescopic shooting, it's best to bring a standard 35mm SLR camera and some "long glass" – good telephoto lenses. Professional wildlife photographers use lenses in the 500mm to 800mm range, but this is generally impractical for the casual visitor. Two zoom lenses – one ranging from 28mm to 100mm, the other from 100mm to 300mm – should suffice.

Whether you are shooting from a hide, a motor vehicle or on foot, you should try to brace the camera with whatever support is available, especially if you are using a long lens. A tripod is best, but very cumbersome

you'll need. Africa inevitably stimulates a shutter-snapping frenzy in even amateur photographers, and locally sold film – if you can find it – is expensive. Transparencies provide better clarity than prints and are essential if you plan to give slide shows. Otherwise, print film is the best choice.

The best times to take pictures in the bush are before 9am and after 4pm, when the sun is low and not too fierce. In the middle of the day, unless it is overcast, the light is simply too bright, "bleaching out" colours, and shadows are impenetrably black. Faster film – from 200 to 400 ISO – is best in low-light situations at dawn and dusk, particularly if you're using a telephoto lens. When the sun is blazing down, polarising filter can help to diffuse the worst of its rays; a "warm" amber filter such as an 81A is useful, too, to correct the "bleaching out" of colour. At the very least, you should always have an ultraviolet filter fitted. Not only does it correct the blue blur you sometimes see on the distant horizon, but it also protects your lens.

Video cameras are increasingly seen on safari. They're a good choice, because they usually have powerful telephoto lenses, they're easy to use, and they perform well in low light. Digital cameras are gaining in popularity, too: all the above rules for film photography apply,

ing and unloading film. Keep all your cameras, lenses and film in sealed polythene bags when not in use.

Respecting wildlife

Human beings have destroyed wildlife habitats and ecosystems the world over, and now all that remains of wild Africa are its national parks and game reserves. The only way to preserve them for future generations is to treat them with respect. As the saying goes, "Take nothing but pictures, leave nothing but footprints." Carry out your rubbish and campfire ashes (better yet, forgo the fire and use a portable camping

although only the most expensive digital cameras allow for the use of filters. If you are using a camcorder or digital camera, take plenty of rechargeable batteries.

Many camps and lodges have recharging facilities, but you may have to wait your turn in a queue of other visitors. At dry times of the year, dust can be a hazard to photographic equipment. It is particularly important to protect your camera from wind-blown dust when you are load-

LEFT: a thrilling photo opportunity for safari visitors.
ABOVE: camel safaris are good for getting off the beaten track, especially in semi-arid areas of Kenya, and offer a superb vantage point

stove). Resist the temptation to collect natural objects. Every feather and seedpod is food or a home to some creature.

Animals can be easily stressed, especially those with young or predators at a kill. Keep your distance and always carry binoculars. They permit safe viewing without intrusiveness. Protest if your driver leaves the prescribed roads to get a better view of wildlife (in some areas they anticipate larger tips in return for close encounters) and resist the temptation to do so yourself. Above all, remember that wild animals are unpredictable. Don't feed them and never try to herd them into a better position for viewing or photographing.

Walking safaris

Seeking wildlife on foot is the most intimate way to experience Africa, because you're on the animals' level. It's important to remember, however, that if you're walking – or on horse-back – you're engaging wildlife on its own terms. Some precautions are in order.

Imagine the world from the wildlife's point of view. Most mammals rely on scent and sound rather than eyesight to gather information about their environment. To enhance your chances of approaching game closely, keep your voice down and avoid perfume and scented sunblocks and insect repellents. Watch your step and

(especially when encountered away from water), and elephant, particularly cows with young calves.

It's generally possible to escape from all these animals – except lions – by climbing a tree, or hiding among rocks or the tangled branches of a large windfall. Few animals will pursue a charge once they've determined that an intruder has been driven off or is in hiding. Lions, however, can be problematic. Never run from a lion, as that merely excites its predatory instincts. Instead, face the animal, stretch out your arms to look as large as possible, shout loudly, and slowly back off.

where you put your hands. Breaking twigs and rolling rocks disturb game – as well as venomous snakes and scorpions. The latter, by no means uncommon in Africa, can be very venomous indeed and naturally get testy when they are trod upon or otehwise threatened.

Though many animals have poor eyesight, they can still detect movement, which they invariably find alarming. Like people, they resent having their private space invaded, especially if the intruder appears suddenly.

Most species will flee in panic, but a few will react aggressively and attack. Animals in this category include lion, rhinoceros (particularly black rhinos), lone bull buffalo, hippopotamus

Professional guides should keep you perfectly safe, but Africa isn't Disneyland; wildlife is unpredictable, and unexpected things do happen in the bush. To a significant degree, you are responsible for your own safety. Determine the wind direction regularly by kicking up dust to see which way it drifts; this will tell you where your scent is going. Regularly check the surrounding terrain for refuges and escape routes. Generally speaking, if an animal is aware of your presence from a distance it will not attack, unless provoked. That's why people sleeping in tents are seldom molested.

Not every outing will produce sightings of large, charismatic species. But one of the great joys of walking in Africa is the opportunity to appreciate all the small things you would otherwise miss from a vehicle: the clacking call of guinea fowl, the various spoor and scat (droppings) of beasts great and small, termites constructing their massive mounds, dung beetles rolling balls of dung.

Ultimately, these are the greatest pleasures of safari: immersing yourself in a land and its inhabitants that have remained largely unchanged since the end of the last ice age.

AFTER DARK

Driving at night is forbidden in most national parks and reserves, but many camps and lodges offer night drives just outside the perimeter – where the action is often just as plentiful.

Small eyes, bobbing about under bushes, are likely to be those of an elephant shrew, while those that seem to bounce may belong to a spring hare, a rodent resembling a small kangaroo which slips into an underground burrow when disturbed.

Large eyes close to the ground probably belong to a small cat – African wild cat, genet or caracal – or a large member of the mongoose family, the civet. The huge eyes of bush babies and owls can be seen shining from high branches. A lucky few may

The changing seasons

To everything there is a season, including African wildlife. A safari in the rainy season is a wondrous experience – the bush vibrant with new foliage, the grass electric green and knee-high, panoramas of wildflowers to the horizon, animals plump and fit, with most of the herbivores giving birth at this time.

Birds breed and nest during the rainy season, and often display extravagant breeding plumage. One drawback: the dense vegetation tends to conceal animals, making sightings difficult.

Once the rains stop, water sources begin shrinking. The game concentrates at waterholes and along rivers; the vegetation desiccates, making it easier to spot animals. By the end of the dry season, virtually all the animals in a given area gather around the few available sources of water. A great variety of species can typically be seen in a short period of time, and predator and prey interactions are common, making this the most exciting time of year for wildlife viewing.

Night safari

A night drive, under huge, starry skies, reveals another side of the bush, one that's alive with scurrying nocturnal creatures. The person behind the spotlight swings the beam back and forth, checking under bushes and trees and among the branches, looking for shining eyes. A knowledgeable guide should be able to identify the owners of those eyes, passing quickly over the diurnal species who need their sleep.

LEFT: walking safaris are the best way to engage wildlife on its own terms.
RIGHT: male crickets produce a chirping sound by rubbing together leathery forewings.

catch sight of a scaly anteater called a pangolin, a honey badger, or even an aardvark.

But the biggest thrill is spotting one of the big cats or other predators. Lions, usually seen lazing around during the day, pace menacingly through the bush at night. Hyenas whoop and jackals yap as they prowl around the fringes of a kill. Most exciting of all is an encounter with that quintessential denizen of the night, the leopard. Rarely seen in daylight, it will completely ignore the interruption, moving purposefully along, lithe muscles rippling under its magnificent coat until, with a haughty flick of a white-tipped tail, it slips silently into the night. ❏

WILDLIFE

The diversity and abundance of East African wildlife, from towering elephants to tiny spiders, is astonishing

East Africa's savanna, grasslands, mountains, woodlands, rainforests, deserts, rivers, lakes and coral reefs are home to an amazing diversity of creatures. Few places in the world have such a variety of habitats and climates within such a (relatively) small area – which explains the amazing biodiversity. And nowhere in the world has such an abundance and variety of large mammals.

In the days of the old-style hunting safari, where the principal purpose was to shoot wild beasts for trophies, some creatures came to be regarded as more desirable targets than others. They were rated according to the skill it took to track them, the risk involved in confronting them, and the quality of the trophy produced by a successful kill. In time, five mammals which qualified on all counts were recognised as the ultimate objectives of a hunting safari: the elephant, rhino, buffalo, lion and leopard – the "Big Five". Our survey of animals and plants begins with profiles of these five creatures.

Successive chapters look at some of East Africa's many other mammals, large and small. The full roster includes over 40 carnivores (cats, dogs, hyenas, mongooses, otters and relatives of the weasel), about 30 primates (monkeys and apes), 60 or so herbivores (including hippo, giraffe, zebra and 46 species of antelope), oddities such as hyraxes, pangolins and aardvarks, and literally hundreds of species of rodents, shrews and bats. There is no room in a book such as this to describe them all: before setting off, you should arm yourself with a comprehensive field guide to all the mammals *(see Further Reading on page 338 for suggestions)*.

The same is true, only more so, for the birds: there are roughly 1,500 species in the region – about 15 percent of all the world's bird species. Our chapter looks at a few of the most impressive, curious or downright beautiful, but you should get another field guide to help you identify the scores, or hundreds, of different birds you will see. Then there are the reptiles, ranging from the world's largest (the Nile crocodile) to tiny chameleons and skinks. And the invertebrates – tens of thousands of insects, spiders, millipedes, scorpions and others, which all play their part in the ecology of East Africa. Not forgetting the offshore coral reefs, which are host to a range of species as numerous, diverse and spectacular as those on land. ❑

PRECEDING PAGES: female lions are highly sociable and work together as a group.
LEFT: there are an estimated 110 mountain gorillas in Parc National des Volcans, Rwanda, where they are the star attractions.

THE AFRICAN ELEPHANT

The charismatic African elephant is not only the largest land animal,
it is also an intelligent, social and compassionate creature

The African elephant *(Loxodonta africana)* is the largest living land animal: it grows to a height of 3 metres (10 ft) or more at the shoulder and up to 5 tonnes in weight. Most of its special characteristics are a consequence of its unique body size. It has a disproportionately large head; toenails instead of hooves; two breasts between the forelegs; internal testes, next to the kidneys; specialised grinding teeth; tusks nearly worth their weight in gold; a unique trunk; enormous ears and a 60-year life span.

Elephants once roamed throughout Africa. Now they occupy only one-fifth of the continent. In the 1920s, the elephant population numbered around 10 million – then poaching for ivory began to take its toll, particularly in the decade 1979–89, when numbers nearly halved from 1,300,000 animals to 750,000. In Kenya alone, the elephant population was reduced from 150,000 to 30,000. Since the late 1980s, an international ban on the trade in ivory has helped to reverse this trend in East Africa, where most elephant populations have increased dramatically over the past 20 years. However, rapidly increasing human population and the resulting loss of habitat continue to threaten elephants, and they are listed as an endangered species. Exact population figures are very hard to ascertain, but the African Elephant Specialist Group, responsible for maintaining a database on populations, reported in 1998 that the continent-wide total may have dropped below half a million.

Mobile beasts

The elephant occupies all African habitats from near desert to closed-canopy forest. It's inherent mobility allows it to select foods from a variety of habitats over a home range which may be thousands of square kilometres. The availability of grass for a good part of the year is important; the presence of perennial water within its range is essential. Elephants move daily and seasonally between different parts of the habitat: from woodland to grassland, from bushland to swamp, and back again. Elephants are active both night and day, since their 16- to 20-hour waking period must necessarily spill into the dark hours. A herd will spend most of their waking time feeding. They often take a midday siesta in shade, and at night, if the group feels secure, they may indulge

in a period of deep sleep, even lying down.

Elephants bathe, wallow or dust whenever possible, at least once a day, for cooling and to help get rid of parasites. They blow trunkfuls of liquid or dust between their legs, on top of their head or along their flanks. As a result of frequent mud bathing and dusting, elephants appear more the colour of local soil types than the natural grey of their skins. Adopted colours range from light grey through red to dark brown, allowing the observer to guess from where a group of elephants has recently come.

The only serious threat to an adult elephant is man, who may eventually either displace all wild elephant populations as he spreads into marginal

LEFT: elephant mother and her calf.
RIGHT: elephants bathe or wallow daily to cool down.

lands, or kill them directly in poaching for ivory. Elephants do, rarely, get their own back. An unarmed human has little chance at close range against an angry elephant. The frequently observed head shake, accompanied often with an audible ear snap, is a warning to keep away. A serious charge is strangely quiet: the elephant runs at 35 kph (22 mph), ears out, head lowered, trunk curled under.

MAKING THEIR MARK

Like many other herbivores in Africa, elephants of both sexes may urinate or defecate to mark their territory and for recognition.

Elephants are as sociable as primates. Greeting elephants will either put their trunks in each others' mouths, or touch and therefore smell each

have no leadership role in the group, although they will assist in defence.

Bulls drift from family unit to family unit, and from time to time into loosely knit bull groups: two to 20 males who move together for a day, a week or a season. The membership of bull groups changes continually. Larger bulls go off to inspect females and mate: young bulls, newly ousted from their family unit, quickly find companionship, teachers and safety in numbers in bull groups.

A family unit of 15 is large. If it grows any

others' temporal glands. These greeting gestures probably reveal subtle states of mood as well as identity. When two family units reunite after several days or weeks of separation, there is much squealing and trumpeting, pirouetting, backing up, greeting and excreting.

Family values

The basic social unit is the family group, comprising several related adult females and their immature offspring. The group is led by the eldest cow, the matriarch. There is no dominant herd bull. Adult males tag along with family units for short periods to inspect females for their readiness to mate. These visiting bulls

THE CALL OF THE WILD

Research has shown that elephants are highly vocal animals. Low-frequency sound, well below or at the very edge of human perception, is a very efficient means of communicating over great distances – even amid thick vegetation. It enables elephants to maintain contact for up to 10 km (6 miles).

The deep rumble we hear from time to time is a contact vocalisation ("Here I am – where are you?") which just enters the range of human hearing. Elephants also roar and scream audibly through the trunk to produce the classic trumpeting, either in anger or exultation, depending on the situation.

larger, the group is likely to split into two, each new group going its own way, one led by the old matriarch, the other by one of her sisters or cousins. Family units may show strong associations with certain other groups in a particular area – often because of a blood relationship between the matriarchs: they are probably sisters or cousins in a family unit that split.

With the rains and abundant grass growth, however, family groups are likely to join together in larger herds which, in places like the Serengeti, Selous and Tsavo, have numbered more than 1,000 elephants in sight from the same hill top. Bull groups satellite such assem-

Check mate

Females may come into season every two or three months, if they are not pregnant or lactating. This, and the wide dispersal of an elephant population, makes it necessary for males to move between family units, constantly testing for female readiness to mate. It was once thought that only Asian elephant males came into sexual season, a period of ill temper called *musth*. Recent studies show that African elephant males also show seasonal fluctuations in their temper and sexual motivation and display conspicuous physiological indicators, known to elephant watchers as the "green penis syn-

blages, and many bulls are within them testing females. The frequency of mating is high. Seasonal gathering of the clans may facilitate breeding in a wide-ranging and mobile beast.

Old elephants provide the family unit with a historical memory of watering holes, the location of seasonally available fruits, and other dispersed features of the elephant's world. Even a menopausal cow can retain her role as matriarch, suggesting that wisdom, and not just sex appeal, is a predominant quality for an elephant herd decision-maker.

LEFT: herds are led by the eldest cow, a matriarch.
RIGHT: crossing the river to a new habitat.

drome". The annual two or three months of irascibility is accompanied by the penis dangling, dribbling, and taking on a characteristic greenish hue and strong smell. The odour is detectable to human observers, so it must be nearly overwhelming to other elephants.

The signs of *musth*, usually attributed only to irritable males, are now known to be inherent in both sexes. A liquid oozes from the temporal gland, a modified tear gland halfway between the ear and the eye, leaving a conspicuous dark stain along the side of the face. The secretion, called temporin, accompanies a state of excitement, such as when there is a frightening disturbance or if close relatives reunite after a period of separation. A bull in *musth* is more likely to displace his peers when it comes to winning the favours of a female.

Occasionally, a female in oestrous and a large courting bull will consort for a time: they stay close together, pay attention to one another, and exclude others from any intimacy. Consorting may be very subtle, or actually take the pair some distance away from the family unit and other bulls. This may account for the old tale of elephant "marriages".

Consorting may not always be so tender – and the male may have to catch her first. If the consorting female breaks into a run, the male

Growing up

Elephant calves spend several years dependent on and learning from the adults. There is nearly constant contact between mother and young. Calves suckle from the side, reaching for the teat just behind the mother's front leg. A young elephant that can walk under its mother's belly is probably less than a year old. A calf may suckle for up to five years. Young bulls stay with their family units until puberty, perhaps 10 to 15 years, after which they are encouraged to establish themselves elsewhere, but young females may stay with the group for life. Young elephants in a relaxed, undis-

takes after her. Females mostly outrun males if they wish, and getting caught is probably the female's way of choosing who catches her.

The female usually stops when the male touches her, particularly if he is able to lay his trunk along her back or across her shoulders. He then rests his head and tusks on her rump and heaves himself up on his hind legs. By squatting slightly and hooking upward his highly mobile erect penis, he is able to enter her. Copulation lasts less than a minute. The rest of the family unit is either indifferent to the copulation, or capable of reacting with great excitement – vocalising, ear-flapping, head-shaking, turning, backing and excreting.

CAUSE FOR CONCERN

If an elephant is wounded or falls ill, it causes great concern and excitement in the group. Faltering animals which find it hard to walk will be kept upright between two or more adults. Fallen animals will be fussed over with trunks and feet, and tusk-breaking attempts to lift a downed elephant have often been observed. The strange habit of burying a dead or immobilised fellow is also well-documented. Trunkfuls of dirt are tossed over the animal; branches are broken off and laid tenderly over the body, until it is completely covered. Extraordinarily, human victims of elephant attacks have been treated in a similar manner. The reason is not known.

turbed and healthy population are a pleasure to watch playing with each other: chasing, play fighting, tug-of-wars and mounting. Their long childhood is only matched by higher primates, including man.

Group defence is common. If simply moving away does not work, the next line of defence is to draw up a formidable wall of adult females to face the intrusion with heads high, ears out, looking to and fro as if trying to make out the exact source of the annoyance. Young members of the group are pushed towards the rear. In full retreat, the group runs off in a tight bunch with the young in the middle.

Energetic eating

Elephants feed up to 16 hours a day, using a variety of feeding techniques. They eat most vegetable material, from staples such as grass, trees and shrubs, to delicacies like fruits, seeds, herbs and creepers. In certain seasons, they strip the bark off acacia trees. They are attracted to over-ripe fruit and often gorge themselves to the point of intoxication on fermenting fruit. Even while feeding on grassland, elephants detect the occasional herb or creeper by smell, and pluck them out. In this way, odd individuals break the feeding pattern as they come across an interesting "side dish" or a new bulk food. The entire group may then shift to the new delicacy.

The trunk is their principal feeding tool, capable of reaching food from ground level to nearly 5 metres (16 ft) up. Its main function is to reach downwards to harvest grass, the bulk of the elephant's diet. The trunk evolved from the nose and upper lip combining. It is an astonishingly mobile and dextrous collection of muscles. It has a "two-fingered" tip, used for smelling and for picking and plucking. Tusks are also important tools, and are modified front biting teeth (incisors), not eyeteeth (canines), as might be expected. Tusks are used for chiselling, digging, prising, levering and stabbing. Elephant ivory grows about 10 cm (4 inches) per year, so the frequently broken tips are continually replaced by new growth. This has inspired suggestions of "live harvesting" of ivory to save elephant lives. No more than one or two percent of elephants are naturally tuskless.

The remaining elephant teeth, the molars, are

also unique. In its lifetime an elephant has only six teeth on each side of each jaw, 24 in all. The teeth are large, 20–30 cm (8–12 inches) long, so only one, or two halves, end to end, are exposed on each jaw side at a time. Molars grow progressively forward, which provides scientists with a means of telling elephants' ages. Chewing is forward and backward: the lower jaw grinds against the upper in the forward stroke. Since elephants spend most of the day eating, they are almost continuously chewing.

An adult elephant can eat 150–200 kg (68–90 lb) of vegetation a day. Water is essential – 70–90 litres (15–20 gallons) per day – both for

helping digestion and for cooling. Water is sucked into the trunk and then tipped and released into the mouth. Animals less than about six months old have generally not learned the trick; they drink from their knees, sucking water directly into the mouth. If water is not within a half day's march, elephants may use their trunks and tusks to dig for it, for example, in the bed of a sand river. Elephant wells, as much as a metre (3 ft) deep, provide numerous other animals with access to water during dry periods. At these wells, or at a normal watering hole, elephants easily displace all other animals, including buffalo and rhino, and have been known to kill them if it comes to a fight. ❑

LEFT: the average life span of an elephant is 60 years.
RIGHT: play-fighting by Ewaso Ngiro River, Kenya.

THE RHINOCEROS

Almost poached to extinction, the prehistoric-looking rhino is
on the critically endangered list – its future very much in the hands of man

In our lifetimes, black and white rhinoceros *(Diceros bicornis* and *Ceratotherium simum)* are doomed to extinction, outside of contained protected areas. Rhinos' horns are leading the beast to the brink of extinction *(see panel below right)*. The alleged pharmaceutical qualities of rhino horn – as a nerve tonic and general restorative rather than an aphrodisiac – have supported ancient markets in the Far East. Much of the poaching in Africa, however, has been to fulfil the demand for dagger handles, a male status symbol in south Yemen. One well-wrought *jambia* made from one life-long grown horn can fetch up to US$20,000 in Sana'a.

Rhinos are odd-toed ungulates, like horses. Their footprints are unmistakable, with three large toes. There are two distinct species of rhinos, the so-called black and white rhino. Both are in fact grey. The latter's name is a corruption of the Afrikaans word for "wide", referring to its broad upper lip, which is designed for grazing. Black rhinos have longer necks than whites which helps them to reach up into vegetation for browsing. The white rhino's relatively longer head enables it to reach the ground to graze.

African rhinos have two long horns, one set behind the other. These are not bone, but tightly packed bundles of hair-like structures, similar to hooves and toenails, mounted on roughened areas of the skull. Apart from this, rhinos are virtually hairless.

The rhinos' keen senses of smell and hearing compensate for their weak eyesight. They can turn their ears to locate the source of any disturbance. Like other large-bodied animals, rhinos have potentially long lifespans – up to 50 years.

There are two distinct population ranges of white rhinos. The northern range *(Ceratotherium simum cottoni)* extends from southern Sudan west through Zaire towards Lake Chad. The southern species *(C. s. simum)* occurs south of the Zambezi. There are marked differences between the two subspecies in the concavity of the forehead. Populations have not been contiguous in recent historical times.

Some populations of black rhino developed characteristic traits. "Gertie" and "Pixie" of Amboseli were famous for their remarkably long, straight horns. The gene for such horns has now been poached out of existence.

LEFT: face-to-face with *Diceros bicornis* (black rhino).
RIGHT: a black rhino in solitary pose.

GOING, GOING, GONE?

The population figures for both rhino species make depressing reading. The northern white rhino once had a wide distribution; as late as 1960, there were more than 2,000 roaming the savannas of central Africa. But widespread poaching ravaged the population and today there are probably fewer than ten left in the wild – all in Garamba National Park in the Democratic Republic of Congo. The black rhino has not fared much better: from around 70,000 in the 1960s, numbers dwindled to about 15,000 in 1980 – and around 5,000 today, 40 percent of them in South Africa. Both the northern white and the black rhino are classified as critically endangered.

Habitat and habits

The black rhino ranges from moist, montane forest to semi-arid bushland. The white rhino prefers the drier habitat of grassland and wooded grassland. Both species characteristically seek shelter and shade in dense undergrowth and thickets. The white rhino is partly nocturnal; the black rhino more strictly diurnal.

The shape of the mouths of the two species reflects the differences in their feeding habits. The black rhino is a browser, and it has a pointed, nearly prehensile upper

> **NEED FOR WATER**
>
> Rhinos are seldom found far from a source of water, but during a period of drought they can go for up to five days without drinking.

Man is the rhino's main predator, although lions and hyenas may try to attack very young calves. Rhinos are able to rout or dispatch most disturbances after a short 50-kph (30-mph) charge. Disturbed rhinos are prone to attack, often before they have properly located the source of disturbance, so the initial charge may not be directly towards the intended target. Other charges may stop short, as though the real purpose is to get close enough to identify and intimidate the disturbance. In such a case the rhino is more likely to

lip, which allows it to choose and pluck small twigs, leaves, fruit and vines. The black rhino eats most plants except grasses – nearly 800 species in some areas. The white rhino is a grazer, with a broad mouth, and upper lips and teeth suitable for grinding grass. Both have lost the front biting teeth altogether and rely on their lips to gather vegetation.

Rhinos are fond of rolling on their sides in mud or dust wallows. They cannot roll on their backs because of the elongated, blade-like protrusions on their spines. They frequently rub their belly, flanks or face on rocks or stumps and "polished" rubbing sites are dotted throughout rhino country.

wheel about and run off than follow through with the attack.

Rhinos are not very sociable, especially black rhinos. White rhinos may form small, family groups including several females and youngsters, but the most commmonly seen group is a female with her calf. The territories of mature males vary from 3 sq. km (1½ sq. miles) in forested areas to 90 sq. km (35 sq. miles) in open grasslands. Old territorial males rarely stray from their familiar area. Territory is marked both around the edges and throughout the middle with large, conspicuous dung piles, or middens. Middens may be a couple of square metres in extent. They are approached and sniffed by most passing rhinos, but only the dominant male defecates and scatters his latest addition on to the pile with his hind feet. They commonly rub their horns in the pile. A white rhino territory may have 20 to 30 middens around the boundaries. Scientists think that middens might be a sort of range "mailbox", allowing all rhinos in an area to keep track of who is in the neighbourhood and their reproductive state.

White rhino females often engage in friendly nose-to-nose greetings when they meet. Males however, especially black rhino males, tend to be less amiable. When they encounter each

Mating games

Their territories ensure that white rhino males have access to receptive females. Once a female is found, she is continuously, but gently, herded within the boundaries of the territory for up to two weeks, often accompanied by her most recent calf. This may in part explain the length of time the male spends manoeuvring and tagging her – as much to get away from the "teenager" as to get close to her. Once close, the male prods the female gently with his horn, rests his chin on her back, rubs his face on her flank, and generally softens her up for the final approach. Mating may last as long as an hour,

other, serious fighting can result if one rhino does not give way. Sometimes gaping wounds are inflicted by the upward sweep of an opponent's horn. White rhinos appear to be more phlegmatic than black: two males may spend an hour staring at each other from a short distance, sometimes nose to nose, as if greeting, occasionally wiping their horns on the ground. They then turn around suddenly and trot back to the centre of their respective territories.

LEFT: black rhino browse on branches and leaves broken off by their horns.
ABOVE: Ngorongoro Crater, Tanzania, is one of the best places to view black rhinos.

during which the male ejaculates several times. This does little to dispel the popular perception of the qualities of rhino horn.

Single calves are born – most commonly in the rainy season – after a gestation of some 16 months. Newborn animals are very small at birth, only one-twentieth of the female's weight. Females seclude themselves at the time of birth and female white rhinos, after calving, may isolate themselves from other animals for a month. It is said that white rhino calves run in front of their mothers; black rhino calves run behind. Calves stay with their mothers from two to four years, depending on the birth of the next offspring. ❑

BUFFALO

Buffalos have a bad reputation, and lone bulls can be extremely dangerous when provoked, but generally they are docile, grazing herd animals

The African buffalo *(Syncerus caffer)* is widely regarded to be the meanest beast in the bush, prone to launch a killing charge at the drop of a hat. Such aggression is understandable when the buffalo has just been shot at, especially coming from a short-tempered solitary male. But the majority of buffalos in cow-calf

herds are nearly as docile as cattle. All African buffalos are classified as one species, but three distinctive races are accorded wide recognition. The most common and widespread is the savannah buffalo *(S. c. caffer)*, a very large (up to 850kg/1,850lb) black-pelted resident of grassland and woodland. The less-bulky forest buffalo *(S. c. nanus)* is a rainforest dweller with a striking chestnut coat, while the western buffalo *(S. c. brachyceros)* of northwest Africa is intermediate in colour and size. The only race to occur in most parts of East Africa is the savanna buffalo, but some interbreeding with forest buffalo occurs in the national parks of western Uganda. Buffalos in general favour grassland, either open,

wooded or bushed. They are most active in the evening, night and early morning, which is when they feed and move from place to place. The rest of their time is spent lying down and ruminating, in shade, if available, rather like cows in a field. Buffalos must drink daily, so are never found more than 15 km (9 miles) from water. As with domestic cattle, buffalo probably sleep not more than an hour a day.

Buffalos are strictly grazers. Different species of grass and even their parts – leaves, stems, inflorescences – are selected. Seasonal changes in grass availability and nutritional value dictate the local movements of buffalo in semi-arid areas. In the rains they will feed on open plains; in the dry season, they retreat to woodlands, hill slopes and river fringes.

The massive, bossed horns and exceptional size of the animal afford considerable protection. This has allowed blind, lame, even three-legged individuals to survive longer than could have been expected. Solitary bulls, without the redoubtable protection of numbers, commonly fall prey to prides of lions. It is not uncommon, though, for lions to be fatally injured during a prolonged battle with a wounded buffalo. A buffalo herd, when in danger of attack by lions, will form a defensive semicircle, protected by bulls on the flanks, with the cows and calves grouped in the centre of the formation.

An explosive snort heralds alarm. This is followed by a nose-up posture orientated at the intruder, who should begin looking for the nearest tree if the buffalo is a lone male. An alarm in a cow-calf herd will bring the others to attention, and those close to the intruder may even move forward in a shortsighted manner, as if to have a better look. If the intruder stands his ground or even advances a few paces, the buffalos will invariably turn tail with high head tosses and the entire herd will run off.

Herd mentality

Buffalos live in herds which have a relatively stable composition, changed only by births and deaths. Herds may be as large as 2,000 for the savanna buffalo but are rarely larger than 20 for its forest counterpart. A figure of 350 was estimated as an average in Serengeti National Park between the wet and dry seasons. Large herds tend to fragment during the dry season and regroup in the wet. This spreads the grazing load when grass is in short supply. In the dry season, they tend to concentrate along the rivers; in the wet season, they spread out over the habitat. Each herd has its own range, and there is little overlap between adjacent herds. Despite their strong herding instincts, the basic social unit appears to be an adult female, her suckling calf and her two-year-old from the previous season's breeding. When any one of the three is incapacitated, the other two will remain with the injured one. Vocalisations play only a small role in social encounters: calves bleat, cows grunt to call calves, and short explosive snorts may be made when alarmed. Otherwise buffalos are rather silent, without the typical bovine lowing sounds.

HERD DECISION-MAKING

Decisions about which way a resting group of buffalos should move next seem to be taken after individual females stand up and face a particular direction: the whole herd moves off in the most popular direction.

Male buffalos

Bachelor groups of 10 to 15 are common, and may consist either of old, retired bulls who no longer bother to compete for females, or younger bulls nearing their prime during the off-season for matings, usually when it is dry. Solitary old males or small bull groups are the ones likely to charge intruders.

Fighting males circle each other for long periods, head-tossing and pawing the ground. The major threat is a lateral display with the head lifted and nose pointed to the ground. Presented side-on, the thickness and power of the neck and shoulder muscles are shown to full advantage. Seen from the front, the posture emphasises the size and raised surface edge of the horns.

Two males squaring off will accentuate their horns with tossing, hooking movements, and by thrashing nearby bushes. Such displays usually end with one animal giving up by simply walking away. Actual fights are rare, which saves potentially serious damage. When

fights do occur, they consist of terrific head-on clashes.

Wallowing in mud holes appears to have a social function as well as keeping animals cool and discouraging skin parasites. A particular wallow, apart from being foul-smelling in its own right, may take on the scent of the bull which lays claim to it. The wallow thus serves as a passive territory marker. Cattle egrets can often be found in the company of wallowing buffalos. These birds give away the pres-

ence of buffalo concealed within a swamp.

Males test for females in heat by sniffing their urine and genitals. Male competition for females does not entail much fierce fighting. Posturing and mock fights serve as substitutes for conflict, which helps keep these large, powerful animals from injuring one another. Courtship entails a temporary male-female bond which lasts only until soon after mating. The principal calving period is between December and February. Calves are carried for 11½ months, and are dropped in the midst of the herd, usually in the rains. The afterbirth is eaten, the calf is licked clean, stimulated to defecate and suckled. After this procedure the calf joins the grazing herd. ❑

LEFT: an African buffalo cow, with a perching red-billed oxpecker.
RIGHT: a herd congregates at the aptly named Buffalo Springs National Reserve in Kenya.

LION

Lions are the only really social cats, with the females doing most of the hunting while the males ward off attacks from nomadic rivals

The lion *(Panthera leo)* is the largest of the big cats, two to four times the weight of its cousins, the leopard and cheetah. It is more social than other cats and also shows greater differences between the sexes. The male weighs up to 50 percent more than a female and has a mane which is fully developed by four years old.

Young lions have a spotted coat which gradually, over the first two years, becomes a nearly uniform tawny. Like many of their prey, lions have a slighty countershaded colouration: a pelage darker on top grading to lighter underneath. This tends to neutralise the three-dimensional shadowing created by overhead lighting from the sun, as the shadow is lightened by the whitish belly fur. The overall effect is to enhance camouflage by flattening form.

Lions are widespread in wooded and bushed habitats. Although they are often seen in completely open grasslands, they prefer areas which have cover for hunting and hiding their young. They appear to succeed in maintaining healthy populations in most game parks and reserves.

Lions are predominantly active in the evening, early morning, and intermittently through the night. They tend to spend nearly all daylight hours resting or asleep in the shade.

Roaring success

Both lions and lionesses roar, the males louder and deeper. Roaring typically consists of long moaning grunts followed by a series of shorter ones, the whole lasting 30 to 40 seconds. Roaring is most common at dawn and dusk or during the night. Its purpose appears to be to define and maintain territories, although it may well also be used to keep in contact on dark nights: a roar can be heard up to 2–3 km (1½–2 miles) away. Individual lions can recognise one another's roars. Cubs may make noises while older lions are roaring nearby. Lionesses often encourage their cubs by softly moaning to them.

LEFT: a lion in Uganda's Queen Elizabeth National Park.
RIGHT: the lion as pet, from the 1996 film *Born Free.*

All in the family

Lions are the only really social cats. Prides are built around two to 15 related lionesses. These are accompanied by a coalition of males, many of whom are probably brothers unrelated to the females. The pride also contains dependent offspring. Young females mature and join their

mothers and aunts as breeding pride members; young males emigrate and seek unrelated prides to attempt to take over.

Lion prides are ever-changing: males only hold sway over a group of females for an average of 18 months, before they are ousted, sometimes even killed, by stronger or more numerous newcomers. Only large male coalitions can aspire to control a pride over a period of relative stability, measured in months rather than years.

Females may produce as many as six litters during a lifetime. Lionesses come into season sporadically; the periods between heats vary from a couple of weeks to months. Oestrus lasts about a week, during which time males compete over receptive females. Male coalition partners, who test females as they wander over the pride's range, are rarely aggressive towards each other in competition over potential mates. They seem to operate an agreed first-come-first-served system.

Either partner may initiate mating. The male initiates with the so-called mating snarl, which has been described as a sneeze-like grimace. The mating snarl may or may not convince the female to stop and crouch. The female, if she initiates, keeps unusually near the male and may rub her head on his shoulders and sides,

20,000 times in his lifetime: the King of Beasts indeed. Gestation is relatively short: 3½ months. In a secluded, well-hidden spot, often among rocks or dense riverside vegetation, the lioness gives birth to two or three cubs on average. She suckles and remains with them for long periods, only occasionally returning to the pride to hunt and feed. Litters are sometimes lost at this stage. After a month the cubs are led to the pride.

Lionesses appear to synchronise breeding activity; it is not unusual for several females in a pride to have litters at the same time. Unlike other mammals, lion mothers will commonly tolerate suckling by cubs of others in the pride,

emitting a deep, sensuous rumble, walking sinuously around him and flicking her tail. She may even back into the male and crouch to stimulate his interest.

Copulation is unmistakable, though perfunctory. The female yowls and the male often bites her neck in a similar manner to the subduing neck bite of domestic cats. After ejaculating, the male leaps off, often to avoid a blow from the female who may spin around when his weight is removed. Both animals then lie down. During one consorting week, the pair may copulate over 300 times, an average of once every 15 minutes during the waking hours. A successful pride male may mate

because they are generally all related. By providing milk to cubs belonging to her sisters and half-sisters, a female feeds young lions that carry some of her own genes. But females do more readily nurse their own offspring, who tend to approach boldly, mewing, purring and pushing their mothers' faces before proceeding to suckle noisily. Cousins are more prone to sneak in from behind.

Nomadic males regularly kill cubs, presumably to eliminate from the population rival genetic material. Cubs are also at risk from other predators, such as spotted hyenas and leopards. Lionesses keep their brood well hidden and move the hiding places if disturbed.

Collective predators

Lions' predatory habits have enhanced the evolution of a large head and powerful jaws equipped with long canines. Feet are large and retractable claws are unsheathed to present a catching tool as wide as a squash racquet head. Lions are the biggest African carnivores and routinely tackle prey, such as buffalo, that is beyond the ability of other predators. They stalk and ambush rather like cheetahs and leopards, but like hyenas and hunting dogs, they also hunt collectively.

GETTING THE WIND UP

Experts disagree on whether or not lions pay attention to wind direction when hunting, though hunts made upwind are usually more successful.

Females in the pride do most of the hunting but males, with their superior strength and weight, gain first access to a kill once the dirty work is done. There is a reason beyond sheer laziness: males have a distinct disadvantage in stalking with their manes, which appear like small haystacks moving though the grass.

Hunting tactics depend on prey and habitat. In open habitats lions tend to hunt at night, though they can be active during the day when there is enough vegetation to hide their approaches. River

Most of their prey consists of medium to large ungulates, such as wildebeest and zebra, although there is considerable seasonal and regional variation. In the Serengeti, for example, lions often hunt warthogs in the dry season when the wildebeest and zebra have migrated north towards Kenya.

At all times lions are opportunistic and take rodents, fledgling birds, ostrich eggs, etc. Males need to eat approximately 7 kg (20 lb) of meat a day; females 5 kg (11 lb).

crossings and watering places are favourite sites for ambushes. Stalking and rushing prey demand that lions get as close as possible. When several lions hunt together they usually try to encircle prey to cut off lines of escape. Although lions can eventually reach nearly 60 kph (37 mph), most of their prey can sprint faster. Lions must get within 30 metres (100 ft) before charging, overtaking, slapping down and grabbing the victim. Once grabbed, the victim is subdued and suffocated with a quick neck bite or a sustained bite over the muzzle. Larger prey may be overcome by several lions and members of the pride may begin to open the victim while one lion is still suffocating it. ❏

LEFT: during a consorting week, a pair may copulate over 300 times, an average of once every 15 minutes.
ABOVE: a lioness get to grips with one of her cubs.

LEOPARD

The solitary leopard is notoriously hard to find, but it is more common
than most people think, and is still the world's most widespread big cat

The leopard *(Panthera pardus)* is the largest of the spotted cats. Its heavy build, pugmark spots and thick, white-tipped tail distinguish it from the more slender cheetah. It is also the most elusive of the large cats, principally because of its nocturnal and secretive habits. It has been little studied, so not much is

Blending in

The leopard has few natural enemies, and its skill in climbing trees assures it protection from all but the most aggressive lions. Anyone who has scanned the branches and canopy of a tree for a leopard knows just how well it can blend into the blotched light and shade. Even the certain knowl-

known of its behaviour in the wild. It is active day and night, but veers strongly towards nocturnalism, due to harassment.

The leopard is found in all except the driest African habitats – woodland, bushland, wooded grassland and forest. It is the most widespread member of the cat family, occasionally even occurring in suburban areas. Large rocks and kopjes and large trees along rivers are favourite resting sites. As long as there is an adequate food supply and a minimum of persecution, the leopard is at home. Despite its adaptability, numbers have been greatly reduced due to the fur trade and by competetion with man for living space.

edge that a leopard is in a particular tree is no guarantee that it will be discovered. The twitch of a hanging tail is sometimes a giveaway.

The leopard's characteristic call is a deep, rough cough, repeated 10 to 15 times, sounding like a saw cutting wood. The male has a distinctly deeper voice than the female. The sawing call serves to advertise a leopard's presence and to discourage others from trespassing into defended territory, thereby avoiding destructive territorial fights.

Greetings are often accompanied by a short growl. The beginning of an agressive charge may be heralded by two or three short coughs, and those foolish enough to corner a leopard never forget the beast rearing up on its hind legs and uttering a blood-curdling scream. Leopards are solitary animals. They occupy and defend home ranges which vary from 1 to 30 sq. km (up to 12 sq. miles) depending on the availability of food. Males and females defend their own, often over-lapping, territories from members of their own sex.

> ## BRANCHING OUT
>
> Of all the African cats, the leopard is the most adept at climbing trees, which assures it protection from lions, concealment for ambush and a safe place to store its kill for later consumption.

Female territories tend to be smaller and several may be encompassed within one male territory. Males often fight over their space and mark trees and logs throughout their area by clawing the bark of trees and spraying urine.

Brief encounters

Breeding can occur at any time of year. Leop-ards, like all other cats except lions, are soli-tary breeders. The only long-term social bond is between a leopardess and her cubs. Females come on heat for about a week every 20 to 50 days. They advertise their receptiveness with the sawing call which soon attracts the nearest territory-holding male. A pair will then consort during the week of heat when matings are fre-quent. Males court, consort and mate, but there the honeymoon ends: they leave and take no part in cub rearing.

Gestation lasts around 100 days. Between one and six (average three) young are dropped in solitary retreats such as rock crevices and caves. At birth the cubs are blind and do not emerge from their birthplace to follow the female until they are six to eight weeks old. Young are weaned after three months and inde-pendent after two years.

The leopard's diet is wide-ranging and indi-vidualistic: most small- to medium-sized her-bivores, including antelopes, warthogs, monkeys and hyraxes, large birds, reptiles, rodents and primates (baboons are a favourite), as well as smaller carnivores such as servals and jackals are fair game.

Leopards use mainly stealth and surprise to capture their prey. Like cheetahs and lions, they are stalkers, but their tree-climbing habit

LEFT: a magnificent female leopard in her tree lair.
RIGHT: leopards usually rest during the day but are active by dusk and hunt at night.

adds a third dimension to their hunts: it is a common tactic to leap out of trees onto prey. But the leopard, surprisingly, is not keen on long chases. If the prey is not secured after a rush of a few metres, the leopard will give up the pursuit and the victim will invariably get away.

Spotting leopards

Leopards are present in con-siderable numbers throughout East Africa, but their reclusive and nocturnal habits mean that sightings are rare and pre-

cious moments. However, success is more likely in certain locations.

Lake Nakuru National Park contains a large population of leopards, including animals relo-cated from other parts of Kenya. Other likely spots in the country include the wooded banks of the Talek and Mara rivers, Tsavo West National Park where Ngulia Lodge leaves bait out at night and Samburu National Reserve.

In Tanzania, the Ngorongoro Crater, espe-cially around the wooded rim; the Seronera River valley in the Serengeti; and the riverine bush in Ruaha National Park are all celebrated leopard hang-outs, as is Queen Elizabeth National Park in Uganda. ❑

LARGE MAMMALS

This chapter discusses some of the larger mammals to be found in East Africa, ranging from the elegant cheetah to the nimble gazelle

There are more large mammals in East Africa than virtually anywhere else on earth. (By "large", zoologists mean anything from the size of a domestic cat.) As well as the lion and leopard *(see pages 67 and 70)*, the carnivorous predators include half a dozen other species of cat, a similar number of dogs (including jackals and foxes) and two species of hyena. Then, among the herbivores, there are African specialities found on no other continent (creatures such as the hippopotamus, giraffe and zebra), several members of the pig family, and finally an astonishing range of antelopes – over 40 different species, from the mighty eland to the tiny dik-dik.

The cheetah

The cheetah *(Acinonyx jubatus)* is a lean, muscular cat, approximately 40 to 60 kg (90–130 lb) in weight. It has a spotted coat and a "tear stripe" running from eye to cheek. Its silhouette is long and lanky. Unlike the rest of the cat family, it does not have retractable claws.

You have a reasonable chance of observing a cheetah in Tanzania's Serengeti and Kenya's Amboseli, Maasai Mara and Nairobi parks. It is most common in savanna and wherever there is a sufficient stock of its preferred prey – small antelope such as Thomson's gazelles. They are the most endangered of the three large cats, perhaps because, unlike leopards, they are unable to adapt easily to the changes wrought to their habitat by man, who is gradually forcing them into marginal areas.

Cheetahs are diurnal animals that are most active around dawn. But in some game parks where they are hassled by tourist vehicles, they have taken to hunting during the heat of the day, at noon when tourists return to the camps or lodges for lunch.

They are generally silent, solitary animals except for consorting pairs and females with dependent offspring. Young animals that have just left their mother tend to stay together for a time, and males often band together temporarily to defend a territory. Males and females only socialise while the female is in heat. They select breeding areas that have a reasonable number of gazelles, with good hiding places for cubs, perennial water and relatively low densities of

possible cub predators. Males congregate in these areas, which allows them to mate with local females.

After a gestation period of three months cheetah cubs are born blind, naked and helpless. Litter size varies from one to eight (usually three) cubs. The female hides them away for two to three weeks in dens, often in dense vegetation or among rocks on kopjes. She hunts for food leaving the cubs in hiding, periodically returning to suckle them. Every few days she moves her litter between dens. Although adults are not very vulnerable to predators, cheetah cubs are preyed on by hyenas and other big cats, including lions and leopards. Cubs may

LEFT: migrating wildebeest crossing the Mara River.
RIGHT: the speed, power and grace of a cheetah.

be born at any time of year, but there is a peak which coincides with the appearance of gazelle fawns, which are easy prey for females. In the Serengeti most litters are born between January and April, coinciding with the long rains.

Cheetahs prey on relatively small animals such as hares and Thomson's gazelles, relying on sight to locate, stalk and initiate pursuits. Groups of males can take on larger animals such as wildebeest, especially calves which are often taken during the mass calving on the Serengeti plains.

They select the least-vigilant animal on the edge of a group of animals as victim. Although cheetahs are the fastest land mammal, they cannot maintain their top speed of 95 kph (56 mph) for more than 200 to 300 metres (215–325 yards), so unless they can get undetected to within about 30 metres (33 yards) of the prey before starting their chase, they are rarely successful.

In a typical kill cheetahs use their forefeet to knock the running animal off balance then clamp tightly on to its neck to strangle it. The dead prey is invariably dragged into cover where the cheetahs will feed. Females will call their cubs to the kill with a soft, bird-like chirrup. Adults will not hunt again until about four days after a successful kill.

EDUCATION IN SURVIVAL

At five to six weeks cheetah cubs venture out after their mother to join her at kills. This is an important period for the cubs since, unlike other young cats, they do not know instinctively how to stalk, chase, catch and kill their prey.

A cheetah cub, when presented with a mouse for the first time, will stare dumbfounded at it, or perhaps even run away. In contrast, other young cats, such as leopard or serval, will pounce on the mouse without hesitation. Therefore, cheetah mothers must bring dazed or half-dead young gazelles or hares to their offspring and patiently instruct them in the process of being a hunter.

Small cats

The cat family (*Felidae*) includes a number of small cats that are relatively common but infrequently seen. These include the African wild cat (*Felis silvestris lybica*), the sand cat (*F. margarita*), the golden cat (*F. aurata*), the caracal (*Caracal caracal*) and the serval (*Leptailurus serval*). Their sizes vary from the 2- to 3-kg (4–6-lb) sand cat to the 15-plus kg (over 33 lb) serval and caracal.

Small cats are generally found in all habitats with perennial water. Only the caracal ranges into semi-arid country to the edge of deserts. All species are active during the night or early hours of the evening and morning.

As with domestic cats, small wild cats communicate with a number of variations on the "meow" theme. They snarl and spit when warning and purr when content. Servals have a characteristic little bark when calling to members of their own species.

In general, cats do not have a very good sense of smell, but their hearing is excellent and keenly directional; their eyesight is acute in dim light. Their main enemies are large raptors and other big predators. Their basic defence is alertness and

FELINE LINE

The African wild cat is the ancestor of the modern domestic cat. Indeed, when wild cats live anywhere near human habitation, they often interbreed with domesticated cats.

Killing techniques depend on the size of the prey: very small animals – insects, lizards, mice – are simply bitten to death or squeezed in the jaws until suffocated. Larger animals – rats, hyraxes, large birds – are characteristically killed with a prolonged bite to the nape of the neck, which effectively breaks it and eventually severs the spinal cord.

The caracal, serval and other larger cats are able to bring down large birds, such as bustards, and the kids of gazelles and other small antelopes.

avoiding open areas in which large birds of prey can fly. All small cats are solitary except for short periods of consorting with a mate and during suckling and weaning of young. Individuals have a hunting range of 1.5–3 sq. km (⅔–1 sq. mile). Males are territorial to other males within their range but permit females to wander in the territories unhindered.

Small cats are overwhelmingly carnivorous. Small living prey is stalked, pounced upon, hooked with extended claws, and then killed.

LEFT: young cheetahs rest using a termite mound as an observation post.
ABOVE: spotlights are used to view the serval cat.

In some cases wild cats take domestic stock. It rarely becomes a habit, however, and such small depredations are more than offset by their importance in controlling rodent pests.

Jackals and foxes

The *Canidae* group comprises smaller, dog-like carnivores, including three jackals – the side-striped *(Canis adustus)*, golden *(C. aureus)* and black-backed or silver-backed *(C. mesomelas)* – and the relatively common bat-eared fox *(Otocyon megalotis)*.

All of them have a striking similarity with domestic dogs in the way they move, lift their legs, raise their hackles, scratch, bury food and roll in something rotten. The senses of *Canidae* are all very well developed. Small *Canidae* are fairly common throughout East Africa, most especially within the Serengeti-Mara ecosystem where all four species are present. They are active 24 hours a day; their tendency to be active at night is reinforced by human persecution. Black-backed and side-striped jackals frequent open wooded and bushed grassland. Golden jackal and the bat-eared fox prefer more open and arid habitats, from grasslands to semi deserts.

EXCEPTIONAL EARS

The bat-eared fox has very acute, directional hearing. It can pinpoint termites moving underground and digs furiously to unearth them before they can burrow away.

and mutual grooming some months before actual mating. Behavioural observations indicate that pairs tend to persist beyond one season – for at least six years in the black-backed jackal, and probably longer. Bat-eared foxes, for example, pair for life. The young are born helpless, just like domestic dog puppies, and will stay in the safety of the burrow, suckled by the mother. When they emerge from the den, they are still suckled and begin to feed on regurgitated food by adults.

Black-backed jackals, golden jackals and

All are vocal to a degree: black-backed jackals yapping is a familiar sound on the plains. They are prey to larger carnivores and to rock python and large birds of prey, such as martial eagles. Alertness and speed are their main defences. All the dogs are very sociable animals. The basic social unit is a pair, either permanent or for a few seasons. Occasionally they team up with the young of that year or with some of the previous year's offspring. Several breeding and non-breeding adults form more or less permanent social groups within a home range, but essentially a pair marks and may defend a small territory which includes one or more subterranean dens. Pairing up begins with consorting

probably the other species have non-breeding "helpers", usually the young of previous seasons, which assist in the care of the current young. This ensures a higher rate of survival of the pups.

Although perhaps not as sophisticated as with lions, hyenas and wild dogs, cooperative hunting is important in jackals. In general, jackals and foxes are opportunistic carnivores. They will feed on almost anything they can catch or unearth – small vertebrates, invertebrates of any size, young animals, eggs, carrion, even some fruits. Bat-eared foxes are highly specialised: the great bulk of their diet is insects, mainly *Hodotermes* termites, and their teeth are highly adapted to an insect diet. Scavenging is one of the main elements of the jackals' search for food. As many as 30 jackals can be seen, often along with vultures, at the fringes of a lion or hyena kill, waiting for a chance to dash in and grab a piece of meat from the carcass.

Pack hunters

The African wild dog (*Lycaon pictus* or "painted wolf"), also called the hunting dog, is a medium-sized carnivore. Adults are approximately the size of a labrador, but are slimmer and light for their size, weighing an average of 25 kg (55 lb). These distinctive dogs have brindled coats of brown, black, yellow and white. They all have

ingly vocal. A bird-like yittering is often heard when the dogs greet one another. Alarmed dogs will bark: distressed puppies occasionally give a squeaky call. Packs consist of a dominant breeding pair, five to six other adults and dependent young. With litters averaging 10, and bitches capable of producing 16 pups, packs can build up to number as many as 50. Young females emigrate at between 18 months and three years of age: males normally remain in their family pack.

Wild dogs are most active in the early morning and evening and lie in shade during the day. They hunt cooperatively, preying primarily on large ungulates including antelope, gazelle, zebra and

similar black face masks and white-tipped tails. The rest of the pattern is unique for each dog. Large, rounded ears allow dogs to hear over long distances. They have very sharp shearing teeth.

Wild dogs are typically found in savanna grassland and woodland. They have also been seen at altitudes of 5,600 metres (18,480 ft) in the snow of Kilimanjaro or in the heat of deserts. Nowhere are they common (see page 43) but there is a sizeable population in southern Tanzania, notably in the Selous Game Reserve, as well as in Laikipia District, Kenya. Wild dogs are surpris-

LEFT: no two wild dogs have the same markings.
ABOVE: wild dogs crowd round a kill.

wildebeest. Most predators stalk or ambush their prey, but these animals make no attempt to hide. They simply approach a herd until it stampedes, then single out an individual – usually one that's slowed by old age or disease – and chase it until it's exhausted. The dogs are swift, tireless runners. They have been known to chase prey for an hour, for as far as 5 km (3 miles). Packs normally hunt once a day – more often if the group is large or there are puppies to be fed. Prey size also influences the number of hunts: a wildebeest will obviously satisfy more dogs than a gazelle. Like their hunting behaviour, the breeding system of wild dogs is an example of remarkable cooperation. In each pack only the dominant pair breeds: the other dogs help to rear their offspring. This is for the good of the pack since all dogs are related but only the strongest genes are passed on. Breeding coincides with the rains. Gestation lasts about 10 weeks and the dominant female whelps in a den. For the first fortnight the female suckles the litter, spending long periods underground with them. After two weeks in the den, puppies make their first unsteady forays outside and begin to feed on meat regurgitated to them by all the pack members. Within a month

MIGHTY BITE

The hyena, with the strongest jaws of any mammal, can eat large bones – a source of nutritious marrow. Hyena droppings are often white because of all the calcium they contain.

or so, they are feeding on meat alone. The wild-dog population may be dwindling, but even more seriously threatened with extinction is the Ethiopian wolf *(Canis simensis)* or Simien fox. Probably numbering less than 400, and confined to five isolated pockets of heathlands in Ethiopia, this once-common canid is now classified as critically endangered.

Hyenas

The spotted hyena *(Crocuta crocuta)* is the most common and visible of the two distinct hyena species that inhabit East Africa. It is distinguished by its rounded ears, spotted coat, powerful forelegs and shoulders, long neck, and heavily built skull with formidable teeth. A young spotted hyena has darker spots than the adult, which may appear almost spotless when quite old.

The spotted hyena occurs widely in most open habitats, ranging from light acacia woodland to open plains or rocky country. It is less numerous in thickly wooded areas (an exception being the forested Aberdare Mountains, where it is common), but can live at altitudes of up to about 4,000 metres (13,000 ft). The spotted hyena's only important enemy in the wild is the lion, but like most other African predators it is currently in numerical decline due to poisoning and other forms of human persecution.

The spotted hyena lives in large permanent social groups called "clans", which may consist of up to 100 individuals where sufficient prey exists. Females stay in the same clan for life, but young males will leave their birth clan for another clan. There is a strong hierarchy in each sex, but all females are absolutely dominant to all adult males. Dominance rank is "inherited": young females attain their mother's rank in the clan, and retain it for life. Thus the different female families *(matrilines)* that form the core of the clan have very stable relations among each other: high-ranking matrilines still rank highly after many generations. Feeding is extremely competitive, with high-ranking females and their young taking precedence. Furthermore, high-ranking females are survived by far more offspring, since those of a lower rank are seldom able to raise their cubs to adulthood.

When in season, a female will attract a number of males, but usually only the highest-ranking males mate with her. A long gestation period (110 days) allows the foetuses to develop their large size, fully erupted teeth, and very advanced muscular and behavioural development. Litters are usually twins, and this prolonged foetal development is an adaptation for the ferocious fighting between siblings that starts within seconds of birth, and lasts a few days until one emerges dominant.

Females give birth at the mouth of abandoned aardvark holes, and the cubs live (and fight) in the burrow; the female cannot enter to intervene. After about one month at the natal den, the mother brings her cubs to the communal den, where all females keep their small young together. Food is not carried to the den, so the young hyenas depend entirely on their mother's milk for approximately eight months and are weaned only at 12 to 16 months, when they can compete at kills to feed by themselves.

Contrary to myth, the spotted hyena is a very successful hunter, cooperating with other clan members to chase and bring down large grazers such as wildebeest, zebra and more occasionally buffalo. Like most predators, the spotted hyena will scavenge, but it kills the great majority of its prey itself. The whoop of the spotted hyena is a characteristic sound of the African night. When squabbling over a kill, it makes a large variety of

The striped hyena inhabits the drier parts of East Africa, preferring rocky country and often ranging into deserts where water is unavailable for many miles. It lives in small social groups, but forages singly. The female gives birth to 1–3 cubs, which are born in aardvark holes or under rocky overhangs. Unlike its spotted counterpart, the striped hyena is seldom heard, and is primarily a scavenger, occasionally taking prey such as hares, small carnivores and small antelope.

Hippopotamus

The hippopotamus (*Hippopotamus amphibius*) is the second-largest non-marine mammal,

sounds, including the maniacal "giggle" that has given it the nickname of "laughing hyena". A giggling hyena is not having fun, however, but usually being attacked by a more dominant hyena or by a lion.

The striped hyena (*Hyaena hyaena*) shares the spotted hyena's powerful shoulders and head, but it has more pointed ears, longer legs, and forefeet much larger than its hind feet. It also has a crest of hair running down its back to merge with a very bushy tail. The body is dark, with white stripes on the flanks and outer surface of the legs.

LEFT: the fearsome jaws of the spotted hyena.
ABOVE: hyenas mainly rest during the day.

weighing up to 2,000 kg (4,400 lb), with a barrel-shaped body and short legs. Its head is adapted for life in water, with eyes, ears and nose all on the upper side. A hippo's jaw can open up to 150 degrees wide, which makes a very impressive sight when this is all that can be seen of the semi-submerged animal.

Hippos live in still or slow-running water with frequent bends in the shoreline and deep pools with shallow-sided banks, in the midst of open wooded or bushed grassland. The preferred water temperature is 18–35°C (64–95°F) and they have been seen along the sea coast. In the rainy season, males may take up temporary residence in seasonal water holes.

Hippos spend the whole day in water, totally or partially submerged, floating beneath the surface and bouncing from the bottom to come up to breath every few minutes. Dives generally last less than five minutes, but can be as long as 15. Hippos rarely leave the water, except at night to feed on land. Their skin is very thin and lacks sweat glands, which means that if they are exposed to the sun they can easily overheat and dehydrate, and suffer from sunburn which cracks their skin. An overheated hippo looks as if it is sweating blood as glands in its skin secrete a sticky red fluid that acts as a natural sunscreen.

Hippos have a variety of vocalisations, among them the dominant male's: "MUH-Muh-muh"; bellows and roars when fighting; a high-pitched "neighing" when attacked and a sort of snort when submerged. Hippos are gregarious and territorial. Group size averages 10 to 15 females with young, led by one dominant male. When water resources become scarce during droughts, groups of 150 have been observed. Dominant males space themselves out along the lake shore or river course advertising their dominance with the familiar "MUH-Muh-muh" call. Sexually mature males are kept on the edges of the group with threats and fights until, at eight to 10 years old, they feel strong enough to take on

A DANGEROUS GIANT

Man is the hippo's only real threat, although a pride of lions will attack a solitary hippo on land, and crocodiles undoubtedly take the occasional baby hippo in the water. Females defend their young by making use of their long tusks (actually canine teeth).

Despite their benign look, hippos probably account for more wildlife-induced human deaths than any other animal, including lions and snakes. They specialise in capsizing boats which get too near, either drowning or biting the people inside. Hippos are also dangerous on land at night, since they will run over anybody standing between them and the water.

a territory-holder. As the flow of river changes with seasons, territories may break down. In more stable lakes, territories may persist for years. Courtship and mating occurs in the water. In theory, territorial males have exclusive mating rights, but they are continuously challenged by other males. Fights are common, leaving animals visibly scarred along their back and flanks. Females give birth in shallow water; suckling occurs on land or in ankle-deep water and lasts for eight months. Hippos are grazers and feed at night, coming out of the water along well-worn trails. They do not eat aquatic vegetation. During the rainy season when grass is abundant they feed near the shore. In the dry season they may walk up to 10 km (6 miles) from water in search of food. Their half-metre (19½-inch) wide lips allow them to eat very short grass. Fallen fruits, like water plants, are rarely taken. Hippos have a curious habit of spraying their dung around a 2-metre (6-ft) radius by rapidly whirling their stubby tails as they defecate. Defecation spots are communal and it is thought that they are used as a display to other hippo groups. The total amount of food taken by an adult hippo (only 1 to 1.5 percent compared

MATCH THE PATCH

The Maasai giraffe is the subspecies with the most ragged, blotchy markings. Rothschild's giraffe has paler, less jagged patches. The reticulated giraffe has a well-defined network of white lines on dark red-brown.

their distribution (the Maasai is found in Tanzania and southern Kenya, the reticulated in northern Kenya, Rothschild's in northwest Kenya and northern Uganda). All other characteristics are the same.

The pattern of a giraffe's coat is fixed for life, making it possible for human observers to distinguish one animal from another, though it tends to get darker with age. It is not easy to distinguish males from females, although males tend to be a little bigger and seem to spend more

with 2.5 percent of body weight) is less than that ingested by other cloven-hoofed animals. This is only possible because of the hippo's undemanding lifestyle: floating around the pool all day does not take much effort.

Giraffe

There are three subspecies of giraffe in East Afica: the Maasai (*Giraffa camelopardalis tippelskirchi*), reticulated (*G. c. reticulata*) and Rothschild's giraffe (*G. c. rothschildi*). These subspecies differ only in their blotch pattern, and

LEFT: hippos spend all day in the water.
ABOVE: reticulated giraffe among the acacias.

time feeding from tree canopies than females, which prefer to feed on low-lying vegetation. Giraffes have very long necks which have only seven bones, no more than the necks of any other mammals, although giraffe vertebrae are elongated. Both sexes are born with horns which are covered by skin and topped with black hair. Giraffes weigh up to 1 tonne. They have a high centre of gravity and this, together with their weight, may account for their strange gait. Walking is almost a "pace": both legs on one side appear to move at the same time making it look as if the giraffe is rolling. When galloping, the hindlegs swing forward together to plant in front of the forefeet. Giraffes can reach a maximum speed of 60 kph (37 mph). They inhabit open woodland and wooded grassland, but may also be seen in bushed grassland and occasionally at a forest edge. They often frequent drainage-line vegetation in the dry season. Riparian thickets are the only place you are likely to see them in dense vegetation.

Giraffes are diurnal, but also move about at night. They sometimes utter snorts and grunts, but are normally silent animals. Often the only noise to be heard when giraffes move by is the click of their hooves when the foot is lifted clear of the ground. These long-

legged animals have few enemies. They are most vulnerable when drinking when they splay their front legs and lower their heads, often in the vicinity of thick, waterside vegetation. Animals will only drink after carefully looking around. Young animals may be taken by lions if the adults are not around. Females will defend their young against any attacker by kicking with their front legs. The mortality rate up to the age of three is about 8 percent , as compared to the 3 percent adult average.

Giraffes are not much hunted by man. They only rarely raid local maize farms and their feeding habits make them almost impervious to drought. This might be the reason why, in some places, as other wildlife species continue to disappear, the giraffe seems to have become the only remnant of a formerly impressive wildlife array.

LINGUAL LENGTH

The giraffe's black tongue is the longest of any mammal – 45 cm (18 inches) – and mobile enough to curl round the tips of branches.

The individual is the basic social unit in giraffe society. Animals are loosely gregarious, with a usual group size of between two and 12 (usually six or fewer). The composition of herds changes constantly as adults come and go. The home range of a female may be 120 sq. km (48 sq. miles) but it spends most of its time in the central part of this range where it feeds. Dominant males wander in and out of female home ranges. Fights between dominant males are a rare event. When two males approach each other, they frequently adopt a threat posture – "standing tall". This is normally enough to persuade the less-dominant male to leave. Serious fighting occurs only when the fixed dominance hierarchy breaks down, for example, when a new nomadic male comes into the neighbourhood.

A ritualised form of fighting, known as "necking", is carried out by young males, normally between three and four years old. The animals intertwine necks, often accompanied by light blows with the head. The "winner" of the bout often climbs on the back of the "loser". This frequently leads to the erroneous conclusion that necking is a courtship ritual. Giraffes breed all year round. Females reach maturity at five years, males not until eight. Dominant males patrol the home range looking for females that come into heat. Males test females by smelling their vulvas or sampling their urine to see if they are receptive. If a dominant male finds a female in oestrus he will displace lesser males and consort with her until mating. During their lifespan, females may have up to 12 calves weighing approximately 100 kg (220 lb) each at birth. Calves are usually two metres (6 ft) high. Twins are very rare. Births normally occur in a calving ground. This might lead to the formation of "creches" in which the unweaned calves spend the day together unaccompanied by adults.

Feeding occurs generally between 6 and 9am and 3 to 6pm. Giraffes are ruminants and spend a good portion of the day resting and chewing the cud. They are exclusively browsers, with 95 percent of their feeding confined to the foliage of bushes and trees, mainly acacias. All parts are taken – leaves, buds, shoots, fruits.

Acacia fodder is harvested in a couple of different ways depending on the strength of the thorns: young, flexible thorns are flattened and the leaves stripped off with a sideways sweep: older, more robust thorns may also be flattened, engulfed in mucous and swallowed along with the branch. Very woody branches may simply be nibbled at selectively. The lips are used as agilely as the tongue. Giraffe saliva is especially thick and viscous, which undoubtedly helps in dealing with thorny branches. Normally, giraffes drink once a week, taking up 30 to 50 litres (63 to 105 pints) at a go. If vegetation is particularly dry, they may need to drink every two days.

of northern Kenya and south-central Ethiopia, Grevy's zebra has been in numerical decline for decades, largely due to competition with livestock for grazing and drinking resources, and it is now listed as endangered by the IUCN, with an estimated wild population of around 5,000.

The more widespread Burchell's (or common) zebra occurs throughout eastern and southern Africa, with the Serengeti ecosystem alone estimated to support a population of at least 500,000, possibly a lot more. A denizen of open and wooded grassland, it is never far from perennial water, and is active around the clock, sometimes resting in the shade at midday and

Zebra

Punda milia, the Swahili name for zebra, means "striped donkey". There is quite a controversy about the function of the stripes but the general opinion is that they serve as a form of visual anti-predator device, either as a camouflage or to break up form when seen from a distance.

Two species are found in East Africa: Grevy's *(Equus grevyi)* and Burchell's zebra *(Equus burchelli).* Grevy's zebra is far bulkier than Burchell's, with more prominent ears and much narrower stripes. Endemic to the arid badlands

LEFT: Maasai giraffe necking in the woods.
ABOVE: a Burchell's zebra mare suckles a foal.

taking the odd short nap during the night. It makes a typical equine neighing sound.

Among the zebra's enemies are lion, hunting dog, spotted hyena and, of course, man. A common response to alarm is bunching. Zebra stallions are fierce fighters and kick back with great ferocity. Mares are as brave as stallions when their foals are involved.

Burchell's zebra lives in groups with more or less permanent membership: there is a dominant stallion and a number of females with their offspring. The tightest social bond is naturally between mare and foal. Young females stay with the family group: as they approach maturity males wander off with bachelor groups. In the

Serengeti groups get together and participate in the great migration when the grazing begins to deteriorate in the dry season.

Grevy's zebra have temporary associations that rarely last more than a few months. Territorial males defend large territories during the breeding season and attempt to keep female groups within their boundaries. At other times, they mix with other male groups.

Breeding in both species is linked to the rains. Sexual maturity in males occurs at about one to

TOUGH DIET

Zebras have evolved stomachs that allow them to feed on coarse, stemmy grass largely passed over by other members of the grazing community, so they can survive where other grazers cannot.

short necks. They have coarse, bristly coats, small eyes, long ears, prominent snouts and tusks (elongated lower canines). The flattened face and broad snout, ending in the characteristic, naked pig nose, are related to both the search for food and fighting style. Despite their heavy bodies, pigs can swim and are agile and quick. All male pigs are larger than females of the same species and have larger tusks and warts. Sight is, in general, the poorest of the senses.

Three species can be found in East Africa,

two years but social maturity – the ability to take and defend a territory or female herd – does not come until about six years. Courtship is followed by repeated matings at one or two hour intervals over two days. Gestation takes around a year.

Young foals are surprisingly independent, even at one month old. They may be left alone while the mare grazes hundreds of metres away or walks several kilometres to water. Animals up to about the age of six months have stripes that are reddish-brown rather than black.

African pigs

African pigs (family *Suidae*) are medium-sized herbivores with compact bodies, large heads and

namely the giant forest hog (*Hylochoerus meinertzhageni*), covered with shaggy, dark, coarse hair; the bushpig (*Potamochoerus larvatus*), varying in coat colour from reddish-brown in the forests to blackish-brown in the drier bushland; and the warthog (*Phacochoerus aethiopicus*), which is less hairy, but covered with sparse bristles, with hairs along the neck and back that can be raised like a crest and serve as a signal during social interactions. Pigs can be found in a series of habitats ranging from grassland to bushed grassland (warthog), bushland to dry forest (bushpig), to moist evergreen forest (giant forest hog).

The warthog is an accomplished and compulsive digger and may dig its own burrow using its forefeet. Most other pigs seem to modify existing holes for their burrows. Bushpigs do not live in burrows. Warthogs are diurnal, but forest hogs and bushpigs are mainly nocturnal.

Continuous, soft grunting serves as a contact sound to keep members of a foraging family group together. Tooth-grinding may be heard when the animal is aroused, presumably angry. Alarm and distress are expressed with porcine squeals. The most important pig predators are lions and cheetahs. The largely nocturnal forest hog is susceptible to leopards. Pigs will defend themselves from predators by using their lower tusks (enlarged canine teeth) which are pointed

rial, males mark their home ranges of 10–20 sq. km (4–8 sq. miles) with secretions from lip glands, pre-orbital glands (warthog) or foot glands (bushpig) by rubbing them against tree trunks and stumps. Pigs are frequently seen rubbing their necks and spreading their saliva with their faces. Greetings are mostly a matter of sniffing: nose to nose, to mouth, to pre-orbital region or rear end. They sniff the ground in places where another animal has stepped, presumably to smell the gland secretion. This may lead to a friendly greeting to the pig.

Pigs are rapid breeders. Females are able to conceive at the age of 18 months, and the size

and very sharp. Nevertheless, their main line of defence is retreat at speed, usually towards the nearest hole. Bushpigs are often very destructive to local agriculture. Warthogs live in a more pastoral setting and therefore do not cause much damage to agriculture.

The main social group consists of temporary female-young bonds and more lasting female-female associations. Such associations account for the joining up of litters. There is no herd boar in a functional sense, although an adult male is usually in attendance. Although not very territo-

of their litter can be as many as a dozen young, which are either born in a grass "nest" constructed by the sow or, more commonly, in a borrowed aardvark hole. Males, meanwhile, mature at around the age of three years. This may explain why breeding males usually ignore fully grown yearlings.

As there is no marked male dominance among the pigs, conflicts between males are fierce when associated with a female in season. The strongest pig is the one that will mate. Fighting between male bushpigs may involve upraised snouts and tusks slapped from side to side, accompanied by whirling around. Side blows may be followed by biting. It seems that hierarchy is based on tusk

LEFT: Grevy's zebra have slim stripes and large ears.
ABOVE: mating warthogs, Kenya's most common pig.

length; if a tusk breaks, as frequently happens, then the pig loses status. The male warthog's threat display is characterised by stiff-legged strutting, an erect mane and tail, and head and shoulders raised with the snout pointed downwards and towards the opponent to present the tusks to full advantage. Female fights are less common than male encounters and consist of rushes and displays if two family groups happen to come too close together. As farrowing approaches, pregnant sows may become more solitary and quick-tempered,

> ### COUNT THE BUMPS
>
> You can tell the sex of an adult warthog by the number of wart-like protuberances on its face: the male has four, the female two.

engaging in male-like head-on encounters.

Females farrow in burrows. The piglets develop rapidly and can leave the burrow and begin to eat grass after only one week. However, they suckle for as long as four months. Suckling is generally done while the sow is standing, although she has to lie down in the burrow. The previous young may try to rejoin their newly far-rowed mother but will be roundly chased off. This is a vulnerable time for yearling males since they have problems finding burrows to share with adults of either sex: mortality from predation is correspondingly high. If, however, the female fails to conceive, then the young will stay with her until she conceives the next time. Shared bur-

rows are uncommon, especially for farrowing, and are only occasionally used by first-time breeders. Males and females take up compan-ionship again after farrowing, and are likely to mate again the next season.

African wild pigs are basically vegetarians. They eat a wide range of plants, grasses, ferns and fungi, and consume almost any part of the plant – but they will also consume small vertebrates and invertebrates when they find them. All pigs are dependent on water and will always be found near a source. The manner in which different species search for food is largely dictated by the habitat in which they live. Warthogs are the most specialised feeders and eat mainly grass. While feeding, they walk from tuft to tuft, or move slowly forward in a charac-teristic "kneeling" or "bowing" posture, by low-ering their short-necked front end and settling on their fore carpals ("wrists"). Tusks are used only occasionally to root out food: most digging is done with the rough upper and leading edge of the nose. The bushpig spends more time rooting by digging with its nose. It can dig several centi-metres deeper than warthogs by taking full advantage of its more flexible snout. Giant forest hogs feed mainly in grassy forest clearings. In the forest, however, they like to eat a variety of herbs and plant parts. They rarely root with their snouts. The combined length of their head and neck allows them to reach the grass sward with-out kneeling.

The antelope families

The grasslands and bushlands of East Africa support the most splendid variety of antelopes in the world – more than 40 different species, ranging in size from the majestic eland, the world's largest antelope, to the tiny blue duiker, standing about 30 cm (12 inches) tall at the shoulder. Some of them graze on grass indis-criminately; others graze very selectively, choosing their habitat according to their diet; others both graze grass and browse for shoots and leaves of trees and shrubs; and a few are almost exclusively browsers.

Whatever they eat, all antelopes are rumi-nants – that is, they have several stomachs for fodder in varying stages of digestion and they reprocess already-swallowed fodder by chew-ing the cud, like buffalos and domestic cattle.

All species are diurnal (active in the day), with a preference for the cooler mornings and evenings for feeding. Except for impala and some of the very small antelopes, most breed in a very narrow time period, usually dropping their calves just before the rains. Antelopes rely on alertness and flight to escape their enemies – predators such as lions, leopards, cheetahs and hyenas.

Wildebeests and their relatives

The size of an antelope is no guide to its zoological classification. The *Alcelaphinae* family, for instance, includes the largish wildebeest or white-bearded gnu, the hartebeest and the topi, but also the much smaller impala, which looks more like a gazelle.

They favour mostly open and wooded grassland, and generally avoid bushland and thickets where grass growth is relatively weak and there is more cover for predators. Impalas, however, prefer woodlands, riverine strips and zones between vegetation types (transition zones).

You are likely to see the lugubrious-looking wildebeest *(Connochaetes taurinus)* in large numbers – possibly hundreds of thousands – if you visit the Serengeti in Tanzania or Kenya's Maasai Mara when they are passing through on their annual migration.

The Serengeti and the Mara are also the places to see the kongoni or Coke's hartebeest *(Alcelaphus buselaphus cokii)*, a long-faced, fawn-coloured antelope with coat-hanger horns and a whitish rump. It is widespread on the grassy plains of southern Kenya and Tanzania, from sea level to around 2,000 metres (6,500 ft). Slightly larger than the kongoni, and tawny-red in colour, is Jackson's hartebeest *(A. b. jacksoni)*, which is more common in Uganda.

The topi *(Damaliscus korrigum)* is similar in build to the hartebeests, but is easily distinguished by its rich rufous colour and black or purplish patches on its flanks. Topi are sometimes seen alone in areas such as the Serengeti – where they are fond of standing on termite mounds as a lookout point – but also sometimes join up with the wildebeest in The Migration.

The smallest and most delicate of the *Alcelaphinae* family is the impala *(Aepyceros melampus)*, a reddish-fawn antelope that's

common in southern Kenya and throughout Tanzania. Impalas are graceful, nimble and capable of prodigious leaps when threatened by a predator. Only the male sports the elegant lyre-shaped horns.

Regardless of their size, all the *Alcelaphinae* have social characteristics in common: they are rarely seen alone, except for the occasional territorial male wildebeest forlornly standing his ground outside the breeding season. Most herds are usually made up of less than 100 animals, with the exception of large, migratory populations of wildebeest, which may be seen during the migrations in tens of thousands.

Their herds spread over the landscape, often without any apparent structure. Breeding is polygamous with one male fertilising many females. Births are synchronised, particularly in wildebeest, into a calving peak which lasts only a few weeks. This floods the predators' market and, even though they eat their fill, the percentage of calves that they can take is much smaller than if calving were spread throughout the year.

Lyrate horns

Close relatives of the *Alcelaphinae* are the *Reduncinae* – medium-sized antelopes whose males have lyre-shaped horns. This group includes two sub-species of waterbuck, two

LEFT: roan antelope are identified by their striking facial markings and coat.
RIGHT: the long-faced Coke's hartebeest in Tsavo.

species of reedbucks and the Uganda kob. The common waterbuck *(Kobus ellipsiprymnus)* and the Defassa waterbuck *(K. e. defassa)* are robust, thick-set antelopes with a shaggy grey-brown coat and heavily ringed, backwards-curving horns. The main difference between them in appearance is at their rear end: the Defassa waterbuck has a solid white circle on its rump, while the common waterbuck has a pronounced white ring, as if it had sat on a freshly painted toilet seat.

As their name implies, both are happiest near water, and live in small groups in riverine woodland and well-watered grassland. Reedbucks are

has a more complex social structure, with several hundred animals often congregating in one breeding herd on the short-grass plains of Queen Elizabeth and Murchison Falls national parks.

Antelopes like horses

The *Hippotraginae* tribe includes the larger, thick-necked, "horse-like" antelopes that sport impressively long, swept-back or straight horns. They include the oryx *(Oryx gazella)*, the roan *(Hippotragus equinus)* and the sable *(H. niger)*. The broad-chested *Hippotraginae* run with powerful, sure-footed strides, hence the name "horse-like antelopes". The roan's scientific

smaller and more spritely, with shorter, forward-pointing horns. The Bohor reedbuck *(Redunca redunca)* is found singly or in small groups, in marshy surroundings or areas of lush grass. Chanler's mountain reedbuck *(R. fulvorufula chanleri)* prefers higher country and is found on grassy hillsides up to 3,600 metres (12,000 ft).

Slightly larger than the reedbuck, the Uganda kob *(Kobus kob)* is a thickset antelope with bright red-brown body with black and white markings on the face and legs, including a white ring around the eye. Males have lyre-shaped horns similar to impalas. Whereas the reedbuck moves around in pairs, and the waterbuck in small family herds of five to 12 animals, the Uganda kob

RESPONSIBILITIES OF LEADERSHIP

Impalas generally live in two sorts of herds. A breeding herd (sometimes called a "harem") consists of females and their young, with just one adult male in charge. A "bachelor herd" is one in which all the other males travel around together, each waiting for a chance to challenge a ram for the right to lead his harem.

After a successful challenge, the loser retires to a bachelor herd, and it is the new ram's responsibility to fend off future challengers, to direct the harem to sources of food and to service any female in season. It's small wonder that his tenure as herd leader rarely lasts more than a few weeks.

name labours the point: "horse-like horned horse". The oryx is happy in extremely arid habitat, and is able to survive in near-desert conditions. It digs up succulent roots and eats wild melons for the water they contain, and grazes at night when lower temperatures lead to an increase in the vegetation's water content. Even dead grass that has been baked by the sun all day can take up to 40 percent of its weight in airborne moisture during the night.

By using these sources of water, producing

LEAP FROM DANGER

When an oribi senses danger, it gives loud whistling snorts to alert others, then leaps straight up in a stiff-legged jump before racing away. It makes more vertical leaps as it runs, perhaps to get a better view over long grass.

prefer grasslands with good bush and tree cover, and they both are frequently found in well-watered grasslands and wooded valleys. The sable and the roan are considerably less common than oryx in Kenya, but are widespread in Tanzania.

All the *Hippostraginae* have an established system of matriarchal hierarchy, resulting in small herds of five to 20 animals with varying degrees of male participation. In sables, female herds range over adjacent male territories: in roan, a single male

concentrated urine and allowing its body temperature to rise rather than sweating, an oryx is able to survive without ever drinking.

There are two distinct races of oryx in East Africa: the beisa oryx, which lives north of Kenya's Tana River and westwards into Uganda, and the fringe-eared oryx (very similar but with a tuft of black hair at the tips of its ears), which is found in the south of Kenya and northern Tanzania. Roan and sable, by contrast,

accompanies the females; in oryx, male groups satellite female ones for most of the year. Only the dominant male in a group of oryx mates with the females in the group.

Spiralling horns

The *Tragelaphinae* are a group of slender, longish-necked antelopes characterised by well-developed spiralling horns on the males. They include the eland (*Taurotragus oryx*), the bushbuck (*Tragelaphus scriptus*), the lesser kudu (*Tragelaphus imberbis*), the greater kudu (*Tragelaphus strepsiceros*), the sitatunga (*T. spekei*) – and the bongo (*Tragelaphus euryceros*), though this is extremely rare. They are

---

LEFT: this sable antelope has perfectly proportioned horns.
ABOVE: the oryx, with its straight horns and distinctive facial markings.

all russet to grey-brown in colour, often with vertical white stripes or lines of dots on their sides and flanks.

Males are larger and often darker or greyer than the females. They all share a delicate, high-stepping gait, even the 2-metre (6-ft) tall eland. Most of the antelopes in this group live in small groups in sub-humid areas, in regions of thick cover, such as forest (bongo), bushland (bushbuck, lesser kudu) and hill thickets (greater kudu).

CATCHING GAZELLE

Gazelles can reach speeds of up to 80 kph (50 mph). They are one of the most agile of creatures but are no match for cheetahs and can overheat if escaping a pack of hyenas or wild dogs.

Dainty gazelles

There are some 20 species and subspecies of gazelle in the *Antilopini* family. All have long legs, slender bodies that are fawn on top and whitish underneath, a white rump and a black-tipped, constantly wagging tail. Males are larger than females and have better-developed S-shaped horns. The main species are Grant's gazelle *(Gazella granti)*; Soemmering's gazelle *(G. soemmerringi)*; Thomson's gazelle *(G. thomsonii)*, distinguished by the black stripe along its side; the

They are all naturally diurnal creatures, although bushbuck will sometimes become nocturnal in areas of persecution. The magnificent eland is an exception to most of the *Tragelaphinae* rules.

For one thing, it is much larger than all the others; for another, both male and female eland have thick spiralled horns. And it is the only real plains grazer in the group, frequenting open grasslands and often roaming as high as 4,500 metres (14,800 ft).

The sitatunga lives in a very restricted habitat in the swamps and has evolved long, splayed hooves to assist in making its way over mud and boggy vegetation.

gerenuk *(Litocranius walleri);* and the dibatag or Clarke's gazelle *(Ammodorcas clarkei)*. The dibatag and gerenuk differ from the rest in having conspicuously long, slender necks. The gazelles both graze and browse, but prefer well-watered grasslands where there is plenty of grazing. The gerenuk, however, is a specialist browser, with a distinctive long slender neck that enables it to reach high up on bushes and small trees.

Smaller antelopes

At the other end of the size scale from the mighty eland are the *Antelopinae* family: dainty, round-backed antelopes that include duikers (genus *Cephalophus*), dik-diks (genus *Madoqua*), the oribi *(Ourebia ourebi)* and the klipspringer *(Oreotragus oreotragus)*. They all look rather similar and are all less than 80 cm (31 inches) high; males have horns, females are either hornless or have small, poorly formed horns.

The smallest of the *Antelopinae* is the pygmy antelope *(Neotragus batesi)* of western Uganda and the Democratic Republic of the Congo, which measures a mere 25 cm (10 inches) at the shoulder. The largest is the rare and elusive yellow-backed duiker *(Cephalophus sylvicultor),* which can reach a height of 80 cm (31 inches). The rest, however, are 40–60 cm (15–23 inches) at the shoulder. Females can be larger than the males by as much as 20 percent in height and weight. The relatively large size of the females may arise from the fact that these antelopes form a permanent pair bond, meaning the male does not have to fight continually with others for a mate.

Females also share in the defence of territory and greater size in territorial conflicts is an advantage. They are found in forests (duikers, suni), in thickets (dik-dik) or on kopjes or rock outcrops (dik-dik, klipspringers). The duikers' and dik-diks' short-necked, arched-back profile assists in rapid movement through thick bush. Oribis, which inhabit open grasslands, have a more upright posture, as do klipspringers, which must balance upright as they spring nimbly from rock to rock.

There are several species of duiker, the rarest (and one of the smallest) being the Zanzibar or Aders' duiker *(Cephalophus adersi).* This tiny antelope, bright chestnut in colour and standing only 30 cm (12 inches) high at the shoulder, retains a precarious stronghold on Zanzibar, where an estimated 1,000 individuals remain, but it has been reported as extinct on its only known mainland haunt, Kenya's Sokoke-Arabuko Forest Reserve. It is elusive, shy and partly nocturnal – so you will need luck and patience to spot one.

The small antelopes are generally active all day, with peaks in early morning and evening. Their enemies are all the large predators, plus

---

LEFT: the horse-like roan antelope with its swept-back horns.
RIGHT: a pair of impalas, among the most agile and graceful of the antelopes.

an array of medium-sized and small predators, including cats, snakes, birds of prey, ratels and baboons. Their only defence is to take flight.

All species live in very small groups centred around lifelong pairs, and are very territorial; all mark their territories with secretions from conspicuous glands in front of their eyes. Their territory sizes may vary from 50–500 metres (165–1,650 ft) in diameter, depending on the season and local conditions.

Such a relatively small territory has its

WARNING WHISTLE

Most antelopes whistle urgently as an alarm call, to warn of predators. The exceptions include the smallest antelopes, which use a high-pitched "zick-zick" sound, hence the name dik-dik.

advantages as it allows the animals to know precisely both the location and season of food plants, the best escape routes and the most effective hiding places from predators.

Sexual maturity may be reached in less than a year: gestation is about six months. Two births a year are therefore possible, given a relatively constant food supply. At less than two years old, the young animal will leave its parents' territory.

Dwarf and small antelopes are almost exclusively browsers and nibblers on fine-structured vegetation. They eat the most nutritious plants and parts that provide a high degree of nutrition. They are not normally seen drinking: moisture comes mainly from food plants. ❑

SMALL MAMMALS

There are many groups of small mammals in a number of families, ranging from small carnivores, such as genets, to herbivores such as hyraxes, to monkeys

E ast Africa is home to many species of small mammals in a number of families, ranging from small carnivores, such as genets, to herbivores such as hyraxes, to a variety of omnivorous and versatile monkeys. They can be grouped into classes according to similar characteristics.

Weasels and their relatives

These small, carnivorous mammals belong to the family *Mustelidae*, which includes the African striped or white-naped weasel *(Poecilogale albinucha)*, zorilla or African striped polecat *(Ictonyx striatus)*, ratel or honey badger *(Mellivora capensis)*, spotted-necked otter *(Lutra maculicollis)* and the Cape clawless otter *(Aonyx capensis)*. They have elongated, flattened bodies, powerful jaws and relatively large brains. Except for otters, all these mammals have a striking horizontal black and white pattern.

They inhabit woodland, bushland and grassland and tend to use one or more dens (holes in the ground) as bases. Otters are rarely far from river banks. Weasels and zorilla are mainly nocturnal; otters are diurnal; ratels are active at most times except noon.

In general, mustelids are quite vocal, especially when annoyed. Otters are very vocal and have a range of twitters and chirps which serve as contact calls. Few other animals will attack them due to their repulsive anal gland secretion and, in the case of ratel, its ferocity. Weasels may be at risk from large owls; otters are taken by crocodiles and rock pythons; zorillas are often run over by cars.

Otters live in small family groups of fewer than 10. Not much is known about their breeding behaviour except that a pair may consort temporarily for several months during the breeding season.

Mustelids take almost any living prey smaller than or equal to their own body size. The zorilla's diet consists of nearly 50 percent insects, with the rest made up of small mammals, birds, amphibians, spiders and plant material. Rodents are the main item in the ratel's diet although it may catch small antelopes. Otters feed mainly on aquatic food – crabs, fish, frogs, molluscs and insects which they catch during dives of about 1½ minutes each.

Mongooses and more

The family *Viverridae* are low-slung, long-tailed, largely nocturnal carnivores, with a variety of striking spottings, stripings or conspicuous tails. All members of the group have large eyes, facing front, and outstanding night vision.

The *Viverridae* contain three sub-families: mongooses, the true civets and genets, and the palm civet. There are some dozen species of mongooses (subfamily *Herpestinae*), a dozen genets (subfamily *Viverrinae*), one African civet *(Civettictis civetta)*, and one two-spotted or African palm civet *(Nandinia binotata)*. Their habitat stretches from forest edge to semi-desert. Genets and palm civets are semi-

LEFT: the large-spotted genet is a nocturnal animal…
RIGHT: …and so is the greater galago.

arboreal; true civets and mongooses, with the exception of the slender mongoose, are more likely to seek refuge in crevasses, holes in the ground, tree trunks or tree roots.

Genets, civets and most mongooses are nocturnal, occasionally crepuscular. Both Egyptian and slender mongooses are active by day, in the evening and on moonlit nights. The marsh mongoose is largely diurnal.

Vocalisations are used for contact (genets: "uff-uff-uff"; civets: "tsa-tsa-tsa"), as well as

NIGHT RAIDER

The large-spotted genet *(Genetta tigrina)* has learnt to scavenge from humans, and in places has become semi-tame around camps and lodges at night.

ings last three to five minutes; gestation is some three and a half months and two or three young are born in tree holes. They are weaned after two to three months and become independent after nine.

Viverrids are carnivorous, almost omnivorous. They are generally opportunistic feeders but also function as quick and efficient predators. Their diet includes all manner of invertebrates and vertebrates up to the size of antelope calves and domestic cats (in the case of the civet).

for alarm, excitement or threat, when they growl, spit and hiss.

Their enemies include medium-sized predators such as African wild cats and large owls. When threatened they rely on stealth and early warning. Genets have very good eyesight, especially at dusk. If disturbed, they will take to the nearest tree.

Viverridae, except for the social mongooses *(see right)* are generally solitary and only occasionally seen in pairs. Their striking black and white markings on the face, body and tail are undoubtedly used in sexual and social signalling. Breeding occurs throughout the year, with some indication of seasonal peaks. Genet mat-

Social mongooses

Two mongoose species do not lead solitary lives: the dwarf mongoose *(Helogale parvula)* and the banded mongoose *(Mungos mungo)* are grouped together because they share ecological characteristics and are highly social, unlike the rest of the *Viverridae* family.

They are small, lively mammals, often seen moving through the bush with weasel-like gait, pausing from time to time to stand upright and look around. Both the dwarf and the banded mongoose frequent wooded and bushed grassland; the latter prefer a somewhat more open habitat. The pack's home range includes a number of burrow sites, such as termite mounds or loose rock piles which are used for night-time dens, as breeding sites and as look-outs. Social mongooses are very vocal, and communicate with a wide range of squeaks and twitters. Their main enemies are larger carni-vores and birds of prey. Alertness, speed and the propensity to dive into nearby holes are their main defences.

Social mongooses occur in packs averaging around a dozen animals, but up to as many as 30 in the dwarf mongoose. Dwarf mongoose packs are led by a dominant female which is the oldest adult female of the group. She is nor-mally the only one that conceives in a pack.

from the depredations of the ravening hoard. Social mongooses eat virtually any small terrestrial living creature, both vertebrate and invertebrate, as well as eggs and occasionally fruits. Poisonous snakes are frequently killed by the pack.

Elephants' cousins

Unbelievable as it may seem at first glance, the rather dull-looking hyraxes, medium-small, brownish-grey creatures are the closest living relatives to elephants and dugongs (sea-cows). Many hyrax characteristics are elephantine: toe-nail-like claws which are really hoofs; two teats

Both dwarf mongooses and banded mon-gooses synchronise their breeding within the pack which ensures that the season's brood can be fed and protected together. In sub-humid regions, such as western Uganda, social mon-gooses are capable of producing four litters a year. Mongoose young are born underground.

Mongoose packs tend to change their dens every few days. This has two functions: it ensures that a particular predator cannot focus its attention on restricted areas and it allows the neighbourhood food supply to recover

LEFT: the African civet is normally nocturnal.
ABOVE: an inquisitive pair of dwarf mongooses.

between the forelegs; internal testicles; a long gestation period of seven months (remarkable for such a small beast); and a somewhat myste-rious gland that is active during states of arous-al. Hyraxes have rudimentary tails and numerous long, tactile hairs over their bodies. Their feet are shod with rubbery pads which sweat when running. The tacky surface allows them to climb up near-vertical rock faces or tree trunks.

Three species of hyrax are found in East Africa. The rock hyrax *(Procavia capensis)* lives in colonies on rocky hillsides or kopjes, feeding by day on leaves, flowers and fruits. The bush hyrax *(Heterohyrax brucei)* is similar in appearance and habits, and the two are often seen together. At night they may sleep together for safety and mutual warmth. Both species become tame when accustomed to people, for instance around lodges. The tree hyrax *(Dendrohyrax arboreus)* is a nocturnal forest animal with an eerie shrieking call.

Their most dangerous predator is Verreaux's eagle, which feeds almost exclusively on rock and bush hyraxes. Other large birds of prey, rock pythons, civets and baboons are also a threat. At an alarm call – an unmistakable, high-pitched shriek emitted by any member of the group – all hyraxes of both species dive for cover in rock clefts. Rock and bush hyraxes

hyraxes on a kopje is determined by the number of sleeping holes and retreats from predators as well as the quality of the local food supply.

Breeding is year-round, with a slight preference for the rainy season. Females are receptive once or twice a year and have a gestation period of seven or eight months. All females in a family group usually give birth within three weeks, to litters of up to six (usually two or three) young which can feed themselves immediately and run about as soon as they are dry. Sexual maturity in both sexes is around 18 months. Like elephants, females stay with the group: newly matured males wander off. Rock hyraxes eat

are extremely social and gregarious. Social organisation seems to be dictated by the size of kopjes. On small kopjes, both species live in family groups rather like harems, with one adult male overseeing three to seven (up to 17 in the bush hyrax) adult females and a number of juveniles of both sexes. The male is usually old and large, intolerant of immigrating adult males, and prone to frequent, raucous territorial display calls. Dominant males chase subordinant ones away.

On larger kopjes groups of females move within overlapping circles around core areas, which are dominated by a territorial male and younger, peripheral males. The numbers of

mainly grass and other vegetation. Bush hyraxes are predominantly browsers. Both species can eat, without apparent harm, many poisonous plants distasteful to other herbivores. They are rarely seen drinking and it is thought that most water is taken from leaf surfaces during feeding.

Baboons

Baboons are the largest and most terrestrial of the *Cercopithecidae* family. They are heavy-shouldered monkeys with rounded heads and protruding dark muzzles. Their arm bones are relatively longer than other *Cercopithecidae* members. Their coat is shaggy and the colour varies from the yellow baboon's light sandy yellow to the near-green of the olive baboon.

Africa has five main species of baboon but only these two are found in East Africa. The yellow baboon *(Papio cyno-* ✓ *cephalus)* lives in bush country, rocky outcrops and woodland in the east of Kenya and Tanzania; the larger olive baboon *(Papio anubis)* is more widespread, in a variety of habitats from rocky bush and acacia woodland to open plains (provided there are trees or rocky outcrops nearby).

Baboons are strictly diurnal and sleep in ✓

PRIMATE RIVALRY

Baboons' main enemy is man, with whom they compete for agricultural crops. They are also prone to human diseases, such as tuberculosis and yellow fever.

They are very gregarious and live in family troops from 10 to 150 strong, with a mixture of all ages and sexes.

At the centre of the groups are females and daughters who stay with the family group as long as they live. Males leave the family group on reaching sexual maturity. There are generally several reproductive males in an average troop but one is dominant until killed by an outside agent or displaced in a fight by a younger, stronger male. Certainly the largest male gets

trees at night. They also take to the trees for defence purposes, but otherwise spend most of their waking time on the ground, foraging for shoots, roots, seeds, flowers and insects, and making an occasional kill – hares or young gazelles being common prey. They exhibit a wide vocal repertoire, from sharp barks of alarm or warning, to squeals and titterings when siblings play together, to screams as subordinate animals are chased off by superiors, to murmuring between mother and young.

LEFT: rabbit-sized rock hyraxes are related to elephants.
ABOVE: a female olive baboon with her offspring.

most, but not all, opportunities to mate.

Baboon society is based on enduring bonds between individuals, especially core friendships which are probably formed between females as they grow up. However, young baboons and even males exhibit close ties to one another. Although males are generally promiscuous, adult females in a troop will have close ties to just two or three males, normally mating with the most dominant. These males will defend her offspring against predators.

Baboons breed the whole year round. Newborn infants have short, nearly black soft fur which changes to colour of an adult's coat at around three months.

Other monkeys

Several other monkeys live in East Africa, but most of them are localised in their distribution – the blue monkey *(Cercopithecus mitis)*, for instance, in forest areas of Kenya, Tanzania and Uganda; the patas monkey *(Erythrocebus patas)*, occasionally seen on the savannas of northern Tanzania and Kenya but more common in Uganda; and the black and white colobus *(Colobus badius)*, a noisy and flamboyant treetop-dweller which rarely ventures onto the forest floor.

WARNING SIGNALS

Vervet monkeys use at least 36 vocal calls, including different alarm calls to warn of the presence of a snake, an eagle, an owl, a leopard, a hyena – or a human.

altitudes from sea-level to 4,000 metres (13,200 ft). They are strictly diurnal animals although they may also feed on moonlit nights. They have acute eyesight and excellent hearing, but a poor sense of smell. As well as vocal calls, they communicate with a wide range of facial expressions – lowering their eyebrows, baring their teeth, raising or jerking their heads.

Vervets are prey to large raptors, snakes and cats ranging from servals to leopards. Their basic defence lies in alertness and flight. They

But the monkey you are most likely to meet anywhere in the area is the vervet *(Cercopithecus aethiops)* – also known as the green monkey, black-faced monkey, tantalus monkey or grivet. Vervets are archetypal monkeys – slight of build, agile and long-tailed – and are always seen in noisy, bickering, family troops containing lots of young animals. Both sexes are generally similar, although males are about 40 percent heavier, with conspicuous red, white and blue genital colouration.

Vervets generally inhabit well-wooded and well-watered grasslands but can also be found from semi-arid regions (generally near rivers or swamps) to evergreen forest edges, and at

are very gregarious and live in troops of between six and 60 animals, composed of adult males and females and young of all ages and sizes. Troops are territorial and defend their range against neighbouring troops with noisy group displays at the territory boundary.

Vervets are omnivorous with a predilection for vegetable matter. Their preferred tastes include fruits, flowers, grass seeds, shoots and bark, both wild and cultivated, as well as insects, reptiles, small mammals, young birds and eggs.

Breeding occurs all year round, although local peaks may be apparent depending on local nutrition conditions. Gestation is relatively long –

180 to 200 days. A young vervet starts eating solid food at a very early age by reaching up and taking morsels from its mother's mouth while she is feeding. It will ride on her back and suckle until six months or until the arrival of the next sibling, often a year later.

Bush babies

Galagos are small nocturnal primates, distant relatives of the lemurs of Madagascar. The greater or thick-tailed galago *(Galago crassi-caudatus)* is by far the largest: it measures around 65 cm (25 inches) and the bushy tail adds about 30 cm (12 inches) to the overall length. Its fur is thick and brownish or silvergrey. Its large eyes are surrounded by a ring of darker fur and stare out from a pointed muzzle: the ears are cupped and rounded and its senses of hearing, sight and smell are excellent.

Greater galagos have small "hands" with long, thin fingers with flat nails, and an extended claw on the second toe. They are treedwellers, living in a range of habitats including rain-forested mountain slopes up to a height of 4,000 metres (13,200 ft), bamboo thickets, wooded savanna grasslands and eucalyptus, mango and coffee plantations. Galagos can sometimes be seen in suburban gardens. Their territories vary in size according to season, with between 70 and 130 animals per sq. km (112-208 per sq. mile). Territories are marked out with excretions from breast, anal and foot glands which are rubbed on the ground, trunks and stems of trees and bushes. Neighbouring territories may sometimes overlap and family groups often share the same sleeping hole, located in dense foliage.

There are more than 20 other species of galago in East Africa. One of the most common is the lesser bush baby *(Galago senegalensis)*, much smaller than the greater galago – only 40 cm (15 inches) long – with a comparatively longer, slimmer tail. Bush babies have huge ears and eyes, and feed by night on sap and insects in all types of wooded habitat from coastal bush to acacia woodland to dense forest.

The curious ant bear

The aardvark *(Orycteropus afer)* or ant bear is a peculiar-looking nocturnal animal with a

humped back and a long snout and tail. An adult's body may be 1.3 metres (4 ft 6 ins) from snout to rump, with the tail adding another 60 cm (2 ft). They can weigh up to 65 kg (143 lb). Males and females are the same size but can be distinguished by the female's slightly lighter colour. Local soil colour often masks their true yellowish grey. Since they are entirely nocturnal, aardvarks are very difficult to see except when caught in the glare of car headlights. Then, they appear to be a light grey colour.

They are accomplished diggers, and can completely bury themselves in less than 10 minutes. Their eyesight is poor, but their sense

of smell and hearing is very good. They inhabit open grassland, woodland and bushland but are rare in forests. When moving, they make a snorting grunt sound.

Aardvarks are relatively vulnerable to predation from all large mammalian predators and rock pythons. They invariably escape by running into a hole. Although they are basically solitary, only coming together to mate, several animals may sleep in one burrow. Most likely these are related: a female and nearly grown young or a courting pair.

Their staple diet is termites, either looped up from the ground with their long, sticky tongues, or dug out of the ground. ❑

LEFT: a young vervet checks out the view.
RIGHT: 60 vervet visual gestures have been identified.

BIRDS

With its extravagant diversity and corresponding abundance of bird life,
East Africa is one of the best places in the world to observe birds

The enormous variety and concentration of bird life in East Africa is often overlooked by first-time safarigoers intent on ticking off the big five. Roughly 1,500 bird species have been recorded in the region to date and scientists believe that many unrecognised birds are yet to be discovered, especially in remote areas. Compare this figure with the 250 or so recorded bird species in Great Britain or the 850 in Canada, Mexico and the United States and you will understand why ornithologists are so attracted to Tanzania (1,112 species at last count including 30-plus national endemics), Kenya (1,083 species), Uganda (1,005 species) and Ethiopia (850 species including about 60 actual or virtual endemics).

Nature has provided East Africa with a tropical environment with every conceivable type of habitat. Equatorial snow on volcanic mountain ranges, cool lush forests on their slopes, vast open temperate plains, harsh dry deserts and lowland equatorial forests, seashores and mangrove swamps providing perpetual food supplies, all contribute to this unique region. The vast majority of birds live and breed here year round, but several hundred species come from northern latitudes when harsh winters destroy their food sources.

Age-old migrations

It is estimated that up to 6,000 million birds make the annual journey to Africa from as far east as the Bering Straits and as far west as northern Scandinavia, with some birds flying as far as the southern tip of the continent. Those that survive make the return journey each spring to breed in their chosen latitudes.

In East Africa there are only wet and dry seasons and even these vary dramatically from place to place and year to year. Driven by some ancient instinct, birds know when to leave their breeding areas to seek a better place to live.

LEFT: ground hornbills are conspicuous and noisy.
RIGHT: saddle-bill storks are seen on Lake Baringo, Lake Naivasha and in Queen Elizabeth National Park.

This is instinctive, not learned behaviour. Many species that breed in the northern latitudes and migrate to Africa each year actually leave their young to find their own way south, or perish in the attempt. Those that survive the long journey over harsh deserts, flying mostly at night, find rest and feeding grounds in the

amenable climate of East Africa. There is a sudden influx of birds almost overnight as huge numbers appear in the bush country, forests and even surburban gardens.

Bird migration has fascinated man for centuries. Their ability to navigate over thousands of miles with none of man's sophisticated technology, and to return repeatedly to the same nest site to breed is a remarkable achievement.

Bird enthusiasts throughout the world have cooperated to study this extraordinary phenomenon. They trap birds in nets, identify and weigh them, and record wing length and other data. Then a small numbered ring is attached to one leg and the bird is released. By making ringing details available to all, it's possible to build up a picture of migration patterns.

The sophistication of the migratory phenomenon is just beginning to be understood. We know why birds migrate, but much work needs to be done before we understand the complexities of birds' highly tuned navigation systems.

Conservation

Birds play an important role in the lives of man, not least for their aesthetic value. We all know how much pleasure can be derived from watching them in our gardens, but birds also perform an essential function in keeping the number of

on the birds of prey was to weaken their egg shells, effectively destroying their ability to reproduce. Once this was realised and conclusively proven, DDT was banned.

Birds on the coast

The East African climate is controlled by two major factors: a meteorological phenomenon known as the intertropical convergence zone, which produces the two main rainy seasons with specific wind directions, and the various ranges and altitudes of mountains in relation to these winds, at different times of the year.

On the coast the climate is tropical all year

insects and pests under control. Perhaps most important, though, is the way birds serve as an indication of man's destructive activities on the environment.

The classic example is the effect of DDT (dichlorodiphenyltrichloroethane) on the eggs of birds of prey. This was widely publicised in the 1960s, and alerted governments throughout the world to the perils of using long-term insecticides. Birds of prey are at the end of a food-chain. Their prey, be it mice, rats, lizards or other birds, all feed on grains or insects which, in this case, had been treated with DDT. The compound built up in their bodies, without serious effect, to very high levels. But the effect

round, and the beaches, with wide tide differentials (up to 4 metres/13 ft), provide massive food supplies for migrating waders or shore birds. At low tide from September to March, thousands of these birds can be seen feeding along the beaches, coral pools and mud flats.

The sanderling *(Calidris alba)*, whimbrel *(Numenius phaeopus)*, ringed plover *(Charadrius hiaticula)*, turnstone *(Arenaria interpres)*, greenshank *(Tringa nebularia)*, Eurasian oystercatcher *(Haematopus ostralegus)* and other migrants live and feed here, storing up energy for the long flight back to their northern breeding grounds in the spring. Resident birds are also much in evidence. The grey heron *(Ardea cinerea)* feeds in the shallow pools, gulls of several species are ever-present, and in the evening large flocks of terns come to roost on the coral cliffs. Breeding colonies of roseate tern *(Sterna dougallii)* establish themselves on offshore islands, and there is a confusing variety and large numbers of egrets. In shallow water without coral cliffs, mangrove swamps develop. Here the mud attracts mangrove kingfisher *(Halcyon senegaloides)*, black-crowned night heron *(Nycticorax nycticorax)* and other species of heron, including the strange black heron *(Egretta ardesiaca)*, with its unique feeding behaviour. It paddles in the mud with bright yellow feet and then brings its wings up

sea, create a third environment, known as riverine forests. Birds take advantage of this narrow strip of permanent water where food supplies are always available. Weaver birds of all kinds nest in the overhanging trees. Eight species of stork are found in East Africa's waterways and lakes. They all have large bills adapted to a carnivorous diet consisting of small animals such as frogs, fish and rodents. The largest of them is the saddle-billed stork *(Ephippiorhyncus senegalensis)*, one of the world's largest flying birds, with a 2.7-metre (9-ft) wingspan.

Tawny eagle *(Aquila rapax)*, martial eagle *(Polemaetus bellicosus)*, Wahlberg's eagle

over its head in umbrella fashion to shade the water underneath. There is also crab plover *(Dromas ardeola)* and yellow-billed stork *(Mycteria ibis)*, which feed by sticking their partly opened long bills into shallow water and, with a sweeping action, snap them shut the moment they touch something edible.

Along the rivers

The great rivers flowing east from the mountains, across semi-desert country down to the

(Aquila wahlbergi) and others nest in the treetops and feed off small mammals, dry-country game and birds such as guinea fowl and francolin which come to the water to drink. The blacksmith plover *(Vanellus armatus)* nests on the sand bars, and huge flocks of sand grouse come to quench their thirst and bathe.

On each side of these rivers stretch vast areas of semi-desert and scrub. This is harsh land at relatively low altitude, with scarce and erratic rainfall. For most of the year it is extremely dry. When rain does fall, however, the land blooms: every living thing from plants to elephants takes advantage of the increase in food supply. Insects flourish, plants flower and seed madly, and the

LEFT: black-headed weaver and elaborately woven nests.
ABOVE: a superb starling – one of Africa's 30 species.

bird life erupts to match. Trees are suddenly full of nesting birds: red-billed buffalo-weaver (*Bubalornis niger*), white-headed buffalo-weaver (*Dinemelalia dinemelli*), thousands of queleas (*Quelea spp.*), yellow-necked francolin (*Francolinus leucoscepus*), hornbills of many types, and those that prey on this new abundance. Pairs of secretary birds (*Sagittarius serpentarius*) nest on the top of flat trees, while the black-crested snake eagle (*Circaetus es pectoralis*) snatch lizards and snakes.

VAST FLOCKS

The red-billed quelea *(Quelea quelea)* is the most abundant bird on the planet. A flock of these little seed-eaters can number hundreds of thousands, and can destroy crops faster than locusts.

fish. They feed by sweeping their bills through the water, sieving out tiny organisms.

The same fish-free lakes, paradoxically, also support the African fish eagle (*Haliaeetus vocifer*), a magnificent raptor closely related to the American bald eagle. Where there are no fish, the fish eagle preys on other birds – sometimes as large as pelicans. Elsewhere, on rivers as well as lakes, it efficiently seizes fish from the water with its mighty talons.

Lakes and rivers are also the place to find

Lake-dwellers

Lakes Victoria and Tanganyika, and Kenya's string of lakes along the Great Rift Valley, are home to many of the same water birds as inhabit the river banks, and many more besides. White and pink-backed pelicans (*Pelecanus onocrotalus* and *P. rufescens*) gather in flocks of up to 100, often intermingling with white-necked cormorant (*Phalacrocorax carbo*). Even more numerous – and more spectacular – are the greater and lesser flamingos (*Phoenicopterus ruber* and *P. minor*). These distinctive long-legged waders congregate in flocks of thousands – sometimes a million or more – in shallow lakes that are too alkaline to support

East Africa's 20 species of heron, egret and bittern. The largest is the goliath heron (*Ardea goliath*), 1.5 metres (5 ft) tall and the world's largest heron. The one member of the family often seen in large numbers away from water is the cattle egret (*Bubulcus ibis*), which follows big game and cattle, feeding on insects disturbed by their hooves.

Birds of the plains

In the north of Kenya and into Ethiopia lie vast areas of almost true desert, most of it uninhabited by man. Here are the true dry-country birds which have evolved to take advantage of their enivronment: large Heuglin's bustard (*Neotis heuglinii);* sand grouse *(Pterocles spp),* which fly up to 50 km (30 miles) each day to scarce water holes; and the tiny, short-crested lark *(Galerida cristrata).*

Vast areas of Kenya and Tanzania are covered by savanna – great open grass-covered plains, where rainfall is erratic, but usually good when it does fall. Watercourses, some permanent, others only seasonal, create tree-lined valleys which slice through the plains where larks *(Alaudidae)* and pipits *(Motacillidae)* of all types, plovers *(Charadriidae),* longclaws *(Mac-*

> ### HIGH FLYER
>
> The Rüppell's vulture *(Gyps rueppellii)* is credited with being the world's highest-flying bird, having attained a height of 11 km (37,000 ft, or 7 miles).

ally kills its food, including smaller birds and lizards. The commonest vulture on the savanna is the white-backed *(Gyps africanus).*

The crowned crane *(Balearica regulorum)* is the only crane widespread in East Africa, and the national bird of Uganda. It stands just over 1 metre (39 inches) tall, with a straw-coloured spiky crest on its head. It feeds in open or wooded grasslands, stomping on the ground to scare up insects. Along the valleys cutting through this region, heavier growth of trees and scrub provide shelter

ronyx) and a vast variety of cisticolas *(Cisticola)* breed and live.

The ugly scavenging marabou stork *(Leptoptilos crumeniferus)* is often seen, and overhead soars almost every species of vulture; all species of scavenger have long, broad wings that enable them to reach great heights on thermals, and acute eyesight with which they search for dead flesh. Vultures are birds of prey adapted to eat carrion. An exception is the white-headed vulture *(Trigonoceps occipitalis),* which occasion-

LEFT: a striking red-and-yellow barbet.
ABOVE: the bateleur bird of prey
is identified by its short tail.

and nest sites for other birds, who feed on the plains: colourful barbets *(Captonidae),* fruit- and seed-eating birds, bush shrikes *(Malaconotus),* francolins *(Francolinus),* guinea fowl and doves of all kinds. Birds of prey, notably the chanting goshawks *(Melierax poliopterus, M. metabates),* find this environment much to their liking, and bateleur eagles *(Terathopius ecaudatus)* effortlessly soar for hours at a time.

Ostrich

One unmistakable bird of the savanna is the ostrich – the largest bird in the world, measuring up to 2.5 metres (8 ft) in height and weighing up to 135 kg (300 lb). Males have attractive black and white plumage and are bigger than females, which have the same dull, grey-brown feathers as their young.

There are two species in East Africa: the Maasai ostrich *(Struthio camelus)* can be distinguished by the male's flesh-coloured head, neck and legs which turn bright red during the mating season; the Somali ostrich *(Struthio molybdophanes)* male has greyish-blue flesh.

Ostriches prefer the lush, open grasslands of the savanna plains, dry thorn-bush country and semi-desert. They are generally silent birds, although during courtship rituals males sometimes make distinctive reverberating calls.

succulent plants and berries. Their diet also includes small lizards and insects. Ostrich eggs are very vulnerable to predators, especially hyenas and lions which may brave an attack by adults in search of this delicacy.

Birds of the mountains

Mt Kenya lies on the Equator. Here, altitudes of up to 5,000 metres (16,400 ft), coupled with latitude, create a peculiar habitat – an environment described by scientists as Afro-Alpine, or Equatorial Alpine.

There are permanent glaciers above a height of 4,700 metres (15,400 ft) above sea level, but

Although ostriches still have flight feathers in their wings they cannot fly and have evolved long, powerful legs as their main form of defence. They have two toes on each foot and one kick is enough to kill a man. They can run up to 70 kph (45 mph) and maintain speeds of 50 kph (30 mph) for up to 30 minutes. Their long necks enable them to sight enemies from a great distance and ostriches often serve as early-warning systems for other plains animals. It is true that they sometimes flatten their heads to the ground when approached by another animal. Ostriches live in family troops, small groups (up to 50 have been recorded in arid areas) or couples.

They feed mostly off grass, bushes, leaves,

regular and heavy snowfalls usually melt fairly rapidly in the tropical sun, making it seem like winter every night and summer every day.

From one of Africa's great birds of prey, the Cape eagle-owl *(Bubo capensis)*, down to the tiny scarlet-tufted malachite sunbird *(Nectarinia johnstoni)* or the moorland chat *(Cercomela sordida)*, many of the birds confined to this Alpine zone could probably not survive elsewhere. There are many other species of birds, but the environment tends to keep numbers and variety down. Of great interest, however, is the way birds have evolved to survive in any environment: vultures have been recorded on the snow-line of several East African mountains, although there is no good explanation for their choice of habitat. The lower slopes of Mt Kenya are covered with dense tropical rainforest. The winds blow predominantly from the Indian Ocean, so east-facing slopes tend to have a higher rainfall and more morning mist. The forests, always green, lush and cool, provide a permanent home for bird life.

NEST MYSTERY

In the Arabuku-Sokoke Forest, Clarke's weavers occur in flocks of 100 or more – but their nests have never been found.

erratic but heavy annual rainfall and zero altitude. Much of this forest has now been destroyed by man, but in the Arabuku-Sokoke Forest Reserve in Kenya live three bird species that exist nowhere else in the world. The Sokoke scops owl *(Otus irenae)*, the Sokoke pipit *(Anthus sokokensis)* and Clarke's weaver *(Ploceus golandi)* can all be seen with a little effort.

In the treetops, insect-loving shrikes *(Laniidae* and *Prionopidae)* feed in noisy family parties, often accompanied by starlings *(Strunidae)* of various different species. At lower levels, nearer the moist, cool earth, plant and insect life are abundant. Robin chats *(Pycnonotidae)* of several kinds find this perfect. So do bulbuls *(Pycnonotus barbatus)* and several species of greenbul. From the forest floor to the treetops, turacos, with their long tails, brilliant scarlet wings and raucous calls, feed on the abundant seeds and fruit.

On the forest floor, the scaly francolin *(Francolinus squamatus)* busily scratches and worries the earth, while overhead the great crowned eagle *(Stephanoaetus coronatus)*, possibly Africa's most powerful bird of prey, soars in display – sometimes appearing as only a speck in the sky, its piercing call drawing attention long before it is seen.

This is a place to sit quietly and watch. If the wild fig trees are fruiting, sit under one because the ripe fruit attracts green pigeon *(Treon australis)*, more turacos *(Musophagidae)*, olive thrush *(Turdus olivaceus)*, starlings and barbets of many kinds. When the fruit becomes overripe, it attracts insects, which are followed by a huge influx of insect-eating birds.

Low forest and swamp

True African jungle does not really exist in Kenya – Kakamega Forest in the west, at an altitude of over 1,500 metres (4,920 ft), cannot properly be called lowland forest. But along the coastline are the sparse remains of a once-vast forest, created by unique local conditions. Situated 5 km (3 miles) inland from the sea, this forest evolved to take advantage of fertile coral-based soils, an

Swamps appear in deserts in years of unusual rainfall and immediately attract the attention of birds not generally found there. Since the swamp holds water long after the surrounding country has returned to normal, the birds will stay. Other swamps are more permanent. Water-loving birds always appear where there is food and disappear when the water dries up.

When to visit

The rainy season in East Africa is the equivalent of spring elsewhere. Rain triggers food, which in turn triggers breeding. So if you want to see bird-nesting sequences and mating behaviour, you should plan to visit between April and May or in November and December. If you are more interested in seeing local birds rather than migrants, then come between March and September. ❑

LEFT: Hartlaub's turaco can be found in the forests of Kenya and Tanzania at 3,000 metres (9,800 ft). **RIGHT:** an Egyptian vulture uses stones to crack open other birds' eggs.

REPTILES

From the ferocious Nile crocodile to the gentle leopard tortoise,
East Africa has a remarkable abundance of reptiles

The richness of reptile fauna in East Africa compares favourably with any other part of the world. The region is a meeting ground for a number of zoogeographical zones, each with its own selection of species. Yet much of the region, including the whole of eastern Ethiopia, is largely *terra incognita* to the student of reptiles. Fortunately, reptiles have no significant commercial value here. A few are killed for skins and smuggled out individually but, at least with snakes and lizards, the trade does not flourish. However, many reptiles are killed on sight by local people as a matter of principle. Sadly, the numbers of individual animals and species are being reduced by habitat devastation and by the expanding population.

Crocodiles

Where there was enough water the Nile crocodile *(Crocodylus niloticus)* used to be fairly ubiquitous at middle and lower altitudes. Although its range has been substantially reduced it is still far from uncommon in many areas. It grows to an average of 5 metres (16 ft), although some can attain 7 metres (23 ft) and weigh 900 kg (2,000 lb). Though crocs rarely venture far from water, their muscular legs can propel them at 45 kph (28 mph) across the ground. Up to 70 percent of an adult's diet is fish, but they also take unwary mammals including baboons, antelope, wildebeest, young hippos – and humans. Females lay a dozen eggs in a hole dug in the ground, which they cover with vegetation.

Two other smaller species of crocodile occur in East Africa but both are from the western limits. One is the long-nosed crocodile *(Crocodylus cataphractus),* which grows to a little more than 2 metres (6½ ft) in length. It is reminiscent of the Asiatic gavial with its narrow nose and quite large teeth. It feeds almost entirely on fish and lives in Lake Tanganyika and associated waters. The other is the dwarf crocodile *(Osteolaemus tetraspis),* a west or central African species whose

range extends to western Uganda. It seldom reaches 2 metres (6½ ft) in length. Neither of the two smaller crocodiles is hazardous to man.

Lizards

More than 180 different species of lizard exist in East Africa – significantly more than the 150

to be found in North America. They range in size from the 2-metre (6½ ft) monitors to the tiny cat-eyed coral-rag skink *(Ablepharus boutonii),* which lives on outcrops of coral-rag and maintains an osmotic balance by having very saline blood.

The Nile monitor *(Varanus niloticus),* Africa's largest lizard, ranges in colour from grey-brown to olive-green, with bands of yellow spots. It grows up to 2 metres (6½ ft) and is an aggressive carnivore, preying on anything from insects and birds to mammals as large as a mongoose. Eggs are a favourite, and monitors will dig up unguarded crocodile eggs or climb a tree to raid birds' nests. They are strong

LEFT: the formidable Nile crocodile.
RIGHT: the monitor is the largest of Africa's lizards.

swimmers and can remain under water for an hour. Females dig open termite mounds and lay their eggs inside, for protection against predators. There are many kinds of agama lizard *(Agama spp)*, some with bright red or orange heads, others with steely purplish blue or shiny green heads. Agamas are often seen around human settlements and lodges. They feed mainly on ants, grasshoppers, beetles and termites, which they catch with a long sticky tongue. About 40 forms of gecko are to be found here, including two transplants from Madagascar which probably arrived many generations ago with the dhow trade. The Madagascan geckos are the brilliant emerald green common to the genus *Phelsuma Gray*. Native geckos are neither very large nor strikingly coloured.

Giant plated lizards *(Gerrhosaurus major)* are handsome, with skin that looks like chain mail, reddish brown in colour. Males are orange-tinted on the head and neck during the courting season. They are largely fruit-eaters but will eat insects and mice if opportunity allows. These lizards can become very tame and sometimes will hang around campsites begging for scraps.

There are far too many other lizard species to

A KALEIDOSCOPE OF CHAMELEONS

East Africa's chameleons come in many sizes and shapes, from the cat-sized Meller's chameleon *(Chamaeleo melleri)*, which sometimes catches birds, to the tiny pygmy chamaeleon *(Rhampholeon kerstenii)*, the size of a small mouse, which lives on tiny insects.

There are chameleons with three horns on the nose such as Jackson's chameleon *(Chamaeleo jacksonii)*. Others, such as Fischer's chameleon *(Chamaeleo fischeri)*, have two side-by-side protuberances that are rather like small pineapples. Still others have a single little spike on the nose – and some even have plain, unadorned noses.

begin to describe individually but one deserves special mention: the serrated-toed lizard *(Holaspis guentheri*, sometimes called the Tanzania forest lizard). This is a small lizard of the high primary forest, conspicuously marked with bright yellow longitudinal bars. It can glide from tree to tree like the Asiatic Dracos.

Turtles and tortoises

There are two freshwater varieties of turtles which have flattish rubbery shells and narrow pointed heads. Be careful when handling them as they have little sense of humour and bite like weasels. The first of the pair is the widely distributed Nile soft-shelled turtle *(Trionyx triunguis).* This occurs in the northerly end of East Africa and grows to a very large size. The other is the Zambezi soft-shelled turtle *(Cycloderma frenatum)* which comes from the southern regions.

Only three species of land tortoise can be found here. The leopard tortoise *(Geochelone pardalis)* is the largest and can grow to well over 45 cm (18 inches). This good-natured, rotund animal is a dull yellow colour with black flecks and lives in the savanna.

The forest or hinge-backed tortoise *(Kinixys belliana)* is quite carnivorous and can close up the back opening in its shell by a hinge more

quite flat and has a flexible papery shell. Unlike most tortoises which retire into their shells when threatened, these fellows gallop off at a good speed and hide among the rocks like a lizard. Even when you find their hiding place they usually wedge themselves in so tightly that they are difficult to extricate.

Snakes

East African snakes are very varied with representatives from many families. The giant snake of the area is the African rock python *(Python sebae),* which can reach a length of 6 metres (20 ft) and more. As it is heavy bodied, even one of

than halfway to the rear of its carapace. The back end closes down upon the plastron (underside of the shell) protecting the tucked-in hind limbs and tail. Other tortoises which can close their rear ends do so by having a hinge on the plastron which closes upwards. The forest tortoise's hinge is easy to see and looks a little as though the shell has been run over.

From the rocky areas comes the strangest of the three tortoises. The pancake tortoise *(Malachochersus torneiri)* is so called because it is

medium length is quite massive. It prefers to be near water, although it can be found anywhere except at very high altitudes. A large python can be a dangerous adversary for man if it is disturbed, but will not attack unless provoked.

The other family of giant snakes is the boa, represented in East Africa by a small relative, the sand boa *(Eryx colubrinus),* which rarely exceeds 45 cm (18 inches) and lives buried in the sand. Only the tip of its nose and eyes show and it ambushes any unwary, lunch-sized passing animal, which it grabs and constricts before eating.

Some of the most venomous snakes in the world are to be found in East Africa. There are three species of mamba, the largest being the

LEFT: several hundred people are killed by Nile crocodiles every year.
ABOVE: leopard tortoise.

black mamba *(Dendroaspis polylepis),* which can grow to more than 4 metres (13.1 ft). The only black part of a black mamba is the inside of its mouth (its body can be any colour from grey to olive brown), and it is more easily identified by its length (the average is 2.4 metres/8 ft), slenderness, speed of movement and its coffin-shaped head.

The black mamba has a reputation for aggressive attacks but experience shows that unless they are pursued or otherwise annoyed, they behave with the utmost discretion, which is just as well – it can inflict a lightning bite, injecting immense quantities of exceedingly powerful venom.

antagonist. If the eyes are washed out quickly the effect is only temporary but acutely painful; if neglected, permanent damage to the eyesight can result. The three spitting cobras are the common spitting cobra *(Naja nigricollis),* Mozambique spitting cobra *(N. mossambica)* and a sub-species, the red spitting cobra *(N. m. pallida).*

Closely related to the true cobra is Storm's water cobra *(Boulangerina annulata)* from Lake Tanganyika and points west. Although it has adequate fangs and very toxic venom, it swims freely among fishermen waist deep in water, neither fishermen or snake giving each other much attention. The other large near-

The other two mambas rarely reach more than 2 metres (6½ ft) in length. One is the common green mamba *(Dendroaspis angusticeps)* seen along the coast; the other is Jameson's mamba *(D. jamesoni)* from the west of the region. Both are brilliant green but the Jameson's mamba has a velvet black tail. They are quite deadly but their venom is only about one-fifth as toxic as that of the black mamba.

Asia is often considered the home of cobras but Africa has many more and in more varied forms. In East Africa there are five types of true cobra and two closely related genera. Three of the true cobras can spit their venom quite a distance, aiming it accurately at the eyes of their

cobra comes from the forest canopy of the western primary forests of Uganda and western Kenya. It is Gold's cobra *(Pseudohaje goldii),* which is hoodless and only comes down to the forest floor to prey on toads.

Three of the four giant vipers of the world can be found in this area. They are the Gaboon viper *(Bitis gabonica)*; the rhino viper *(B. nasicornis)*; and the puff adder *(B. arietans).* These are all large-bodied snakes with wide heads. In exceptional cases all three can reach a length of 2.5 metres (over 8 ft). The colouring of Gaboon and rhino vipers is striking and beautiful. They can all inflict multiple doses of lethal poison in just one bite.

There are a number of small vipers but three merit special mention. They are all endemic to a small area of Africa around Mt Kenya. The small Worthington's viper *(Bitis worthingtoni)* is related to the three giants. It is an attractive little snake with black, brown, lilac and white markings, horns over its eyes, a saturnine face and an irascible disposition. It comes only from the hills around Lake Naivasha. The mountain or Hind's viper *(Vipera hindii)* is a diminutive snake resembling a tiny melanotic European viper. It can only be found well above the tree-line in moorland on top of the Aberdare Mountains where there is frost most nights.

The last of the trio is the Mt Kenya bush viper *(Atheris desaixi),* which was discovered in 1967. This snake belongs to a West African genus and nobody suspected that a species existed this side of the Great Rift Valley.

Other snakes

There are only two back-fanged snakes in the world known to be deadly, and both are found in East Africa – the boomslang *(Dispholidus typus)* and the twig, bird or vine snake *(Thelotornis kirtlandii).* The former is a medium-sized snake with large eyes. Typically, males are green and females grey or brown. The latter is very slender with a large pointed head. The body looks exactly like a lichen-covered twig and the head is white or off-white below and green, red or brown on top.

A third species of back-fanged snake, though not known to have inflicted a fatal bite on a person, must be considered suspect due to the high toxicity of its venom. This is Blanding's tree snake *(Boiga blandingii)* from the western forests. It is a long soggy-looking snake with a huge head which, when threatened, suddenly becomes very unsoggy indeed, expanding its neck and flattening its head into a very intimidating display.

There are too many harmless snakes to mention in detail, including specialist feeders such as centipede eaters, slug eaters, egg eaters and even a little shovel-nosed snake which lives off gecko eggs. Others are more general feeders, such as the sand snakes *(Psammophis)* which, paradoxically, don't normally live in sand.

LEFT: the male common agma is brightly coloured; females are well-camouflaged.
RIGHT: a spitting cobra usually aims for the eyes.

Where to find reptiles

Reptiles are difficult to find unless you know where to look. Fortunately, each area in East Africa has its resident *Bwana Nyoka* (snake man), most of whom are excellent and well worth their hire. Reptiles can be found almost anywhere but places to hunt are by river or lake sides, forest edges, and where one type of habitat merges into another.

There are few places to go to ask questions: the National Museum in Nairobi (PO Box 40658, Museum Hill Road, Nairobi; tel: 02-374 2131; www.museums.or.ke) runs a long-established snake park opposite the main build-

ing with two additional satellites in Kisumu and Kitale. Mamba Crocodile Village (PO Box 85723, Mombasa; tel: 011-472709) has an excellent display of reptiles and successfully combines an educational and conservation programme with commerce. Bio-Ken (PO Box 3, Watamu, Kenya) has a reptile farm and runs a technical and advisory service for universities and museums.

The University of Dar es Salaam in Tanzania (PO Box 35091, Dar es Salaam; tel: 022-241 0500/9; www.udsm.ac.tz) has a good herpetological section, and Makerere University (PO Box 7062, Kampala; tel: 041-532631; www.makerere.ac.ug) serves Uganda. ❑

INVERTEBRATES

One way or another, insects will be part of a visitor's East African experience, from beautiful butterflies to glossy spiders and scorpions

Apart from dazzling butterflies and irritating flies that bite, it is easy not to pay much attention to East Africa's myriad insects and other creepy-crawlies. But invertebrates (creatures without internal skeletons) are an important and fascinating element of the wildlife tapestry. There are tens of thousands of

species – far more than all the mammals, birds, reptiles and amphibians added together – and they are integral to the ecology of the region, either as part of the food chain or as architects of the environment itself.

Many birds, reptiles and small mammals feed largely or entirely on invertebrates; many plants* rely on insects for pollination; the tsetse fly has been an important if unwitting agent for wildlife conservation; the largest consumer of grass on the savanna is not an antelope but a creature that measures less than 2-cm (¾-inch) long; and if it were not for the assiduous dung beetle, the savanna would look very different after a herd of wildebeest has passed through.

The invertebrate population is so vast and so varied that this chapter can only mention a few of the more conspicuous, or important, or downright fascinating species.

Butterflies

East Africa is home to hundreds of different butterflies, most of them seasonal and confined to a very particular choice of habitat. One of the most widespread and easily spotted is the African monarch *(Danaus chrysippus)*, also known as the plain tiger and the lesser wanderer – two names that do it less than justice. Its wings, with a span of 8 cm (3 inches), are bright orange-yellow with black and white markings (hence the "tiger"), and far from plain. As for the "wanderer", monarchs are strong fliers, sometimes soaring high to take advantage of wind currents and thermals, and often cover great distances during their life-span, which may be up to 8 months.

Many butterflies need flowers on which to feed. But in the grassy plains, butterfies of the *Colotis* genus thrive on dry vegetation. These white butterflies with brilliant red or orange wingtips are some of the most common in the region. So too are the pansies (genus *Precis*), which are usually blue and yellow and can be seen settled on territories of dry earth among the grass.

Winged nuisances

Not all flying insects are as attractive and harmless as the butterflies, and several pose a particular threat to mankind. There are literally hundreds of species of mosquito in East Africa. The males, and sometimes females, feed on nectar and other plant juices. But in most species the female also feeds on blood, often favouring a particular host animal. The genus *Anopheles,* however, prefers human blood – and it is these that carry the parasites that cause malaria.

The tsetse fly (family *Glossinidae*) looks like an overgrown housefly, but does a lot more damage. It has a long, stiff proboscis that can pierce the skin of mammals to suck blood. Some species of tsetse carry the parasites (trypanosomes) that cause sleeping sickness in humans and a deadly disease called nagama in domestic cattle and horses. Over thousands of years, wild game has developed an immunity to the sickness, but the domestic livestock introduced more recently has not: as a result, the presence of the tsetse has deterred large-scale ranching in much of East Africa – thus preserving the habitat for native game animals. It is no exaggeration to say that, but for the tsetse fly, many of today's national parks and reserves would simply not exist.

is scarce – in a dry year or because a growing locust population has reached a critical point – they come together in swarms numbering hundreds of thousands, which can devastate large areas of crops within hours.

Masters of disguise

Some insects are harder to spot than others. The many species of stick insects (order *Phasmida*) are masters of camouflage. Most of them look like twigs (some also have flattened wing-cases that resemble leaves) and usually live on plants that mirror their colouration – yellow, brown or green. Some even lay eggs

Another flying insect that makes an impact on agriculture is the locust. Locusts are large short-horned grasshoppers, which occasionally swarm in huge numbers, destroying vegetation in their path. The red locust *(Nomadacris septemfasciata)*, one of the most destructive, measures up to 8 cm (3 inches) and is beige and brown with red hind-wings. When food is plentiful, they live as solitary individuals, slow-moving and relatively harmless. But when food

that look just like seeds. Adults vary in length from 8–20 cm (3–8 inches) but even the largest are hard to spot in their natural habitat. They feed almost exclusively on leaves, creeping slowly around a plant to avoid detection.

Another well-disguised insect is the praying mantis, a predator that catches smaller insects with its specialised, spiny front legs, which it holds in an attitude of supplication (hence its name). East Africa's most common species, *Heterochaeta reticulata*, grows up to 15-cm (6-inches) long (the male is longer and thinner than the female), and resembles green twigs and leaves. It adds to the camouflage by remaining motionless until it strikes – amazingly fast.

LEFT: there are very few spiders in the region that are dangerous to man.
ABOVE: industrious dung beetles bury their eggs in balls of dung.

Unlike most insects, the mantis does not have a grub or caterpillar stage: infants are tiny replicas of their parents.

One common insect you are more likely to hear than see is the cicada *(Cicadidae)*. There are many species, measuring 2–5 cm (¾ inch–2 inches). They are flying insects, usually grey-green or brown in colour, with two pairs of transparent wings. They feed on sap which they suck from plants, and are very common wherever there is lush vegetation – yet their camouflage and secretive habits make them difficult to spot. However, you cannot fail to hear them: male cicadas pro-duce a characteristic loud humming, especially during the heat of the day, by vibrating membranes near the base of the abdomen.

Beetles and ants

There are many species of dung beetle *(Scarabaeinae)*, in all shapes and sizes. Most are black or metallic brown-green and between 5- and 40-mm (¹⁄₁₀–1½-inches) long. They all feed on the droppings of herbivores, which they mould into a sphere (the size of a golf ball or larger) with their shovel-shaped head, and roll away to bury. The dung provides food for the beetle, which can eat its own weight in 24 hours, and also serves as a brood chamber into which the female lays her eggs. The beetle itself is food for mongooses and bat-eared foxes.

Biggest of all the beetles is the Goliath beetle (genus *Goliathus*). They grow to over 10 cm (4 inches) long and weigh up to 100 gm (3½ oz). Despite their size, they are vigorous flyers, making a sound like a small helicopter. They feed on anything sugary, particularly fruit and sap. The Y-shaped "horn" on the male's head is used in battles with other males over feeding sites or for mates. Females use their wedge-shaped head to burrow when they lay their eggs.

Fireflies *(Lampyridae)* are soft-bodied bee-tles ranging from 5 to 25 mm (up to 1 inch) in length, with special light organs on the under-side of the abdomen. Their speciality is pro-ducing short, rhythmic flashes of light in a pattern characteristic of the species. The rhythmic flash is part of a signal system that brings the sexes together. It may also warn predators of the fireflies' bitter taste – although some frogs eat so many fireflies that they glow from the inside.

Termites, often called "white ants", are in fact beetles, related to cockroaches. The spec-tacular termite mounds that rise to 3 metres (10 ft) or more are "cities" containing up to 3 million individuals – workers, soldiers, larvae and, at the heart of it all, a single breeding queen. The queen may lay 6,000 to 7,000 eggs per day, and may live 15 to 50 years.

Unlike most termites, harvester termites *(Hodotermes mossambicus)* do not build mounds but live in underground nests con-nected over a wide area by a network of tun-nels. Workers emerge in their millions at night to collect dried grass, which they carry back to feed the queen and her brood. So numerous

EDIBLE INSECTS

Although most insects and their grubs are highly nutri-tious and provide food for many animals, very few are part of the human diet. One exception is the so-called mopane worm *(Imbrasia belina)*, the larva of the large mopane emperor moth. This spiny, red, yellow and black striped caterpillar feeds exclusively on the protein-rich leaves of the mopane tree, and is in turn a source of food for local people, who eat it raw, baked, boiled or fried. Other insect delicacies include grilled grasshoppers (served on thin wooden skewers) and the flies that swarm in their millions on Lake Victoria, which are gathered by the bucketful by the Sese Island people.

and indefatigable are they that they devour more grass than all the wildebeest and other large herbivores put together. The forest-dwelling driver ants (genus *Dorylus*) are the largest of all ants: workers measure 33 mm (1⅓ inches), while the queen grows to a massive 52 mm (2 inches). She can lay broods of up to 3 million eggs every 25 days. During egg-laying periods, driver-ant colonies lead a quiet, sedentary life. But in between they become nomadic, moving to a new spot every day in ferocious columns numbering millions. Using their powerful cutting jaws, they attack everything in their path – other insects, spiders, millipedes and even snakes and small mammals.

Arachnids

Among East Africa's thousands of arachnids, there are very few harmful spiders and scorpions. Indeed, there are very few you will actually see, unless you are looking for them. One of the more conspicuous is the golden orb spider (genus *Nephila*). It is a huge yellow and black creature (the female's body may be 5 cm/2 inches, the tiny male's only 6 mm/¼ inch), which spins amazingly strong golden-yellow webs up to 2 metres (6½ ft) across. The silk is the toughest organic fibre known – stronger than steel of equivalent diameter – and the web is so strong that it can catch small birds (which the spider does not eat) and can last for two years. The spider has a poisonous bite, but it is not fatal to humans.

More dangerous is the brown widow spider *(Lactrodectus geometricus)*, a relative of the American black widow. Its bite is venomous, but not necessarily fatal if medical treatment is administered. Fortunately, it is by no means common.

There are many scorpions in East Africa, most of them small with disagreeable but harmless stings. In dry bush country they can reach up to 20-cm (8-inches) long, but some of the smaller species are more venomous. Most are very elusive, preferring to run for cover rather than attack a human. One species you may encounter is the glossy black Tanzanian long-claw scorpion *(Iomachus politus)*, which is also found in Kenya and Ethiopia. Its tail does contain venom, but it is not very powerful and, in any case, this species is not aggressive and does not attempt to sting when provoked. Its flat profile enables it to hide upside-down beneath rocks.

Millipedes and snails

There are at least 1,000 species of millipede found around the world. The several giant species of East Africa (genus *Archispirostreptus*) grow up to 30-cm (12-inches) long and thicker than a human thumb.

A giant millipede looks like a fat black worm, but has several hundred short legs, two pairs on each segment of the body. They feed on dead and decaying vegetable matter and, when

threatened, curl into a spiral, to protect the head and soft underside, and secrete a noxious fluid that can irritate human skin.

The giant African land snail *(Achatina fulica)* is, quite simply, huge. Its conical brown shell, streaked with yellow, black or purple, is normally around 10 cm (4 inches) – although the largest-known specimen measured 30 cm (nearly 1 ft) fully extended, with a 20-cm (8-inch) shell. It feeds on all kinds of vegetation, rasping at food with its "tongue" (radula), which carries several hundred teeth. In some areas the giant snail is a major agricultural pest. It can live up to 9 years, and lays eggs in batches of 100 to 400 – up to 1,200 in one year. ❏

LEFT: praying mantis remain motionless while hunting.
RIGHT: the East African rainforest has hundreds of species of brilliant butterflies.

FISH AND MARINE MAMMALS

The marine life of East Africa is spectacular, and you don't have to be an experienced diver to explore the colourful creatures of the coral reef

All continents are edged by waters not more than 200 metres (660 ft) deep, covering the so-called continental shelves. In East Africa, this shelf is very narrow, not more than 75 km (47 miles) at its widest at Zanzibar, and often not more than 2–3.5 km (1½–2 miles). The East African coast has a series of continental islands, which are part of the continent, separated only by the sinking of the intermediate land. Zanzibar is one of these islands.

Pemba and Latham are oceanic islands, rising straight out of the water, and the flora and fauna found here is quite different from that of continental islands. On Pemba, for example, the fruit bat found is a genus found in Asia and Madagascar, but not on the African mainland.

Africa at one time is thought to have been part of a much larger continent, called Gondwanaland, which split into what is today known as India, Australia, Antarctica and South America. The existence of this larger continent helps to explain the presence of so many species common in East Africa which are also found on the Great Barrier Reef in Australia.

The distribution of plants and fish is affected by the currents impinging upon the continent. The South Equatorial Current which flows westwards towards the East African coast turns right once it reaches a point on the Somalia coast north of the Equator. The effect of the current changes with the season of the year and the winds. Between April and October, the southeast monsoon *(Kusi,* in Swahili*)* blows in the same direction as the current, strengthening the flow westwards and turning the current to push great water masses as far as Malindi in Kenya.

This effect is reversed between October and March when the northeast monsoon *(Kaskazi)* blows against the flow of the current. The temperature of the water is correlated to this water flow, being relatively lower in September – 24–25°C (75–77°F) – compared with about 28°C (82°F) in March when the water is at its hottest.

In the open water

Open sea fish are the ones most affected by the currents. These fish, among them marlin, sail-

fish, kingfish, tunny, runners, bonito and dorado, are called pelagic fishes because they continually swim around the open water. They are most abundant during the fishing season from September to March off the north coast of Kenya as well as off Shimoni on the south coast. The narrow Pemba Channel is an excellent place for fishing during this time of the year.

Pelagic fish are generally streamlined, with smooth bodies, slim tails, strong caudal fins and with dorsal and pectoral fins reduced in size. They swim mainly by rapid lateral movements of their tails and not with the movement of their fins as is common in fish that live in sheltered waters. They are generally dull

LEFT: a deserted beach on Kenya's north coast.
RIGHT: tranquil reef fish.

coloured, blue and silver with darker bars or markings. Manta ray or devil fish *(Manta birostris)* and the whale shark *(Rhincodon typus)* are two of the largest fish. The ray may measure up to 6 metres (20 ft) across and weigh up to 1,350 kg (3,000 lb). Whale sharks (the world's largest fish) can grow up to 12 metres (40 ft) in length and can weigh a tonne or more. Both are quite harmless if left alone. Despite their formidable size and appearances, they both feed on plankton.

MARINE MENACE

Sharks occur off the East African coast, but present little danger to humans – with the exception of those present in places like Kilindi or Dar es Salaam harbours, where they live largely by scavenging.

even at low tide. Coral reefs are the richest ecological environment in the world.

A typical coral garden can support some 15 families of fish containing up to 60 species which, if added to the fish in the surrounding water and those in rock caves and the seagrass beds, would come to more than 200.

Odd fins

In an easy morning's snorkelling around an undisturbed coral head you can expect to find globe fish and puffers *(Diodontids and*

Reef life

All reefs off the East African coast are fringing reefs. These reefs grow in warm, clear, shallow water on platforms of the continental shelf. They follow the outlines of the land and enclose lagoons. The reefs are corals, which are colonies of animals (polyps) of the same species as anemones and jellyfish. Polyps resemble small sea anemones and belong to the same *Coelenterata* phylum. They extract calcium carbonate from the sea to form a skeleton of lime on which they perch. When the polyps open to feed, they cover the skeleton with a filmy mass of tentacles. Corals grow continually, adding to their skeleton as long as they are covered with water,

Canthigasterids), which inflate themselves with water when disturbed and are poisonous to eat unless prepared by an elite cook. Keep an eye out for the queer-looking file and trigger fish *(Monacanthids* and *Balistids)*, which anchor themselves into the coral with their dorsal spines to keep from floating away whilst asleep. Then there are parrot fish *(Scaridae)*, which graze on the living coral and help to convert the coral into sand. Parrot fish are elongated, usually rather blunt-headed and deep-bodied, and often very brightly coloured. They use their characteristic bird-like beak to scrape algae and the soft parts of coral from the reef. Colours vary, and the male of a species often looks quite different from the female. In the surf parrot fish *(Callyodon fasciatus)*, for instance, the male is green and orange-red, the female blue and yellow.

Further on, you might swim past shoals of snappers and gaterins. Single, territorial damsel-fish *(Pomacentrids)* in a variety of colours and sizes, defend tiny parcels of the coral head. One genus, the *Abudefdufs*, are particularly belligerent and all 10 cm (4 inches) of indignant fish will dash out to threaten a passing snorkeller.

Larger fish are kept parasite-free by cleaner wrasse *(Labroides)* which have conspicuous

happened, the impostor has taken a bite out of the proffered flank and made good his escape.

The distinctive zebra fish (also known as lion fish and turkey fish) have extremely large pectoral fins, numerous extremely poisonous spines, and colourful vertical stripes. When disturbed, they spread their fins and, if further pressed, attack with the dorsal spines. One of the best-known species is *Pterois volitans*, an impressive fish with bold red, brown and white stripes, which grows to 30 cm (12 inches) long.

Red, black and white soldier or squirrel fish *(Holocentrids)*, jewel fish *(Anthiid)* and yellow and black butterfly fish *(Chaetodontid)* can

black and silver lateral stripes and approach potential customers with an undulating "invitation dance". A large angel fish *(pomacentrid)* may partially roll over to allow the wrasse to pick skin parasites off its belly. In a classic example of aggressive mimicry, sabre-toothed blenny have evolved an almost perfect imitation of the cleaner wrasse's colouration and invitation dance. This combination allows the mimic to get close to otherwise wary fish. Unfortunately for them, blenny eat fish flesh, not skin parasites, and before they know what has

also be seen. Surgeon fish *(Acanthuridae)* are oval and laterally flattened. They have a razor-sharp "scalpel" protruding from either side of the base of the tail and if handled or touched, they can flick it to make a nasty incision.

Serranids are generally duller but very tasty. The largest of the group, sea bass or groupers, may grow to 300 kg (660 lb) with a mouth that most people would feel nervous about swimming too near. Groupers wait quietly camouflaged in rock crevices and when something edible appears, usually a small fish, they open their enormous mouths so rapidly that anything in the immediate neighbourhood gets sucked into the temporary vacuum.

LEFT: zebra fish and staghorn coral.
ABOVE: a shoal of coral fish off Malindi.

The ocean floor

The bottom of the lagoon is white sand often covered with a dense growth of weeds, spotted with dead coral that is being eroded away. *Cymodocea ciliata* is the most common weed growing on sandy or coral rubble. The weed is not an algae but a marine Angiosperm. The bright-green wrasse *(Cheilio inermis)* and a small olive-green fish *(Leptoscarpus vaigiensis)* are two of the few that live here.

Where there is more sand and some coral rubble, a greater number of fish are found, among them the rabbit fish *(Siganus oramini)* and snappers *(Lutjanus fulviflamma)* with yel-

most excruciating pain. Medical help has to be sought immediately before the poison can act as the sting can be fatal in some cases. Luckily, the fish will usually move out of the way of the unsuspecting walker.

Marine mammals

Two marine mammals, dugongs and dolphins, live in the Indian Ocean off the East African coast. Dugongs *(Dugong dugon)* are heavy bodied, vaguely seal-like animals with almost atrophied hind limbs and a body that ends in a single flat flipper. Dugongs cannot move well out of water as their front flippers are weak and

lowish fins and a big black spot on their sides. The sandy bottom is favoured by species like red mullet *(Pseudopeneus macronema)* and sting ray *(Taeniura lymna)*. The ray is brown, with blue spots and a long tail with a sting which has serrated spines and is very painful. The ray will take flight when you approach it, so it is not very common to be stung by one. Far more dangerous is the stonefish *(Synanceja verrucosa)* which is found on the edges of lagoons and in pools. This brown, ugly and perfectly camouflaged fish lies at the bottom, often among rocks where it is very difficult to spot. Its sharp dorsal spines that have poisonous sacs will penetrate any beach shoe and cause the

they must raise their bodies by the strength of their breathing muscles alone. They hide in mangrove swamps by day, coming up only to breathe and feed on marine plants that grow on the bottom of the swamp, normally some distance offshore.

It takes some imagination and perhaps several months at sea to understand how dugongs could have given rise to the mermaid myth. Nowadays, dugongs and dolphins are threatened throughout their habitat although several species of dolphin, including the bottlenose, can be found off the East African coast. ❑

ABOVE: a manta ray glides across the ocean floor.

Snorkelling

Snorkelling offers much of the pleasure of scuba diving with few of the complications. It's inexpensive, requires little equipment, and is easy to learn. Most people, including children, can do it fairly well the first time, although it may take some practice to become accomplished. Among the skills you'll need to master is clearing water from your mask and snorkel, kicking efficiently with fins, and equalising water pressure against your inner ear when you dive beneath the surface. The absolute golden rule when snorkelling is not to touch anything with any part of your body.

When selecting a mask, move the strap and any hair out of the way and push the mask onto your face. If the mask remains unsupported, then it is making a good seal. Choose a mask with good visibility. Fins aren't a necessity for snorkelling but they do help you dive more quickly. Large fins may help you to swim faster but they will take more leg power to operate and you are also more likely to damage the underwater environment so select small fins.

To stop the mask from fogging up while snorkelling, before you enter the water spit on the inside of the mask and smear the spit fully over the optical surface with your finger. Then give the mask a quick rinse with seawater. The snorkel strap will need to be adjusted on the mask strap. Most people find the most comfortable position is to have the snorkel strap well forward, almost against the mask. Keep the snorkel upright while you are swimming face down on the surface.

Wade out into the water until you can float and hold your arms along the side of your body. Swim along the surface of the water, breathing through the snorkel and kicking gently with your fins. When you see something interesting hold your breath and dive down to get a closer look. When returning to the surface tilt your head back and watch where you are going. You should reserve enough air in your snorkel so that after you break the surface of the water you can send a quick burst of air through the snorkel to help expel any remaining water.

If you are diving more than a couple of metres down you will start to feel some pressure in your ears and you need to equalise before going much deeper. Pressure on the ears is equalised by holding your nose and blowing gently. You should hear

a crackling sound and the pressure subside. Under no circumstances should you do anything that is painful for your ears. The best time to snorkel is at low tide; however, if this is early in the morning, the water will to be too much disturbed by the wind. In between tides, currents can be strong and the water tends to be murky.

Don't touch or remove anything from underwater. Coral is very fragile and easily damaged but it is also razor sharp so avoid all contact and be aware what you're doing with your fins. A single branch of coral can take decades to regrow. Another hazard is sea urchin whose black spines, which contain a mild venom, can break off and embed in the skin

if they are contacted. The strength of the sun is often underestimated by snorkellers: sunscreen is essential and a T-shirt worn over your swim gear to protect your back is a very good idea.

The coral reefs around the coasts of Kenya and Tanzania offer some of the best snorkelling sites. In Kenya head for the marine national parks and reserves inluding the clear waters of Kisite MNP, Watamu, and the country's first marine park, Malindi, noted for its north reef. The islands near Lamu offer some of the best diving on the coast. Tanzania's best underwater spots are around the islands of Pemba *(see page 247)* and along Zanzibar's east coast. Several islands near Dar es Salaam also offer snorkelling trips. ❑

RIGHT: extravagant coral shapes on the Shimoni reef.

FLORA

*East Africa contains an astonishing variety of plants, each perfectly adapted
to its habitat, from Alpine peaks to humid coastal swamps*

The diversity of flora in East Africa is a result of the wide range of differing ecological and climatic conditions. Rainfall and altitude are the two major factors affecting the distribution and growth of different species of plants. The region rises from sea level to nearly 6,000 metres (19,600 ft), and varies in rainfall from 125 mm (5 inches) to 2,500 mm (100 inches) per annum.

Geographical zones

Recognition of these geographical zones helps in identifying plant species. The coastal zone running along the Indian Ocean from north to south, extends approximately 16–24 km (10–15 miles) inland, with a moisture index rarely below 10. In semi-desert, often covered with arid bushland or dwarf-shrub grasslands, rainfall is generally below 250 mm (10 in) per annum. There are no true deserts in East Africa.

Bushland (*nyika* in Swahili) is generally found below 1,650 metres (5,445 ft) and is sometimes interspersed with grasslands. Rainfall varies between 250 mm and 400 mm (10 and 16 inches) per annum. Grasslands are medium to dry rainfall areas with 400–600 mm (16–25 inches) per annum. They are found at altitudes of 760–1,800 metres (2,500–5,900 ft).

Areas with medium to higher rainfall – 625–1,000 mm (25–40 inches) – at altitudes of 1,100–2,000 metres (3,600–6,560 ft) are usually covered with wooded grasslands with acacia, albizzia and combretum trees.

Highland areas between 1,800 and 3,650 metres (5,900 and 12,000 ft) contain moorland, upland grassy plains and higher rainfall forest which can be divided into two regions: on the main high-altitude massifs, including Kilimanjaro, Kenya, Elgon and the Ruwenzoris where there is considerable cloud cover and rainfall exceeds 1,000 mm (40 inches) per annum; and

dry forests which, although evergreen, have an average rainfall of less than 750 mm (30 inches) per annum. Examples can be seen around Nyeri district, the Chyulu Hills and Langata near Nairobi in Kenya. There is no true rainforest in East Africa, except possibly a small area on the Usumbara Mountains in Tanzania.

Above 3,650 metres (12,000 ft) lies the Alpine zone with its own species of plants adapted to the extreme conditions. Altitude has a great influence on the distribution of flora throughout the region. Plants tend to extend their altitude range upwards as you move westwards. Here the climate is influenced by both the mellowing effect of the great bodies of water in Lake Victoria and Lake Tanganyika and their attendant satellite lakes, and by a reduction in the effect of glaciers on mounts Kenya and Kilimanjaro.

In the southern and extensive northern latitudes of the region, plants extend their range to lower altitudes due to the movement of the sun and its effect on mean temperatures. It must

LEFT: tussock grass and a type of "red hot poker" growing high in the Aberdares in Kenya.
RIGHT: a black rhino grazes under a giant euphorbia.

always be remembered that as altitude increases, the effect of rain is proportionately enhanced, and that on the highest mountains the rainfall is often less near the summit than on the slopes.

Plant families

Many families of flowering plants such as the mallows *(Malvaceae)*, composites *(Compositae)* and orchids *(Orchidaceae)* have a wide tolerance of changing ecological conditions and can be found throughout the region. For example, orchids both terrestrial and epiphytic can be found from sea level to altitudes around 3,600 metres (11,800 ft) in conditions ranging from

In all the drier areas the grasses *(Gramineae)* have an unusually plentiful supply of seed to enable them to survive long periods when no rain falls and seed germination is doubtful or impossible.

Similarly, the flowers of many plants have a higher than average nectar content to attract bees to stimulate fertilisation. Others such as the aloes *(Liliaceae)* and the parasitic *Loranthaceae* (related to the mistletoe) have bright orange or red flowers to attract birds, because in dry conditions there is a marked shortage of the insect life that normally performs the function of pollination. Many plants in semi-

high humidity and warm temperature ranges, to dry conditions at high altitudes with wide variations in the nocturnal and diurnal temperatures. On the other hand, succulents such as the genus *Caralluma* are generally found in semi-desert and bushland where rainfall is limited and temperatures are distinctly high.

Where ecological zones have marked characteristics flora has adapted itself to meet them. In grassland areas often extending over a hundred miles or more, the thorn tree (genus *Acacia*) has evolved to cope with fire and drought. In many species the seed germinates more easily after fire and leaves are thin, often turning their narrower margins towards the sun to limit transpiration.

desert and bushland regions have grey and aromatic foliage: the colour restricts transpiration and the scents attract moths and other insects for pollination.

Higher ground

In high montane and Alpine areas there are three curious evolutions, all growing to extraordinary heights. The groundsel tree *(Dendro senecio)* reaches 10 metres (33 ft), with a flower that's 1 metre (39 inches) long. Tree groundsels are selective in their altitude: none of them grows below 2,550 metres (8,365 ft) and most of them are found at 3,200 metres (10,500 ft) or more. They are also selective in their habitat and each mountain area, such as mounts Kenya, Kilimanjaro, Elgon and the Ruwenzoris, has evolved its own subspecies.

In these high altitudes giant heather *(Erica arborea)* can also be found. This many-branched tree grows up to 8 metres (26 ft) with white flowers clustered at the end of the branches. The related giant heath *(Philippea keniensis keniensis)* is found up to 4,250 metres (13,940 ft) on Mount Kenya. The giant lobelia *(Lobelia giberroa)* has evolved into a

HOW MANY PLANTS?

No-one knows just how many plants exist in East Africa, but when botanists complete their survey into the region, it's probable that more than 11,000 species will have been described.

cus, abutilon and pavonia which can be found mainly in grassy plains and, strangely enough, in rocky terrain and lava flows.

The pea family *(Papilionoideae)* is also prominent in grasslands, wooded grasslands and highlands. Represented strongly by the genus *Crotalaria*, of which there are probably more than 200 species in the region, they are widely distributed and can often be seen in considerable drifts of colour, mainly with yellow or yellow and orange

veritable tree which grows to 4 metres (13 ft), and has an inflorescence 3 metres (10 ft) long. This lobelia has evolved an exaggerated deep calyx in which the blue flower is almost hidden, to help it withstand the wide variations in temperature, which may range from 60°C (140°F) at midday to several degrees below freezing overnight. In the medium-altitude zones of grassland and wooded grassland there are 14 genera and 137 species of *Malvaceae*. Notable among them are hibis-

LEFT: giant lobelia and tree groundsel in the Ruwenzoris, Uganda.
ABOVE: golden flowers cover the *Cassia didimobotrya.*

flowers, though there are one or two species which are predominantly blue.

Lilies of the field

Among the lily family *(Liliaceae)* are three outstanding species. *Gloriosa superba*, sometimes known as "the flame lily", is a particularly beautiful plant with a red, red and yellow or red and green striped flowers whose outside petals bend abruptly backwards. It is widespread in the area below an altitude of 2,500 metres (8,200 ft). There is a singularly fine variant at lower altitudes with lemon-coloured segments and a deeper violet meridian stripe. The plant grows from a V-shaped tuber and can reach 5 metres (over 16 ft). *Albuca wakefieldii* or *abyssinica* is the most common lily in East Africa.

This robust plant up to 1 metre (3 ft) tall has bell-shaped flowers rather widely spaced on the stalk. Though they never open fully, these flowers are yellowish green in colour with a darkish stripe down the middle of each petal with off-yellow on the margins.

Among the *Liliaceae,* aloes are most widespread in the middle and lower altitudes. Red, orange or yellow with green spotted or striped leaves, they form dense groups of beautiful colour, especially in grassland areas where

tubular flowers. It grows throughout East Africa and is often seen at the sides of roads and in ditches.

The carpet flowers

A notable feature from sea level to more than 3,350 metres (11,000 ft) is the convolvulus family *(Convolvulaceae)* which has no less than 22 genera and 170 species in the region. Prominent everywhere is the *Ipomoea* genus whose myriad flowers scramble over coral at the coast, in semi-desert scrub, in wooded grasslands, forest glades and even on the moorlands.

Cycnium tubulosum tubulosum, with white

grazing has reduced competition. Elephants are particularly fond of the aloe.

In the *Amaryllidaceae* family are two beautiful species. The fireball lily *(Scadoxus multiflorus)* is an arresting sight. Growing from a deep-rooted bulb in rocky places, riverine forest and open grassland, often in the shade of trees or on the side of ant heaps, the flower spike arises before the leaves and is crowned with up to 150 small flowers making a single magnificent red or pink head, looking like a gigantic shaving brush.

Crinums often flower at the same time, notably the pyjama lily *(C. macowanii),* so called after the pink stripes marking its long

"pocket handkerchief" flowers, a member of *Scrophuliaraceae,* is dotted all over the grassland plains, especially on black cotton soils. *C. t. montanum* often grows alongside its near relative. It has large pink flowers and extends to slightly higher altitudes. Both are parasitic on the roots of grasses and speckle the countryside for mile after mile where grasses have been burnt or grazed heavily.

In dry open bushland is another parasitic plant from the broomrape family *(Orobanchaceae)* – *Cistanche tubulosa*. An erect, unbranched spike of yellow flowers like a large hyacinth springs out of a bare patch of soil drawing its nourishment from the roots of neighbouring shrubs or trees. There are three beautiful species of gladiolus in the *Iridaceae* family: *Gladiolus natalensis* grows at altitudes of up to 3,050 metres (10,000 ft) throughout the region and south to South Africa. It has yellowish-brown to orange flowers and is a relative of the garden varieties derived from *G. primulinus*.

Above that altitude, the finest species of them all, *G. watsonioides* with bright red flowers, grows in stony soils only in Alpine and sub-Alpine regions on mounts Kenya, Kilimanjaro and Meru. *G. ukambanensis* is a delightful species with white, delicately scented flowers, produced copiously but capriciously in wet years. It is restricted to stony soils in the Machakos district of Kenya, the Maasai Mara and coastal areas of Tanzania.

Throughout shady and damp places in higher rainfall regions, nestling in banks or decorating the sides of streams will be found members of the *Balsaminaceae* family, allied to "Busy Lizzies" of temperate gardens. There are more than 70 species in the region, ranging from near the coast, inland through the Ruwenzoris all the way to Cameroon in West Africa, and from the Red Sea Hills to the Drakensburg.

The desert rose *(Adenium obesum)* is found in semi-arid areas, often among inhospitable rocks. From the *Apocynaceae* family, this plant has magnificent long red to pink tubular flowers and fat fleshy branches: it appears a glowing mass of colour in a semi-lunar landscape.

Flowering trees

East Africa also has beautiful flowering trees. The Nandi flame *(Spathodea campanulata,* of the family *Bignoniaceae)* is a magnificent sight when in flower, growing up to 18 metres (60 ft) in height with large open chalice-like orange flowers. Originating in areas from western Kenya to the Congo, it is now widely planted as an ornamental tree.

The Cape chestnut *(Calodendrum capense)* is another beautiful tree, recorded throughout East Africa and as far south as the Cape. It grows in heavy stands which set the whole area alight with its cyclamen-coloured flowers. In drier

bushland areas *Cassia singueana* and *C. abbreviata* (*Caesalpinioideae* family) both flower before their leaves appear, and look as if golden sheets have been thrown over their branches. In contrast, in the wetter forest areas in the middle altitude range *Cordia africana* (*Boraginaceae* family) is a resplendent tree growing up to 24 metres (80 ft), with stalkless white flowers massed inside a strongly ribbed soft brown calyx.

When flowering, thorn trees *(Acacia* family*)* are covered with a mass of highly scented globular to elongated flowers. There are more than 50 species to be found in East

Africa: in particular, *A. senegal* and *A. mellifera*, which grow in medium to low rainfall areas and decorate the bush for miles. *A. seyal*, a species found in colonies on stony ground or black cotton soils, has lovely spherical flowers which appear in great profusion before the leaves.

If you are fascinated by the slightly grotesque do not miss the euphorbia. Numbering more than 20 species and growing up to 30 metres (100 ft) in height, these trees have twisted triangular, quadrangular or hexangular fleshy branches. They exude copious amounts of latex and their flowers look like blobs of squashed plasticine. ❑

LEFT: bright flowers attract birds, which play an important role in pollination.
RIGHT: golden flowers cover the *Cassia didmobotrya*.

PLACES

*East Africa's diverse environment and climate supports
an amazing variety of large animals*

There is no drama to compare with the unscripted antics of wildlife
in its natural habitat; no arena better for watching this drama unfold
than the vast and spectacular national parks and game reserves of
East Africa. A herd of elephants trudging away across a grassy plain,
hippos wallowing in a mud pool, vultures riding the air currents above
a group of grazing gazelles – all are part of the animal kingdom's daily
cycle of life and death. East Africa's game parks give a fascinating
glimpse of animal life in a series of pristine habitats.

This amazing combination of animals and scenery brings thousands of visitors each year to some of the most famous reserves in the
world. Kenya and Tanzania are at the heart of the safari experience
and the majority of visitors head for destinations within these two
countries. Both countries possess the tourist infrastructure, facilities
and variety of wildlife to pamper visitors who want to combine their
adventure with luxury, although arrangements can also be made for
anyone who wants to reap the rewards of roughing it in the lesser-
known regions.

Political and economic uncertainties in recent years, coupled with
poaching, have complicated the wildlife picture in Uganda, Rwanda
and Ethiopia. Uganda is arguably Africa's best place to observe birds
and the country has recently gazetted six new national parks while
the wildlife numbers are returning to their pre-Idi Amin levels. The
country's tourism industry has also revived and there are perhaps
some 30 hotels and tented camps that bear comparison to their peers
in Kenya or Tanzania.

The conservation of wildlife in Ethiopia is low on the government's
list of priorities but the spectacular Bale and Simien mountains
national parks are very accessible and are home to many unique
species. Many visitors to Ethiopia will want to combine a safari with
time exploring the nation's many cultural and historical attractions. In
the past, Rwanda's turbulent political history has kept visitors away,
but since 1994 the country has enjoyed relative stability and travel
conditions are as safe as anywhere in Africa. The country has a good
infrastructure to support its three diverse national parks. Famed for its
mountain gorilla population in the Parc des Volcans, Rwanda now
attracts significant levels of cross-border tourism from Uganda.

Wherever you choose to visit in this fascinating region, there is
nowhere else on earth with such varied environmental and climatic
conditions supporting such a large range of large animals. ❑

PRECEDING PAGES: a striking view of Kilimanjaro's Mawenzi peak at dawn;
the Mara River winds its way past a tented camp; a herd of wildebeest head
off on their great migration.
LEFT: birdwatching in the Semuliki Valley Wildlife Reserve.

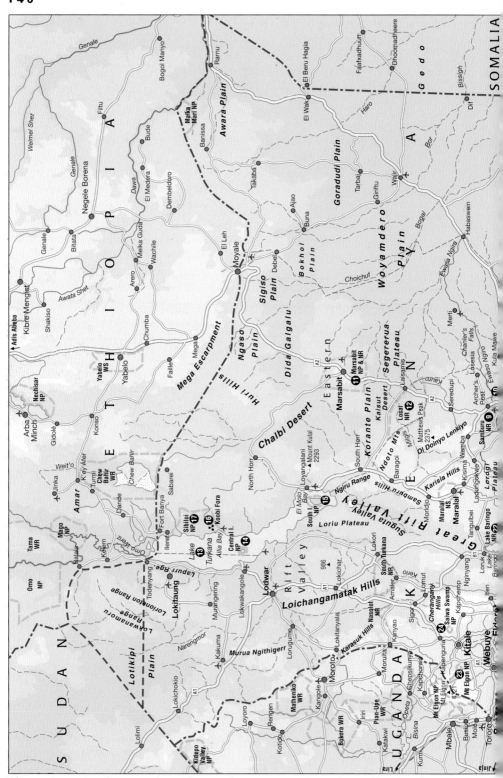

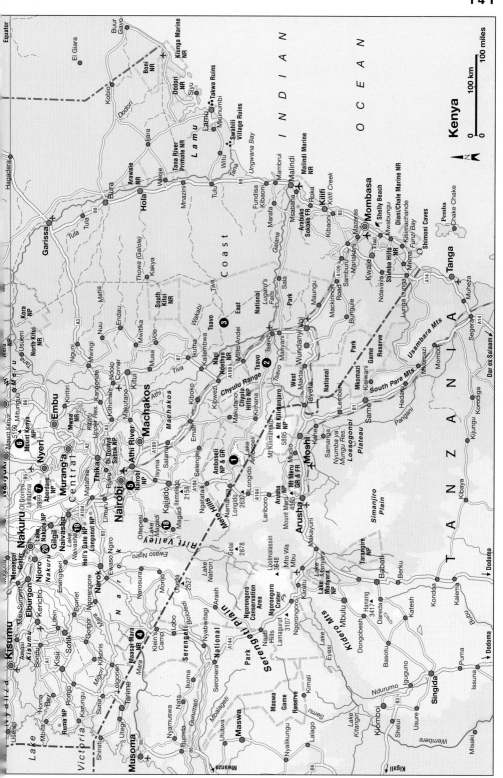

Kenya

KENYA

From mountain peaks to beaches via forests and plains, the Kenyan landscape encapsulates the entire African continent

Kenya is a country of dramatic extremes and classic contrasts. Desert and Alpine snows; forests, both lowland and montane; acacia woodlands and open plains; vast freshwater lakes and the superb coastline pounded by the Indian Ocean. Overall, it can be seen as the African continent in microcosm.

It is bordered by five countries. To the north lie the high plateaus of Ethiopia. To the northeast is Somalia, a hot, arid lowland of semi-desert. Most of Kenya's eastern border is warm unruffled and translucent ocean. To the south is Tanzania, the border a division between people of the same tribal origins – the Digo on the coast, and the Maasai and the Kuria in the west, where the frontier ends at the inland sea of Lake Victoria. On its western flanks are Uganda and a short stretch of Sudan.

Geophysically, Kenya divides into a number of distinct zones, by far the largest of which is the low-lying arid land in the north and northeast. This comprises about two-thirds of the country, most of it at an altitude of up to 900 metres (3,000 ft). Kenya's coastal plain is well-watered in two monsoon seasons, and the land is lush and fertile, but cultivated only in patches with coconut groves, sugar and other crops.

The third and by far the most productive sector of Kenya is the high tableland in the southwest, much of it above 1,500 metres (5,000 ft). This raised, volcanic block is split from north to south by the Great Rift Valley, leaving one-third of the land area in the east, two-thirds in the west. Of the two parts, the east is the more dramatic since it is dominated by the mass of Mt Kenya, a giant extinct volcano once higher than Everest.

Constitutionally, Kenya has been a republic since 1964. The first president, Jomo Kenyatta, has gone down in history as one of the most outstanding politicians of the 20th century. His successor, Daniel arap Moi, remained in power for 24 years. Under his autocratic rule, Kenya fell victim to rising poverty and corruption. When Moi stepped down in 2002, the Kenyan people, desperate for change, voted in Mwai Kibaki. Within a week, Kenya's new head of state had declared free primary education and health care and was soon being hailed by some as Kenya's first genuinely democratic leader. It remains to be seen however if Kibaki will fulfil his electoral promises to eradicate the corruption that is endemic to Kenyan government on practically every level. ❑

PRECEDING PAGES: a family of elephants.
LEFT: a buffalo calf in the Shimba Hills National Park.

Maps:
Area 140
Park 146

AMBOSELI NATIONAL PARK

Amboseli is everyone's picture of Kenya: open plains, woodlands and swamps, with an abundance of wildlife, all set against the spectacular backdrop of Mt Kilimanjaro

Amboseli National Park ❶ is seen at its best just after dawn and around dusk. The animals are up with the sun and Mt Kilimanjaro, across the border in Tanzania, is usually exposed for an hour or so before pulling up a blanket of cloud. At sundown Amboseli can be as unreal as a pantomime set. On the vast stage, the mammals are lit by strong pink and amber tones, with the mountain a gradually darkening cycloramic backdrop. Looming above that is perhaps a ruff of cloud, the black hump of high moorlands and the snowy speckled edge of Kilimanjaro's summit – the famous Kibo cone reaches an elevation of 5,895 metres (19,340 ft).

Amboseli is one of the oldest national parks in East Africa, having enjoyed more or less protected status for more than 50 years. It was originally part of the Southern Maasai Reserve, which also encompassed the **Kajiado** and **Narok** area where several clans of the nomadic Maasai people lived. The park became the Amboseli Reserve in 1948, when the right of the Maasai people to live there was recognised and a special area for wildlife was set aside. In 1961 the Amboseli Reserve was handed over to Maasai Tribal Control and became a Maasai Game Reserve, together with the much larger Maasai Mara Reserve.

However, competition for grazing increased and in 1970 a sanctuary around the swamp was preserved for game only and the Maasai were not allowed to enter. This aggrieved them so much that they killed many of the rhino population without even taking their horns. Consequently, a ring of bore holes around the park and a portion of the swamp was given back to the Maasai in exchange for an area to the north. Eventually, in 1977, Amboseli achieved full national park status, a comparatively small protected area of 392 sq. km (160 sq. miles).

Lake Amboseli

The national park is famous for its tranquil beauty and easily approachable wildlife. The Amboseli elephant population, only about 600 strong, is one of the few in all of Africa which has not been ravaged by poachers. It is also one of the longest studied and best researched by Cynthia Moss and her colleagues, who know every elephant by face and name and have written about them in the book, *Elephant Memories*. The **Amboseli Elephant Research Centre** ❹ can be visited by arrangement (staff sometimes give lectures): enquire at the lodges in the park.

Lake Amboseli ❸, from which the park takes its name, is a dry lake, some 10 by

FT: an
Amboseli
ture gazes
Mt
Kilimanjaro.
RIGHT: zebra
and wildebeest
are often
companions.

16 km (6 by 10 miles), and is flooded only during the rare occasions when there are heavy rains. The maximum depth in the wettest years is about half a metre (18 inches), but the surface is more usually a dry, caked expanse of volcanic soil – boring to look at, if it were not for the frequent appearance of a phantom lake in a genuinely spectacular mirage. The entire horizon seems liquid, with perhaps a file of wildebeest reflected on itself in a shimmering mirror image. Mirages aside, the lake's fine, alkaline dust has a habit of creeping into every crevice, so photographic equipment should be protected in plastic bags.

Clouds of dust blow up from the perennially dry bed of the lake and provide a stark contrast to the lush vegetation of the marshy areas such as Enkongo Narok, which form the heart of the ecosystem. These swamps are fed by the melting snows of Kilimanjaro, which percolate through porous volcanic soils, forming underground streams which rise close to the surface in the ancient lake basin.

Where the water reaches the surface, the desert is suddenly green, sprouting wild palms and enough grass cover to attract the fauna for miles around. Forests of towering yellow-barked acacias ("fever trees") used to surrounded the Amboseli swamps, but their number was gradually reduced by elephants, which stripped off and ate the bark and were initially blamed for all the damage.

However, it was then discovered that the naturally rising water table, induced by a period of good rains, was bringing toxic salts to the surface, which were "pickling" the tree roots. This caused physiological drought because the trees could not absorb enough water through their roots to compensate for the moisture lost from the leaves through transpiration. Even today you can see moribund fever trees which appear to be dying from the top down. Overall, however, the park has a varied habitat with open plains, acacia woodland, swamps and surrounding marsh areas.

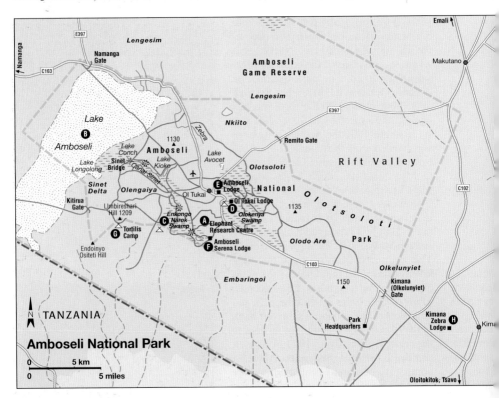

Amboseli National Park

Map
on page
146

Large mammals

Due to the open nature of most of Amboseli, lions are easily found and can occasionally be watched stalking their prey. Buffalo numbers have increased and plains game such as zebra, giraffe and gazelle abound. Small groups of gerenuk can occasionally be found in the arid bush standing on their hind legs to browse upon more succulent leaves on the higher branches. Hippos live in the open waters and swamp channels formed by seeping waters from Kilimanjaro. Buffalos feed in the shore-line swamps and elephants penetrate deeper, often emerging with a high-tide mark of vegetation on their flanks.

For years ecological and behavioural studies of elephants have been carried out in the park, so animals are accustomed to cars and visitors will be able to observe these large mammals at close range from inside their vehicles. However, aggressive encounters with Maasai warriors have left the animals wary of people on foot. An elephant feeding peacefully 3 metres (10 ft) from your car will run off in alarm – or attack in a rage – if someone suddenly gets out.

The density of visitors has had negative impacts on wildlife. Cheetahs, for example, have been so harassed by crowding vehicles that they have abandoned their usual habit of hunting in the early morning and late afternoon, and have taken to hunting at midday, when most tourists are back at the lodge having lunch and a siesta. Since this is not the best time of day to hunt, the result has been a reduction in the cheetahs' reproductive success.

Vultures and weavers

The 1951 film *Where No Vultures Fly*, based on the true story of how the Kilimanjaro Game Preserve was born, was shot in Amboseli. Its title seems somewhat at odds with the location since six species of vultures – often airborne on hot up-drafts from the desert – are recorded in the park's checklist of over 420 bird

LOW:
elephants
able across
Amboseli.

species. Of these, the kingfishers are per-haps the most photogenic, especially when caught making a strike. The Taveta golden weaver is the most distinctive, or emblematic, as it occurs only in this gen-eral region. The swamps and marshy areas support a wide variety of waterfowl, with no less than 12 species of heron. Birds of prey are also represented with over 10 varieties of eagle, as well as kites, buzzards, goshawks and harriers.

The most productive game runs are nor-mally around the main swamps of **Enkongo Narok** **C** ("black and benevo-lent"), where icy water bubbles out of fis-sures in black lava. Another favourite run is up the solitary **Observation Hill**, up which one may be chased all the way – as has happened – by a mad, rogue elephant with ants up its trunk. Otherwise, the hill is for long-range lion spotting.

Practical facts

Amboseli can be reached from Nairobi by two main routes, the most common

one being along the main Kajiado–Namanga road, turning left at **Namanga**, entering the park through the main gate nearby and following the road to **Ol Tukai Lodge** **D**. The distance from Nai-robi to the lodge is 240 km (150 miles).

The second access point is along the main Mombasa road, turning right just beyond the railway bridge past **Emali** and then following the Oloitokitok road for approximately 65 km (40 miles), tak-ing another right turn near the flat-top **Lemeiboti hill** and following this road for 32 km (20 miles) before reaching Ol Tukai Lodge. This route is shorter than the other, but the Namanga road is in bet-ter condition. Daily flights from Nairobi are also available.

The original camp at Ol Tukai was built as a film-set amenity in 1948 for *The Snows of Kilimanjaro*, and used the fol-lowing year by the crew of *Where No Vul-tures Fly*. The original huts have now been demolished and replaced by the new Ol Tukai Lodge, informal buildings of wood, stone and slate offering first-class accommodation and panoramic views of Kilimanjaro. Nearby **Amboseli Lodge** **E** offers international standards of accom-modation and cuisine.

Other lodges include the **Amboseli Ser-ena Lodge** **F**, built in the style of a Maa-sai *manyatta* (village) near one of the springs feeding Enkongo Narok swamp. The three campsites within the park have only very basic amenities.

Just outside the bounds of the park, on the south side, lies the luxury **Tortilis Camp** **G**, which has beautiful tents, excellent food and a swimming pool. Also outside the park is the **Kimana Zebra Lodge** **H**, to the east of the boundary about 15 km (9 miles) from the **Kimana Gate** on the Oloitokitok road, set in a Maasai community-owned reserve on the banks of the Kimana River.

There are advantages to staying in accommodation outside a national park : visitors are not restricted by game-park regulations, and so you are allowed to take game walks and night drives (both of which are forbidden within national parks and reserves). ❑

Map on page 146

LEFT: young cheetah cub. **RIGHT:** camping in Amboseli.

TSAVO NATIONAL PARKS

Tsavo is one of the largest wildlife sanctuaries anywhere in the world. Once famous for its man-eating lions, it now provides luxury accommodation for viewing wildlife of all kinds

The route to Tsavo from Amboseli (about 130 km/80 miles) is out through Kimana village on a straightish southeasterly line of dirt roads and tracks to Tsavo West and on to **Kilaguni**, the traditional centre of the park. As a useful point of reference, a high-folded range of green hills – an unusually vivid, velvety green – stays on the left but gets gradually closer. This is the **Chyulu Range**, which is incorporated within the **Chyulu Hills National Park** and may be among the world's youngest mountains, finally formed perhaps not more than a few hundred years ago. It's obviously a comparatively recent happening since one of the spur ridges is still black cauterised pumice.

Overall, the range is approximately 80 km (50 miles) long, 7 km (4 miles) wide and just over 2,200 metres (7,000 ft) at its highest point. A scenic track on the crest looks over the expanse of Tsavo Park but is seldom used and becomes downright dangerous when the mists descend. In among the hills is **Ol Donyo Wuas**, a small luxury camp with superb views of Mt Kilimanjaro, and another small camp, **Kampi ya Kanzi**. Here you enjoy Africa with an Italian touch and your days are not predetermined by a set programme.

Tsavo West National Park

Much of **Tsavo West National Park ❷** is of recent volcanic origin and is therefore very hilly. Entering from the Tsavo Gate, you come across the palm-fringed Tsavo River, from where the country rises through dense shrub to the steep, rocky **Ngulia Hills** which dominate the area. Of the volcanic cones, rock outcrops and lava flows that you can see, the most famous is Shaitani ("devil" in Swahili) – the black scar of lava that looks as if it has only just cooled, near Kilaguni Serena Safari Lodge. The Ngulia range peaks at close to 1,800 metres (6,000 ft) and on the south-

ern side drops a sheer 600 metres (2,000 ft) to the Tsavo River valley. Apart from the permanent spectacle, the Ngulias stage a special nocturnal show towards the end of the year. Thousands of birds appear out of the nightly mountain mists. They are palearctic migrants, flying out from the European winter, and about 40 species have been recorded. More than 60,000 birds have been netted and ringed – some subsequently tracked back as far north as St Petersburg.

The famous **Mzima Springs ❹** are found in this volcanic zone. The springs gush out 225 million litres (50 million gallons) of water a day, of which 30 million litres (7 million gallons) are piped down to provide Mombasa with water. The rest of the water flows into the Tsavo and

Galana rivers. The water originates on the snowcap of Kilimanjaro and in the Chyulu Hills as rain which percolates rapidly through the porous volcanic soils to form underground rivers.

Hippos followed by shoals of barbels and crocodiles can be watched from an **underwater observation chamber** at Mzima Springs. The best time for viewing is early in the morning; during the day hippos move to the shade of the papyrus stand and remain out of sight. East of the springs (downstream) is a stand of wild date and raphia palms, the latter with fronds of up to 9 metres (30 ft).

North of Mzima Springs are numerous extinct volcanoes, rising cone-shaped from the plains. Mt Kilimanjaro dominates the western horizon. To the south is a beautiful picnic site at **Poacher's Look-out** on the top of a hill. The view across the plains to Kilimanjaro is worth the trip. Tsavo West stretches further south to the **Serengeti Plains** which, despite their name, have nothing to do with the Serengeti National Park, although the landscape is similar. This part of the park, lying at the foot of Kilimanjaro, is crossed by the road and railway from Voi to Taveta.

Birds and baobabs

Tsavo West has spectacular baobab trees, which used to be far more numerous. In the mid-1970s, there was an enormous and as yet unexplained attack by elephants on baobabs. Some claim it was because of the drought, others believe that there were "too many" elephants. Whatever the reason, the remaining baobabs are quite safe today.

The variety and sheer numbers of birds in Tsavo are incredible. **Lake Jipe ❸**, at the southwest tip of the park, is surrounded by tall reeds and is one of the most important wetlands in Kenya, providing a sanctuary for a number of water and marsh birds, including migrants from Europe. Some of the birds commonly seen at the lake are knob-billed duck, pied kingfisher, white-backed night heron, black heron, palm-nut vulture and the African skimmer. To expe-

LEFT: baobab trees are widespread.

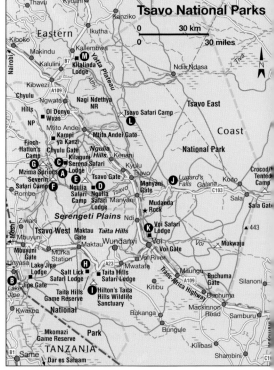

Map
on page
152

rience this wetland at its best, around dusk or dawn, you need to camp on the lakeshore or stay at the basic **KWS** *bandas* there. Unfortunately, the more up-market Lake Jipe Safari Lodge, a few faded signposts notwithstanding, has been closed for years.

Tsavo's most famous inhabitants are the black rhino. Just 30 years ago, around 8,000 of them roamed through the park – the highest concentration in all Africa. In the 1970s and '80s they were almost poached out of existence. Thanks to on-going rehabilitation programmes, numbers are picking up again. The majority of Tsavo's black rhino population are now contained within a secure fenced sanctuary at the foot of the Ngulia Hills, but if you take an early-morning game drive you might catch a glimpse of one of the few that roam free.

Other wildlife in the park includes lion, cheetah, leopard, buffalo, spotted hyena, warthog, Maasai giraffe, kongoni, duiker, waterbuck, klipspringer, impala, Grant's gazelle, oryx, eland and zebra. The lions of Tsavo are legendary but after the rains, when the grass grows very long, they are difficult to spot. Among the rarer fauna are caracal, kudu and Hunter's hartebeest, relocated from Tsavo East a few years ago from the Tana River area, where they were in danger of extinction. Also in the park is a herd of the bat-eared, pinstriped Grevy's zebra, which was brought in as a refugee group to escape poachers in Samburu. They seem to have confounded the dismal prognosis of zoologists by surviving out of their normal desert habitat.

Lodges in Tsavo West

Accommodation is available at a series of lodges within the park. The floodlit waterhole at luxurious **Kilaguni Serena Safari Lodge C** attracts an incredible variety of animals, especially in the dry season. **Ngulia Safari Lodge D**, sited on the edge of a great escarpment, is visited most nights by baited leopards, some of which have been studied by scientists, who have tagged them to track their movements. Only 5 metres (16 ft) from the veranda there is a waterhole and salt lick where elephants converge to within touching distance and dig at the salt-bearing earth with their tusks. **Ngulia**

Safari Camp **E**, not far from Ngulia Lodge, has six *bandas* on the side of a hill overlooking a small dam that's visited by elephants. Just south of Mzima Springs is **Severin Safari Camp F**, with the bar and main dining room overlooking two watering holes. Outside tthe park, **Finch-Hatton's G** is a luxurious tented camp, situated at the foot of the Chyulu Hills near a series of hippo pools and natural springs.

On the outskirts of Tsavo West, **Salt Lick Safari Lodge H** is built on top of stilts and linked by walkways for elevated views of the animals that converge at the salt-lick waterholes. Set within **Hilton's Taita Hills Wildlife Sanctuary I**, it offers excellent game viewing in a luxury resort atmosphere. The **Taita Discovery Centre** is a community centre and an educational facility that explains conservation issues in the Tsavo environment. The Taita Hills, which rise to the north of the sanctuary, are the only known haunt of the endemic Taita thrush, a critically endangered forest bird of which just 1,000–1,500 individuals survive.

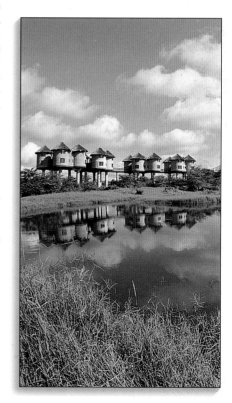

Tsavo East National Park

The outstanding physical feature in **Tsavo East National Park** ❸ is the **Yatta Plateau**, which runs almost parallel to, and is easily seen from, the Nairobi –Mombasa road. The plateau, which is between 5 and 10 km (3–6 miles) wide and about 305 metres (1,000 ft) high, originated as a lava flow from Ol Doinyo Sabuk east of Nairobi. Natural erosion over the millennia has exposed the flow to form the striking plateau seen today.

Around Voi, close to the road boundary, extends flat, dry, semi-desert thorn-bush country stretching as far as the eye can see. Running east from Voi is the Voi River, which is partly swamp and does not flow all year round. It meanders to **Aruba**, where a large man-made dam, the remains of a defunct fish-farming scheme, makes an oasis for both animals and birds. Along the banks of the river is the dependent riverine woodland and numerous wildlife paths leading down to waterholes. The road between Aruba Dam and Buchuma Gate on the Mombasa road is heavily populated with weavers, starlings and lilac-breasted rollers with iridescent wings.

One of the most spectacular sights in the park is **Lugard's Falls** ❶, 40 km (25 miles) north of Voi. Here the Galana River, which in its early stages borders Nairobi National Park, rushes through water-worn coloured rock. It is said that you can step across it at its narrowest point; perhaps the crocodiles downstream look forward to meeting those who try. A good spot to see them is **Crocodile Point** further along the river. Lesser kudu hide in the dry bushland along the river banks.

Mudanda Rock, a 1.5-km (2-mile) long rock between Voi and Manyani Gate, is a water catchment area which supplies a natural dam at its base. It is a vital watering point during the dry season and one of the park's best wildlife-viewing areas. Large numbers of elephants used to congregate here before the population was drastically reduced by ivory poachers.

BELOW: zebra are the common prey of lions.

Maps:
Area 140
Park 152

Wildlife in Tsavo East

Tsavo's lions were made famous by Colonel Patterson in his book, *The Maneaters of Tsavo*, which records the havoc caused by marauding man-eating lions to the imported Indian labour force brought in to build the Mombasa–Nairobi railway during the early part of the 20th century. Today's lion population keep a guarded distance. Grant's gazelles, zebra, impala, kongoni, giraffe and lion have replaced elephants as the most common animals in Tsavo East. Large herds of buffalo can also be found. Buffalo have enjoyed a well-deserved reputation in the past as being extremely dangerous when wounded or hunted. But since the banning of hunting, buffalo no longer associate danger with man or vehicles so they are generally quite docile.

Some of the more rare and unusual animals include fringe-eared oryx, lesser kudu and klipspringer; the latter can be seen standing motionless on rocky outcrops. The rock hyrax, improbable first cousin to the elephant, can be seen sunning on rocks and chasing one another in and out of rocky crevices.

The conspicuous white-headed buffalo weaver (the most striking characteristic of which is the red rump and not the white head) and red and yellow bishop birds are found everywhere. Some of the more unusual local birds include pale chanting goshawk, carmine bee-eater, red and yellow barbet, palm-nut vulture, African skimmer, yellow-throated longclaw and rosy-patched shrike.

The roads north of the Galana River and east of the Yatta Plateau are closed to the public, except when special permits are granted by the park warden. The country is wild and woolly, and spotted with outcrops such as Jimetunda and seasonal rivers such as Lag Tiva.

Lodges in Tsavo East

Various accommodation is available. **Voi Safari Lodge ⓚ** clings to the side of a hill overlooking the vast expanse of Tsavo and is literally built into the rock – many of the floors are natural rock. There are two waterholes and even during the

hottest times of day various wildlife, such as impala and warthog, come here to drink.

Other accommodation can be found at a number of tented camps such as Epiya Chapeyu Tented Camp, Galdessa, Satao Camp and Tiva River Camp. There is also Crocodile Tented Camp on the road to Malindi, just outside the park beyond the **Sala Gate**. Every night, there is a ritual in which huge crocodiles are "called" out of the Galana River with chants and drums, up to the veranda to be fed on offal.

A dirt road from Mtito Andei runs to the west bank of the Athi River opposite **Tsavo Safari Camp ⓛ**, which was reached by boat, prior to its recent and hopefully temporary closure.

Up-river, within its own Maasai Wilderness Trust area overlooking the Yatta Plateau, on the border of Tsavo East, is the luxury accommodation of **Kilalinda Lodge ⓜ**. Public campsites with minimal facilities are available throughout both Tsavo East and West.   ❑

Map on
page
140–141

THE MAASAI MARA

*The Mara is a natural continuation of the famous Serengeti
Plain: undulating grassland, dramatic escarpments, beautiful
acacia forests – and the greatest wildlife show on earth*

The **Maasai Mara National Reserve** ❹ was established in 1961 and covers 1,800 sq. km (720 sq. miles). The southern boundary lies on the border with Tanzania's Serengeti National Park. The Loita Hills mark the eastern boundary; to the west lies the splendid Esoit Oloololo (Siria) Escarpment, while the north is bordered by the Itong Hills. The Mara's wide horizons are unforgettable and game are clearly visible. It is also the scene of the greatest animal show on earth, known simply as The Migration.

In terms of statistics, no Broadway extravaganza has ever come close to the show provided by the Serengeti-Mara: a company of 3 million animals, an arena 3,200 km (2,000 miles) round and a non-stop year-long spectacle – every year for hundreds of thousands of years. At last count, there were 1.4 million wildebeests in the main cavalcade, 550,000 gazelles, 500,000 zebras, 64,000 impalas – and so on down the checklist of East African grazers and browsers. These are the moving herds of The Migration.

In this extraordinary natural circus, the wildebeest (or white-bearded gnu) is regarded as the clown, largely because of the way it looks: a head far too big for a spindly torso and legs. An over-long snout, a pair of over-small horns and a wispy white goatee beard complete the assembly. Wildebeests also play the fool much of the time. Arching their backs, they buck up and down in a straight take-off of the Maasai *ipid* dance, or then spin and fall, or generally charge about for what looks like the sheer fun of it.

But there is also something of the operatic about the gnu, some off-stage worry which is serious and often tragic. An animal endlessly pirouetting on itself may be a terminal casualty of a botfly embedded in its brain. A hundred may die in a crazy nose-dive into a ravine.

The word *mara* means "spotted". Why the Maasai applied it to this area is anyone's guess, although one theory is that it relates to the landscape, which is patched or mottled with groves of acacia and thickets of lesser whistling thorn. More likely, however, the Mara was named for the spotty, speckled inundation of the wildebeest and a million other herbivores that occurs any time between the end of June and the middle of September.

The Migration

Given the option, the wildebeest would probably never come up to the Mara. They would stay down south, on the vast alluvial short-grass plains of the Serengeti, which they prefer because there is virtu-

LEFT: a cheetah and her cubs on the Mara plains.
RIGHT: a Grant's gazelle and her calf.

ally no cover for the predators. But they soon mow the grazing to stubble, the land dries up and they are forced to move out following the northwesterly bearing of the "long rains".

The great journey generally has a disorderly start. None of the animals seems to know what's happening, except for a few individuals in the 1.4 million who must sniff the air, decide it's time and amble off towards Lake Victoria. The others follow, straggling individuals and small groups, but eventually bunching in broad lines which look like columns of safari ants. They wheel before the lake, moving due north to cross the Mara, Sand and Talek rivers at exactly the same places each year.

This brings them into Kenya, where there will be good grazing in the best-watered section of the ring from the Mara and the dozen other rivers that flow off the western wall of the Rift. The herds tend to break up and scatter across the hills, but also on to valley fields of "golden grass" – actually russet red

Themeda triandra – which contributes to the Mara's motley appearance.

The wildebeest are highly vulnerable to predators launching out of the thickets, so whenever they smell the October "short rains" moving up from the south, the hordes reform and restart the migration. This time, for some still unknown reason, the lines are narrower and more dispersed for the southeasterly arc, back to where it all started.

Resident game

The lush grasslands interspersed with silver- and russet-leaved croton thickets, hillocks and forested river banks provide a good variety of habitats for wildlife. There are many buffalo and quite a few rhino in the Mara, as well as herds of Thomson's and Grant's gazelles, topi and impala. The larger predators include Kenya's densest lion population, often encountered in prides of 20 or more animals, alongside healthy numbers of cheetah, leopard, spotted hyena, black-backed jackal and bat-eared fox.

BELOW: a herd of Burchell's zebra.

Map on page 160

There are over 450 recorded species of birds in this reserve, including the rare Verreaux's eagle owl. Other common birds include ostrich, kori bustard, martial eagle and various other birds of prey.

The Mara is the archetypal arena of conflicts between man and nature in modern Africa. Wheat schemes and livestock improvement programmes to the north meet the greatest remaining wildlife migration to the south. At the interface, conservationists and ecologists strive to reconcile the needs and aspirations of the Maasai landowners.

Although fraught with problems, many of the results have been encouraging – apart from elephant and rhino poaching, which is a blight thoughout Africa. Many tourism-based enterprises, such as tented camps, are run by local landowners who recognise that wildlife can be a resource worth husbanding.

Arriving from Nairobi

There are two ways to reach the Maasai Mara from Nairobi, either the high or the low road west towards Nakuru. "Up" is a reasonable tarmac highway across the top of the Rift escarpment; "down", formerly a minefield of potholes, has recently been resurfaced and is a pleasure to drive on. Either way, the route leads to the northern end of the **Kedong Valley** about 50 km (30 miles) from Nairobi. In the old days, this was "Blood Valley", where the Maasai massacred 550 caravan porters and, later, lost many lives in a reprisal raid.

At the bottom of the escarpment, in the village of Mia Mahiu, a left turn is signposted to **Narok**, the town that administers the northern half of Maasailand. It is full of strolling *moran* buying very little from shanty *dukas* (stores). Sixteen km (10 miles) out, on a good tarmac road, is a game department barrier at **Ewaso Ngiro** ("brown river" in Maa). At this point, there is a confusion of tracks, especially if the signpost is missing, which it frequently is.

Take the left turn to **Sekenani Gate**, then straight ahead to **Aitong**, for Governor's Camp and the western end of the Mara. However, to **Keekorok**, the tradi-

tional centre of Maasai Mara Reserve, the compass bearing is southwest on the centre track for about 72 km (45 miles) of bumpy, all-weather dirt.

Altogether, the drive from Nairobi is a rough 231 km (145 miles), so that charter or light-aircraft scheduled services to Keekorok or another Mara airstrip are worthwhile – if you can afford it.

Staying in the Mara

Keekorok Lodge 🅐, in the east of the reserve, was a traditional resting place on the long safari from the Serengeti to Nairobi. These days, it is well laid out with cottages and good facilities, including car mechanics – sometimes essential after the rough and bumpy roads.

Mara Serena Safari Lodge 🅑, in the west, is set high on a saddle overlooking rolling grasslands and the far-off Esoit Oloololo escarpment. Bedrooms are stylised mud *manyattas* grouped in outward-facing rings. The Mara area has numerous tented camps, including **Governor's**

LIGHT: the powerful martial eagle.

Camp **C** on the Mara River, where old colonial governors used to pitch their tents; it is now a very up-market retreat. The same company also owns **Il Moran O** private camp and **Little Governor's E**.

On the boundaries of the reserve are **Kichwa Tembo Camp F** (*kichwa tembo* means "elephant's head" in Swahili) and **Fig Tree Camp G**, both offering romantic settings where you can lose yourself in the true safari atmosphere.

Mara Intrepids Club H is situated in the centre of the reserve, and thus offers great views of The Migration when it comes through. **Mara Sarova Lodge I** is about 5 km (3 miles) into the reserve from the Sekenani Gate.

Outside the reserve, the **Mara River Camp J** lies about 8 km (5 miles) north of the Oloololo Gate, on a forested bend of the Mara River. Further to the northeast, on the road to Ngorengore, **Mara Buffalo Camp K** consists of thatched *bandas* situated near a hippo pool that's supposedly one of the best-popuated in Kenya.

Also outside the reserve is **Siana Springs Intrepids Camp L**, a lodge about 20 km (12 miles) from Sekenani Gate. **Mara Sopa Lodge M**, just outside the reserve's eastern boundary, blends in with its surroundings in the Oloolaimutia Valley, and puts the accent on the Maasai people as well as the flora and fauna.

To the southeast of the Mara, in a private concession bordering on the Serengeti, is the classic **Cottar's 1920s Camp N**, an old-style tented camp run by the great-grandson of Chas Cottar, one of the great white hunters who led the very first photographic safari in East Africa in 1919.

There are a number of semi-permanent camps and homestays around the reserve – for example, the **Cheli and Peacock Mara Camp**, a seasonal camp in the protected Koyiaki wilderness area. **Rekero Ranch**, in the wheatlands that border the Mara, caters for eight guests in thatched bungalows. ❑

Map
on page
160

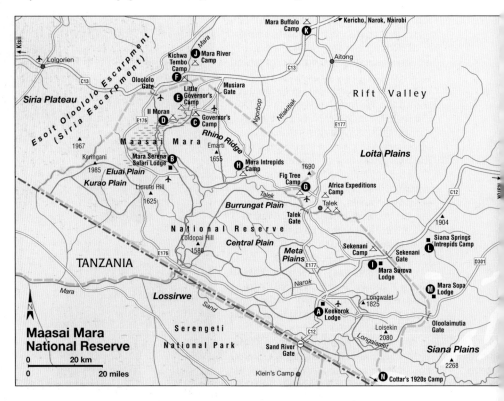

Up, Up and Away

Jules Verne's novel *Five Weeks in a Balloon*, published in 1862, was the first to mention ballooning in Africa and was the inspiration for English gas balloonist Anthony Smith's visit more than 100 years later. Using a hydrogen-filled balloon, he successfully crossed from Zanzibar to Tanzania, and also completed flights over the Serengeti and the Great Rift Valley.

Accompanying Smith as cameraman during these early flights was Alan Root, now a renowned wildlife film maker. He realised that, if problems of expense and manoeuvrability could be overcome, a balloon basket was the perfect place from which to appreciate the majesty of the African landscape.

Root had a hot-air balloon delivered to Kenya and, with the aid of a trained pilot, set about learning to fly it. Early flights were hazardous until European flying techniques were adapted to African conditions. The result of Root's efforts was one of his most popular films, *Safari by Balloon*.

While on location Root was several times asked by passing travellers for rides over the savanna. It was these visitors to Kenya, wanting to see the game from a different perspective, who prompted him to set up Kenya's first balloon company, Balloon Safaris. Based at Keekorok Lodge in the Maasai Mara Game Reserve, the company has flown 35,000 passengers since its inaugural flight in 1976. The original five-passenger balloons with their cramped baskets have been superseded by balloons three times bigger, with baskets containing seats for 12 passengers.

Since the first flights, balloon safaris have become a major attraction for many visitors in Kenya. Other balloon companies have sprung up in the Mara based at Governor's Camp, Sarova Camp and Fig Tree Camp. Wherever you stay in the Mara, you're close to a balloon base if you wish to take a trip. Although open year-round, the optimum time to balloon in the Mara is from July to October during the annual wildebeest migration, when over one million animals cross the open plains. The daily flights lift off with the rising sun for an hour-long journey over an average distance of about 12 km (8 miles). Being highly manoeuvrable, the balloons can skim treetops or rise to over 300 metres (1,000 ft) for panoramic views of the rolling Mara plains.

All balloon companies serve a luxurious champagne breakfast wherever they land in the park, something which can be as memorable as the flight itself.

Because balloons are moved by the prevailing winds they cannot return to their take-off point. After breakfast passengers are driven slowly back to the lodge by retriever vehicles. All companies return passengers to their respective lodges by mid-morning after presenting them with a certificate to mark the occasion.

In 1988, balloon companies started flying in two other game parks. In Samburu Game Reserve balloonists have the chance to enjoy the magnificent scenery with Mt Kenya in the distance. Ballooning in the privately owned Taita Hills Game Sanctuary near Tsavo West offers views of Kilimanjaro as well as a variety of game.

RIGHT: looking out over the savanna.

Map
on pages
140–141

NAIROBI NATIONAL PARK

*Barely 6 km (4 miles) from the city centre, wild animals can be seen
grazing or hunting against the Nairobi skyline
in this unique national park*

Created in 1946, **Nairobi National Park ❺** was the first park in Kenya and stretches a modest 120 sq. km (48 sq. miles) south from Nairobi to the Mbagathi-Athi River system. To the west, at the very edge of the Great Rift Valley, the gently saw-toothed Ngong Hills rise to an altitude of 2,458 metres (8,070 ft). On the northern horizon, beyond the city, one can see the Aberdares mountain range and to the east, on a clear morning, the peak of Mt Kenya. Being so close to the city, the park attracts many visitors on day trips and earns enough money to help subsidise some of the more remote protected areas.

Almost 37 km (23 miles) of fencing along the park's western boundary prevents wildlife from straying into human settlements and the rapidly expanding and not very attractive industrial area. To the south, migratory wildebeest, zebra and Coke's hartebeest (kongoni) enter and leave the park more or less freely through the **Kitengela** portion of the northern **Athi-Kapiti plains**. Their movements depend on the availability of grazing and water: the animals are mostly out of the park during the short (November) and long (April) rains. As the pastures dry out, the animals pull back north into the park, until their density appears to rival that of the Serengeti herds.

Absolute numbers are much less, however, and there are now fewer wildebeest and zebra than there used to be in the whole ecosystem that once stretched as far as Thika and the whale-shaped hill, **Ol Doinyo Sabuk**, which can be seen in the distance to the northeast.

Developments of farm buildings, rural residences and fences along the south-western edge of the park have raised fears that this free movement of animals could be affected, which would make Nairobi's famous park no more then a big zoo. It is hoped that land-use development policies will take into account the future of the park and its role in the annual movements of the migratory grazers, as well as its enormous potential as a money-earner for surrounding citizens.

Park habitats

Though small, the park has a good variety of habitats. It slopes from about 1,740 metres (5,712 ft) in the western forest down to approximately 1,500 metres (4,900 ft) in the southeastern plains. Forest in the west occupies almost 6 percent of the land and receives a rainfall of 700–1,100 mm (27–43 inches) a year, compared to the much drier southeastern tip. Tree species in the forest include

crotons, Kenya olive, yellow-flowered, long-seeded markhaemia, and Cape chestnut, with its lavender-coloured bunches of blossoms. Forested areas are home to at least a dozen black rhinos (some of which have been transported from less-friendly neighbourhoods) as well as larger numbers of buffalo and giraffe. Smaller wildlife, such as dik-dik, suni, duiker and bushbuck can also be seen here.

Bisected by valleys, the plains have less rainfall – about 500–700 mm (19–27 inches). They are covered with one of the most characteristic grassland types of the region, composed of *Themeda* (red oat grass) and *Setaria*, spotted with acacias, desert dates *(Balanites)* and the occasional arrow-poison tree *(Akocantha)*, which are dark green and often stunted from years of harvesting branches for rendering the bark into poison.

Visitors are allowed to get out of their cars at **Observation Hill**, a spectacular spot on the forest edge overlooking the central plain. From here herds of wilde-beest, gazelle and zebra can be easily observed. In the open grassland just under the hill, a well-studied male ostrich, "Pointy-head", has held his territory for years, and he or his successor can usually be seen entertaining delighted onlookers by dancing to female ostriches or chasing off rival males.

The southern part of the park is criss-crossed by ridges, valleys and plains. Cliffs fall for about 100 metres (330 ft) to the valley floor. In the dry season, wildlife gather to drink at the isolated pools left in the gorges. The gorge cliffs, some of which are quite spectacular and attractive to rock-climbers, have vegetation ranging from cacti and bushes to grasses and moss. They are lined with acacia trees browsed by giraffe. Buffalo and rhino can be found here, together with lion and leopard. The latter feed on the numerous hy-raxes which inhabit the cliff faces in, among other places, **Hyrax Gorge**.

The southern and eastern ends of the park consist of acacia-wooded grassland

BELOW: a topi stands alone on the high plains.

Map
on pages
140–141

bound by the Nairobi–Mombasa road and the **Mbagathi River**. This modest but perennial river becomes the Athi, which runs into the Galana, which becomes the Sabaki and eventually runs into the Indian Ocean just a little north of Malindi.

Game viewing

Visitors can park their cars and follow a 1.5-km (1-mile) **nature trail** along the banks of the river, which leads to a series of hippo- and crocodile-inhabited pools. Hippos usually give themselves away by their loud snorting. During the day animals stay submerged in the water and only come out at night to graze. Hippo trails can be seen etched into the bank. A few crocodiles can also be seen swimming about or sunning on banks, as well as impalas and hundreds of vervet monkeys. Another, slightly longer trail meanders through stands of yellow-barked fever trees *(Acacia xanthophloea)* and their greenish-barked cousins, *Acacia kirkii*.

Birds are abundant at the water's edge, among then the snake-necked African darter, saddle-billed stork, and various herons, kingfishers and ibises. Hammerkop and beautiful crowned crane are also common. The open plain features birds like ostrich, marabou stork, cattle egret, secretary bird and vulture.

The best time of year to visit is during the dry seasons, in February–March and again in August–September, in order to catch the return of the antelope herds that disperse southwards towards the Athi plains during the rains and return to the park to gather around the permanent waterholes. The big cats and impala are permanent residents; wildebeest, kongoni, zebra and to a lesser extent giraffe are migratory. There is a strong chance of seeing lion, cheetah, buffalo and rhino.

Nairobi National Park is an excellent introduction to the art and sport of wildlife viewing. Tours lasting four or five hours are available from most tour companies and can be taken either in the morning or afternoon. They can be arranged through any of the big hotels in Nairobi or tour operators. Roads in the park are not Tarmacked, but are kept in very good condi-

tion, so even small rental vehicles can carry you to an away-from-it-all experience in the morning, and back to the more intense experience of bargaining for local handicrafts in the Nairobi market before lunch.

Ol Doinyo Sabuk

Ol Doinyo Sabuk is a minute reserve of only 18 sq. km (7 sq. miles) which used to be the residence of the American, Sir Northrop MacMillan, who is buried on his reputedly haunted homesite at the foot of the hill.

The park is located just 15 km (9 miles) northeast of Nairobi, near **Thika**. The hill, also known as *Kilima Mbogo* ("buffalo hill" in Swahili), is a granitic kopje rising above the surrounding plain. It is almost entirely forested except for a small patch at the top. The area is inhabited by buffalo and bushbuck, but they are hard to see in the dense undergrowth. Admission is free. There is no accommodation available, but it makes an interesting day trip from Nairobi. ❑

Map on pages 140–141

THE MOUNTAIN NATIONAL PARKS

Kenya's highest region climbs from savanna through rainforest and bamboo jungle to moorland heath and finally snow-capped peaks. It's a unique part of the country

The Mt Kenya and the Aberdare national parks are about 80 km (50 miles) apart and comprise the highest reaches of the country's central highlands. The Mt Kenya park covers an area of roughly 490 sq. km (190 sq. miles) above the 3,470-metre (11,375-ft) contour line, with two salients stretching down the western slopes. The Aberdare park is about the same size and comprises high plateau, moorlands and peaks, with a forested ridge on the eastern flank known as the Treetops Salient, after the world-famous lodge.

Both parks – the country's main watersheds – are surrounded by forest reserves and are home to a wide range of wildlife. They were set up principally as recreation areas for walking treks in the moorland-heath zones and for climbing Mt Kenya, whose highest point, the **Batian** peak, is 5,199 metres (17,058 ft) above sea level. The climb to the top is popular and there are many well-established main routes to the summit and scores of minor ascents for the skilful Alpine mountaineer.

Mount Kenya National Park

The two salients excepted, **Mt Kenya National Park** ❻ begins where the upper forest merges with the heath zones of mostly *Erica arborea,* a weirdly shaped bush often as large as a tree and covered with moss and lichen. At just over 3,300 metres (11,000 ft), this giant heather is replaced by open moorland covered in tussock grass and studded with many species of giant lobelia and groundsel growing to a height of about 4 metres (15 ft). The ground is a rich profusion of everlasting helichrysums and alchemillas, interspersed with gladioli, delphiniums and "red-hot pokers".

The many mountain ridges resemble the spokes of a wheel meeting at a central hub,

formed by the gigantic spikes of Batian and Nelion (the second-highest peak, at 5,188 metres/17,022 ft). These are surrounded by many other smaller peaks, snow fields and glaciers, tarns, lakes, waterfalls and imposing scree slopes. The peaks are the remnants of a central core of an ancient volcanic crater, the rim of which has long since eroded away. Below these jagged summits are intersecting glacier routes up 4,985 metres (16,355 ft) to **Point Lenana**, which are suitable for visitors with little or no climbing experience.

The mountain has a wide variety of avifauna, ranging from the huge eagles to the delicate sunbirds. Among the most distinc-

tive species are crowned eagle, mountain buzzard, Cape eagle-owl, Jackson's francolin, golden-winged and scarlet-tufted malachite sunbirds, and mountain chat.

The forests below the moorlands contain a rich abundance of game animals including elephant, rhino, buffalo, leopard, bushbuck, several species of duiker, giant forest hog, and colobus and Sykes' monkeys. The remains of an elephant and several buffaloes have been found in the peak region above 4,300 metres (14,000 ft) but no one knows why they ventured into these high zones. Leopard and wild dog tracks have occasionally been recorded in the snow at around 4,600 metres (15,000 ft) above sea level. The attractive features of the mountain are 32 small lakes and colourful tarns. **Hall Tarn** is superbly situated, overlooking a valley, and **Lake Michaelson**, well over 300 metres (1,000 ft) below. At the **Curling Pond**, beneath the **Lewis Glacier**, it's possible to skate and have a game of curling.

Dense rainforests cover the lower salients and slopes of the mountain and the main tree species are the cedar, olive and podo *(podocarpus)*. Above this lies a bamboo zone at approximately 2,400 metres (7,800 ft), which in turn gives way to a belt of glorious rosewood *(hagenia)* trees and giant St John's wort *(hypericum)* before dying out at the heath zone at 3,200 metres (10,400 ft). Several vehicle tracks wind their way up the forested ridges. The quickest access to the peaks is via the Naro Moru track, which reaches just over 3,000 metres (9,800 ft) and stops immediately below the moorlands.

All visitors must sign in at the park entrance gate. You are not permitted through the gates unaccompanied – except on a day trip, which must end at 4pm. For longer stays on the mountain, there must be at least two people, guides and porters included. These, together with all climbing equipment, can be hired at the **Naro Moru River Lodge**, a delightful spot in beautiful gardens through which the Naro Moru River flows (regularly restocked with trout

LEFT: a trekker takes a break at the base of Kibo, one of Kilimanjaro's three extinct volcanoes.

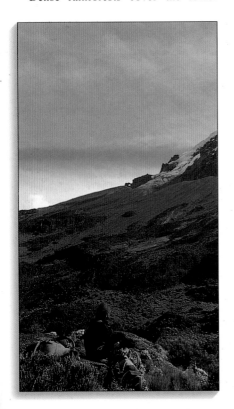

CLIMBING MT KENYA

Mt Kenya with its twin peaks, Batian and Nelion, both over 5,000-metres (16,400-ft) high, are a prime attraction for rock climbers and mountaineers. Climbs here are graded – though definitive grading is impossible because of variable seasonal and meteorological conditions. Climbs are only usually attempted during the two dry seasons: late December to early March, and July to early October. It is still possible to climb during the off-seasons but the climbs are usually one grade harder and take several hours longer. A tent is not usually required, as all routes can be approached from established huts, but bivouac equipment should be carried on all climbs and is essential on the longer, harder routes. Tourist lodges around the mountain provide everything you will need: guides, porters, cooks, pack animals, tentage, climbing and camping equipment, food and transport to roadheads. Altitude problems remain the most serious limitation to good performance on the mountain. Conditioning is important, technical competence essential, and acclimatisation at high altitude for a few days before ascent is required. Technical climbing on the main peaks is not for everyone. Point Lenana, the third peak at 4, 985 metres (16, 355 ft), offers spectacular ridge walks.

Map on pages 140–141

for fishermen). There is also accommodation at the **Met Station Lodge** (at 3,000 metres/10,000 ft) and at Mackinder's Camp, also known as **Teleki Lodge** (4,330 metres/14,200 ft), which is warm and staffed by qualified guides.

Another approach to the mountain is from **Chogoria** on the eastern side – perhaps the toughest and most demanding route, as it goes through thick forest. You can stay at the **Meru Mt Kenya Lodge**, which is just inside the park and offers self-catering *bandas*.

You don't need to camp at altitude to enjoy the spectacle of Mt Kenya's snow-capped peaks gleaming in the sun. **Serena Mountain Lodge**, on the forested south-western slopes, overlooks a watering hole and has great views of the mountain. Near **Nanyuki** to the west is the famous **Mt Kenya Safari Club**, established by a Texan oil baron, a Swiss millionaire and film star William Holden. There are superb views of the mountain from its beautifully manicured gardens. There's also a nine-hole golf course and the only heated swimming pool on the Equator. Surrounding the club is the Mt Kenya Game Ranch, a wildlife sanctuary which incorporates the William Holden Wildlife Education Centre.

Another place to stay within sight of Mt Kenya is **Ol Pejeta Lodge**, on the Laikipia Plateau on the way to Nanyuki. The ranch, formerly owned by millionaire Adnan Kashoggi, is now run by Lonrho Hotels, who also operate the lodge and the neighbouring Sweet Waters Tented Camp.

Aberdare National Park

The mountain range in **Aberdare National Park ❼** has in fact been renamed the Nyandarua but the old name – Aberdares – persists. The mountains rise in the north to the highest moorland peak of **Ol Doinyo Lesatima** at 3,999 metres (13,120 ft), and some 40 km (25 miles) to the south stands the well-known summit of **Kinangop** at 3,906 metres (12,816 ft). Between these two peaks is a plateau of moorland – gently undulating country covered in tussock grass

BELOW:
elephants at
the waterhole
of The Ark.

and large areas of mixed giant heath. Ice-cold streams, well stocked with trout, thread their way across the moorlands and cascade over a series of waterfalls to form the headwaters of several of the major rivers.

The Aberdares are well-endowed with a great variety and quantity of wild animals despite the occurrence of periodic cold and mist. The western slopes of the range are principally part of the Rift wall, and are therefore relatively steep and generally not as attractive to game as are the more gentle slopes of the eastern side.

Elephant, buffalo, rhino, eland, waterbuck, bushbuck, reedbuck, several species of duikers, suni, bushpig, warthog, serval, lion, Sykes' monkey and hyena occur in varying numbers, and most of them are easily seen. Rhinos are sparse here, as everywhere else in the country, but they can be seen on the moors and particularly on the **Treetops Salient**.

The Aberdares also form the last stronghold for the endangered eastern race of bongo, an outsized forest antelope that is seldom seen but whose numbers are reputedly on the increase within the national park

Herds of elephant and buffalo migrate with the rain, occupying the bamboo and rainforest zones during the dry seasons. When the rain begins, the game migrates to the plateau moorlands and the lower areas of the Treetops Salient, where the forest is not so dense and the ridges are less steep.

The park is criss-crossed with tracks, many of which were made by British troops during the Mau Mau rebellion in the 1950s. The most important of these is the road from **Nyeri**, which climbs the eastern slopes and crosses the moorlands, reaching a height of 3,170 metres (10,400 ft), and finally descends the western slopes and crosses the Kinangop farmlands to Naivasha.

The Outspan Hotel in Nyeri offers distant views of Mt Kenya, has tasteful guest rooms with fireplaces and serves meals in a baronial-style dining room. Lord Baden Powell, the founder of the scout movement, spent the last three years of his life in a cottage here, which is now a small museum. Visitors to **Treetops** meet at the Outspan and are transported by the hotel through the coffee plantations, to the famous lodge overlooking a waterhole and salt lick. This is where, in February 1952, Princess Elizabeth learned of her accession to the British throne.

On the road northwest from Nyeri is the **Aberdare Country Club**. Set on the side of Mweiga Hill, it affords great views of Mt Kenya and the Laikipia plains. The club grounds are attractive, with a golf course and horse riding among other outdoor activities. Visitors to **The Ark**, another forest lodge, assemble and board transport here. The trip is 18 km (11 miles) from the club into the Aberdare National Park through the Ark Gate. The Ark is situated over a natural waterhole, illuminated at night so that nocturnal visitors can be viewed.

Back on the main road, heading north, is **Solio Ranch**, a private sanctuary that has been successful in breeding both white and black rhino. Patrick's Camp in Solio is modelled on a turn-of-the-20th-century hunting camp.   ❏

Map on pages 140–141

LEFT: Sykes' monkeys can be found at the roadside in the Aberdare National Park. **RIGHT:** Mt Kenya is a challenge for rock climbers

Map
n pages
40–141

MERU NATIONAL PARK

In an area formerly popular with hunters, this reserve was established for the rehabilitation of wildlife. It lies off the beaten safari trail, but offers spectacular game viewing

Meru National Park ❽ achieved international recognition with Joy Adamson's novel *Born Free*, the story of Elsa the lioness that was rehabilitated to the wild (Elsa's grave lies within the park and can be visited by tourists). Despite being one of the major national parks in Kenya, and a very beautiful one, Meru is off the mainstream circuit for the majority of visitors. But it is well worth a visit. The park covers an area of 800 sq. km (320 sq. miles), lying to the west of Mt Kenya in the semi-arid area of the country. It straddles the Equator and ranges from an altitude of 1,000 metres (3,300 ft) in the foothills of the Nyambeni Range (the northern boundary) to less than 300 metres (990 ft) on the Tana River in the south.

Two routes lead from Nairobi to Meru National Park: one around Mt Kenya, through **Nanyuki**, and the other one through **Embu**. Both roads go to **Meru** town, from where it is 78 km (48 miles) to the park. If you go via Nanyuki, you can enter the park from the west using the **Murera Gate**. Some visitors prefer to fly in to avoid the slow and winding road.

The main tourist roads are in the western part, with only a few roads in the remote east. The eastern park boundary is bordered by the Bisanadi National Reserve; to the southeast are the North Kitui and Kora national reserves; while to the north of Kora is the Rahole National Reserve. Together with Meru, they create a wildlife sanctuary that encompasses 4,670 sq. km (1,868 sq. miles).

Vegetation is mainly bushland, with combretum bush prevailing in the north and commiphora in the south. The northeast is dominated by grassland with borassus palms and acacia woodland. There is plenty of water, the main perennial river being the Tana, which is the longest in Kenya. There are many small streams in the park; most are bordered by riverine forest. Some valleys are partially flooded during the rainy season, providing a swampy grassland habitat favoured by buffalo and waterbuck.

The wildlife

Large numbers of buffalo can usually be found around the swamps and the Tana River, which also provides a sanctuary for hippopotamus and crocodile. The big cats are abundant, but difficult to see because of the tall grass cover and thick bush. The reticulated giraffe is commonly seen, while the elephant comes here in the dry season but disappears with the rains. Baboon and vervet monkey are easy to spot. Dik-dik and gerenuk browse the

T: a wary
male leopard.
HT: the
reticulated
giraffe is a
common sight.

woodlands; eland and kongoni prefer the wetter grassland areas. Lesser kudu, either alone or in pairs, can be found in thickets or in valley bottoms in the evening. Bird-watchers should look out for the palm-nut vulture, which feeds on a mixture of palm nuts and carrion. In addition, the palm swift can be seen building its nest on the underside of palm fronds. Pel's fishing owl and the elusive African finfoot live near the Tana River; they are very secretive and are usually seen swimming under over-hanging trees close to the bank. With its brilliant cobalt-blue breast, the vulturine guinea-fowl stands out in the crowd.

Wilderness area

The backdrops at Meru are picturesque. At **Adamson's Falls** on the Tana River, blocks of granite have been weathered and watered into weird shapes, like modern sculptures. On clear mornings, the snowy peaks of Mt Kenya appear in the south-west, but perhaps the definitive skyscape for the park is with the sun directly behind the high bordering Nyambeni Range, the light shafting through the summits for an impression of a romanti-cised religious painting.

Geologically the park is extremely interesting. Most of the land surface is olivine basalt lava flows from the Nyam-benis, overlaid with rich brown and grey volcanic or black cotton soils strewn with small pumice boulders. The basement rock occasionally outcrops as low insel-bergs or kopjes (rocky outcrops) to relieve the monotony of the dry bush country.

The park is roughly bisected by the **Rojewero River**, which marks an abrupt change of landscape. On one side, open grasslands stretch out of the Nyambeni foothills; on the other is thick com-miphora bush which spreads north and eastwards 480 km (300 miles) to the coast. This is arid, broken country cut by innumerable sand *luggas* (dry river beds).

There are 19 rivers and streams in the park, 15 of them permanent. In addition, numerous swamps and springs occur where

BELOW: a pa chanting goshawk sto for directions

Map pages 140–141

the lava is spread thin on the basement system and in the line of a fault running southwestwards from Kinna to Kilimakieru. The main feeder springs and swamps are the Kithima ya Mugumu ("fig tree springs"), Murera Springs, Bisanadi and Buguma swamps, and Mulika Swamp.

One section of the park has been designated a wilderness area, in which there are no roads. This area can only be reached by four-wheel-drive vehicles, accompanied by an experienced ranger. Similarly, the 600 sq. km (240 sq. miles) of the **Bisanadi National Reserve**, which adjoins Meru National Park, is undeveloped for tourism. Access is difficult even with four-wheel-drive vehicles. The habitat, flora and fauna are similar to Meru, with more spectacular elongated rocky outcrops.

Neither the Kora National Reserve, which borders the middle reaches of the Tana River, nor the Rahole National Reserve on the other side, are suitable for tourists: there are no roads, no camps and a real risk of banditry.

Lodges and campsites

The most up-market accommodation in Meru is the stunning **Elsa's Kopje**, consisting of eight stone and thatch cottages situated on Mughwango Hill, with breathtaking views over the sweeping plains of Meru. Near the Mulika Swamp, on the banks of Murera River, is **Leopard Rock**, a lodge which has been largely rebuilt in the form of 14 *bandas* (rustic cabins with bathrooms). The *bandas* and main building have views across the river to a salt lick.

There are a number of campsites in Meru National Park, which are marked on most maps. The **Murera Gate Campsite** and the **Park Headquarters Campsite** both have toilets and water. The eight other campsites in the park do not have any services. *Bandas* run by the Kenya Wildlife Service can be booked at KWS headquarters in Nairobi *(see Travel Tips page 343)*. Just outside the park on the western boundary is the self-catering Kindani River Camp with five well-equipped rondavels. ❏

LOW: driving for a Meru ne drive.

Map
on pages
140–141

NORTHERN GAME COUNTRY

*North of Mt Kenya is a vast area of desert and semi-desert
that stretches all the way to Sudan and Ethiopia. It's a
magnificent and largely unexplored wilderness*

The region that used to be called the Northern Frontier District is a stark, rugged landscape where nomadic pastoralists, whose lifestyle has changed little over the centuries, still drive their cattle in search of an ephemeral growth of grass. It is the emptiness and wildness that makes a visit to the Samburu, Buffalo Springs and Shaba national reserves such an unforgettable experience. To reach this wilderness area, drive northward from Nanyuki on a rather rough tarmac road; Mt Kenya lies on your right, with vast stretches of open bush country ahead of you. Not far from Timau is the turning to Borana Ranch, which takes you (after about an hour's drive) through the wildlife area to **Borana Lodge**. The lodge offers first-class accommodation in six unique cottages built of cedar and glass, with fine views of Mt Kenya. This retreat (where the writers of *The Lion King* supposedly got their inspiration) sits on a private game ranch in a valley running from the Laikipia Plateau down to the Samburu plains.

Back on the main road to Isiolo, about 2 km (1½ miles) from the Meru junction, is the entrance to the **Lewa Wildlife Conservancy**. This encompasses both the Ngare Sergoi Rhino Sanctuary for endangered black rhinos and the **Lewa Downs Ranch**, where visitors can stay at Wilderness Trails, the home of the Craig family since 1924, which offers a relaxed, understated homestay in the ranch house or at the Lewa Safari Camp. The Craigs and their staff offer game walks, horse riding and game drives by day and by night.

Northwest of Lewa Downs is the **Il Ngwesi** group ranch, home of the famed Il Ngwesi self-catering lodge, which has won awards for ecotourism. It is constructed out of local driftwood and clay, and has no windows. There is a full contingent of staff who will do your cooking. The furnishings are in keeping with the

theme of the lodge – simple but elegant. Income from the lodge goes to community projects. On Lekueeuki Community Group Ranch there's another eco-lodge, Tassia, with breathtaking views towards Samburu and Shaba. Just north of Wamba is **Sarara Camp**, located in the Namunyak Wildlife Conservation Trust, which is also promoted and supported by the Lewa Wildlife Conservancy. You can either self-cater or pay for an all-inclusive stay.

Samburu and Buffalo Springs

The two reserves, **Samburu** ❾ to the north of the Ewaso Ngiro ("brown water") River and **Buffalo Springs** to the south, are usually treated as one unit by both tour companies and local wildlife. A bridge

across the Ewaso Ngiro a little way upstream of Samburu Lodge connects the two areas.

From Nairobi to the reserves, it is approximately 300 km (186 miles) on tarmac up to **Isiolo**, then on a dirt road for about another 50 km (30 miles). The most convenient entrance to the reserves is the **Ngare Mara Gate**, 20 km (12 miles) north of Isiolo, through the Buffalo Springs Reserve. Another entrance, 3 km (2 miles) before reaching Archer's Post, is called **Buffalo Springs Gate**. The road directly into Samburu National Reserve, reached from the township of Archer's Post, is fairly rough, and should be attempted only in a four-wheel-drive vehicle, but the journey is made more interesting by the several Samburu *manyattas* (enclosed villages) passed on the way. There's also a tarmac airstrip for tourists who do not wish to endure the long drive.

Physically dramatic, with a great table mountain called **Ololokwe** in the background, the 100-sq. km (40-sq. mile)

Samburu National Reserve is baked red-brown for most of the year. A permanent relief is in the broad green ribbon of trees along the Ewaso Ngiro, which originates on the Laikipia Plateau in the west, is fed by the runoff from the Aberdares and Mt Kenya, and vanishes beyond Samburu in the recesses of the Lorian Swamp in the east towards Somalia.

The river is a permanent source of water for animals and is lined by acacias, tamarind and doum palms. The major, central part of both reserves is dry, open, thorn-bush country, which becomes green only during the rains.

A variety of animals can be found, including diminishing numbers of elephant and numerous buffalo and waterbuck that feed on the vegetation around the river and in the adjoining swamps. Impala herds, with one male guarding up to 50 females and young, graze along the riverine vegetation. Grevy's zebra, beisa oryx, reticulated giraffe and gerenuk are found only in this sort of semi-arid coun-

BELOW:
Samburu
sights – a
termite moun
and weaver
birds' nests.

Map
on pages
140–141

try. Oryx are very shy, relatively scarce animals with beautifully marked heads and long, straight horns. Dik-dik are far more common and particularly like the rocky hills and dry acacia woodland to be found here.

Dinner guests

Crocodiles sun themselves on the banks of the river. Lion, cheetah and leopard are also fairly easy to see, thanks to the sparse grass cover. Smaller mammals include the ground squirrel, which is common around the lodges, and dwarf mongoose, which is frequently seen scampering across the open ground looking for food.

Birds are abundant, with more than 365 species recorded, including the Somali ostrich, whose blue legs are particularly conspicuous during the breeding season. Numerous flocks of helmeted and vulturine guinea-fowl can be seen, especially in the afternoon as they go to the river to drink. The martial eagle, one of the largest aerial predators, is often seen perching on a vantage point scanning for movements in the grass indicating potential prey. Other birds of prey, such as bateleur and pygmy falcon, are also common. Along the banks of the rivers, various kingfishers and black-headed weavers are found. The elusive Narina trogon, a bird with a bright green and red breast, distantly related to the parrot, is also seen in the riverine woodland.

The comfortable **Samburu Lodge** is on the north side of the river near the western boundary. You can watch crocodiles being fed on leftovers, and there is a platform where goat carcasses are hung from trees to attract the big cats, especially leopards. Downstream from Samburu Lodge is **Larsen's**, the ultimate in luxury tented camps. This is a small 17-tent camp, situated on the bank of the Ewaso Ngiro, offering high style with colonial elegance, game viewing from a tree platform over the vast Samburu Plain, game drives in the late afternoon, dinner by candlelight and coffee around the campfire.

GHT: a young Samburu warrior.

THE SAMBURU

A nomadic Maa-speaking people, the Samburu (73,400 of them) live mainly in northern Kenya between Lake Turkana and the Ewaso Ngiro River. As with other pastoralists of the north, their lifestyle has changed little over the years. They live in low huts carefully crafted with interwoven sticks and plastered with mud and cattle dung. An extended family of brothers, wives and parents live in a circular formation of huts surrounded by a high thorn-branch fence called a *boma*. Livestock is herded inside at night where the thorn forms an effective barrier against marauding predators. The smallest animals are brought into the huts. The Samburu live on the livestock – more specifically, on a thick curdled milk which tastes like smoke-flavoured yoghurt. Sometimes this is mixed with cattle blood and, on special occasions only, they eat meat. Their entire lifestyle is centred on cows, camels and goats, which they refer to as their wealth and only sometimes slaughter for ritual events. Unlike the warlike Maasai, whose language and cultural heritage they share, the Samburu do not adopt an aggressive and dominant cultural stance towards other tribes. Instead they place a high social value on a mature sense of respect.

In the northwestern section of the reserve is **Samburu Intrepids Club**, a luxury lodge that's reminiscent of a fantasy tree house set on stilts with its vaulted thatched roofs, sprawling wooden terraces and 25 tents elevated on individual decks overlooking the river. **Samburu Serena Safari Lodge** is situated outside the reserve to the west. A short distance from the eastern gate are the clear pools of Buffalo Springs. The story goes that during World War II an Italian bomb, dropped by a plane from occupied Somalia, missed Isiolo township and formed the pool.

Shaba National Reserve

The third and largest of the reserves in this region lies to the east of Buffalo Springs and Samburu, across the Isiolo-Moyale road, and on the south bank of the Ewaso Ngiro. **Shaba National Reserve ⑩** (240 sq. km/96 sq. miles) is reached by a turn-off 2 km (1½ miles) short of Archer's Post through the **Natorbe Gate**. Shaba has a particular place in the history of Kenyan

game conservation. It was there that author Joy Adamson was murdered early in 1980, leaving behind her unfinished trilogy of books on the rehabilitation of lions to the wild.

The reserve's central attraction is again the wide, sauntering Ewaso Ngiro on its way to the Lorian Swamp, as well as the tall trees of the stark riverine forest that provide a sharp contrast to the rugged and pitted tracts which make up much of the sanctuary. Many small hills crisscross Shaba and, with four springs, the reserve is better watered than its neighbours. Heavy downpours often render the already rough tracks accessible only for four-wheel-drive vehicles. All this serves only to enhance the traveller's sense of the reserve's isolation, which is the essence of Shaba – a place for the connoisseur, where an authentic African experience is the objective.

Shaba National Reserve takes its name from **Mt Shaba**, a copper-coloured sandstone hill which lies partially in the reserve and is famous for its lava flows that oozed down from the **Nyambeni Hills** only 5,000 years ago. The western side of the reserve is bushed grassland savanna, dotted with thorn bushes, gradually becoming acacia woodland nearer Mt Shaba. Beyond the mountain the vegetation becomes grassland plains. A series of springs bubble up in the river in the northeastern side of the reserve. One spring, **Penny's Drop**, was named after Joy Adamson's leopard, Penny, which she released back into the wild in Shaba Reserve. Filming of the American "reality TV" series *Survivor III* was carried out mainly in Shaba.

Although heavy poaching in Shaba has made animals very shy, you might be lucky enough to see elephant, lion, cheetah, leopard, waterbuck, as well as all the animals specially adapted to the dry region: beisa oryx, gerenuk, Grevy's zebra, reticulated giraffe and Somali ostrich. The only accommodation in the reserve is the **Sarova Shaba Lodge**, which has 80 thatched-roof bedrooms, a restaurant, two bars, a swimming pool and conference facilities. ❑

Map on pages 140–141

LEFT: beisa oryx and passenger.

Marsabit & Losai National Parks

Marsabit National Park and Reserve ⑪ is situated in what used to be known as Kenya's "Northern Frontier District". Marsabit itself is an improbable forested volcanic mountain which rises like an oasis out of the dry black lava-strewn surrounding semi-desert. The park encompasses the mountain and is only some 20 sq. km (8 sq. miles) in extent. The much older surrounding reserve covers approximately 2,100 sq. km (840 sq. miles). The eastern slopes of Mt Marsabit are dry and barren, whereas the western slope is covered in perpetual mist and enjoys heavy rainfall which has given rise to dense rainforest. The reason for this climatic oddity is that when hot air blown off the surrounding desert rises and cools over the mountain, clouds are formed and rain occurs. The mountain microclimate allows for the growth of lush, tropical, evergreen forest in which elephant and greater kudu can be found. Herds of buffalo – some claim a smaller "mountain" variety – are also common. Lake Paradise, at the bottom of one of the mountain's craters, hosts a variety of waterbirds. Some of the biggest elephant tuskers have lived here, including the famous Ahmed, now sadly dead. In the 1970s he was assigned a ranger to watch over him and keep his location known for visitors. He died when he was 65 years old and his position was filled by another tusker called Mohammed II.

Marsabit National Park is 560 km (347 miles) north of Nairobi. The asphalt road finishes at Isiolo which means that 270 km (167 miles) has to be driven on corrugated dirt road. In order to drive to Marsabit one must obtain permits from Provincial Headquarters at Isiolo. From here, it is recommended you drive in convoy and carry petrol, water and supplies for the journey. Various charter companies at Wilson Airport in Nairobi will arrange flights to the reserve.

Accommodation in the park is provided by the Marsabit Lodge at the edge of the forest, overlooking the swamp and lake in the Sokortre Dika crater. The lodge is comfortable and food is provided as well as lunch boxes for game drives. Nights are cold, so a sweater is needed for when you are not sitting around the lodge fireplace. Rooms face the crater lake where greater kudu, reticulated giraffe and, if you are lucky, the elusive lammergeyer can be seen. Campsites are available – the most beautiful is the one located at Lake Paradise.

Losai National Reserve

Located to the southwest of Marsabit, across the Kaisut Desert, the 1,735-sq.-km (694-sq.-mile) **Losai National Reserve** ⑫ is an area of impenetrable mountain forest on the northeastern edge of the central highlands. The Great North Road runs through the eastern section, but it is a wild area and is generally inaccessible, except by four-wheel-drive vehicle in the dry season. For the more intrepid visitor, a walk up the seasonally dry bed of the Milgis is an incomparable experience. It is like a broad avenue, bordered by some of the most magnificent umbrella acacias *(Acacia tortilis)* in Kenya. ❑

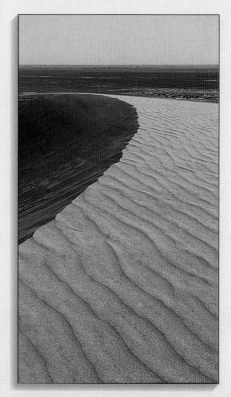

LAKE TURKANA

The algae that abound in Lake Turkana turn its water a spellbinding, beautiful deep green in the sunlight, giving the lake the name of "Jade Sea"

Logipi's northern neighbour, **Lake Turkana** ⓭, is the final destination for every safari in this area – after a journey of at least two days from Nairobi. The lake, which is about 300 km (185 miles) long and 50 km (30 miles) wide, has its northern tip in Ethiopia. It is a place of spellbinding beauty. The algae that abound in the lake change their colour from charcoal grey to Delft blue as clouds scud overhead. But most often its surface dances deep green in the sunlight, giving it the nickname "Jade Sea".

With air temperatures touching 63°C (145°F), Lake Turkana's cool depths look tempting. But note that the bitter alkaline waters can never quench your thirst, and swimming is a pastime to be treated with a certain amount of caution. There are plenty of crocodiles here, and they can be seen basking along the shore, seldom venturing far from the beaches.

For the most part they are fish-eaters, hence the belief that the saurians in Turkana *never* eat humans. However, when a scientist, Alistair Graham, conducted a study of crocodile behaviour at the lake in 1965–67, and in the process lost his colleague to one of the reptiles, it was accepted that the crocodiles of Lake Turkana *do* eat large mammals, albeit rarely. Indeed, such is the infrequency of attacks on humans that Turkana can be considered relatively safe to swim in.

Anglers head for the Lake Turkana Fishing Lodge or the Oasis Club while

BELOW: the "Jade Sea".

Map
on pages
140–141

campers stay at the Sunset Strip Camp, southeast of the village, with drinking water and showers. Anglers in search of sport try for the great Nile perch *(Lates niloticus)*, a melancholy but enormous fish that can tip the scales at 100 kg (220 lb). As an angling challenge, however, it is a disappointment, providing about as much fight as an outsized goldfish. Less spectacular but more exciting are the tiger-fish that can be reeled in from the shore.

Central Island National Park ⓓ, in the middle of Lake Turkana, can be reached by boat from Ferguson's Gulf. The island's main crater lake is a nesting point for an extremely large number of crocodiles and many water birds. Once you're on the island, the rest of the trip has to be undertaken on foot, which can be very strenuous in the heat of the day. Until recently, the island was populated more by immigrant Luo fishermen from Lake Victoria than by crocodiles.

South Island National Park ⓔ is the birdwatcher's and Nile-perch fisherman's paradise of Lake Turkana. Care must be exercised if you are camping rough since the large population of crocodiles can be dangerous. The airstrip on the island is a twisted, rock-strewn horror – a challenge for every bush pilot in Kenya.

The first human?

It is ironic that Lake Turkana, where today men and animals struggle for survival, may have been the birthplace of mankind itself. Kenyan palaeontologist Richard Leakey *(see page 17)* and a team of international scientists have spent many years carefully brushing away sand and dust from a treasure trove of hominid bones and stone tools. These finds prove that man-like creatures with a relatively high level of intelligence inhabited the lake shores as far back as 2 million years ago.

Koobi Fora ⓕ, the name given to the heart of this palaeontological site that fans out over 2,500 sq. km (1,000 sq. miles), burst into the public arena in 1972. This was when Bernard Ng'eneo, a member of the Leakey team who was passing through a gully he had often walked before, caught a glimpse of a tiny frag-

ment of skull. Eventually more than 300 segments were sifted from the sand. When reconstructed, the skull – simply known by its archaeologists' index number of "1470" – was recognised as the earliest firm evidence of human's evolution from apes, replanting our ancestral roots by half a million years. Visitors can reach the site by a chartered plane or on a track from Loyangalani, although this is rough even by northern standards. There are self-catering cabins at Koobi Fora, which can be booked through the National Museums of Kenya in Nairobi*(see Travel Tips page 349)*.

Koobi Fora is a part of **Sibiloi National Park ⓖ**, a little used wildlife sanctuary where visitors can watch lion, cheetah, oryx, zebra and topi in almost guaranteed solitude. Just before the park's entrance, on the right, is **Sibiloi Mountain**, where giant petrified trees 125 cm (4 ft) in girth are strewn like building blocks of the gods. Seven million years ago, these junipers stood at 15 metres (50 ft) and could have flourished because of high rainfall. ❏

THE LAKES OF THE GREAT RIFT VALLEY

*The largest split in the earth's crust runs through Kenya, making
a mighty valley characterised by volcanoes and lakes
that – when they aren't empty – mostly contain undrinkable water*

Tectonic theory has it that the earth's crust is a set of plates floating on liquid magma deep down below. Sometimes the plates break up and the parts drift away from one another. These breaks are usually below the ocean surface, but one of them splits the earth. It runs from the Jordan Valley in the north, takes in the whole of the Red Sea, sheers through Ethiopia, Kenya, Tanzania and Mozambique and finally reaches the sea near the Zambezi delta.

This **Great Rift Valley** is more than 8,700 km (5,400 miles) long – a crack in the African plate that, in length, exceeds one-quarter of the earth's circumference.

An arm of it runs through much of the Nile Valley, scours across western Uganda and Tanzania and joins the main Rift in southern Tanzania. In places, the walls of the Rift rise little more than 30 metres (100 ft) above the valley floor. Elsewhere, there are steep, often sheer cliffs to above 1,200 metres (4,000 ft), but nowhere is the Rift more sharply defined than where it cuts through the highlands of Kenya. In addition to the towering walls, the whole length of the valley in Kenya is studded with volcanoes. Also scattered along the length of the Kenya Rift is a chain of seven lakes. These are unusual in that not a single one of them has an obvious outflow. Water pours in from the rainfall on the surrounding land and more or less stays there in the shallow pans. While a high rate of evaporation keeps the levels fairly constant, it also causes an accumulation of salts and minerals in the waters of the lake. As a result, all but two of the Rift Valley lakes are so saline that they are virtually undrinkable.

The most alkaline of all these lakes is **Magadi ⓗ**, in the extreme south of the country but easily accessible from Nairobi. The drive on a good road, which climbs up to the southern shoulder of the Ngong Hills before dropping precipitously into the Rift, takes little over an hour.

The descent to the valley close to Magadi occurs in stages, down scarp after steep scarp through a harsh, stark landscape that is increasingly dry and hot as the altitude falls. At the end of the road, shimmering in temperatures above 38°C (100°F) in the shade, is Lake Magadi itself. At first glance, the term "lake" seems a misnomer since there is little water evident. The lake bed appears white; in fact, it's an enormous pan of trona – an agglomeration of mixed salts – over 100 sq. km (40 sq.

LEFT: soda washed up on Magadi's shores.

**Map
on pages
140–141**

miles) in extent. Around the periphery is a series of hot springs, highly charged with salts and bubbling out of the ground at temperatures of about 45°C (113°F). They flow into the huge evaporation pan, where the sun and searing winds leave nothing but the thick white deposits of sludge. But in this is an almost endless source of potash, salt and related chemicals which have been exploited by the Magadi Soda Company since before World War I – Kenya's oldest mining venture, with a company township built up on a peninsula into the lake.

At the far southern end of Lake Magadi, where the largest springs occur, is an area of open water. Although undrinkable, it produces a wealth of microscopic aquatic life which, in turn, attracts many water birds and birdwatchers. Many African species are permanently on show, including flamingos, and the lake also hosts waders and many others escaping the winter in Europe. Situated on the western side of Magadi up in the Nguruman

Escarpment is **Shampole**, a new community eco-lodge, with wide vistas of the surrounding savanna and swampland.

A freshwater exception

Going north from Magadi, the next lake along the Rift is **Naivasha ⓭**, which is easily accessible from Nairobi (80 km/50 miles) on the main Nairobi–Kisumu road, which snakes down the eastern Rift Valley wall following an ancient elephant trail. As you descend, there is a magnificent view of the lake and the extinct Suswa and Longonot volcanoes in the valley bottom. The lake lies on the valley floor at about 1,890 metres (6,200 ft) above sea level.

Its area has fluctuated a great deal over the centuries, but currently covers about 170 sq. km (60 sq. miles). Fence posts stand forlornly way out from the shore as mementos of the days before 1961 when farmers and ranchers grazed their cattle far beyond the present shore.

An oddity characterises Lake Naivasha: although it has no visible outlet, it is one of

**BELOW:
secretary birds
live on a diet
of snakes and
other reptiles.**

the two freshwater lakes (Baringo is the other) in the Rift. Many theories have been forwarded to explain the phenomenon, but none is entirely satisfactory. The most obvious is that there must be massive underground seepage through the lake flow – a diffused outflow that takes the place of a conventional discharging river. Whatever the reason, Naivasha water is indeed fresh, potable, abundant and excellent for irrigating the surrounding fertile volcanic soils. Not surprisingly, it is also ringed by agricultural land, from which spring many tons of vegetables and flowers harvested for both Nairobi and overseas markets.

On the eastern end of **Crescent Island** sailing is possible at a private boating club. Sunday regattas are an incongruous sight on the bottom of the Rift Valley and the view of the valley walls from the lake is an altogether exhilarating experience. Among the resident birds are fish eagle, osprey, African jacana, black crake and a variety of herons. Hippo also live in the lake. A number of mammals can be seen grazing in the surrounding lake environs, such as zebra, impala, buffalo, giraffe, kongoni and, at night, hippo.

Accommodation is available at **Lake Naivasha Country Club**, where the resplendent traditional Kenya Sunday lunch is recommended, even if you are not staying there. The view over the lake, from the well-manicured lawn, in the shade of yellow-barked fever trees, will not be soon forgotten.

For an experience in the bush, stay at the well-appointed **Crater Lake Tented Camp**, enclosed by the walls of the crater and its own game sanctuary.

There are a series of campsites on the southern side of the lake, probably the best known being **Fisherman's Camp**, where you can rent a *banda* or pitch your own tent. There are also a number of excellent homestays around the lake, including **Longonot Game Ranch**, offering horse riding over the plains.

Hell's Gate National Park, a dramatically beautiful slice through the volcanic

BELOW: hippos abound in Lake Naivasha.

Map
on page
140–141

ridge south of Lake Naivasha, was created in 1984. It lies some 13 km (8 miles) southeast of Naivasha and is about 68 sq. km (27 sq. miles) in area.

The park is an impressive gorge with towering cliffs. Close to the entrance is **Fischer's Tower**, a lone 25-metre (82-ft) high rock. Powerful geysers, which gave the park its name, have been harnessed with foreign aid to generate electricity. The geothermal electricity project has been carefully executed so that it does not affect the beauty of the park.

Hell's Gate supports an interesting selection of birds, with raptors such as Egyptian vulture, Rüppell's griffon vulture, peregrine falcon and Auger buzzard breeding on the cliffs alongside large flocks of swifts and swallows. Note, however, that the park's much-vaunted reputation for lammergeyer (bearded vulture) sightings is somewhat historical – the lammergeyer haven't been recorded here since the solitary breeding pair resident in the gorge moved on in the early 1980s. There are also Verreaux's eagles, invariably seen soaring in pairs, and many other notable birds of prey. Mammals found in the park include Thomson's gazelle, zebra, hyrax, cheetah and leopard. Camping is the only available accommodation in the park. It is wise to enter into a private arrangement with a local Maasai warrior to guard your vehicle for the night.

To the southeast of Hell's Gate is the **Longonot National Park**, to which access is from the bottom road to Naivasha. The young volcano rises to 2,776 metres (9,105 ft) above sea level. Mt Longonot offers a wide range of attractions for those who are keen on activity holidays, including hiking, rock climbing, cycling and birdwatching. There is no accommodation to be found at Longonot, but Kenya Wildlife Service rangers are available as guides. North of Lake Naivasha, on the slopes of Ol Doinyo Eburru ("the mountain that steams" in Maasai), the luxurious **Great Rift Valley Lodge** has an 18-hole golf course, tennis courts and unequalled views over the lake and valley.

BELOW:
white pelicans
on a fishing
expedition.

Lakes Elementeita and Nakuru

You have only to drive a further 80 km (50 miles) up the Trans-Africa Highway from Naivasha to view two more lakes also situated in the highland part of the Rift, at about the same altitude. Both are highly saline. Like Naivasha, they vary enormously in size and sometimes disappear altogether, during which time they are reduced to white salt flats, swirling with dust-devils.

The first, **Lake Elmenteita**, about 40 km (25 miles) from Naivasha, is one of the stop-off points for millions of flamingos en route to Magadi, Nakuru or Lake Natron in Tanzania. **Lake Elementeita Lodge** overlooks the lake and offers horse riding and game walks. A homestay can be arranged at River House just outside nearby Gilgil.

Then, another 40 km (25 miles) to the north, comes **Lake Nakuru**. When this lake regularly dried up in the mid-1950s, strong daily winds swept up the dust into a dense white soda smog which blew 65 km (40 miles) away up the Rift Valley. But when heavy rains fell in 1961, the lake filled to its brim and the soda smogs were soon forgotten. However, 1997 saw Lake Nakuru dry up again, with the same strong winds and daily soda smog blowing around the agricultural town of **Nakuru** and the surrounding area.

The alkaline constitution of Lake Nakuru supports a vast flowering of the blue-green algae and diatoms on which flamingos live. The waters are so rich that the birds assemble there in their millions. The roseate mass they create along the shorelines is a spectacle of immense beauty. Over 400 varieties of birds can be seen altogether, although not at the same time since many are migrant visitors from the northern hemisphere. Great numbers of pelican can be seen at the southern and eastern shores.

Lake Nakuru National Park [20] was created in 1961 as a bird sanctuary. Originally, it comprised only the lake and its immediate surroundings, including the escarpment at its western side known as

BELOW: greater flamingos on Lake Nakuru.

Map on pages 140–141

Baboon Cliffs. It was expanded in 1974 with help from WWF, and now includes an extensive area of savanna to the south. Now the park – total area about 200 sq. km (80 sq. miles) – has been fenced in to make a rhino sanctuary. Other species of mammal include lion, leopard and hyena. It is the best place in Kenya to see Bohor reedbuck and Defassa waterbuck. A herd of Rothschild giraffe was introduced in 1977. **Sarova Lion Hill Lodge** is perched on high ground by the eastern boundary overlooking the lake. It is also adjacent to Kenya's finest euphorbia forest, filled with the grotesque, giant cactus-like trees. On cold evenings a fire is lit by the bar. **Lake Nakuru Lodge** used to be part of Lord Delamere's estate and, apart from the main manor house, there are new *bandas* for visitors. Safari vehicles are available for hire and an airstrip is close by. There are also two well-maintained campsites with good water supplies, a self-catering KWS *banda* site and four picnic sites within the park.

Bogoria and Baringo

To the north of Nakuru, the land falls away from the highlands. At this point, the Trans-Africa Highway veers to the west to break out of the Rift, whereas the way to the next valley lake is straight on. **Bogoria** was formerly known as Lake Hannington in Kenya's colonial era, after the missionary bishop who was murdered in Uganda. It's a slender stretch of blue water under towering cliffs, like a splinter sticking into the northern foot of the highlands. Also saline-charged, this body of water has an added attraction of shoreline hot geysers spouting up from the bowels of the earth. **Lake Bogoria National Reserve ㉑** was gazetted to protect the herds of greater kudu that live mainly on the western slopes of the Laikipia Escarpment, which towers over the lake to the east. The reserve covers approximately 110 sq. km (44 sq. miles) and includes the shallow soda lake, which attracts huge flocks of flamingos.

Accommodation is available at **Lake Bogoria Hotel**, which has the only spa in Kenya. There are three campsites at the southern end of the lake near Emos Gate. No facilities are available, and all necessary water has to be brought along, since the lake water is not drinkable. Another campsite (with water available) is just outside the northern entrance to the reserve, as well as a picnic site at the hot springs.

No one who travels a few more kilometres north from here misses Lake **Baringo National Park ㉒**, the second freshwater lake in the Rift. It is twice the size of Naivasha, and poses the same question: why, with no outlet, does it stay fresh? Baringo is home to great numbers of birds and hippo, which can be seen in the evenings grazing by the shore.

First-class accommodation is available either at the **Lake Baringo Club**, which offers guided birdwatching walks, boat trips, water-skiing and camel rides, or at **Island Camp**, on Ol Kokwa Island, a luxury tented lodge with swimming pool and water sports. Camping facilities, as well as *bandas*, are available at Robert's Camp on the lake shore.   ❑

LEFT: a giant Nile perch, Lake Turkana.

WESTERN KENYA

Western Kenya is dominated by tea and coffee plantations. There are three small areas of interest for wildlife watchers: Mt Elgon on the Ugandan border, the Saiwa Swamp and Kakamega, Kenya's last jungle

Map on pages 140–141

The Trans-Africa Highway climbs the western wall of the Rift Valley by a less spectacular route than its descent on the eastern side. It is a steep climb nonetheless since **Nakuru**, lying on the valley floor, is around 1,800 metres (6,000 ft) above sea level, while the highest point the road reaches above the western wall is well over 2,700 metres (9,000 ft).

At that point, 8 km (5 miles) off the main trunk route, is the small farming town of **Molo**. The town is set in high-altitude open downs which are more reminiscent of Scotland than Africa – more so with the chill and mists of the morning. It's not surprising that the Molo area attracted the early white settlers, who saw it as prime sheep country. Now the white settlers have all gone, with their large farms subdivided and given out to the local African community.

Close by Molo, near **Mau Summit**, the trunk route splits. The Trans-Africa Highway heads northwest across the highland plateau west of the Rift to Eldoret, eventually reaching the Uganda border at Malaba. The other heads southwest as the main route to Lake Victoria.

Eldoret and Elgon

Not far from the fork, the highway crosses the Equator and the wide level plain of the Uasin Gishu Plateau to the town of **Eldoret** – or "64" as it's sometimes called, since it was set up by milepost 64 of the ox-wagon route from Londiani once used by the local "voortrekker" South Africans.

When they arrived before World War I, the plateau was teeming with wildlife, rather like the Athi Plains around Nairobi or the Mara-Serengeti. The game soon disappeared, however, since the settlers turned the Uasin Gishu into Kenya's

main granary. Maize and wheat fields stretched from horizon to horizon, and still do in parts.

Eldoret is now a major farming town, with an airport of international standard. Beyond Eldoret, filling much of the western horizon is the massive extinct volcano of **Mt Elgon National Park ㉓** which straddles the border of Kenya and Uganda. Mt Elgon is around 880 metres (3,000 ft) short in height of Mt Kenya, but the circumference of its base makes it a bigger massif.

At its foot stands Kitale, the northernmost of the agricultural towns built by the settlers in the colonial era. In its upper, forested reaches, Mt Elgon is a national park, but dense, tall forest and a lack of

LEFT: black-and-white colobus monkey in Aberdares National Park. **RIGHT:** a ostrich, sunset.

roads inhibit game viewing, though it is possible to hike up to the summit across moorlands of giant heather. However, Mt Elgon's peaks are on the Ugandan side of the border, which is far more organised for hikes and ascents than the Kenyan side *(see page 281)*.

While the volcanic soils of Kenya's mountain ranges are fertile, they don't seem to yield the minerals the elephant crave – except at rare salt licks, one of them in the distinctive **Kitum Cave**, in the forested lower slopes of the mountain, which has attracted the big mammals for centuries. Quite literally, the elephant mine the cave, gouging out the walls and extending the shafts hundreds of feet into the mountain.

Saiwa Swamp National Park ㉔, to the east of Kitale, is Kenya's smallest, at only 3 sq. km (1 sq. mile). It was opened in 1974 to protect the semi-aquatic sitatunga antelope, notable for its wide-splayed hooves which allow it to walk on the soggy surface of the swamp. Saiwa is

also home to the locally endangered De Brazza's monkey, two species of otter, giant forest squirrel, black-and-white colobus monkey, bushbuck and grey duiker. There are three nature trails, bridges for walking, three sitatunga viewing platforms and two campsites within the park.

Kenya's last jungle

From Elgon, the country to the south falls away fairly gently towards Lake Victoria and the Nile Valley. The road passes **Webuye**, where Kenya's fledgling paper industry is located in an area of dense settlement, principally of the Luhya peoples. Their headquarters are in the township of **Kakamega**, which is 42 km (26 miles) to the south of the road.

Not far from the town is the **Kakamega Forest Reserve ㉕**, a centre of significant conservation interest since it is a relic of the Equatorial rainforest which once spread from West Africa to the East African coast. Kakamega is Kenya's one true jungle. The forest canopy is the habitat for black-and-white colobus, red-tailed and blue monkeys, red-legged and giant forest squirrels.

It is prime birdwatching territory, with over 300 species including various bee-eaters, hornbills and turacos. Butterflies are also abundant. Accommodation is available in the reserve in the form of a guesthouse, self-catering *bandas*, two campsites and the Rondo Retreat, as well as at the Golf Hotel in Kakamega town.

About 48 km (30 miles) south of Kakamega is the town of **Kisumu**, on the shores of Lake Victoria, Kenya's third-biggest town after Nairobi and Mombasa. Its atmosphere is distinctly nautical, which is not surprising given the vast size of Lake Victoria – its area of 63,000 sq. km (26,500 sq. miles) makes it the largest lake in Africa and the world's second-largest freshwater lake.

On the far side of the gulf from Kisumu, in the lee of **Homa Bay** town, lies the **Ruma National Park**. This is mostly uninhabited because of tsetse fly and the sleeping sickness it carries, which is no worry to in-and-out tourists. At

LEFT: tusk marks in a salt cave.

Map
on pages
140–141

some stage, this refuge for Kenya's remaining roan antelope will be integrated into the country's wildlife circuits. For the moment, however, it's something of a backwater for the specialist.

Tea plantations at Kericho

Back to the fork at Mau Summit, the southern highway runs some 50 km (30 miles) through forest reserve and plantations before reaching the "tea capital" of **Kericho**. High ground, a temperate climate and high rainfall off Lake Victoria make the district ideal for the production of tea. Kenya is the world's third-largest tea producer after India and Sri Lanka, and more than half the output is collected from thousands of individual African planters on small plots of tea-growing land. Because the southwest of Kenya generally is so densely populated, it's not wildlife country and thus off the most popular tourist circuits.

When the Europeans first arrived, much of the area was under tall montane forest.

With a massive import of capital, the land was cleared and planted so that ridge after ridge is now patterned a bright, almost apple-green as one of the most productive tea areas on earth. As a consolation for the conservation purists, who regret the loss of natural forest, there is no erosion. The tea plants retain the soil and anyway have an attraction of their own in a distinctive greening of the hills.

From Kericho a major road descends to Kisumu, while another holds to the high ground through Sotik, **Kisii** and eventually to the Tanzanian border.

From Kisii, it is possible to travel south to the Tanzanian border, which is 98 km (61 miles) away at Isebania. From there, you can continue down to the lakeside town of Musoma. However, most visitors turn off east on the way – at **Suna**, 77 km (48 miles) from Kisii – and then head through **Lolgorien** (the scene of a minor gold rush in the inter-war years), down the Siria Escarpment and into the Maasai Mara National Reserve. ❏

IGHT:
rigation
chemes
ave brought
rosperity
the west.

THE LUO

The second-largest of the non-Bantu ethnic groups in Kenya after the Kikuyu, the 2.7 million-strong Luo of the central and south Nyanza districts, around the Winam Gulf of Lake Victoria, represent the most vigorous of southward drives of Nilotes from the Sudan. Cattle and constant migrations in search of pastures for their herds dominated the life of the first Luo immigrants. But they adjusted to growing population pressures by adopting a sedentary way of life in relatively isolated homesteads. Although cattle continued to dominate ritual and economic activities, agriculture and fishing became increasingly important for subsistence. Foremost among Kenya's people in their fishing skills, the Luo today mainly use gill nets and long-line fishing to catch tilapia and other fish. They also use dhow-type fishing boats and canoes to fish. The head of the homestead has his own hut *(duol)* built near the cattle enclosure. The Luo are an articulate, community-conscious people, and were prominent in Kenya's struggle for independence, providing many leading trade unionists and politicians, including the late Tom Mboya and the former Vice President of Kenya, Oginga Odinga. Luo folklore has been imaginatively captured in the modern fiction of Grace Ogot and Tom Okoya.

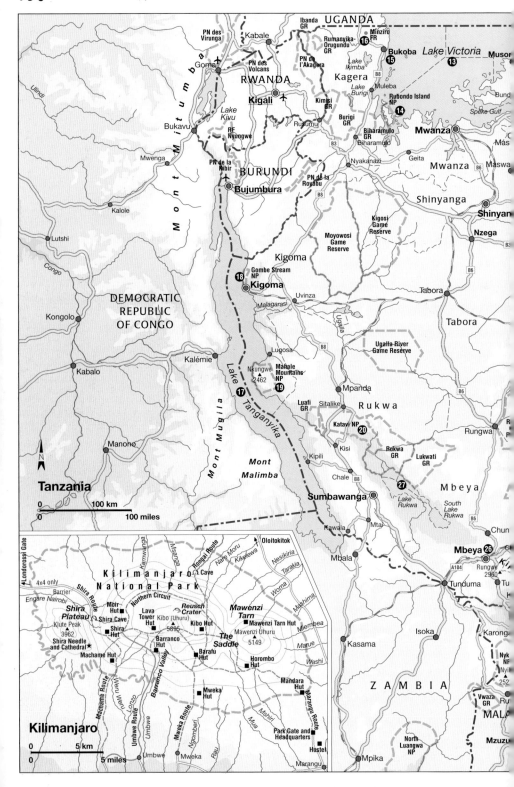

UGANDA

PN des Virunga
Kabale
Ibanda GR
Rumanyika-Orugundu GR
Minziro FR **16**
Bukoba 15
Lake Victoria **13**
Musor

Goma
PN des Volcans
PN du l'Akagera
Lake Ikimba
Kagera
B8
Muleba
Bund

RWANDA
Lake Kivu
Kigali
Kimisi GR
Lake Burigi
Rubondo Island NP **14**
Speke Gulf

Ulindi

Bukavu
RF Nyungwe
Rusumu
Burigi GR
Biharamulo GR
Mwanza
Más

Mwenga
PN de la Kibir
BURUNDI
PN de la Ruvubu
Biharamulo
Nyakanazi
Geita
Mwanza
B6
Maswa

Bujumbura
B8
Shinyanga
Shinyan

Kalole
Kigosi Game Reserve
Nzega

Lutshi
Moyowosi Game Reserve
B3

Congo
Kigoma
B6

DEMOCRATIC REPUBLIC OF CONGO
Gombe Stream NP **18**
Kigoma
Uvinza
Tabora

Kongolo
Malagarasi
Ugalla
Tabora

Kabalo
Lugosa
B8
Ugalla River Game Reserve
B6

Kalémie
Nkungwe 2462
Mahale Mountains NP **19**
Mpanda

Mont Mugila
17
Luafi GR
Sitalike
R u k w a

Lake Tanganyika
Katavi NP **20**
Rungwa
R P

Manoho
Kisi
Rukwa GR
Lukwati GR

Kipili
Mont Malimba
Chale B8
27
M b e y a

Tanzania
Chale
Sumbawanga
Lake Rukwa
South Lake Rukwa
B6

0 ___ 100 km
0 ___ 100 miles
Kawala
Mtai
Chun

Oloitokitok
Mbala
Mbeya 26
Rungwe 2960
Tu

Londorossi Gate
Kamwanga
Msanga
Rongai Route
Nare Moru
Kikelewa
Nesikiria
Tarakia
A104
Tunduma

4x4 only
Barrier
Engare Nairobi
K i l i m a n j a r o
1 Cave
Woma
Mashima

Shira Route
N a t i o n a l   P a r k
Northern Circuit
Mawenzi Tarn

Shira Plateau
Moir Hut
Lava Tower Hut
Reusch Crater
Kibo (Uhuru) 5895
Kibo Hut
Mawenzi Tarn Hut
Mlembea
Isoka
Karong

Klute Peak 3962
Shira Cave
Shira Hut
Barranco Hut
Mawenzi Uhuru 5149
The Saddle
Marue
Kasama

Shira Needle and Cathedral ★
Machame Hut
Barafu Hut
Horombo Hut
Washi
Z A M B I A
Nyk NF
Nyi
252

Kilimanjaro
Machame Route
Weru Weru
Lonzo
Umbwe Route
Barranco Valley
Mweka Route
Ngomberi
Mweka Hut
Mandara Hut
Marangu Route
Mshiri
Mua
Vwaza GR
MAL

0 ___ 5 km
0 ___ 5 miles
Umbwe
Mweka
Rau
Park Gate and Headquarters
Hostel
Marangu
North Luangwa NP
Mpika
Mzuzu

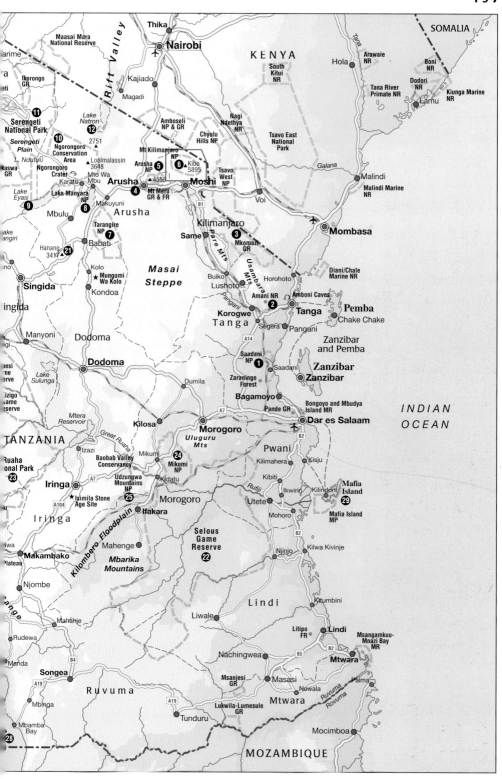

SOMALIA

Thika
Nairobi
KENYA

Maasai Mara
National Reserve

arime
Ikorongo
GR
eti
Kajiado
Magadi

Arawaie
NR
Hola
Boni
NR
South
Kitui
NR
Tana River
Primate NR
Dodori
NR
Kiunga Marine
NR
Lamu

11
Serengeti
National Park
Lake
Natron
12
2751
Amboseli
NP & GR
Nagi
Ndethya
NR
Tsavo East
National
Park
Malindi

*Serengeti
Plain*
10
Ngorongoro
Conservation
Area
Loolmalassin
3648
Chyulu
Hills NP

Mt Kilimanjaro
NP
aswa
GR
Ngorongoro
Crater
Mto Wa
Mbu
Arusha
NP **5**
6 Kibo
5895
Tsavo
West
NP
Galana
Malindi Marine
NR

L. Ndutu
*Lake
Eyasi*
Karatu
Arusha
4
4550
Moshi

Lake Manyara
NP
Mt Meru
GR & FR
Voi
9
Makuyuni
Arusha
Mbulu
8

Tarangire
NP **7**
Babati
Kilimanjaro
Same
3
Mkomazi
GR
Mombasa

ake
angiri
Hanang
3417 **21**

no
Kolo
*Masai
Steppe*
Buiko
Horohoto
Diani/Chale
Marine NR

Mungomi
Wa Kolo
Lushoto
Singida
Kondoa
Amani NR **2**
Amboni Caves
Pemba

ingida
Korogwe
Tanga
Chake Chake

Manyoni
Dodoma
T a n g a
Segera
Pangani
*Zanzibar
and Pemba*

iesi
ne
erve
Lake
Sulunga
Dodoma
A14
Saadani
NP **1**
Saadani
Zanzibar
Zanzibar

izigo
ame
eserve
Dumila
Zaraninge
Forest

Mtera
Reservoir
Bagamoyo
Pande GR
Bongoyo and Mbudya
Island MR
INDIAN
OCEAN

ΤΑΝΖΑΝΙΑ
Great Ruaha
Kilosa
A7
Morogoro
Dar es Salaam
B2

Ruaha
onal Park
Izazi
Mikumi
*Uluguru
Mts*
Pwani
Kilimahera
Kisju

23
Baobab Valley
Conservancy
24
Mikumi
NP
Kibiti
Iringa
Udzungwa
Mountains
NP
Kidatu
Rufiji
Ikwiriri
Kilindoni
**Mafia
Island**

A7
*Isimila Stone
Age Site*
25
Morogoro
Utete
29

A104
I r i n g a
Ifakara
Mohoro
Mafia Island
MP

wa
Makambako
Mahenge
*Selous
Game
Reserve*
22
B2

Plateau
*Mbarika
Mountains*
Njinjo
Kilwa Kivinje

Njombe

ange
L i n d i
Kitumbini

Mahánje
Liwale

Rudewa
Litipo
FR
Lindi
Msangamkuu-
Mnazi Bay
MR

Manda
B4
Nachingwea
B5
B2

Songea
Msanjesi
GR
Masasi
Mtwara

A19
R u v u m a
Newala
Palma
Mtwara

Mbinga
A19
Lukwila-Lumesule
GR
Ruvuma
Rovuma

28
Mbamba
Bay
Tunduru
Mocimboa

MOZAMBIQUE

TANZANIA

*The combination of wonderful scenery and magnificent
wildlife has boosted the safari business in Tanzania*

Laid out in front of you is a vast, almost perfectly circular volcanic caldera, shadows of the clouds chasing across the short-cropped golden grassland on its flat floor. Near the centre, a cloud of pink overlaps the shining ice blue of a small lake; to one side are some splashes of red and here and there are dots of white or charcoal grey. Use the binoculars and the pink turns into a flock of flamingos; the red into Maasai tribesmen taking their cattle to water; the white dots are safari vehicles; the grey, the rocky bulk of black rhinos. If the light is right and your eyes are keen you may just see a prowling pack of hyenas encircling a herd of wildebeest.

This is the Ngorongoro Crater, one of the most beautiful and outstandingly rich game sanctuaries in the world. A few hours' drive to the west and you reach the broad Serengeti plains, home to the great migration of some 2 million wildebeest, zebra and antelope. A few hours' drive to the east and you are standing at the foot of Mt Kilimanjaro, for all the world like a giant Christmas pudding, its rounded top iced with streaming glaciers, peering out from a festive dish of clouds.

Head south to Tarangire, where lions loll in the shade of the trees and giant fleshy baobabs stand like sentinels above the rolling red dust. Further south still, you pass the rock paintings of Kondoa, left by bushmen centuries ago, as you head towards the great Rufiji River that slices through the Selous Game Reserve.

In the west, you reach the great lakes – the clear, deep waters of Lake Tanganyika, home to hundreds of species of brightly decorative fish, with snorkelling as a main attraction. Along the shoreline, the primeval forests of Gombe Stream and Mahale Mountains protect some of the world's last thriving colonies of chimpanzees. By contrast, the steel grey waters of Lake Victoria, shrouded in an almost perpetual haze, are less forgiving and more mysterious – fitting for the source of the Nile.

Perhaps, instead, you choose a short plane ride across to Zanzibar, the off-shore coral paradise with its gleaming beaches, turquoise seas and fragrant clove forests, its ancient cities and full-bellied fishing dhows, blowsy in the afternoon breeze. It doesn't really matter where you go. Whichever direction you take, Tanzania offers inspiration. It could take a lifetime to explore. ❑

PRECEDING PAGES: dominating the landscape of Tarangire National Park, baobab trees can have trunks of up to 10 metres (33 ft) in diameter.
LEFT: Kirk's red colobus monkey, sometimes called the Zanzibar colobus, is restricted to areas of southern and eastern Zanzibar.

THE NORTH COAST

*The north coast is not renowned for its wildlife but the
incredible variety of plants found in the Eastern Arc Mountains
more than makes up for any lack of game viewing*

Map
on pages
196–197

Tanzania is one of the few countries where the bush meets the beach and before breakfast you can safari and then swim in the warm waters of the Indian Ocean. The mainland north coast is almost entirely undiscovered by tourists, but a significant part of the slave trade and the first Christian mission are to be discovered in dilapidated Bagamoyo, the largest botanical garden in Africa at Amani, and a superb stretch of undeveloped and little-used beach between Dar es Salaam and the Usambara Mountains. In addition, the necklace of the Eastern Arc Mountains offers wonderful walking and what has become known as the Galápagos of the plant world. The journey begins 70 km (43 miles) north of Dar es Salaam, along a newly constructed road which connects the city with **Bagamoyo**. In Swahili, Bagamoyo means "lay down your heart". This was the end of the caravan route and it was here that captured slaves arrived and often died after an exhausting march, usually well over 1,000 km (620 miles) from their homelands, carrying ivory and rhino horn to the coast. Initially its name applied to the porters; ultimately it became a reminder that this was also the end of the road for the one and a half million East African slaves who were captured and transported from this port to Zanzibar.

Saadani National Park

Situated less than 50 km (31 miles) from Bagamoyo as the crow flies, but divided from it by the uncrossable Wami River mouth, **Saadani National Park ❶** can either be reached by charter flight from Dar es Salaam, or by a circuitous four-hour drive through Chalinze and Mkange. There is nothing but the bush running down to the beach, Maasai people nearby and the sound of the warm sea gently sliding across the soft sand. Two small and exclusive lodges, **Tent With A View** and **Saadani Safari Lodge**, operate in the park,

Saadani, upgraded to national park status in 2002, covers about 1,000 sq. km (400 sq. miles) of flat land covered in coastal scrub, acacia grassland and miombo forest. The wildlife is not abundant but there are excursions that take visitors to see hippos and crocodiles on a Wami River boat safari and to the village of **Saadani** itself, a once-important trading centre, which now survives on fishing and donations from visiting tourists.

A walking safari reveals a good deal about the flora, especially the desert rose, but is not too hot on the fauna. There is relatively little game as yet, though there are plans to build it up, and many species, including elephant and lion, are finding their way into the sanctuary. In the mean-

time, look out for animals such as eland, kudu, sable and the tiny red duiker, as well as normal plains species. It's possible to go on a birdwatching expedition by boat on the Wami River.

Uniquely among Tanzania's parks, Saadani also has a 20-km (12-mile) stretch of sea front with fine sandy beaches interspersed by mangrove swamps. The thickets and palms that fringe the beach are home to white-browed coucals and tropical boubous. Green turtles nest at Madete, while bottlenose dolphins are frequently seen offshore. Humpback whales cruise past in season, and hundreds of soft pink flamingoes fish by the salt flats. And if you are really fortunate, you may even see lions or elephants trailing along the beach.

Amani Nature Reserve

Back on the coast road, it's an 85-km (53-mile) drive from Saadani to Pangani, a small town, once a dhow port, about 290 km (180 miles) from Dar. It enjoyed affluence during the 1960s, when the Pangani

River became a transport route to the interior, and in the late 19th century when it was a terminus of the caravan route from Lake Tanganyika. From here slaves, ivory, sisal and copra were exported. Today it still has a strong Arab feel. Relics of its prosperous past can be seen in the carved doorways and colonial buildings, two dilapidated Omani mansions and a coconut market in what was once a German castle.

Tanga, 46 km (28 miles) north of Pangani, is Tanzania's second-largest seaport. Today, it is a pleasant waterfront town with a number of attractive colonial buildings. The **Amboni Caves**, 8 km (5 miles) northwest of Tanga off the Horohoro–Mombasa road, is the largest cave system in East Africa, rumoured to be up to 200 km (120 miles) long. Only about 1 km (⅔ mile) of the system is generally open to the public but this is not for the claustrophobic; in parts you have to crawl, sometimes in procession, through to a stalactite-clad cave. Locals believe the main cave is the home of a fertility god. There is camping nearby.

BELOW: fishing in the Saadani National Park

Map
on pages
196–197

The reason for coming here is the **Amani Nature Reserve ❷** in the heart of the East Usambaras, 66 km (41 miles) from Tanga. The botanical gardens, set up as part of an agricultural research station in 1901, were once the largest in Africa, with almost 1,000 species of plant life. Although once neglected they have been renovated by the East Usambara Catchment Forest Project. In 1997, the beautiful gardens were incorporated into a 10,000-hectare (24,700-acre) nature reserve that also includes the Nilo Forest Reserve, Nilo Park, and a trek called a Climb into the Clouds (a 1,360-metre/4,460-ft climb up Lutindi Peak). The guided trails through the montane forest offer a collection of woodland vegetation, black-and-white colobus monkeys and birdlife, with some 340 species identified, many of them, such as the long-billed tailorbird, the Usambara eagle-owl and the Amani sunbird, rare and/or endemic. Check the website, www.usambara.com, or the information centre in the old stationmaster's house (tel: 027-264 6907; email: usambara@twiga.com). Six-room resthouses are available.

The Usambaras

Divided by the 4-km (2-mile) wide Lwengera Valley, the East and West Usambara form part of a sequence of 14 isolated mountain ranges that arc through the eastern interior between Kenya's Taita Hills and the Udzungwa Mountains of southern Tanzania. Known collectively as the Eastern Arc Mountains, this "archipelago" of ancient montane forests is ranked as one of the world's top 20 biodiversity hotspots, and is sometimes referred to as the African Galápagos due to the extraordinary degree of plant and animal endemism it supports.

The main town of the West Usambara, **Lushoto**, is about 160 km (100 miles) from Tanga along a good Tarmac road through Muheza, Segera and Mombo. There are a number of hotels in town and from here you can walk through the arboretum, take forest hikes and visit the **Irente Viewpoint**, which has a 1,000-metre (3,300-ft) drop to the plains below and offers a panoramic view of the Maasai Steppe. There is also a herbarium housing plants and birdlife.

Mkomazi Game Reserve

Situated to the north of the Pare Mountains, the 3,702-sq. km (1,429 sq. mile) **Mkomazi Game Reserve ❸** abuts the Kenya border and forms a southern extension of that country's vast Tsavo migratory ecosystem. Mkomazi harbours low densities of lion, cheetah, elephant, giraffe and various antelope, including dry-country "specials" such as fringe-eared oryx, gerenuk and lesser kudu, as well as introduced populations of the endangered black rhino and African hunting dog.

Partly because the reserve is so seldom visited by tourists, wildlife tends to be shy, though this may well change following an announcement that Mkomazi is likely to be upgraded to national parks status in 2006–7. And while mammals are sometimes thin on the ground, a tally of more than 400 bird species, including several dry-country specialists found nowhere else in Tanzania, provides a real inducement to birdwatchers. ❑

Map
on pages
196–197

ARUSHA NATIONAL PARK

*With Africa's highest mountain, the gateway to the great
gameparks of the north, and the cultural delights of
Arusha, this little district packs a big punch*

Dubbed the "Geneva of Africa", due to the United Nations' presence at the International Criminal Tribunal for Rwanda, which has been taking place in the Arusha International Conference Centre (AICC) since 1994, Arusha's prime function is as a hub for the buoyant safari industry. Nestling at the foot of the steep slopes of Mt Meru, **Arusha ❹** is the first stop on the northern safari circuit *(see page 211)*, as well as being close to the parks of Arusha and Kilimanjaro.

International flights arrive at Kilimanjaro International Airport, 45 km (28 miles) away, but there's also a busy domestic airport on the edge of town, with regular flights to the national parks, Zanzibar and Dar es Salaam, and a shuttle service to Nairobi.

On the outskirts of Arusha at **Tengeru**, 2 km (1½ miles) south of the Moshi road, and a short walk from Serena's Mountain Village Lodge, is **Lake Duluti Forest Reserve**. A crater lake, Duluti is said to be 300 metres (980 ft) deep and fed by an underground river. It takes an hour to walk around the lake, shaded by tall trees with straggling lianas. There's a good chance of seeing fish eagles and watching fishermen on home-made rafts fishing for black bass and tilapia.

Further along the Moshi road, you can go horse riding through coffee farms and onto the Mt Meru foothills at Usa River. This area also has some delightful places to stay, such as Moivaro Coffee Plantation and the more homely Rivertrees.

Arusha National Park

Shortly after this, you reach the turn-off to Arusha National Park. Near the Ngurdoto Gate is a snake park and reptile centre which breeds chameleons. It has knowledgeable guides, a comprehensive display of snakes and six types of chameleon, including the exquisite, prehistoric-

looking giant chameleon, together with tortoises and crocodiles. At Mkuru, 12 km (7 miles) from the Momela Gate, at the northern base of Mt Meru, camel safaris are on offer.

Arusha National Park ❺ is small, covering an area of 137 sq. km (53 sq. miles), but has stunning scenery, ranging from the lofty peaks of Mt Meru and its magnificent montane forests, to craters, open glades and the alkaline Momela lakes – from which one can see both Meru and Kilimanjaro on a clear day.

Around 570 species of bird have been recorded in the park, along with a wide variety of butterflies and other wildlife. Only an hour's drive from Arusha, the park is often overlooked in the rush to

LEFT: giraffe at the foot slopes of Mt Meru, Arusha National Park.
RIGHT: waterfall in stunning Arusha National Park.

head off on the Serengeti circuit, but it is well worth a visit. To the left of the park boundary is the area known as the Little Serengeti – a large, open glade with giraffe, zebra, buffalo, warthog and the occasional bushbuck on the woodland periphery. From the gate at Ngurdoto, the road winds up through the forest, where troops of smart black-and-white colobus monkey can be glimpsed in the high canopy, to Ngurdoto Crater. From look-out points along the crater rim you can see herds of buffalo, giraffe and warthog grazing the grasslands on the crater floor, and listen to the less-than-musical cries of the silvery-cheeked hornbill and various woodpeckers.

The road through the park to the Momela lakes descends from the Ngurdoto Forest to the Lokie Swamp and two small lakes, Jembamba and Longil, home to hippo, waterbuck, reedbuck, saddle-billed stork, Egyptian goose and various heron species, before reaching the grassland and thornbush around the Momela lakes. A mixture of wildlife, from giraffe to warthog, and a diverse range of birds are commonly seen. Here one appreciates the scale of **Mt Meru**, which, when clear of cloud, looms, dark and threatening.

Mt Meru

Known as *Oldonyo Orok* ("the black mountain") by the Maasai, Meru stands at 4,556 metres (15,000 ft), the fifth-highest mountain in Africa. Walks on the lower slopes and climbs to the summit, **Socialist Peak**, or Little Meru, can be arranged with the park headquarters at Momela Gate. Allow four days for the tough hike to ascend the peak; the best time to go is between July and September. Park guides are well-trained and informative. Walking gives a different perspective on viewing the wildlife.

Skirting past breeding herds of buffalo, getting to within 50 metres (160 ft) of a giraffe, listening to the raucous sounds of Hautlaub's turaco, and searching for colobus monkeys in the trees, is guaranteed to sharpen the senses. Natural attractions **BELOW:** the extinct crater of Mt Meru.

Map
on pages
196–197

include the giant fig-tree arch, the buttress roots of a strangler fig through which an elephant can pass, and the **Tululusia Waterfall**. The word tululusia means sentinel, and the top of Tululusia hill was used as a look-out point by the Maasai during the inter-tribal wars with the Wa-Arusha some 50 years ago. Interestingly, the volcanic rocks give the water a high mineral and fluoride content, staining teeth brown, as can be seen among the Wa-Arusha living on the slopes of the mountain.

The route up the mountain

The track up Mt Meru begins at the **Momela Gate**, at 1,500 metres (4,920 ft). There are two routes to the first hut, **Mirakamba**, at 2,600 metres (8,530 ft). The northern route takes 3 to 4 hours, and can also be driven. The southern route takes a couple of hours longer, but is more interesting and scenic. Crossing streams and open grassland you then climb up through the forest, passing through the fig-tree arch and cross the Jekukumia River to the Njeku viewpoint, with expansive views to Momela lakes and across the park, before continuing to Mirakamba. On the way there's a good chance of seeing monkeys, bushbuck, duiker, baboons and giraffe.

From Mirakamba it's a 4-hour hike to **Saddle Hut**, at 3,600 metres (11,810 ft), passing through glades and forest to **Mgongo wa Tembo** (Elephant Ridge). From here, it's a pleasant afternoon's excursion to the summit of **Little Meru** (3,820 metres/12,530 ft), from which there are impressive views of the crater, the ash cone and the sheer cliffs of the crater's inner wall towering some 1,500 metres (4,920 ft) high.

Look out, along the way, for the agile klipspringer, a small antelope which has adapted to steep and rocky terrain, and the imposing lammergeyer (bearded vulture) soaring on the updrafts.

From Saddle Hut, you can hike to the summit in about 6 hours, traversing a knife-edge ridge. Start early to watch the sun rising behind Kilimanjaro. Descending from the summit, you can stay at Saddle or Mirakamba Hut before the final descent to Momela Gate.

Bush lodges

Of the accommodation next to the park, the smartest option is the recently opened Hatari! Lodge near the Momela Gate. Nearby Momela Wildlife Lodge, by contrast, is a shadow of its former glory. Both lodges make much of their association with the filming of the 1962 Howard Hawks movie *Hatari!*, which featured John Wayne and Hardy Kruger – the latter settled in the area after the film had been made, and owned both lodge properties.

On the western slopes of Kilimanjaro, a 2-hour drive from Arusha, is a private 4,000-hectare (10,000-acre) ranch, called **Ndarakwai**, a pioneer in community conservation work with the Maasai. Dominated by acacia savanna woodland and bisected by riverine forest, there are two resident herds of elephant, and you may see gerenuk and lesser kudu, which are not found in Arusha or Kilimanjaro national parks. Walking with the Maasai and riding safaris are a speciality, and guests stay in a comfortable tented camp.

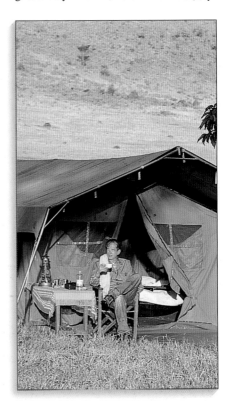

Before independence, western Kilimanjaro was the main centre of European farming in the area.

Moshi

The small, sprawling town of **Moshi**, due west of Arusha and surrounded by wheat, maize and coffee farms, lies at the foot of Mt Kilimanjaro, dwarfed by the twin peaks of **Kibo** (5,895 metres/19,340 ft) and **Mawenzi** (5,149 metres/16,893 ft). Founded in 1911 as the terminus of the Tanga railway line, it is now a major staging post for those inspired to conquer Kili. The main gate of Kilimanjaro National Park is only 30 km (19 miles) away, a steep climb up through the coffee and banana plantations of the prosperous Chagga tribe.

Day trips can be arranged to the **Rau Forest**, visiting Rau village and the Materuni waterfalls. At **Mweka**, there's a small wildlife museum attached to the College of Wildlife Management. **Lake Chala** is a small crater lake, about 1 km

(⅔ mile) wide, on the Kenyan border. Skirting around the eastern slopes of Kilimanjaro, take the road to Taveta, from where a rough road to the lake passes through farmland, west of Holili, with views to Kenya. There's a steep path down the 100-metre (330-ft) crater wall, but there are crocodiles so don't be tempted to take a dip. A large lodge has been under construction for years, and shows no sign of ever being completed.

Less visited is **Lake Jipe**, a shallow alkaline lake some 16 km (10 miles) long. Also sharing a border with Kenya, it is accessible from Kifaru on the Tanga road and offers excellent birdwatching.

Kilimanjaro National Park

The **Kilimanjaro National Park ❺** covers an area of 760 sq. km (293 sq. miles). It was gazetted in 1977 to protect the mountain above the 2,700-metre (8,858-ft) contour. Below this is a buffer zone of forest reserve to the 1,800-metre (5,905-ft) contour. The summit of Kilimanjaro was first climbed in 1889 by Dr Hans Meyer and Ludwig Purtscheller.

Today, more than 20,000 people a year make a bid for Africa's highest mountain, and Kilimanjaro earns more in park fees than all the other Tanzanian parks put together. Numbers have more than doubled in a decade, with a considerable environmental impact on the park's trails. Efforts are being made to counteract the erosion, and the Marangu and Mweka routes have been recently upgraded. Climbing Kilimanjaro can be arranged through tour operators in Moshi and Arusha and at the park headquarters at Marangu. The best months to climb the mountain are January, February and September. July and August are also good, but colder. Prices vary, but it pays to go with a reputable tour operator, as scrimping on price usually equates to poor equipment.

Kilimanjaro is not the best place to spot wildlife, although it is possible to see blue silvery-cheeked monkey, black-and-white colobus and hornbill. Botanists will enjoy the diversity of habitats found on the mountain, which range from forest to alpine desert. ❑

Map on page 196–197

LEFT: Helichrysum flowers are a common sight

Climbing Mt Kilimanjaro

According to legend, the first person to ascend Kilimanjaro was King Menelik I, supposedly the son of King Solomon and the Queen of Sheba. He ruled Tigre, the oldest province in Abyssinia (now Ethiopia) in the 10th century BC and fought battles in the present-day Ethiopia, Somalia, Kenya and Tanzania. As an old man, returning with the spoils of war, he camped between the peaks of Kibo and Mawenzi (4,500 metres/14,760 ft above sea level). Feeling that death was drawing near, he told his followers that he wished to die as a king. He, his warlords and slaves, laden with jewels and treasure, climbed to the crater, where he died.

The legend relates that one of Menelik's offspring will return to the mountain, climb Kibo and find the king and his jewels. Among these will be the Seal of Solomon, a ring which will empower the wearer with the wisdom of Solomon. The legend was so firmly believed by the Abyssinian Christians that when the Rev. Dr Reusch (a missionary who spent many years in the Kilimanjaro area, and who later became president of the Mountain Club of East Africa) reached the summit in 1926, many were deeply sceptical that he had reached the top as he found no trace of the long-dead king.

Although news of a snow-capped mountain was first mentioned in European literature in 1848 by another missionary, John Rebmann, no serious attempts at exploring Kilimanjaro were made until 1861, when Baron von der Decken and Richard Thornton led an expedition. The first successful ascent of the mountain was eventually made by Hans Meyer and Ludwig Purtscheller, on 5 October 1889.

Since then, many have reached the summit. Africa's highest mountain has attracted the rich and famous, and adventurers, including such unlikely people as the former US president Jimmy Carter and the Australian supermodel Elle Macpherson.

Remarkably, wildlife can survive at this high altitude – John Reader, filming on the mountain in 1983, saw eland, buffalo, jackal and wild dog on the Shira Plateau. The explorer Wilfred Thesiger describes being tracked by five wild dogs when he reached 5,750 metres (18,865 ft). Perhaps the most famous was the frozen specimen of a leopard discovered by Dr Donald Latham on his 1926 ascent. This gave its name to Leopard's Point on the crater rim.

In more recent years, just climbing Africa's highest mountain hasn't been enough. In 1962, three French parachutists beat the record for the highest parachute drop by landing in the crater. Others have successfully reached the top on a motorbike or bicycle. Several people have paraglided from the summit – on one occasion, a paraglider got blown off course, and was promptly arrested as a spy.

Another time a father and son engaged in a dual flight – the son descended safely, but the father and his paraglider disappeared into the forest and were never found. Wacky feats are no longer permitted by the park authorities. Disabled climbers are encouraged to take up the challenge however and in 1987 a paraplegic, an ex-British Marine, reached Hans Meyer Cave. ❑

Map
n pages
96–197

THE NORTHERN CIRCUIT

*The stuff of legends, this extraordinary area includes the Serengeti,
Ngorongoro Crater and Olduvai Gorge, world-class
game viewing and much more besides*

There is a well-worn tourist track across northern Tanzania. Almost every first-time visitor to the country will, at some point in their trip, visit the region. Some cherrypick the most famous bits, visiting only the Serengeti and Ngorongoro Crater; others try to cram the whole lot in at breakneck speed. To do the circuit properly, you need three weeks.

However you choose to do it, just make sure you do the circuit – this is one of the most compelling destinations in Africa, a superb blend of magnificent wildlife, stunning scenery, fascinating people, and outdoor activities.

The jumping-off point for the circuit is **Arusha** *(see page 205)*, with flights coming into Arusha or Kilimanjaro international airports. Once there, you have a choice of driving between the main reserves, or taking advantage of the daily scheduled light-aircraft flights that link the many airstrips in the region. Otherwise, it is strongly recommended that you use an Arusha-based safari company to provide a four-wheel-drive vehicle and driver/guide. This may seem like a luxury, but you need good ground clearance and height for game viewing, four-wheel-drive is necessary in some areas, and a driver costs very little more than self-drive hire. Unlike many parts of Africa, very few of the lodges provide game drives, assuming that most visitors have their own vehicle.

Don't expect to do this without spending an appreciable amount of money. The area has a variety of lodges, from small tented camps to large hotels. Most are comfortable, some extraordinarily luxurious, but few are cheap. The only way to bring the costs down is by taking a camping safari. Even then, you will be unable to avoid the high national-park fees, unless you never enter the parks – which rather defeats the purpose of going.

Tarangire National Park

From Arusha, head south on the Dodoma road, through **Makuyuni**, 80 km (50 miles) away. This is part of the Great North Road, the Pan-African "highway" that runs from Cairo to Cape Town. The entrance to **Tarangire National Park ❼** is 115 km (71 miles) south of Arusha, with good tarred roads all the way.

Tarangire is a long, thin park covering 1,360 sq. km (525 sq. miles), roughly running north–south along the line of the Tarangire River. It is made up chiefly of low-lying, rolling hills on the Rift floor, its natural vegetation of acacia woodland and giant baobabs only altered by huge areas of swamp which are a magnet for wildlife – including, sadly, mosquitoes

T:
colourful
erb starling.
HT:
ostrich egg
breakfast.

and tsetse flies. Take precautions. The swamps of black cotton mud produce rich grasslands, while the watercourses are lined by huge trees, including sycamore fig, tamarind and sausage trees.

Although it is relatively small, Tarangire is a highly accessible park, and it has much to offer in terms of game viewing. It is best known for its immense concentrations of elephant, which peak towards October at the end of the dry season, but it also hosts a wide variety of antelope, including elusive populations of fringe-eared oryx, gerenuk and greater and lesser kudu, all of which are very scarce or absent from the more westerly reserves. Coke's hartebeest, claimed by many as a speciality of the area, has long since vanished, as have the rhinos, shot out by poachers in the dark days of the 1970s and 1980s.

Baby boom

The elephants also suffered badly from poaching, but with the CITES ban on ivory trading, they have recovered with a vengeance and hundreds now roam the hills. As yet, there are few tuskers, but for cute elephant babies, this is definitely the place to be. It must be hoped that the decision, in late 2002, to partially lift the ban on the ivory trade won't be at the expense of this magnificent herd.

The park lies at the southern end of a vast migration area which stretches north to Amboseli in Kenya. As the land dries and the smaller rivers cease to flow, the herds head south towards the permanent water in the Tarangire River and its surrounding swamps. First to arrive are the eland and oryx, in June, followed by the elephants, wildebeest and zebra. June to October is the best time to visit. Although the herds remain in the area through until March, and it is great to see the thousands of calves born at this time, you will also have to contend with the rain, luxuriant vegetation and the plentiful insect population that make this less suitable for great game viewing.

The main lodges are all near the gate, overlooking the Tarangire River and

BELOW: plant adapt to the dry landscap

**Map
on pages
196–197**

baobab-clad hills, although there are a couple of smaller luxury camps in the centre of the park. There is no accommodation in the south and few visitors ever get there. Do try and make it at least as far as the **Silale Swamp**, the most northerly of several large swamps in the park. Fuelled by natural springs, they are year-round oases of lush green grass. Many of the animals you see nearby are coated in black cotton mud, having waded in waist-deep to reach the best shoots.

There are also masses of birds, including tawny, steppe and fish eagles, marabou stork, goliath heron, white pelican, spur-winged goose and sacred ibis. Some 300 species are regularly seen in the park, including a number of European migrants who winter here. It is also near the swamps that you may get to see one of the reserve's party tricks – tree-climbing lions.

Beyond the boundaries

Outside the park, large swathes of the areas to the northeast, crucial to the annual migration, are now conservation zones. A considerable amount of effort is going into educating the local populace on living in harmony with the wildlife, and setting up schemes to ensure they share the financial benefits of having the park on their doorstep. Several of the best lodges are found in this region, reached via a rough track just north of the park entrance.

The **Lemiyon Plain**, north and west of Tarangire, is a huge, flat, dry and desolate area, with the occasional village and small town, way too many cattle and goats and so little grass that dust clouds blow for miles. **Kolo**, home of some of the finest of the Kondoa rock paintings, is not far to the south of the park *(see Central Tanzania, page 232)*.

To continue the circuit, head back north to Makuyuni, from where the road turns off to Manyara, Ngorongoro and Serengeti. Once notoriously rough and bumpy, the road running through Mto wa Mbu and Karatu as far as Ngorongoro has now been surfaced – though roads running

LOW:
oi have
stinctive
ack markings.

further west into the Serengeti remain as spine-jarring as you might expect.

Lake Manyara National Park

The agricultural and market town of **Mto Wa Mbu** stands next to the entrance of Lake Manyara National Park, about 50 km (30 miles) west of Makuyuni, at the foot of the Gregory Escarpment, the western wall of the eastern arm of the Great Rift Valley.

Named after Scottish geologist, John Walter Gregory, the first to map and name the East African Rift, this is one of the most dramatic points along its length, rising almost sheer some 800 metres (2,625 ft) from the valley floor. The enormous amount of ground water pouring through the rocks of the escarpment has created a lush, green swamp here, and the locals are excellent farmers, growing everything from bananas and maize to citrus fruits, rice and vegetables. The road is lined with produce stalls and the town has a self-satisfied feeling of wealth – also

helped by the estimated 18,000 souvenir salesmen waiting to pounce the moment you leave your car. The downside of all this plenty is that the area is very malarial – Mto Wa Mbu ominously and accurately means "mosquito creek" – so lash on the repellent and take the pills.

Many people pass by **Lake Manyara National Park ❽** in their rush towards the Serengeti, but although small, this is one of the prettiest, most interesting and game-rich parks in the country. It is only 330 sq. km (127 sq. miles) in size – tiny by Tanzanian standards – and about two-thirds of that is water. The rest is a long thin strip of land sandwiched between the lake and the cliff, fed by a very few extremely rough roads.

There is only one lodge actually within the park, the exclusive **Lake Manyara Tree Lodge** at the far end of the park beyond the reach of most daytrippers. Most of the other lodges are built along the rim of the escarpment, with fabulous views across the lake, and safely out of the way of the mosquitoes.

The park and lake take their name from the manyara bush *(Euphorbia tirucalli)* used by the Maasai to build their stockades. The Maasai actually use the same word, *emanyara*, for a kraal. There is a manyara bush at the park entrance. Once inside, the first part of the park is thick groundwater forest with huge trees, including Cape mahogany, croton, sycamore fig and several sorts of palm. Beneath these soaring canopies, dense undergrowth provides a delightful array of wildflowers and butterflies, but this is not easy country for game viewing. You should see troops of olive baboons and Sykes' monkeys playing beside the road. Bushbuck may emerge from the shade, and as you round a bend, you are quite likely to find an elephant in your path. They frequently choose to use the roads rather than having to struggle through the undergrowth.

Remember to keep looking up. As in Tarangire, the local lions sometimes take to the trees, and there are also plenty of leopards, although you need luck to see them. Even if the cats elude you, there are many birds to see, including the giant silvery-

LEFT: a yellow billed stork catching fish.

Map
on pages
196–197

cheeked hornbill. The further you get into the park, the drier it becomes, gradually opening out into forests of umbrella-topped fever trees and baobabs. As the vegetation changes, so does the wildlife, with plains animals such as buffalo, wildebeest, zebra and giraffe making an appearance. Above, martial eagles and bateleurs circle idly on the thermals as they scan for prey. Near the southern end of the park there are two groups of bubbling, steaming-hot springs that have dyed the surrounding ground a rainbow of colours with their chemicals.

Like most other Rift Valley lakes, Manyara is a shallow soda lake, fed by groundwater, and varying hugely in size according to the season. As it shrinks back, a broad floodplain opens up. Many animals choose to graze the new shoots, and wallow in the muddy shallows. Among them paddle waterbirds such as pelicans, flamingos, cormorants and herons, while a little further out, pods of hippo grunt and puff their way through the heat of the day.

Karatu Highlands

At the top of the Manyara Escarpment, you enter a lush area of richly fertile farmland and superb mountain scenery, with purple hills ringing rich red earth and neatly ordered fields of wheat, sweet potatoes, beans and coffee, carved up by high green hedges of spiky manyara plants. In the distance are the imposing cones of the great volcanic craters, Ngorongoro *(see page 216)* and Ol Doinyo Lengai *(see page 222)*.

The largest town in the area is **Karatu**, a bustling market and business centre that is a useful stop for travellers, with several campsites, phones and internet cafés. If you have time, spend a day detouring down to **Lake Eyasi ❾**. Look for the turning to the left, 10 km (6 miles) west of Karatu town. The 60-km (37-mile) road is poor almost from the start and gets increasingly bad until, at times, it disappears altogether. It is just passable without four-wheel-drive in the dry season, as long as you have good ground clearance. As the road drops down from the plateau, the

GHT: a
dza man.

THE HADZA

The Hadza represent a precious link with human pre-history. They are among the last adherents to the hunter-gatherer lifestyle that sustained the world's entire human population for perhaps 99 percent of its existence. Their language belongs to the dying Khiosan linguistic group, distinguished by punctuating clicks that many linguists believe to be a preserved element of the first human language.

The Hadza refuse to adopt a settled lifestyle, so a tract of state land fringing Lake Eyasi has been set aside for their use. Here, small nomadic family bands construct temporary grass shelters, moving according to weather conditions, game movements, or the location of a kill. Anything from sparrows to giraffes is fair game, but the local delicacy is baboon flesh. Meat accounts for only 20 percent of Hadza food intake; the remainder consists of vegetable matter gathered by women.

The Hadza philosophy of living for the moment is encapsulated in their favourite gambling game. A wooden disc, with rough and smooth faces, is thrown down together with one similar disc per participant. This action is repeated until only one person's disc lands same-face-up with the master, deciding the winner.

lush farms of the highlands give way to bare earth crisscrossed with erosion canyons, and to acacias and baobabs powdered white by flying dust, and herds of goats and skeletal cows.

Lake Eyasi is a long, skinny soda lake that stretches up to 80 km (50 miles) when the rains are good and virtually dries up at other times.

Above it soars the 800-metre (2,625-ft) **Eyasi Escarpment**, one of the more spectacular cliffs in the Tanzanian Rift Valley. At certain times of year, the water can be thick with clattering pink flamingos, while numerous other birds call from the shores. The locals fish in the lake, smoking their catch on the foreshore.

Ngorongoro

The **Ngorongoro Conservation Area** ❿ stretches from the Karatu Highlands to the Serengeti and down to the northern tip of Lake Eyasi, covering some 8,300 sq. km (3,205 sq. miles). **Lodoare Gate** is 29 km (18 miles) west of Karatu. The new tarred

road ends here so the rest of your circuit will be done on gravel roads that range from bumpy to diabolical.

Be warned – the hefty daily park fee only gets you as far as the rim of the crater. If you wish to drive down into it, you need to pay an additional fee per car. The only road to the Serengeti runs through the conservation area so you have to pay even if only passing through. Remember that you need to reach the gate before it shuts for the night.

From the entrance, the road climbs steeply up through the thick montane forest to a T-junction and **Heroes' Point**, from which you get your first, mind-blowing view of the crater itself. In the parking area is a memorial to rangers killed while protecting the crater from poachers.

The right fork leads to Sopa Lodge, the only hotel on the eastern rim, and beyond that to the **Empakaai Crater**, a 6-km (4-mile) wide, 300-metre (980-ft) high volcanic crater largely filled by a soda lake. There is a road around the rim and

BELOW: bat-eared foxes hunt at dusk and dawn.

Map
on pages
196–197

into the crater, but both are rough and four-wheel-drive is strongly advised. The much shallower **Olmoti Crater** can only be reached on foot. Rangers can be hired at the ranger station in the nearby village of Nainokanoka. Back at the crossroads, the left fork leads to all the other hotels, the main access routes to the crater, Olduvai and the Serengeti.

Maasai territory

Formed by the same immense geological upheavals as the Great Rift Valley, Ngorongoro was once a mountain as high as Kilimanjaro. About 3 million years ago, it blew itself to bits, covering the Serengeti in ash while the crater floor sank into the mountain. Today, the rim stands at a crisp 2,285 metres (7,497 ft). The **Ngorongoro Crater** is the world's largest complete volcanic caldera, with a diameter of about 18 km (11 miles) and an area of 260 sq. km (100 sq. miles). The sheer-sided rim is just over 600 metres (1,969 ft) at its highest point. From the top, it is impossible to see the animals without binoculars, but the ever-changing play of light across the flowing grasslands can be hypnotic.

Ngorongoro is a Maasai word; some say it mimics the clatter of cow bells, others that it is a traditional name for a type of bowl, similar in shape to the crater. The colourful Maasai are the traditional owners of the area, although they are relative newcomers, having forced the Mbulu and Datoga out of the area around 200 years ago. Two German brothers farmed the crater floor for a short while in the early 20th century, but when the area was first incorporated into the Serengeti National Park in 1951, around 12,000 Maasai lived in the crater.

A deal was struck that turned Ngorongoro into a conservation area, rather than a national park, allowing them to continue to water their animals on the crater floor, in exchange for moving out and receiving a share of the profits from tourism. Today, with the populations of people, cattle and goats growing exponentially,

LOW:
Ngorongoro
Crater
game drive.

and water and grazing land limited in the surrounding area, some 40,000 Maasai are claiming rights over the crater and demanding a larger slice of the cake. Even though Ngorongoro was declared a World Heritage Site in 1978, there is no room for complacency. To the Maasai the cattle are all important and the game is there on suffrance.

Into the crater

Perhaps the truest indication of how busy the crater can get is that the access roads operate as a one-way system. The crater is only open between 7am and 6pm, and most people prefer to spend the whole day there. There are two picnic and toilet spots, in the Lerai Forest or at **Ngoitoki-tok Springs** in the southeast. Watch out for the aggressive tactics of the black kites who have discovered that chicken sandwiches taste better and are easier to catch than mice. The main descent road twists down the western wall, near the **Seneto Springs**, used by the Maasai to water their

cattle. The crater floor is a true Shangri-La, one of the most densely crowded game areas in the world, home to an estimated 30,000 animals. Because it is enclosed and the flat crater floor is largely made up of open grassland, it is easy to police, with the result that this is a stronghold for endangered species including black rhino and, increasingly, cheetah. The only downside of the open vistas is that you can see other vehicles – although even they can be a useful way of helping you spot something of interest. The best vantage point is flat-topped **Engitati Hill** in the northeastern corner.

There are no giraffe, topi or impala in the crater – they find it too difficult to negotiate the cliffs. The usual prey animals are wildebeest, zebra and buffalo. It is easy to spot and track a hunt across the open plain, although contrary to preconceptions, the local hyenas are aggressive pack hunters while the resident lions regularly chase hyenas off their kills and scavenge them.

In the southwestern corner, **Lake**

BELOW: zebra and wildebees at the edge o Lerai Forest, Ngorongoro Crater Conservation Area.

Map on pages 196–197

Magadi is a large, shallow soda lake, home to a plentiful supply of flamingos as well as hippos and other waterbirds, which can also be seen in the central **Mandusi Swamp**. The **Lerai Forest** of fever trees, in the south, is the best place in the park to see elephants, Oddly, the only elephants resident in the crater itself are old bulls, many with outsized tusks – although the breeding herds do cross the crater floor from time to time, they are more usually to be found on the densely forested rim. The ascent road is near here.

Olduvai Gorge

From the crater rim, the Serengeti road winds gently down the western flank of the volcano, through rolling grasslands and acacia woodland. It is here that you will find the many giraffe and antelope absent from the crater floor, mingling freely with the Maasai livestock. This is probably also your best opportunity to see the Maasai people; there are several local *bomas* that offer expensive guided tours of their *manyattas* (homes) that include photo opportunities. Ask your driver to fix the price for you. About 30 km (18 miles) from the crater, a small road on the right leads to the Olduvai Gorge.

The **Olduvai Gorge Museum** (open daily 8.30am–5pm; entrance fee) is 3 km (2 miles) off the road. The area takes its name from the spiky wild sisal plants known to the Maasai as *oldupai*. The gorge, which is about 90 metres (295 ft) deep, lies on the site of an ancient lake, covered over by thick layers of volcanic ash, which have carefully preserved some of the world's earliest records of mankind.

About 100,000 years ago, seismic activity split the earth, creating the gorge and laying bare the rich fossil beds. These were discovered in 1911 by a German Professor Katwinkle while out hunting for butterflies. He carried out one small dig in 1913, but little else was done until Louis and Mary Leakey arrived in 1931. Archaeologists have been working here ever since, and have made many of pre-history's most famous and influential discoveries in the canyon walls. Standing in the gorge, you are as close as you can get to our earliest hominid ancestors. It is an awe-inspiring thought – especially when you see the cast of footprints made at Laetoli about 3.6 million years ago.

This is just one of the fascinating items on display in the excellent interpretation centre and museum. Although the human exhibits are all copies (the originals are in Nairobi Museum, Kenya), the explanations are fascinating and there are also plenty of animal remains, many belonging to long-extinct species such as the pygmy giraffe.

Guides are on hand to give tours of the gorge and any current excavations, although these generally look pretty unimpressive to outsiders. The area is also a pleasant place for a walk, picnic and a spot of birdwatching, with a wide variety of small, brightly coloured species such as barbets, rollers and glossy starlings patrolling the grounds. A few kilometres from the museum, the extraordinary **Shifting Sands** are a couple of black volcanic sand dunes, which slowly meander

RIGHT: skulls of extinct animals displayed in the Olduvai Gorge Museum.

across the plains, according to the winds. The Maasai regard them as an important place of meditation.

Lake Ndutu

About 40 km (25 miles) further on, a turning to the left leads down to **Lake Ndutu**, still technically part of the Ngorongoro Conservation Area, but right on the southern border of the Serengeti. Like most of the Rift lakes, it is alkaline, although it is still drinkable and is used by a wide array of local wildlife, including many birds. Rather disconcertingly, the black cotton mud around the shores is littered by wilde-

beest and buffalo skulls belonging to animals trapped as they tried to cross the lake.

The main reason for visiting is to stay at **Ndutu Lodge**, a charming small safari lodge set in acacia woodland, which has the benefits of being within the Serengeti ecosystem but outside the park's boundary. It is used as a base by many wildlife film units. Every evening, a posse of genets invades the lodge, peering down at the dinner tables from the rafters.

Serengeti National Park

The **Serengeti National Park ⓫** is quite probably the most famous game reserve

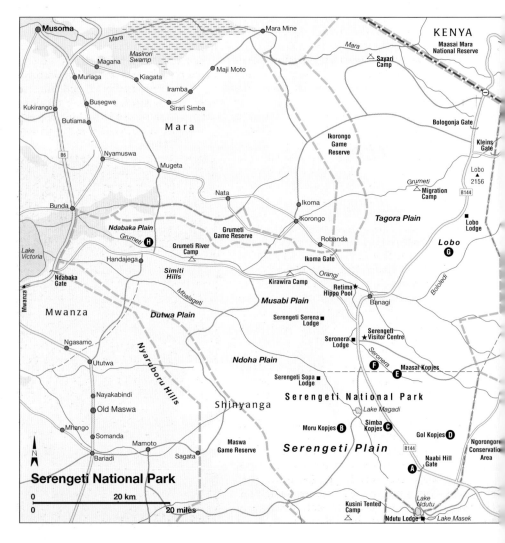

in the world; it achieved legendary status from its inauguration when Professor Bernard Grzimek wrote *The Serengeti Shall Not Die*, the story of the quest to have it declared a national park, an aim finally achieved in 1951. It is now also a World Heritage Site.

The national park covers a vast 14,763 sq. km (5,700 sq. miles). The full Serengeti ecosystem is far larger still, also covering the Maasai Mara in Kenya and the Ngorongoro Conservation Area, totalling a massive 25,000 sq. km (9,650 sq. miles). Animals can wander freely throughout the system.

Only about a third of the park is made up of the flat grassy plains which gave the park its name – *Siringit* is Maasai for "the place where the land runs on forever". However it is these plains and their role in the annual migration of some 2 million animals *(see page 223)* which have made the area so special.

About 3–4 million years ago, during the massive eruptions of Ngorongoro, Sadiman and Kerimasi volcanoes, a thick rain of ash settled over the plains, creating a rock-hard top coat, known as hard-pan. Although richly fertile, it is too tough to be broken by tree roots, leaving the landscape to the shallow-rooted grasses, packed with nutritious minerals which act as a magnet to grazers such as wildebeest, zebra, impala and Thompson's gazelles.

From **Naabi Hill Gate** Ⓐ, the grasslands stretch around you in all directions. There are animals here at any time of year, but from October to May, the area is teeming with life, including wildebeest, zebra, warthog, topi, hartebeest, impala, Thompson's and Grant's gazelles, Kori bustard, secretary bird and ostrich. Hyenas and jackals prowl nearby while vultures circling overhead may indicate the position of a kill.

Lions, almost the exact colour of the grass in the dry season, are more easily visible at some of the rocky kopjes, granite inselbergs scattered across the landscape. The **Moru Kopjes** Ⓑ are favourites amongst many big cats, including lion, leopard, serval and caracal, and you may even find elephant in the area.

Look carefully at the rocks themselves to find the faded centuries-old Maasai paintings. **Simba Kopjes** Ⓒ are frequently used for sunbathing by the lions after which they are named. You may also see baboon, giraffe and a good variety of birds in the area. **Gol Kopjes** Ⓓ are popular with cheetah, while the **Maasai Kopjes** Ⓔ again attract lion and formidably large cobras.

Seronera

At the centre of the park, the **Seronera River Valley** Ⓕ is one of the richest wildlife habitats in the region, not only providing a valuable water source, but also marking the boundary between the grassy plains and the wooded hills to the north, attracting animals and birds belonging to both environments. In addition to plains animals, the woodlands are favoured by baboon and monkey, buffalo, giraffe, eland, bushbuck and dik-dik. Waterbuck and reedbuck hang out along the river banks, overlooked by leopards who love to laze away the heat of the day

in the shady sausage trees. The river provides a home for hippos and crocodiles, while many of the park's estimated 500 species of bird can be found in the area.

Seronera is also home to the **visitor centre** and **Serengeti Balloon Safaris**. There can be few experiences more magical than drifting over this endless scenery at dawn, sometimes low enough to skim the trees, at others, soaring to see the true scale of this vast wilderness.

Heading north, the **Lobo area** ❻ becomes more rugged with craggy hills covered by scrubby bush and open woodland favoured by buffalo, elephant and the rare gingery Patas monkey. In the gallery forest along the watercourses, look out for brightly coloured turaco. Antelope living in the rocky hills include mountain reedbuck, oribi and the grey bush duiker.

The Western Corridor

The **Western Corridor** sticks out like a panhandle, following the line of the **Grumeti River** ❼ and taking the borders

of the Serengeti almost as far as Lake Victoria. A central range of hills is flanked to either side by large areas of plains, their sticky black cotton soil bursting into flower during the rains.

It may look spectacular but is a nightmare for drivers, and the area is best visited in the dry months (June to October) when the non-migratory animals cluster along the river. Eland and roan antelope both live in the area, while the wooded riverbanks are home to black-and-white colobus and some spectactularly huge crocodiles (up to 6 metres/20 ft in length), which spring into a feeding frenzy when the wildebeest come through, usually in May and June.

Lake Natron

From the Serengeti, the quickest route to **Lake Natron** ❶❷, the most northerly of Tanzania's Rift Valley lakes, is to exit the park at Klein's Gate, then follow a rough, dusty road east (past Longido) for 4–5 hours before descending the Rift Escarpment to the small lakeshore village of Ngare Sero. Alternatively, an equally bumpy and even dustier road connects Ngare Sero to Mto wa Mbu near the entrance gate of Lake Manyara National Park, a three- to four-hour drive. This is an excursion for the rugged traveller, into harsh dry landscapes inhabited by hardy Maasi pastoralists and seasonal concentrations of wildlife. The lake is extremely saline, a fact adored by the nearly 3½ million flamingos that flock here from the Rift Valley area of Tanzania and Kenya to breed. The birds are actually hard to see as the lake creates mirages.

Natron Lake Camp will also organise climbs up **Ol Doinyo L'Engai**, a still-active volcano which last erupted in 1983. It stands 2,751 metres (9,026 ft) tall and is sacred to the Maasai. Indeed, Ol Doinyo L'Engai literally translates as God's Mountain, and the Maasai believe it to be the home of *Engai*, a single deity with benevolent and vengeful aspects. The climb takes a very long day (some operators prefer to start at midnight to avoid the baking heat) and you need to be physically fit to complete it. ❑

Maps:
Area196
Park 220

LEFT: grey-breasted spurfowl, endemic to the Mara-Serengeti ecosystem.

The Great Migration

Imagine a column of wildebeest 40 km (24 miles) long and two or three abreast, patiently plodding across the plain for hour after hour. Now multiply that until you have about 1½ million wildebeest, throw in some 300,000 zebras, another 300,000 Thompson's gazelles, and about 30,000 Grant's gazelles, all on the move in the search for fresh new grass.

Imagine it taking over two weeks for the column of animals to pass a single spot, and visualise them all bunching together into protective herds in the evenings or scrambling across each others' backs in their panic to cross the river and stay clear of the snapping jaws of the crocodiles. Imagine the lions and hyenas roaring and cackling as they prowl the outskirts of the herds looking for weakened animals. Now you may just begin to have an idea of the awesome spectacle that is the Serengeti migration.

The various different species that make up the migration live amicably together, part of a carefully balanced cycle that allows them to get the maximum amount of food from any area. The cycle actually begins with the elephants who open up the woodlands, the heavy buffalo and hippo who rip up the coarse, long grass and the antelope such as topi, eland and hartebeest who have their own much smaller migration cycle around the woodland fringes.

The wildebeest are the most dedicated travellers in their quest for the finest shoots. The zebras are less picky, going for quantity rather than quality, so need to travel less far. Behind them come the smaller gazelles, nibbling the delicate new growth. The wildebeests' keen sense of smell, the zebras' fine eyesight and the gazelles' acute hearing together create a formidable early-warning system, while the huge herds make it easier to stay alive. These defences are very necessary – such a smorgasbord attracts the predators in droves.

The Serengeti migration is actually a year-round phenomenon, a broad, slow clockwise route march covering a total of around 3,000 km (1,870 miles). The cycle begins in May when the grass on the southern plains is exhausted and the herds begin to move slowly northwards through the western corridor. This is the time of the rut, the bulls working to the point of exhaustion to build and protect their harems.

The mass migration reaches the Maasai Mara by late June, remaining there until September, when they return south through the Lobo area, following the scent in the air of the small rains. They reach the southern plains by November, remaining there to feed on the nutrient-rich grass during the breeding season.

In three weeks from February to March, over 90 percent of the females (around 500,000 animals) give birth to their young. Calves can stand within 7 minutes and within two days can outrun a lion, but even so the predators grow fat at this time of year. The herds remain in the south, allowing their young time to build strength, before heading north as the grass runs out and the cycle begins again. ❑

Map
n pages
96–197

LAKE VICTORIA

*One of the greatest attractions of Lake Victoria, Africa's largest
lake, is Rubondo Island, which offers wonderful
opportunities for birdwatching*

The world's second-largest freshwater body, the 70,000-sq.-km (27,027-sq.-mile) **Lake Victoria ⑬**, lies within a shallow elevated basin shared between Tanzania, Uganda and Kenya. Characterised by murky, cloud-toned water and (within Tanzania) a somewhat starkly vegetated shore, this shallow inland sea is notable more for its dimensions perhaps than for any great scenic qualities.

Rubondo Island National Park

Despite its proximity to the Serengeti, Lake Victoria has never featured prominently on tourist itineraries, though the recent construction of a proper lodge on **Rubondo Island National Park ⑭**, and the introduction of scheduled flights there from the Serengeti, may yet alter that.

Whether you fly in directly from the Serengeti or come by boat across from the mainland, 240-sq.-km (93-sq.-mile) Rubondo Island is a revelation. Jungle-swathed hills tumble down to a shore of lush papyrus swamps and sandy beaches, lapped by the water of the lake, to create a bewitching and scenically memorable freshwater tropical paradise.

This is the least visited of Tanzania's national parks (only 60 non-residents set foot here in one recent year) and the most underrated: a consummate post-safari retreat for those more interested in low-key wildlife viewing than lazing around at an Indian Ocean beach resort.

The island is best explored along a network of walking trails that lead through tangled jungle to rocky bays and rickety stilted hides overlooking the marshy shore. Here, the handsome sitatunga antelope, a localised and elsewhere elusive swamp resident, is exceptionally easy to locate, as are the all-too-familiar bushbuck and squabbling troops of vervet monkeys. Alternatively, it can be just as rewarding to hang around the lodge,

where exquisite paradise flycatchers flutter their long orange tails through the trees, grey parrots maintain a perpetual mutter and squawk, and pairs of spot-necked otter make dens in the offshore rocks. Further afield, the swampy **Mlaga Bay** – inhabited by scores of hippo and waterbirds – can be explored slowly by motorboat.

Rubondo has an odd history. It was earmarked as a "floating zoo" in 1966, with the idea that the Frankfurt Zoological Society could breed introduced populations of endangered rainforest species such as okapi and bongo. This plan never quite came together, and it was abandoned totally in 1973. But not before troops of chimpanzees and black-and-white colobus monkeys had been settled on the island,

-T: a great
ite egret,
ing.
LOW: tented
ommodation
he Rubondo
nd
ional Park.

together with several non-forest *species including elephant, giraffe, black rhinoceros, suni and roan antelope. All but the last two are still present today.

The chimpanzees of Rubondo are neither as habituated nor as easily located as their counterparts on Lake Tanganyika, but chimp-tracking excursions have become increasingly rewarding following the implementation of a new research project in 2003.

Visited in isolation, Rubondo Island – a forest reserve since German times, its surrounding waters off-limits to commercial fishing – might give a misleading impression of Lake Victoria's ecological state. The Tanzanian littoral has been all but denuded of indigenous vegetation through overgrazing and agriculture. Below the surface, the 200 endemic cichlid species that evolved since the lake dried up 12,000 years ago are undergoing what one biologist describes as "the greatest vertebrate mass extinction in recorded history", due to the introduction of the predatory Nile perch in the colonial era. Fifty years ago, cichlids constituted 80 percent of the lake's fish biomass; today they account for a mere 1 percent.

This change in the lake's species composition, exacerbated by an inflow of chemical waste, has promoted a five-fold increase in algae levels and a comparable drop in oxygenation since records were first maintained. If present trends continue, ecologists fear that Lake Victoria is destined to die, becoming incapable of sustaining vertebrate life.

Set on a rocky peninsula on the southeastern lakeshore, Tanzania's second-largest city, **Mwanza** (population 350,000) is a pivotal regional transport hub, serviced by a good selection of flights, ferries, trains and buses.

Stroll ten minutes south of central Mwanza to the jetty for **Saa Nane Island** (entrance fee inclusive of boat transfer, two-hourly between 11am and 5pm). The island offers a rare opportunity to observe the natural lakeshore fauna. Rock hyraxes

BELOW: lush vegetation in Rubondo Island National Park.

Map
on pages
196–197

and colourful agama lizards bask on the rocks, monitor lizards stalk the undergrowth like diminutive dinosaurs, and the odd crocodile has been known to stretch out on the beach. Vervet monkeys and introduced impalas range freely on the island, and the birdlife – from the vociferous fish eagle to the localised yellow-throated leaflove – is fabulous.

Serengeti National Park

The road following the eastern lakeshore is surfaced for much of its 250-km (155-mile) length to the Kenya border, and it offers regular glimpses across the open water of Speke Gulf. Near Bunda, the road skirts the **Western Serengeti**. Wildebeest and zebra graze complacently on the fringes, while the lodges in Serengeti's western corridor frequently take guests this way for a lakeside lunch.

Most tourists visit the Serengeti on an extended northern circuit safari out of Arusha *(see page 211)*, but – worth knowing if you're on a tight budget – it is also easy to visit the national park from the Lake Victoria side. **Serengeti Stopover**, situated outside the main western entrance gate is the best contact for inexpensive day and overnight Serengeti safaris.

Roads, of a sort, run west from Mwanza through the booming gold-mining town of **Geita**, and the isolated former German administrative centre of **Biharamulo**, to **Bukoba** near the Ugandan border, but it would require a certain perversity of spirit to elect to drive or take a bus ride along them. A far less arduous mode of transport is the overnight ferry (capable of carrying vehicles) between Mwanza and Bukoba – or the daily flights between the ports.

Founded by the Emin Pasha in 1890, **Bukoba** ⓑ was settled three years later by Catholic missionaries, who built the well-maintained cathedral that stands out from the time-worn colonial buildings that otherwise characterise the centre of town. The marshy lakeshore below the town hosts large concentrations of water-birds, while the small fishing village of **Nyamukazi**, 2 km (1½ miles) northeast of Bukoba, provides an enjoyable glimpse into rural Tanzania life. At **Bwanjai**, 25 km

(15 miles) northwest of Bukoba, a mysterious rock-art shelter is daubed with ancient geometric patterns and stylised human figures, the sole surviving legacy of some long-forgotten Stone-Age artists.

Minziro Forest Reserve

Nestled against the Uganda border inland of Lake Victoria, the swampy groundwater forest of the little-known **Minziro Forest Reserve** ⓰ has strong faunal affinities to the West African rainforest. Ornithologists are in for a treat – an incredible 56 Guinea-Congo biome bird species found nowhere else in Tanzania have been recorded at Minziro. High in the canopy, troops of Angola colobus, grey-cheeked mangabey and red-tailed monkey play hide-and-seek with human intruders, while Peter's duiker and bushbuck flit elusively through the dense undergrowth. Permission to visit and camp in the forest, as well as directions, can be obtained at no charge from the forestry office in Bukoba.   ❑

LAKE TANGANYIKA

*The longest freshwater body of water in the world, Lake Tanganyika,
contains over 1,000 species of fish. Along its shore, the
Gombe Stream National Park is famed for its chimpanzees*

Running for a distance of 675 km (419 miles) from Burundi in the north to Zambia in the south, **Lake Tanganyika** ⓱ is the longest freshwater body in the world, and the second deepest, plummeting to depths approaching 1,500 metres (4,910 ft). It is also immensely beautiful. Hemmed in by the mountainous western Rift Valley escarpment, the lakeshore is lined by long sandy beaches, rustic fishing villages, and patches of ancient forest rattling with birds, monkeys and chimpanzees. The aquamarine water – reputedly the least polluted in the world – is so clear that you can wade in chin deep and still see your toes, and harbours an estimated 1,000 fish species, most of them endemic to the lake.

Lake Tanganyika remains resolutely off the beaten track. What differentiates it from most similarly underdeveloped areas, however, is a wealth of world-class tourist attractions. Gombe Stream and Mahale Mountains offer the best chimpanzee tracking in Africa, while the little-known Katavi National Park supports herds of savanna game that compare favourably with almost any other African sanctuary you care to mention. With the arguable exception of Gombe Stream, Lake Tanganyika's major attractions are readily accessible only to those with reasonably deep pockets. There is, however, scope for adventurous budget travel in the region. Heading the list of such possibilities is the historic

BELOW:
watching the
chimpanzees
in the Mahale
Mountains
National Park.

Map on pages 196–197

MV *Liemba*, the weekly ferry that plies from Kigoma south to Mpulungu in Zambia. This handsome old boat has been in non-stop service since 1924, providing a vital lifeline to remote parts of the lake – and an offbeat excursion that embodies the romance of African lake travel.

Gombe Stream National Park

Covering a mere 52 sq. km (20 sq. miles), Tanzania's smallest national park, **Gombe Stream National Park ⓲**, protects a hilly stretch of lakeshore transected by forest-fringed permanent streams. Gombe Stream's fame derives from its association with Jane Goodall's chimp research project. Inevitably, it is the chimp community habituated by Goodall that forms the centre of tourist activities at Gombe, but the olive baboons that habitually beachcomb in front of the rest camp are also relatively tame and easy to photograph. Birdlife is prolific, with normally secretive forest birds such as the lovely Peter's twinspot tame around the rest camp.

Gombe Stream lies on the eastern lakeshore 25 km (16 miles) north of Kigoma. The park is not accessible by road or by air, and accommodation is limited to a basic rest camp.

The easiest way to visit is on a daytrip, using a charter motorboat from the **Kigoma Hilltop Hotel**. A more affordable option, although you will need two nights, is to use a public boat-taxi from **Kibirizi** (3 km/2 miles north of Kigoma). These leave in the afternoon, returning in the early morning, taking 2 hours in either direction. Guided forest walks can be arranged on the spot, with a near-certainty of encountering chimps in the morning. The entrance fee of US$100 per 24 hours is charged only upon entering the forest, so you won't be penalised if you spend a second night at the rest camp.

Mahale Mountains

Mahale Mountains National Park ⓳ extends for 1,613 sq. km (623 sq. miles) across a bulbous peninsula of forested

BELOW: young chimpanzee at Gombe Stream National Park.

mountains, roughly 120 km (75 miles) south of Kigoma. In many respects it is more rewarding than Gombe Stream. The scenery alone is magnificent: rugged mountains rise sharply from sandy beaches, through tangled miombo woodland and montane forest and grassland, to the 2,462-metre (8,077-ft) **Nkungwe Peak**.

This diversity of habitats is reflected in the wide variety of birds, butterflies and mammals. Savanna residents such as lions, African hunting dogs, elephants, giraffes and sable antelopes are resident, though seldom observed, as are West African rainforest species such as the brush-tailed porcupine and giant forest squirrel. Aside from the famous – and easily seen – chimpanzees, smaller primates such as red colobus, red-tailed monkey, Sykes' monkey, vervet monkey and yellow baboon should be encountered by casual visitors.

There is no road access to Mahale Mountains. The upmarket lodges can be visited by charter flight from Arusha or motorboat from the **Kigoma Hilltop Hotel** *(see page 329)*, generally as part of an all-inclusive package. Hardy and self-sufficient independent travellers can get as far as the village of **Lugosa** with the MV *Liemba*, then hike – or hire a local boat – to cover the remaining 15 km (9 miles) to the park headquarters. Forest walks are easily organised on the spot; entrance costs are a reasonable US$50 per 24 hours.

Map on pages 196–197

Katavi National Park

Covering about 5,000 sq. km (1,931 sq. miles), **Katavi National Park ❷⓿** is the most inaccessible and untrammelled of Tanzania's major savanna reserves. It is also inexplicably underrated, offering an undiluted bush experience that's increasingly precious in these days of pre-packaged safaris and over-orchestrated private game lodges.

During the latter part of the dry season, when the Kavuu River and associated tributaries form the only source of water for miles around, the game viewing can be little short of astounding. Thousand-strong herds of buffalo are a daily sight, the park's notoriously aggressive elephants lurk round every other corner, and concentrations of hundreds of hippo huddle tightly in any suitably deep pool. This is one of the few remaining game reserves anywhere in Africa where you can expect to encounter more lions that you will other visitors.

The only comfortable way to see Katavi – short of driving a private vehicle halfway across Tanzania – is by charter package to one of a handful of seasonal tented camps. For genuinely adventurous travellers, there is the option of catching a train from Tabora to Mpanda, then a local bus along the 35-km (22-mile) road to the park headquarters at Sitalike, where modest accommodation can be found, and four-wheel-drive vehicles are available at US$100 per day.

Katavi is best avoided from November to April, when game disperses, roads are impassable, and the heat and insect activity are insufferable. Game viewing is good in May and June, better still from August to October.

LEFT: doum palms a sunset, Katavi National Park.

The Chimps of Lake Tanganyika

Lakeshore Gombe Stream and Mahale Mountain national parks are indubitably the best places in the world to track chimpanzees in their natural environment. Even so, Tanzania cannot be regarded as a major chimpanzee stronghold; its estimated total of 1,500–2,000 chimps – roughly half resident in Mahale, another 100 or so in Gombe – represents less than 1 percent of the global population. Which only makes Lake Tanganyika's pre-eminence in almost every aspect of contemporary chimpanzee research and conservation more remarkable.

The reason can be summed up in two words: Jane Goodall. In July 1960, this academically unqualified (at that time) young Englishwoman arrived at Gombe Stream to initiate what has become the world's longest-running – and arguably most ground-breaking – study of any wild animal population.

Goodall's pioneering research cannot be summarised in a few sentences; her absorbing books are requisite reading for anybody heading to Gombe or Mahale. Perhaps the most significant of her early observations, however, related to the modes of behaviour thought until then to distinguish *Homo sapiens* from other living creatures – for example, the manipulation of twigs to "fish" termites and ants from their burrows; inter-community warfare; the methodical hunting of other primates; and even an orchestrated campaign of cannibalism.

Goodall's work was enhanced by a parallel project in Mahale Mountains, instigated in 1965 by the Japanese primatologist Junichiro Itani. Comparative studies have revealed the fascinating cultural differences in chimp behaviour. For instance, although the palm nut forms a major part of the diet of the Gombe chimps, it is never eaten at Mahale. Up to 40 percent of plants available in both reserves are eaten by one population but not the other.

Chimpanzees are related more closely to humans than to any other living creature. They live in large territorial communities, within which different individuals move around in smaller sub-groups, which can change on a daily basis. Every community is headed by an alpha male, whose dominance is often achieved by the intelligent manipulation of his fellows rather than through brute strength. Male chimps seldom leave their ancestral community, but females regularly migrate outside them.

There are three communities at Gombe, with the largest being Kasekela, the focus of Goodall's studies. Of the 15 communities in Mahale Mountains, the 100-strong Mimikire community is the most habituated, and the one that tourists will normally encounter.

Chimp tracking can be undertaken all year, but the late dry season – July to October – has several advantages: the steep slopes are less treacherous underfoot, and the chimps tend to stick to lower, more accessible altitudes. Of the two reserves, Mahale has better facilities for up-market tourists, and offers a more holistic wilderness experience, while Gombe is more accessible and – despite the higher daily park fee – is a bit more affordable to budget travellers. ❑

RIGHT: chimps are more closely related to humans than any other living creature.

CENTRAL TANZANIA

Not many visitors travel to Tanzania's barren heartland,
but there is some good birdwatching to be had
in the lakes around Mt Hanang

Tanzania's sparsely populated and drought-prone central plateau, all red-dirt plains and mean acacia scrub studded with boulders the size of mountains, does possess a certain austere beauty. Realistically, however, a combination of poor roads, lousy buses, long distances and relatively meagre travel pickings make it difficult to recommend the region wholeheartedly, even to those with an express interest in getting away from the established tourist trails. The only exception to the above is the 500-km (300-mile) road connecting Dodoma to Arusha, where the rock art of Kondoa and forested slopes of Mt Hanang head a list of noteworthy and relatively accessible sites that are unheard of by most local tour operators, let alone travellers. Otherwise, the small proportion of tourists who do travel across central Tanzania are almost without fail putting miles behind them en route from the coast to one of the great western lakes.

With this goal in mind, the only land transport worth contemplating is the 1,500-km (930-mile) German-built railway line connecting Dar es Salaam to Kigoma, Mwanza and Mpanda. Moderately comfortable rather than luxurious – even the first-class sleeping carriages have seen better days – this remains one of Africa's great train journeys, a leisurely two-day chug through Tanzania's barren heartland, the open horizons enlivened by sporadic patches of forest and swamp on the approach to Kigoma. Fascinating, too, to watch how torpid small towns spring into entrepreneurial life as the train pulls in and the hungry passengers spill out, to mill around rows of stalls selling grilled kebabs, chicken stews, and the local staples of rice and ugali (maize porridge).

Lake Babati

Situated on the outskirts of the small market town of Babati, **Lake Babati** practically laps the western verge of the Arusha road 100 km (60 miles) north of Kondoa. The papyrus-fringed lakeshore, encircled by low mountains, attracts a fair variety of waterbirds – orderly flotillas of white pelicans, eagle-eyed herons and egrets, and sweeping spoonbills and yellow-billed storks. Birds are easily seen on foot, but the best way to locate a few of the lake's prodigious hippo is to pay a small fee to be taken out on a boat by one of the local fisherman. This can be arranged informally at the lakeshore, or through the offices of Kahembe Enterprises, a Babati-based company that supervises one of Tanzania's more interesting community tourist projects, designed in collaboration

LEFT: impalas on the move.

Map on pages 196–197

with the national tourist board and a Dutch development agency. Among the excursions organised by this project are overnight cultural trips to the rustic *bomas* of the various nomadic pastoralists that inhabit this part of the ridge: the Barabaig, the Iraqw, the Bulu and others.

Mt Hanang

The focal point of the Babati ecotourism project is the 3,417-metre (11,211-ft) high **Mt Hanang ㉑**, an extinct volcanic that towers like a miniature, snow-free Kilimanjaro above the surrounding flat plains, visible from hundreds of kilometres away on a clear day. The third-tallest mountain in Tanzania, Hanang can be climbed over a very long day – fit hikers will need a minimum of 12 hours for the round trip – or, more realistically, as an overnight hike, sleeping in caves or a tent.

Experienced and properly equipped independent travellers could arrange a hike from the small town of Katesh, which lies at the southern base of the mountain, 50 km (30 miles) from Babati along the Singida road. It is safer, however, to arrange a package through Kahembe Enterprises, whose guides speak English and have vast experience of the mountain. Either way, because Hanang lies outside the national-park system, hikes are light on the pocket in comparison to the Kilimanjaro and Meru climbs.

The Hanang area is also notable for its many lakes. The saline **Lake Balangida**, set at the base of the Rift Valley escarpment immediately north of Hanang, less than an hour's drive from Katesh via Giting, attracts large flocks of waders and flamingos when full, and is reduced to a shimmering white salt flat in years of low rainfall. Roughly 60 km (37 miles) northwest of Katesh, reached via a good dirt road, **Lake Basotu** is an attractive freshwater body where traditionally dressed Barabaig and Bulu pastoralists still bring their cattle to drink. Fringed by the small town of Basuto, this lake harbours large numbers of hippo, and a fabulous variety of birds, including vociferous breeding colonies of pink-backed pelican, reed cormorant and various herons.

The Barabaig are Nilotic-speaking pastoralists who arrived in their present homeland at least 500 years ago. In common with most other pastoralist societies, they measure wealth in terms of livestock and children, and shun centralised leadership. The main social unit is the family stockade, inhabited by a patriarch, his harem of wives, and their offspring.

Staunch traditionalists, the Barabaig refused to be co-opted into the colonial migrant-labour system, ignored former President Nyerere's attempts to outlaw their traditional clothing, and have no time for exotic religions (less than 1 percent of the population practises Christianity or Islam). Most Barabaig women still wear a traditional ochre-dyed, bead-studded hide dress, while men drape dyed cotton cloths over their shoulders and waist.

Where the road from Katesh reaches the southern tip of Lake Basuto, Lake Gida Monyot is sunk within a small volcanic crater, invisible from the road, but only two minutes' walk away. ❑

Map
n pages
96–197

THE SOUTHERN HIGHWAY

*The huge Selous Game Reserve remains relatively unknown to
visitors, yet its still undisturbed wilderness contains some
of Africa's biggest populations of large mammals*

The **Selous Game Reserve** ㉒ exists
on a barely comprehensible scale.
Covering 50,000 sq. km (19,300 sq.
miles), it is Africa's largest protected area:
50 percent larger than Switzerland, situated at the core of a 155,000-sq.-km
(59,800-sq.-mile) cross-border ecosystem
traversed by some of the world's greatest
remaining herds of buffalo (150,000), elephant (65,000), hippo (40,000) and sable
antelope (8,000). And yet such statistics,
thrown about glibly by tour operators,
flatter Selous to the point of deceit.

The life-sustaining waters of the **Rufiji
River** divide this semi-arid wilderness
into two wildly disproportionate sectors:
an immense and practically impenetrable
southern block used exclusively by commercial hunting concerns, and a more
compact northern circuit – about 10 percent of the Selous's total area – dedicated
to less bloodthirsty forms of tourism.
Selous is a fine game reserve; the statistics are so much hyperbole.

Along the Rufiji River

The divisive Rufiji, its constantly mutat-
ing course spilling into a labyrinth of intimate, lushly vegetated channels and open
lakes, defines the Selous experience.
Sandbanks are lined with outsized crocodiles, yellow-billed storks and spoonbills
scoop methodically through the shallows
while pied kingfishers hover overhead,
African skimmers fly low across the surface dipping their bright red beaks into
the water, and carmine bee-eaters swirl in
a crimson cloud around the exposed mud
banks in which they breed. Becalmed
channels flow northward from the main
river, past swampy islets where elephants
browse and waterbuck graze. And, in the
evening hippos enter into earnest grunting debate, and a red-coal sun sinks
behind a neat row of borassus palms – the
quintessential African river scene.

A network of game-viewing roads connects the lakes, where zebra, giraffe and
various antelope slake their thirst during the
dry season. The odds of seeing a lion kill
here are unusually high. In recent decades,
wild dog populations elsewhere in Africa
have gone into rapid decline: the estimated
1,300 individuals that roam the Selous
account for 20 percent of the free-ranging
global population, exceeding that of any
other African country.

The Selous (pronounced "Seloo") is
named after Capt. Frederick Courtney
Selous, the legendary game hunter and
writer who was killed by German sniper
fire near the Rufiji during World War I. A
year after the war ended, P.H. Lamb
trekked to the "wild inhospitable district"

LEFT: the rare
African wild
dog in Ruaha
National Park.
RIGHT: black-
headed heron.

where a plain wooden cross marked Selous's grave, and predicted that "the object of most people who have seen it will be to avoid it carefully in the future". Inherently, the Selous remains as wild and inhospitable today as it was in 1919. By comparison to the more famous Serengeti, it is also free of safari traffic, visited by a mere 1 percent of tourists to Tanzania.

If Lamb were alive today he would doubtless have revised his gloomy prediction had he been staying in one of the six exclusive tourist lodges that scatter the Selous now. With their combined bed space less than that of many individual hotels along the Northern Circuit, these lodges are justifiably known for their luxurious accommodation, personalised service and integrated bush atmosphere.

Guided game walks add vivid immediacy to exploring the Selous: the thrill of emerging from a riverine thicket onto a plain where a surprised elephant bull trumpets a warning, or a herd of buffalos stare down the oddly clad intruders.

Not exciting enough? Then take things one step further and arrange to spend a night or two at a private fly-camp, separated from the pristine night sky by a transparent drape of mosquito netting. As hippos and elephants tread gingerly past the makeshift tent, sleep might not come easily, but this primal African nocturnal experience will never be forgotten.

Ruaha National Park

The Selous features prominently in many seasoned African travellers' top-ten wilderness areas, but ask a Tanzania-based wildlife lover what is their favourite game reserve, and odds are that the reply will be **Ruaha National Park** ㉓. Like the Selous, this rugged 10,300-sq.-km (4,000-sq.-mile) tract of wilderness forms the core of a much vaster ecosystem, extending into half-a-dozen other protected areas. Characterised by parched slopes covered in dense brachystegia woodland, and wide open baobab-studded plains, Ruaha fulfils every expectation of untram-

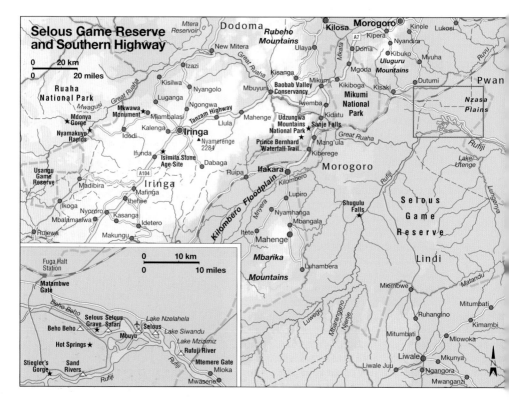

**Map
n pages
96–197**

melled Africa, no less so because its 400-km (250-mile) road circuit has only two small lodges – even the Selous seems crowded by comparison.

Game-viewing roads follow the perennial Great Ruaha River and seasonal Mwagusi River through thick riparian forest frequented by one of Africa's densest elephant populations. Cheetahs pace the open savanna, which is grazed upon by herds of buffalo stretching to the horizon, as well as the usual cast of ungulates: impala, waterbuck, zebra and Grant's gazelle. The woodland, transitional to the eastern savanna and southern miombo biomes, is the most southerly haunt of the shy striped hyena and delicate lesser kudu, as well as two endemic birds: the black-collared lovebird and ashy starling. Ruaha also harbours a trio of lovely antelope that are rare in northern Tanzania: the imposingly horned greater kudu and sleekly handsome sable and roan antelope. Near the Mwagusi River, prides of 20-plus lion reduce a freshly killed buffalo or zebra to skin and bone in a couple of hours.

Ruaha, like Selous, is an important refuge for the endangered African wild dog, which often make their dens in the Mwagusi area over June and July. Fine game viewing indeed, and yet if Ruaha leaves one overwhelming impression, it is the sense of solitude associated with driving for hours through untamed Africa without encountering another human soul.

Selous and Ruaha are linked to each other, and to Dar es Salaam, by a daily scheduled flight, and most tourists who visit one or both reserves fly in from Dar es Salaam. Yet the two reserves also form part of a looser road circuit connected by the **Tanzam Highway** – the endless strip of asphalt that runs southwest from Dar es Salaam, via Morogoro and Iringa, to the Zambian capital of Lusaka (Tanzam being an abbreviation of Tanzania-Zambia). The Selous can be reached from Morogoro along the rough 120-km (75-mile) Matombo Road (named for a buxom pair of peaks known as *Matombo* – "breasts") while a fair 100-km (60-mile) dirt road runs west from Iringa to the main entrance gate of Ruaha.

Bypassed by the Tanzam Highway, 200 km (120 miles) out of Dar es Salaam, **Morogoro** (population 250,000) is a lively town transformed into one of the prettiest cities in Tanzania by the **Uluguru Mountains**, which rise to a majestic 2,635 metres (8,645 ft) on the southern horizon. Clear freshwater streams tumble down the forested slopes of the Uluguru to provide generous sustenance to the local agricultural community, a vital source of fresh produce for Dar es Salaam. Neat, compact and energetic, Morogoro makes for an agreeable, even enervating, stopover, and yet it's somehow surprising to learn that this rapidly growing town is Tanzania's largest landlocked urban centre, surpassed in population only by the ports of Dar es Salaam, Zanzibar and Mwanza.

A pretty, whitewashed, German *boma* and mildly pompous railway station stand as isolated reminders of Morogoro's colonial roots, while the packed central market, stalls laden with succulent papayas, sweet pineapples and candelabras of bright-yellow bananas, reflects its modern agricultural base. A quick 30-minute stroll out of town leads to the **Rock Garden Resort**, a botanical garden situated on the lower slopes of the Uluguru.

The Uluguru Mountains

For a more ambitious day walk, Morningside Camp is a disused German research station set on the higher slopes, amid patches of natural forest and pretty cascades. Morningside is difficult to locate without a local guide – available from the **Uluguru Mountains Biodiversity and Conservation Project** (UMBCP) office in Pamba House, which also arranges cultural visits to **Nugutu**, famed locally for its skilled Luguru craftsmen and powerful traditional healer. The UMBCP office is also the best place to enquire about travel deeper into the Uluguru Mountains, a vast Eastern Arc range inhabited by dedicated Luguru agriculturists who work their fertile, well-watered smallholdings throughout the year. Between the cultivated fields, about

500 sq. km (200 sq. miles) of indigenous forest harbours black-and-white colobus monkey and various small antelope – as well as 40 vascular plants, ten reptile and amphibian species, and more than 100 invertebrate species found nowhere else in the world. The secretive Uluguru bush shrike, a striking canary-yellow bird with a jet-black cap, is one of three endemics to tantalise ornithologists. At present, the forests of the Uluguru are realistically explored only from **Nyandira**, a humble Luguru village situated 25 km (16 miles) from the Tanzam Highway along a four-wheel-drive-only road that forks to the left, 20 km (12 miles) south of Morogoro.

Mikumi National Park

Unprepared travellers driving southwest along the Tanzam Highway towards the town of **Mikumi** (120 km/75 miles from Morogoro) are frequently taken aback at the sight of an elephant emerging from the bush or a herd of buffalos masticating lazily on the verge. This is one of the few **BELOW:** an arid section of Ruaha National Park.

Map
n pages
96–197

LOW:
uffalo in
Kumi
tional Park.

trunk routes in Africa to cut through the heart of a major game reserve, and indeed the **Mikumi National Park** ❷ directly owes its protected status to the construction of the Tanzam Highway, which opened up the formerly remote area to poachers. Gazetted in 1964 and later expanded to share a border with the Selous, Mikumi is the fourth-largest national park in Tanzania, extending over 3,230 sq. km (1,247 sq. miles). Popular with expatriate weekenders, Mikumi has never caught on amongst international visitors.

The extensive Mkata Floodplain, crossed by a 60-km (37-mile) road loop running northwest of the Tanzam Highway, feels like a compressed replica of the Serengeti, its seasonally inundated grassland hosting impressive herds of zebra, wildebeest, buffalo, eland and impala. Giraffes lope preposterously through stands of flat-topped acacias, elephants maintain a perpetual presence at the waterholes below Kikoboga Lodge, and the majestic greater kudu and sable antelope skulk in the thick brachystegia woodland. Mikumi's reputation for wild dog has dipped since the resident pack migrated to the Selous in the late 1990s, but lions and hyenas are reliably heard serenading the night sky.

Mikumi town, on the western border of the national park, was founded in 1914 and named after the borassus palms that flourished in the vicinity. Sadly, no palm groves grace Mikumi today: this scruffy little town, whose shape is defined by the highway along which it seems to creep further with each passing year, has all the aesthetic appeal of an overgrown truck stop. However, it is a popular budget base from which to explore the national park, and it also lies at the junction of the approach road – signposted left – to the marvellous Udzungwa Mountains.

Udzungwa Mountains

The road to Udzungwa runs south from Mikumi for a freshly surfaced 37 km (23 miles), before crossing the white-water rush of the Great Ruaha River to enter the

lively, small town of Kidatu. Another 25 km (16 miles) of rutted road leads south to the overgrown village of Mang'ula, at the entrance gate to **Udzungwa Mountains National Park** ㉕. The 1,900-sq.-km (730-sq.-mile) park protects the most extensive of the Eastern Arc ranges, a craggy, forest-swathed massif that erupted from the plains more than 100 million years ago.

The undemanding self-guided Prince Bernhard Waterfall Trail, named after the Dutch royal who opened the park in 1992, provides a lovely introduction to the magic of Udzungwa's forests. Turkey-sized trumpeter hornbills flap heavily through the canopy, the exquisite green-headed oriole betrays its presence with a repetitive song, pairs of forest weaver flit restlessly through the mid-strata, and dozens of different butterfly species flutter above the shadowy forest floor.

Lucky visitors may catch a glimpse of a shy suni crossing the forest path, or a chequered elephant shrew rummaging its elongated nose through the litter. Com-mon around the waterfall, the endangered Uhehe red colobus is distinguished from the ubiquitous blue monkey by its translucent orange fringe.

A longer guided hike leads from the entrance gate to **Sanje Falls**, which plunge 300 metres (980 ft) down the escarpment in three discrete stages. It was here, in 1979, that two ecologists heard a whooping call similar to that of a mangabey, a West African monkey not known to occur within a 1,000-km (620-mile) radius of Udzungwa. Initially, the ecologists thought they were victims of a prank, but their guide told them that an orphaned monkey of the type that made the call was being tended at Sanje village on the main road to Mikumi. It turned out to be a new species: the Sanje crested mangabey, which, in 2000, achieved the dubious distinction of being the sole East African species on a list of the world's 25 most threatened primates, compiled by the IUCN Primate Specialist Group.

Udzungwa, a contender for East Africa's most important biodiversity hotspot, yields

BELOW: red-billed hornbill

Map
on pages
196–197

previously undescribed species with sensational regularity. In 1991, for instance, biologists working in western Udzungwa noticed a pair of strange feet floating in their "chicken stew". Upon enquiry, they were shown a snared specimen of a wildfowl that more closely resembles the Asian hill partridge than it does any African bird. Named the Udzungwa partridge, this localised endemic underscores the great antiquity of the Eastern Arc forests – the sole living representative of a lineage dating back 15 million years to when Africa and Asia were linked by a forest belt along the Arabian coastline.

Two recent mammalian discoveries have again made scientific headlines. In 2002, the first-ever photograph of Lowe's servaline genet, taken by a trip wire in the forests of Udzungwa, confirmed the taxonomic validity of a race of carnivore described on the basis of a solitary pelt collected by Willoughby Lowe in 1932. Even more sensational, in early 2005, was the announcement of the simultaneous discovery of a new monkey species by Caroline Erhardt in Udzungwa and Tim Davenport on the Kitulo Plateau and Mount Rungwe. Dubbed the highland mangabey (*Lophocebus kipunji*), this presumed Tanzania endemic has a thick brown coat, a black face and a distinctive white lower tail, and has made its way immediately onto the endangered species list, with the total population unlikely to exceed 1,000.

Kilombero Floodplain

Bisected by the Umena River some 40 km (25 miles) south of Mang'ula, the unfocussed small town of **Ifakara** wouldn't win any beauty contests. Continue 5 km (3 miles) south of Ifakara along the Mahenge Road, and you'll reach the **Kilombero River**, a wide and muddy tributary of the Rufiji crossed by a regular motor ferry until April 2002, when the boat capsized, claiming the lives of 100 passengers. The 4,000-sq.-km (1,544-sq.-mile) **Kilombero Floodplain**, an unprotected extension of the Selous ecosystem, is East Africa's largest seasonal wetland, home to 50,000 puku antelope (70 percent of the global population) and attracting up

to 5,000 elephants in the dry season. The area has thrown up three previously undescribed bird species since 1986. Much of the floodplain is inaccessible to all but self-sufficient four-wheel-drive expeditions, but hippos, and, on occasion, the endemic birds, can be observed near the ferry crossing. For a small fee, the dugout-canoe owners will carry travellers upstream in search of elephant and buffalo.

Situated 22 km (14 miles) southwest of Iringa along the Tanzam Highway, the **Isimila Stone Age Site** is a dry watercourse incised through sequential layers of sediment deposited by a lake which dried up 60,000 years ago. The site museum displays tools and weapons used by Stone Age hunter-gatherers, as well as the fossilised remains of the creatures they preyed upon: buffalo-sized swine, giraffe-like ungulates with huge antlers, and gargantuan hippos with projecting eyes. Ten minute's stroll from the museum, a deeper gorge is dotted with a mini-Arizona of tall sandstone pillars carved by an extinct river. ❑

Map
on pages
196–197

SOUTHERN HIGHLANDS AND THE SOUTH COAST

The southern highlands, rich in wildlife and scenery, are tough to travel but can be combined with a trip to the south-coast havens of Zanzibar and Pemba

Tanzania's remote southern highlands climb steeply from the sultry northern shore of Lake Nyasa in a spectacular montane crescent, shaped by the same ongoing tectonic violence that wrenched open the Rift Valley around Nyasa many millions of years ago. Studded with dormant volcanic peaks, mysterious crater lakes, wild tracts of indigenous forest, pretty waterfalls and haunting volcanic rock formations, the southern highlands, seldom visited by tourists, are rich in offbeat pickings for devoted hikers and keen natural historians.

The urban pulse of this lovely region is **Mbeya ㉖**, Tanzania's fifth-largest city: a neat, bustling, well-equipped and climatically pleasing base from which to explore the highlands, yet curiously unmemorable in itself. The **Sisi Kwa Sisi Tourism Office** (corner of School Street and Mbalizi Road; tel: 0741-463471; email: sisikwasisitours@ hotmail.com) offers travel advice and inexpensive guided tours to all accessible sites of interest in the area. Their services are virtually essential for hikes on Ngosi, Rungwe and the Kitulo Plateau.

The Mbeya Range, noted for its wet-season floral displays of orchids and proteas, rises above central Mbeya to the 2,656-metre (8,714-ft) **Loleza Peak**, which can be ascended in two hours along a footpath starting on Hospital Hill Road. The more challenging 2,827-metre (9,275-ft) **Mbeya Peak** is more easily climbed from the out-of-town Utengule Country Hotel (tel: 065 560100).

Lake Rukwa

The roads around **Chunya** offer views across **Lake Rukwa ㉗**, a vast alkaline sump set in an inhospitable arm of the Rift Valley, all but bereft of human habitation. The Rukwa floodplain supports plentiful game, including the localised puku antelope and high densities of hippos and crocodiles, as well as incredible concentrations of waterbirds. Rukwa is a genuine wilderness, and any expedition there should be self-sufficient in spare motor parts, fuel, food, drinking water and camping equipment. From Chunya, a 2-hour drive northwest through Saza and Mbangala leads to the fluctuating lakeshore, as does a rough track from Galula Mission to Totoe. A third approach crosses the Ufipa Plateau west of Sumbawanga (on the Tunduma–Mpanda road).

From Chimala, a small town straddling the Tanzam Highway 78 km (48 miles) east

of Mbeya, a thrillingly scenic southbound dirt road navigates 57 hairpin bends en route to Matamba, gateway town to the proposed 1,300-sq.-km (502-sq.-mile) **Kitulo Plateau National Park**.

Locals refer to Kitulo as Bustani ya Mungu (God's Garden), an apt name for what is to be the first national park in East Africa gazetted primarily for its amazing floral wealth. The plateau is best visited between November and May, when the rains transform the grassland into a dazzling floral kaleidoscope. Bright orange red-hot pokers reach skyward from the crags above a carpet of multi-hued lilies, asters, geraniums and orchids punctuated by otherworldly giant lobelias and pretty protea shrubs.

Large mammals are scarce, but blue swallow, Denham's bustard and mountain marsh widow top a long list of endangered or localised birds and a recently discovered monkey, the highland mangabey – *(see pages 241 and 245)* – is resident in the forests.

The Kitulo Plateau is most easily visited from Chimala, but a second, rougher approach road from Isongole (in the Poroto Mountains) is scheduled for repair once the national park is formally gazetted.

The Poroto Mountains

A fast, surfaced 140-km (87-mile) road runs southeast from Mbeya to Kyela (near Lake Nyasa), passing for most of its length through the scenic Poroto Mountains. The highlight of the Poroto region is **Ngosi Crater Lake**, brooding at the base of a 300-metre (980-ft) deep volcanic caldera. Ngosi's brackish green waters reputedly provide refuge to an enormous serpentine monster, which is able to change colour to disguise or reveal itself according to mood – disappointingly, it's invariably in camouflage mode when travellers come past. Still, the extensive evergreen and bamboo forests around the lake harbour a wealth of less-elusive birds and monkeys, plus an endemic species of three-horned chameleon.

The turn-off to Ngosi is signposted

BELOW: typical forest flora.

Map
on pages
196–197

from Isongole on the main Mbeya–Kyela road. You can drive the first 5 km (3 miles) from the junction, but the final 2-hour ascent to the crater rim is for pedestrians only. Towering over the northern horizon of Isongole, the 2,960-metre (9,711-ft) **Rungwe Volcano** last erupted a century ago, though a spate of tremors in early 2001 may hint at a fresh bout of natural fireworks in the near future.

Rungwe's uninhabited higher slopes, protected within a forest reserve, are home to troops of acrobatic black-and-white colobus monkeys; they also form an important stronghold for the rare Abbott's duiker and recently discovered highland mangabey, while the moorland above around 2,500 metres (8,200 ft) is dotted with colourful ground orchids and protea scrubs. During the dry season, a reasonably fit person should be able to climb to the peak and back within a day. The easiest ascent is from Kagera Estate Timber Camp, set on the northern footslopes 18 km (11 miles) by road from Isongole.

Lake Nyasa

The climatic contrast between the breezy Poroto highlands and **Lake Nyasa 28**, set in the Rift Valley floor at an altitude of 437 metres (1,434 ft), could hardly be more dramatic. Nor, for that matter, could Lake Nyasa itself.

Known as Lake Malawi south of the Malawian border, Nyasa runs for 585 km (364 miles) through a stretch of the Rift Valley hemmed in by a sheer escarpment rising sharply from the shore. The lake's trademark sandy beaches, studded with giant baobabs and whispering palms, resonate with the high eerie cry of the fish eagle, while the startlingly clear turquoise water supports the world's greatest diversity of freshwater fish.

Lyulilo, east of Matema, is the site of a famous Saturday pottery market, while the nearby **Pango Cave** was an important sacrificial site before the missionaries arrived. Thirty minutes from Matema by local canoe, the village of **Ikombe** is the main source of the region's distinctive

BELOW:
dugout canoes
on Matema
beach,
Lake Nyasa.

pale Kisi pottery, sold at Lyulilo for distribution all around the country. A canoe is also the best way to reach the swampy **Lufirio River mouth**, 3 km (2 miles) west of Matema, which offers excellent birdwatching, crocodiles and hippos.

The south coast

With its sticky tropical atmosphere, and generous quota of postcard-perfect beaches and atmospherically timeworn ports, the 600-km (370-mile) coastline that stretches from Dar es Salaam south to the Mozambiquan border shares most of the elements that have made Zanzibar such a popular post-safari chill-out destination with many travellers. What it lacks, however, is any semblance of a conventional tourist infrastructure.

The roads, almost without exception, are bumpy dustbowls that transform into impassable quagmires at the height of the rains. What's more, aside from Mafia Island (which has few travel links to the facing mainland), it would be positively

libellous to advertise any hostelry more than an hour's drive south of Dar es Salaam as an idyllic beach resort.

Mafia excepted, the south coast is about as well suited to package holidays as it would be to dedicated ski parties, but the region has much to recommend it to travellers seeking genuine insight into Swahili culture past and present.

It is not merely that the area's assortment of ruined and living settlements collectively provide a cross-section of coastal trade and history over the past millennium. There is, too, a pervasive aura of cultural continuity hanging over this forgotten corner of Tanzania, the feeling that while its front foot stretches gamely towards the future, the other one remains firmly planted at the cusp of the 19th and 20th centuries.

The Mafia archipelago

Linked to Dar es Salaam by regular flights, Mafia is more realistically viewed as a stand-alone up-market destination than as an extension of the rough-and-ready travel circuit on the south coast.

The archipelago, which lies some 20 km (12 miles) east of the Rufiji River Delta, is comprised of the 50-km (30-mile) long **Mafia Island ㉙** as well as a dozen smaller islets and numerous coral outcrops. Mafia is East Africa's premier diving, snorkelling and game-fishing venue. The extensive offshore reefs, protected within an 820-sq.-km (317-sq.-mile) **marine park**, are comprised of 50 genera of coral, and harbour 400 species of fish. Mafia is a noted breeding ground for giant turtles which lay their eggs on the white coral sands. Recommended for their colourful coral formations and kaleidoscopic shoals of small reef fish are the **Kinasi Wall** and adjoining **Chole Wall**, near the outlet of Chole Bay, while a 12-metre (40-ft) coral pinnacle within the bay is a reliable place for sighting giant cod and moray eels. Further afield, sharks and giant tuna haunt the **Dindini North Wall** and **Forbes Bay** on the main barrier reef. Snorkellers are also well catered for here: the two larger coral islets in Kinasi Pass host a volume and variety of reef fish that compares favourably with any site in East Africa. ❏

Map on pages 196–197

LEFT: bringing home the catch, off Kinasi Camp.

Diving in Zanzibar and Pemba

The Zanzibar archipelago and Mafia Island, to the south, have an excellent combination of shallow water reefs for less-experienced divers and high walls and deep channels for the more adventurous. Both the soft and hard corals are in relatively prime condition, despite El Niño, and the variety of reef fish and larger pelagics is as good as anywhere. In Pemba and Mafia you will have the site to yourself, and while you won't find many sharks, large rays, turtles, whale sharks and whales are wonderful compensations.

Zanzibar Island (Unguja) is the largest of the islands but has the least impressive diving. Two main areas are worth consideration. There are 4 or 5 smallish reefs about 30 minutes from Stone Town where the coral is in good condition but marine life is limited. With nothing deeper than 20 metres (66 ft) and often nothing bigger than a parrot fish, they are fine for a warm-up dive. The highlight is a wreck, thought to be the *Pegasus*, which lies 40 metres (131 ft) down, a 15-minute speedboat ride from town. No coral has developed but there are huge shoals of barracuda and jacks, and what remains of the deck is littered with lion fish. Another recommended site is the Boribu reef, at 15 metres (49 ft).

Mnemba Atoll, some 5 km (3 miles) off the northeast coast, near Matemwe, offers enough variety for two or three days. The reef has a range of good inner and outer wall dives, and some beautiful coral gardens. The best diving is on the south side where big currents can afford great drift dives. The hard corals are in excellent condition and you will find honeycomb, pillar and brain, clouded with shoals of sergeant fish, fusiliers and wrasse. The island is now a marine sanctuary. The highlight of the year is when the migrating whale sharks stop over in about March.

Pemba has more interesting, varied and spectacular diving than anywhere else in East Africa. The coastline is dotted with tiny, uninhabited islands surrounded by almost unlimited dive sites. There is excellent drift diving along the big walls, and some huge independent *bommies* teeming with reef fish.

Njao Gap in the north hosts table-top coral, sea whips and gorgonian sea fans with giant groupers, Napoleon wrasse, titan trigger-fish and regular darting pelagics wahoo, jacks and giant trevally. In the south, **Mesali Island** is the coral jewel in the crown, with shallow water reefs in pristine condition so even snorkellers can indulge. Live aboard enthusiasts should take a trip down the east coast with its strong currents, large pelagics, fantastic soft corals and the likelihood of large shoals of hammerhead sharks. At the right times of year, you can encounter schools of pilot whales and the awesome humpbacks.

At **Mafia Island**, 150 km (90 miles) south of Zanzibar, most of the diving is focused around Chole Bay, and from September to March it is possible to dive the walls outside the reef that protect the bay. Finally, the coral gardens, at a maximum of 20 metres (66 ft), provide possibly the best hard corals in East Africa, with brain and stag horn in abundance, and crocodile fish, turtles and striped barracuda milling around amongst the colourful reef fish.   ❑

RIGHT: fine coral, rich marine life and warm Indian Ocean water.

UGANDA

*Regarded by many as Africa's top ornithological destination,
Uganda also has abundant rainforest and growing tourism*

Arriving from the open plains of Tanzania or Kenya, Uganda appears deliriously moist and green. Some 20 percent of the country's surface area consists of open water, notably lakes Victoria, Albert, Kyoga, Edward and George and the Nile River. And its fertile, well-watered volcanic soils support a luxuriant cover of leafy tropical cultivation and verdant rainforest, rising along the eastern border to the jagged peaks of Mt Elgon and in the west to the Virunga Volcanoes and snow-capped Ruwenzoris. The country has an Equatorial location transitional to Africa's eastern, western (and to a lesser extent southern and northern) biomes, for which reason it harbours a biodiversity without parallel in what, by regional standards, is a fairly small country, comparable to the United Kingdom.

Seasoned safarigoers are attracted to Uganda for its abundance of western rainforest species: the charismatic gorilla, which has been habituated for tourist visits in Bwindi and Mgahinga national parks, a substantial chimpanzee population and several forest-dwelling monkeys absent further east. And yet the country also offers visitors a more conventional safari experience, with Queen Elizabeth, Murchison Falls, Kidepo and Lake Mburo national parks supporting a rich savanna fauna including lion, leopard, buffalo, elephant, giraffe, hippo and a variety of antelope.

Uganda is arguably Africa's premier ornithological destination. The smallest of the four African countries whose bird checklist tops the 1,000 mark, a remarkable 400 species are regularly recorded on dedicated two-week birdwatching tours. Of particular note are the roughly 150 west/central African rainforest species found here at the eastern limit of their range, together with 24 Albertine Rift endemics. The papyrus-dwelling shoebill, arguably the most eagerly sought bird in Africa, is nowhere seen so easily as it is in Uganda.

To some, Uganda remains synonymous with Idi Amin, the despotic general who siezed power in 1971 to embark on a murderous eight-year dictatorship that left the country in economic and social tatters. By 1986, when President Yoweri Museveni came to power, the country's plains wildlife had been poached close to oblivion. Since 1990, however, the wildlife in Uganda's four established savanna national parks has recovered to something approaching its pre-Amin highs, while six new national parks have been gazetted to protect rainforest and montane habitats.

Uganda's tourist industry has revived rapidly since this period so that today its national parks and other recognised tourist attractions are serviced by perhaps 30 hotels, lodges and tented camps that bear comparison to their peers in Kenya or Tanzania. ❏

PRECEDING PAGES: the spectacular Murchison Falls plunges some 350 metres (1,150 ft) into the Nile River.
LEFT: tree-climbing lions in the Queen Elizabeth National Park.

KAMPALA, ENTEBBE AND SURROUNDS

If you're using Entebbe airport and want to explore the surrounding area there are plenty of attractions and wildlife to see, either before or after your main safari

Kampala ❶, the modern capital city of Uganda, doesn't hold much promise to natural-history enthusiasts, though the ghoulish marabou storks that construct their large, scruffy nests on street lamps along even the busiest of thoroughfares seldom fail to impress. A more satisfying place to spend a first night in Uganda is Entebbe ❷, situated on the Lake Victoria shore 35 km (20 miles) south of Kampala, and the site of the country's international airport.

A short walk from central Entebbe, the grassy lawns of the Entebbe Botanical Garden, founded in 1902, are interspersed with vine-tangled stands of indigenous forest leading down a reed-lined stretch of lakeshore. The few resilient troops of black-and-white colobus monkey that cling on in this sumptuous suburban retreat are often seen swinging acrobatically through the trees with their white capes and tails flowing behind them. Among the more conspicuous birds is the monstrous black-and-white casqued hornbill, which flocks between trees with its trademark heavy wing flaps, neighing and braying like an airborne donkey. The dazzling great blue and Ross's turacos are also common, while the majestic fish eagle and superficially similar palm-nut vulture perch on branches above the lake.

A few hundred metres from the botanical garden, the Entebbe Wildlife Orphanage & Education Centre plays an important role in local conservation and education, but the experience it offers tourists is essentially that of a zoo – albeit one overrun by wild vervet monkeys and cackling birds. A visit to the orphanage, though recommended, is perhaps best left until the end of a safari, since close-up views of the likes of shoebill or lion in captivity will inevitably dilute the impact of seeing the same creature in the wild.

A pair of white rhinos (hunted to local extinction in 1982) was imported to the orphanage from Kenya in September 2001, for eventual release onto a ranch north of Kampala.

Excursions from Entebbe

A popular excursion from Entebbe is the boat trip across Lake Victoria to Ngamba Island Chimp Sanctuary ❸, established in 1998 in association with the Jane Goodall Trust. This admirable organisation provides refuge to more than 30 orphaned chimps, many of which were confiscated from smugglers. The chimps

LEFT: ground squirrel.

Map on page 253

have the run of the island, with the exception of a small fenced-off section of beachfront reserved for project staff and visitors. Excursions to Ngamba are conducted at feeding time, when the chimps come close to the electrified fence. A more exciting option – comparable in price to gorilla tracking – is to take a guided walk within the chimp enclosure, an activity that often results in the human participants being jumped upon and relieved of any detachable possessions by the chimps. As with the orphanage, and for much the same reason, a visit to Ngamba is arguably best left to the end of a safari.

The **Mabamba Swamp** ❹ to the southwest of Entebbe is one of the most reliable sites in Africa for sighting the shoebill, regarded by many African bird-watchers as the ultimate "tick". Even for those with a limited interest in birds, the shoebill is an impressively bizarre creature: an enormous slate-grey swamp-dweller whose somewhat prehistoric appearance is underscored by an outsized clog-shaped bill adapted to scooping up lungfish from the muddy swamp floor. Mabamba isn't formally developed for tourism, but the local boatmen will take visitors onto the water for a small fee, and are adept at

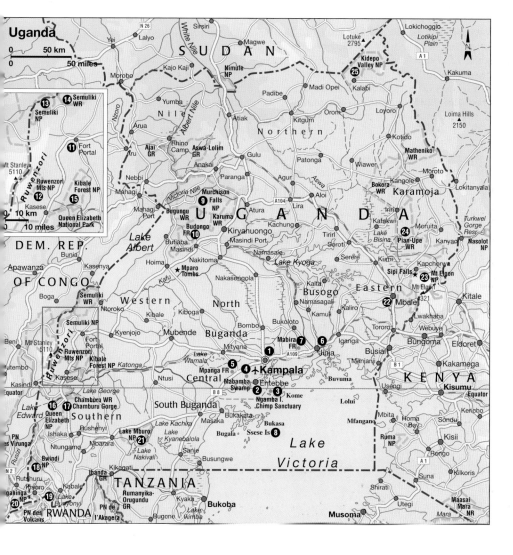

locating shoebills and other localised wetland specials such as pygmy goose, gull-billed tern, white-winged warbler and lesser jacana. The drive from Entebbe to Mabamba takes about one hour. Follow the Kampala Road north for 10 km (6 miles) to Kisubi, turn left onto a dirt road, then after about 25 km (15 miles) turn left again at the traffic roundabout in the small town of Kasanje, from where it's about 13 km (8 miles) to the swamp. Coming from Kampala, a better route entails following the surfaced Masaka road for 30 km (18 miles) to Buyege junction (shortly before Mpigi town), where a left turn leads after 12 km (7 miles) to Kasanje.

An excursion to Mabamba can be followed with a visit to the 45-sq.-km (28-sq.-miles) **Mpanga Forest Reserve ❺**, which flanks the Masaka Road about 3 km (2 miles) past Mpigi town. Gazetted as a forest reserve in the 1950s, Mpanga is serviced today by a low-key community-run *banda* and campsite. Overnight or day visitors are offered a choice of three guided walks, the longest of which leads through the forest to an extensive swamp in which scarce sitatunga antelope are residents. The red-tailed monkey – oddly, the only diurnal primate that occurs in Mpanga – is readily observed, and the forest harbours a huge variety of colourful butterflies. It also provides a good introduction to Uganda's forest birds, with some 180 species recorded, ranging from the vociferous but widespread African grey parrot, blue-breasted kingfisher and black-and-white casqued hornbill to the localised Weyn's weaver and pink-footed puffback.

Jinja and around

Uganda's second-largest city, **Jinja ❻**, lies on the Lake Victoria shore about 80 km (50 miles) east of Kampala along the excellent surfaced road towards the Kenya border. Jinja isn't strictly speaking a wildlife destination, not unless you count the colony of tens of thousands of fruit bats that chatters incessantly in the trees around the golf course. But it is of some

BELOW:
simple *banda*
accommodation
in the Mabira
Forest Reserve

Map on page 253

geographical significance as the site of Ripon Falls, identified by Speke as the source of the Nile in 1863 – and subsequently submerged by a hydroelectric dam. A more in-your-face natural experience (one, again, that admittedly has little to do with wildlife) is a popular grade-five white-water rafting excursion along the Nile, which starts from Bujagali Falls, about 10 km (6 miles) downstream of Jinja.

Situated alongside the Kampala Road some 20 km (12 miles) west of Jinja, the 300 sq. km (186 sq. mile) **Mabira Forest Reserve ❼** has similar facilities to Mpanga Forest – a community-run *banda* and campsite, and several guided day trails. But its biodiversity is much higher than Mpanga's, with more than 200 tree species and a similar variety of butterflies.

The red-tailed monkey, black-and-white colobus and grey-cheeked mangabey are encountered around the camp, as is the pretty blue duiker, and leopard reputedly survive in small numbers.

More than 300 bird species occur in Mabira, with more widespread forest species supplemented by the localised tit hylia (known only in one other East African site), forest wood-hoopoe, Weyn's weaver and Nahan's francolin.

Lake Victoria – the second-largest freshwater body in the world – is a constant but somehow rather peripheral presence as one explores the vicinity of Kampala. An excellent way of seeing more of the lake is to head across to the **Ssese Islands ❽**, a group of 84 forested islands scattered close to the northwestern shore. The largest and most accessible of the islands is Bugala, linked by a motor ferry to Bukakata near Masaka, and serviced by resorts and campsites to suit most tastes and budgets.

The network of roads around the island makes for lovely unstructured rambling – the birdlife and views across the lake to neighbouring islands are fantastic – though large mammals are limited to vervet monkey and (in the swampy southeast) sitatunga and hippo. Another attraction of Bugala is the excellent game fishing for Nile perch. ❏

ELOW: red-iled monkey.

Maps:
Area 253
Park 258

MURCHISON FALLS AND BUDONGO FOREST

The spectacular Murchison Falls compete with the wildlife for best attraction in the national park, and the Budongo Forest Reserve is one of East Africa's most ecologically diverse forests

The 3,840-sq.-km (1,483-sq.-mile) **Murchison Falls National Park ❾** (MFNP) is Uganda's largest protected area, flanking the 100-km (60-mile) stretch of the Victoria Nile that flows downriver from the Karama Falls to Lake Albert. Gazetted in 1952, the national park previously formed part of the Bunyoro Game Reserve, created after a sleeping sickness epidemic forced the authorities to evacuate its human inhabitants in 1910.

Today, MFNP is the core of the greater Murchison Falls Conservation Area, which also incorporates the Bugungu and Karuma wildlife reserves and the Budongo Forest Reserve. Visitor activities in MFNP are focused on Paraa, situated about 10 km (6 miles) west of the 43-metre (141-ft) high waterfall for which the park is named, and the only place downriver of Karama Bridge where vehicles can cross the Nile, using a reliable motor ferry service (hourly from 7am–7pm daily).

The most enduring feature of MFNP is the untrammelled stretch of the Nile that flows through it – a quintessential tropical African river, wide and sluggish, flanked by tall acacia trees and shallow reed banks, and populated by hordes of out-sized crocodiles, snorting hippos and waterbirds. It is easy to believe that the scene here is little changed since 1864, when Murchison Falls was "discovered" by Sir Stanley Baker, the legendary big-game hunter and incidental explorer, who (in what must be the most idiosyncratic honeymoon of the Victorian era) spent years charting the southern course of the Nile in the company of his wife.

MFNP activities

The most popular visitor activity in MFNP is the launch trip that departs from **Paraa ❹** twice daily, travelling upriver to a view-point below Murchison Falls. Spotting vast numbers of hippos and crocs can be taken for granted from the launch, as can buffalo, Defassa waterbuck and Uganda kob, while avian highlights include the African skimmer, Goliath heron and red-throated bee-eater.

Passengers might be entertained by a herd of elephants splashing around in the river, or by a troop of black-and-white colobus monkeys leaping gracefully between the branches of a ficus grove. The truly fortunate might be treated to the sight of a leopard lazing on the riverbank, or a lion pride staring in feline bemusement as the boat floats past. The highly

sought-after shoebill is occasionally seen from the launch, but motorboat trips downriver from Paraa towards Lake Albert offer much better odds – perhaps the best anywhere in Africa – of locating this peculiar bird.

The falls

The launch trip terminates just below **Murchison Falls ❸**, described by Baker as the "greatest waterfall" along the White Nile's 6,700-km (4,160-mile) journey from Lake Victoria to the Mediterranean. In reality, Murchison Falls doesn't so much fall as explode: an immense frothing plume that gathers irresistible momentum as the Nile is expelled, crashing and roaring, through a narrow crack in the Rift Valley escarpment.

It's a thrillingly primal sight as viewed from the launch. Clamber up densely vegetated cliffs to the rocky viewpoint above the falls, and the force of the water is simply devastating and an experience not to be missed.

The history of the park

In the 1960s, MFNP was as busy as any game reserve on the continent: a cinematic slice of African wilderness, serviced by a clutch of popular tourist lodges, and teeming with game. Back then, the park supported Africa's densest concentration of elephants – an incredible 15,000 animals, more than 10 per square mile – while the 1969 aerial census counted 26,500 buffalo, 14,000 hippo, 16,000 Jackson's hartebeest and 30,000 Uganda kob.

Then, in 1971, Idi Amin initiated the 15-year cycle of coup and counter-coup that ground Uganda's economy – and its once-booming tourist industry – to a standstill, and resulted in every tourist lodge in the park being gutted. By 1990, fewer than 250 elephant and 1,000 buffalo remained, and the hartebeest and Uganda kob herds had dwindled to around 3,000 and 6,000 respectively.

Lodges can be resurrected – indeed, there are now three up-market lodges in MFNP, as well as a good budget rest camp.

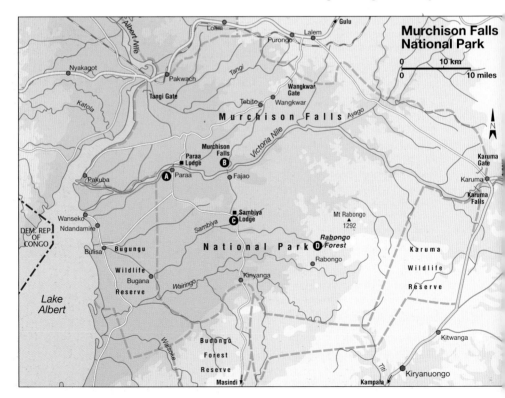

Map
on page
258

So, given the right circumstances, can an ailing tourist industry. But the rhinos that were poached to extinction during the country's years of madness are gone forever, and it will take decades for the other large-mammal populations to be restored to their pre-Amin highs. Still, these things are never as clear-cut as they seem.

Expert opinion is that the park has never been in better ecological shape than it is now, paradoxically a product of the wholesale poaching, which allowed the vegetation to recover from degradation linked to elephant over-population. Furthermore, the relative political stability of the 1990s engendered a sharp reverse in population trends. In 2002, roughly 1,100 elephant, 8,200 buffalo and at least 150 lion were estimated to be resident within MFNP, while numbers of Uganda kob, hartebeest and giraffe have almost certainly doubled, possibly trebled, since 1990. Cheetahs – never before recorded in MFNP – were observed on several occasions in 2002, but have not been seen since then.

BELOW:
storm clouds
approach
the park.

Game-viewing tracks

A fair network of game-viewing tracks runs through the park, though driving through the dense, scrubby woodland to the south of the Nile tends to be rather enervating, due as much to an abundance of tsetse flies – Africa's miniaturised answer to the vampire bat – as to a scarcity of wildlife that makes any sign of mammalian activity cause for minor celebration. By contrast, game drives through the rolling palm-studded grassland to the north of the river – where tsetse flies are mercifully few – can be absolutely superb, evoking some idea of what MFNP was like in its heyday.

The handsome Uganda kob is abundant, while Jackson's hartebeest, a doleful-looking antelope with stumpy spiral horns, often stands sentinel on termite mounds. Oribi are frequently encountered in pairs or trios, freezing at the approach of a vehicle, before sneezing their distinctive alarm call and belting off into the distance. Restricted to the northern sector

of the park, some 500 Rothschild's giraffes constitute what is possibly the last viable breeding population of a race whose markings fall between those of the Maasai and reticulated giraffes of Kenya.

All game-viewing tracks in the north of MFNP converge on a wide grassy peninsula flanked by the Victoria and Albert Niles, an extensive kob breeding ground in which the game viewing ranks with pretty much any African game. Large herds of buffalo, often attended by flocks of insectivorous cattle egret and piacpiac, typically contain a few individuals whose red coloration indicates genetic mixing with the forest buffalo of West Africa. Hippos are often seen out of the water around the delta, while herds of up to 200 elephant congregate at the water from around midday into the late afternoon.

Large ground birds are well represented: Abyssinian ground hornbill, grey crowned crane, saddle-billed stork, Denham's bustard and black-headed lapwing are practically guaranteed, while fortunate visitors might even glimpse a shoebill soaring above the papyrus beds.

The abundance of kob around the delta feeds several prides of lion – most likely to be seen in the early morning along the short anonymous track that connects the Albert Nile and Queen's Tracks. The easiest way to locate lions in this area is by observing the male kobs – listen for their wheezing alarm call, then follow their gaze towards the nearest thicket, and you can be reasonably confident that a lion languishes within. The same track is also frequented by the puppy-like side-striped jackal, and it's probably the best place in East Africa for sightings of the skittish patas monkey, a lanky terrestrial primate primarily associated with the dry West African savanna.

Coming from Kampala, MFNP is reached by following the surfaced Gulu road north for about 170 km (115 miles), then turning left onto the 45-km (27-mile) dirt road to the small town of Masindi. The Gulu road is mostly in good condition, but some stretches are potholed, and

BELOW: the park is one of the best place to spot the rare shoebill.

Maps:
Area 253
Park 258

the dirt road is often slippery after rain, so the drive to Masindi can take up to four hours. Masindi can also be reached from Fort Portal, following an erratic dirt road through Hoima.

From Masindi, two different dirt roads lead to MFNP, branching off from each other immediately north of the town centre, between the police station and the Masindi Hotel. The direct 85-km (50-mile) road between Masindi and Paraa, bypassing **Sambiya Lodge ⓒ**, is the quickest – about 2 hours' drive. More scenic, however, is the 135-km (80-mile) road that heads west towards the Rift Escarpment, then runs north, parallel to the Lake Albert shore for 41 km (25 miles), before veering back east at Bulisa.

Budongo Forest Reserve

The **Rabongo Forest ⓓ** in the remote, tsetse-ridden southeast of MFNP harbours a wide diversity of forest primates, including chimps, but the magnificent 790 sq. km (490 sq. mile) **Budongo Forest Reserve ⑩** to the south of the national park is far more rewarding, and better equipped for tourist visits. Budongo is one of the most ecologically diverse forests in East Africa, with 465 plant, 366 bird and more than 250 butterfly species recorded, along with black-and-white colobus, red-tailed and blue monkey, the sloth-like potto, and the peculiar chequered elephant-shrew.

Gigantic mahogany trees, up to 60 metres (200 ft) high, are a feature of the forest, and their vast buttresses are banged upon, like talking drums, by Budongo's 800 chimpanzees – the largest population in the country.

Kanyiyo Pabidi and the **Busingiro** tourist sites, the two community-run ecotourism sites that operate in Budongo, can easily be visited en route to or from MFNP. Both offer inexpensive camping, *banda* accommodation, chimp tracking and other guided forest walks.

Kanyiyo Pabidi, set alongside the main road between Masindi and Paraa, is the more convenient under most circumstances, though Busingiro – on the Bulisa road – is more accessible using public

transport. Chimp tracking is the most popular activity at both ecotourism sites: the success rate exceeds 90 percent from May to September, when the chimps generally stick close to favoured fruiting trees, but it dips below 50 percent over October to January, when fruit is scarce and the chimps roam more widely.

The ecotourism sites both offer splendid birdwatching, while the so-called Royal Mile, 13 km (8 miles) east of Busingiro, is arguably the single best site for forest birds in Uganda. The main ornithological attraction of Budongo is the presence of some 60 West or Central African bird species known from fewer than five localities in East Africa.

The yellow-footed flycatcher and Puvel's illapopsis (the latter found at Kanyiyo Pabidi only) have been recorded nowhere else in Uganda, while Ituri batis, lemon-bellied crombec, white-thighed hornbill, black-eared ground thrush and chestnut-capped flycatcher are known from just one other forest. ❑

IGHT: a male
'gandan kob.

FORT PORTAL AND ENVIRONS

There is plenty to do around Fort Portal. Its highlights include the Ruwenzori Mountains National Park, the Semuliki Valley and Kibale Forest National Park, noted for its diversity of primates

Sprawling across the northeastern foot-slopes of the cloud-covered Ruwenzori Mountains, **Fort Portal** ⓫ lies at the heart of the Toro Kingdom, a 19th-century offshoot of the older Bunyoro Kingdom. The town and its (now defunct) fort were named in honour of Sir Gerald Portal, the British Consul General of Zanzibar who formalised British protectorship of Uganda in 1892 and died a year later without ever having set foot in Toro. One of the prettiest towns in Uganda, Fort Portal is also an important tourist hub, situated close to three national parks, one wildlife reserve and a number of attractive crater lakes.

Fort Portal lies 320 km (190 miles) west of Kampala, along a road that's surfaced

for all but one-tenth of its length. The main town along this road is Mubende, site of the sacred **Nakayima tree**, a magnificent natural sculpture named for a hereditary line of priestesses who had dwelt in the cavernous hollows of its buttressed trunk for 400 years before being outlawed by the British in 1907. Fort Portal can also be approached directly over one long day from Murchison Falls, following dirt roads through Masindi and Hoima. A worthwhile stop along this route is the traditional **Mparo Tombs**, 3 km (2 miles) outside Hoima, the burial place of the legendary King Kabalega and several other Banyoro dignitaries.

With an afternoon to spare, a pleasant 6-km (4-mile) walk or cycle ride out of Fort Portal, following the Semuliki Road, leads to the **Amabere Caves**, whose name – which means human breasts – refers to a stalactite formation that bears a stronger resemblance to bovine udders. The entrance to the main limestone cave lies behind a small waterfall – it is exhilarating to stand behind the spray – and the fringing riparian forest hosts black-and-white colobus. Two attractive crater lakes, Kigere and Saka, located within easy walking distance of the caves, are reputedly safe for swimming.

The Ruwenzori Mountains

The Ruwenzori Mountains, which run for 110 km (70 miles) along the Democratic Republic of Congo (DRC) border, would dominate the western skyline of Fort Portal were it not that the glacial peaks are almost perpetually shrouded in clouds. Unlike East Africa's other large mountains, the Ruwenzoris are not volcanic in origin, but were formed by a block of rock that was tilted and thrust upwards during the development of the Rift Valley. Six mountains in the range exceed 4,600 metres (15,700 ft) in altitude, with

LEFT: yellow-billed storks are widespread.

Map on page 253

the tallest being the 5,110-metre (16,760-ft) Mt Stanley – the third-highest point in Africa after Kilimanjaro and Mt Kenya. The first expedition to the upper slopes was led in 1906 by Luigi di Savoia, who conquered all of the main peaks.

The cloudy veil that frustrates modern tourists also rendered the Ruwenzoris invisible to the several European explorers who bypassed them prior to 1888, when the glacial peaks were observed by Arthur Jephson and Thomas Parke, members of a cross-continental expedition led by Henry Morton Stanley. Stanley, who claimed personal credit for the discovery, named the mountains the Ruwenzoris and claimed them to be the fabled *Lunae Montes* – Mountains of the Moon – a snow-capped range cited in Ptolemy's *Geography* (*circa* AD 150) as the source of the Nile. The association between the Ruwenzoris and the Mountains of the Moon has endured to this day, but its validity is debatable. Ptolemy's reference to snow-capped peaks was derived third-hand from Indian Ocean traders, and the link with the Nile could have been pure supposition – in which case Kilimanjaro or Mt Kenya would seem a more likely candidate for the *Lunae Montes*.

The Ugandan slopes of the range are protected within the 1,000-sq.-km (390-sq.-mile) **Ruwenzori Mountains National Park ⑫**, which is accessible only to hikers. The forest zone, starting at around 1,800 metres (5,900 ft), supports a varied fauna, including elephant, golden cat, chimpanzee, yellow-backed duiker, giant forest hog and numerous birds endemic to the Albertine Rift, but Angola colobus and blue monkey are the only mammals likely to be seen by hikers.

Spanning altitudes of 3,000–4,500 metres (10,000–15,000 ft), the multi-hued Afro-Alpine heath, studded by desolate stands of giant lobelia and groundsel up to 15 metres (50 ft) tall, possesses a disarmingly otherworldly quality: "a world of fantasy where nothing is real but only a wild and lovely flight of imagination"

RIGHT: fishing boat on Lake Albert.

according to Eric Shipton. Mammals are scarce above the forest zone, but bird-watchers should look out for the bearded vulture, black eagle, Alpine swift and scarlet-tufted malachite sunbird.

The Ruwenzoris are normally explored over seven days along the so-called loop trail, which skirts the base of the glacial peaks to a maximum altitude of 4,370 metres (14,350 ft). Notoriously boggy at the best of times, this trail is not likely to appeal during the rains, with June to August being the best time to hike. The activities of a DRC-based rebel group forced the authorities to suspend Ruwenzori hikes between 1997 and mid-2002. The Ruwenzori Mountain Service (RMS) has an exclusive license to handle ground arrangements for all hikes, charging a fixed fee of US$480 for the standard seven-day, six-night loop trail, inclusive of porters, guides and all park fees.

Based in **Kasese**, 75 km (45 miles) south of Fort Portal, the RMS can also arrange shorter hikes as well as longer ascents to

the peaks – the latter only suitable for experienced and equipped technical climbers. All ascents start from the trailhead at Ibanda, roughly 30 km (18 miles) from Kasese off the Fort Portal road.

The Semuliki Valley

Running west from Fort Portal, a spectacular dirt road skirts the Ruwenzori footslopes before descending into the Semuliki Valley, named after the river that flows along the DRC border into **Lake Albert**. The northern spur of the Ruwenzoris divides the Semuliki Valley into two ecologically divergent sectors.

The Semuliki National Park, immediately northwest of the Ruwenzori foothills, is essentially a Ugandan extension of the vast Ituri rainforest of the Congo Basin. The eastern part of the valley, protected within the Semuliki Wildlife Reserve, supports a cover of open savanna and woodland abutting the southern shores of Lake Albert. The road junction for these two protected areas (often confused with each other due to their similar names) is at Isojo, 30 km (18 miles) past Fort Portal – straight on for the national park; turn right for the wildlife reserve.

The fauna of the 220-sq.-km (85-sq.-mile) **Semuliki National Park** ❸ (known as the Bwamba Forest Reserve before it was gazetted in October 1993) possesses by far the strongest western affiliations of any forest in East Africa. Mammals include the forest races of elephant and buffalo, a substantial population of chimpanzees, eight types of monkey, and 11 species recorded nowhere else in Uganda, notably pygmy antelope, white-bellied duiker, and two types of flying squirrel. Also unique to Semuliki within East Africa is the water chevrotain, a superficially duiker-like relic of an ancient ungulate family that shares several structural features with pigs and is probably ancestral to all modern-day antelopes, deer, cattle and giraffes.

Semuliki National Park is an ornithological paradise. Of the 400 species recorded, more than 40 are Congolese rainforest species recorded nowhere else in Uganda, among them spot-breasted

LEFT: warthogs are prolific breeders.

Map
on page
253

ibis, Hartlaub's duck, chestnut-flanked goshawk, chestnut owlet, African piculet, red-sided broadbill, white-throated blue swallow, fiery-breasted bush shrike, blue-billed Malimbe, Maxwell's black weaver, Fox's weaver, Grant's bluebill, five varieties of greenbul and four types of hornbill. An added attraction for bird-watchers is the possibility of an exciting "first". New discoveries are made here regularly, with Congo serpent-eagle, grey-throated rail and black-throated coucal all recorded for the first time in the late 1990s.

A restricted network of guided trails sur-rounds the **Sempaya Hot Springs**, which lie about 1 km (⅔ mile) from the main road as you enter the park coming from Fort Portal. Ringed by forest and palm trees, the springs erupt geyser-like at more than 100°C (212°F) from two large white mounds comprised of saline deposits from the sulphuric water. Grey-cheeked manga-bey, black-and-white colobus and red-tailed monkey are easily seen around the springs and along the nearby stretch of the

Fort Portal road. It would be wildly opti-mistic to spend a couple of hours at Sem-paya and expect to see more than a handful of "Semuliki specials", but dwarf red horn-bill and the stunning white-crested and black-casqued wattled hornbills are com-mon in this area.

Semuliki Wildlife Reserve

The 3-hour hike to the Semuliki River that runs from Sempaya along the eastern boundary of the park can be undertaken as a sweaty day trip, but it is better tackled as an overnight excursion, assuming that you are carrying camping gear and food.

For birdwatchers, this trail should pro-duce about 10 of the species that are unique to Semuliki, as well as monkeys, hippos and crocodiles, and possibly buf-falo and elephant, along the river. More ambitious – allow at least three nights' camping – but correspondingly likely to yield a significant proportion of Semuliki's most sought-after birds, is the 12-km (7-mile) foot trail that runs from Kirumia

ELOW: Ntandi
ygmy village
Semuliki
ational Park.

Bridge (on the main Fort Portal road) to the Semuliki River via a series of productive oxbow lakes. Also of interest, and readily accessible from the main road, is the Batwa (pygmy) hunter-gatherer encampment near Ntandi, 5 km (3 miles) past Sempaya.

The **Semuliki Wildlife Reserve** ⑭ (500 sq. km/310 sq. miles) is one of the most scenic protected areas in Uganda, hemmed in by Lake Albert, the Ruwenzoris and the sheer eastern Rift Valley Escarpment, and shadowed by the Blue Mountains of the Congo to the west. Formerly known as the Toro Wildlife Reserve (and still marked as such on many maps), this part of the Semuliki Valley supported legendary volumes of plains grazers in the 1960s. Between 1970 and 1990, however, the game was decimated by poaching, and although populations are on the rise, the only ungulates that could now be described as common are Uganda kob, Defassa waterbuck, oribi, warthog and to a lesser extent buffalo and elephant. Leopards are regularly encountered on night drives, and lions – once hunted to local extinction – are gradually re-colonising the area, while in 2002 a spotted hyena was observed for the first time in years.

The exclusive **Semuliki Safari Lodge**, set in a stand of riparian woodland inhabited by black-and-white colobus and redtailed monkey, is the focal point for tourist visits to the reserve. In addition to day and night drives through the surrounding savanna, the lodge offers guided walks through a patch of sub-escarpment forest in which a semi-habituated troop of chimpanzees and small numbers of forest elephant are resident. Boat trips on the marshy southern shore of Lake Albert provide scintillating birdwatching – this is among the most reliable sites in Uganda for shoebill – and the lodge is also the closest tourist-class accommodation to the Semuliki National Park (Sempaya is about an hour distant by road).

The Kibale Forest National Park

To the south of Fort Portal, the 770-sq.-km (300-sq.-mile) **Kibale Forest National Park** ⑮ was gazetted in 1993 to protect an extensive medium-altitude rainforest harbouring at least 60 mammal species, including a substantial population of chimpanzees. Kibale Forest is noted for its primate diversity – more species than any other East African national park, including vervet, red-tailed, L'Hoest's and blue monkeys, grey-cheeked mangabey, red colobus, black-and-white colobus and olive baboon. Roughly 350 bird species have been recorded, notably the mysterious Kibale ground thrush (collected in 1966 but never seen again), Cassin's spinetail, blue-headed bee-eater, masked apalis and the utterly breathtaking greenbreasted pitta. The park is a lepidopterist's dream – dozens of brilliantly coloured butterflies congregate around puddles along the main road and forest footpaths.

All activities within the national park are run from the Kanyanchu Visitors Centre, 35 km (21 miles) from Fort Portal along the Kamwenge Road. The top attraction is the guided chimp-tracking excursions that depart from Kanyanchu twice daily (7.30am and 3.30pm), offer-

LEFT: walkway through a papyrus swamp, Bigodi Wetlar Sanctuary, Kibale Forest National Park

Map
on page
253

ing the best chance of close-up encounters with these fascinating apes of any African reserve after Tanzania's Gombe Stream and Mahale Mountains national parks. Visitors may walk unguided along the stretch of the Fort Portal–Kamwenge road running past Kanyanchu, where a good selection of forest birds are likely to be seen, along with legions of butterflies and a variety of monkeys. A unique feature of Kibale Forest is the night walks that leave Kanyanchu at 7.30pm and offer a great opportunity to search for nocturnal primates such as the wide-eyed bushbaby and sloth-like potto.

Bordering the national park only 5 km (3 miles) south of Kanyanchu, the **Bigodi Wetland Sanctuary** is an exemplary ecotourism project, with all proceeds directed towards community development. The 4.5-km (3-mile) circular trail through the forest-fringed swamp offers a fine introduction to Ugandan forest birds, partially due to the knowledge and enthusiasm of the local guides.

In addition to flagship rainforest species such as black-and-white casqued hornbill, African grey parrot and great blue and Ross's turaco, this is a good place to look for the brightly coloured papyrus gonolek, and a reliable site for the likes of yellow-billed barbet, yellow-spotted barbet, speckled tinker barbet, brown-eared woodpecker, blue-throated roller, snowy-headed robin-chat and red-headed bluebill. Up to five primate species are likely to be seen in the course of the walk – notably red colobus and L'Hoest's monkey (both very localised in Uganda) but also red-tailed monkey, black-and-white colobus and grey-cheeked mangabey.

The lush hilly country immediately north and west of Kibale Forest is studded with at least 30 gem-like crater lakes, relics of the brutal volcanic forces that shaped this part of Uganda. The pretty Lake Nyabikere, overlooked by the CVK Resort, lies amid tea plantations precisely 20 km (12 miles) south of Fort Portal along the road to Kibale Forest and Kamwenge. The other lakes mostly lie further west, and are reached by following the Kamwenge Road out of Fort Portal

for 12 km (7 miles), then forking to the right instead of continuing straight ahead to Kibale Forest. The forest-fringed Lake Nkuruba, 8 km (5 miles) south of this junction, is the site of a budget-friendly community-run nature reserve and campsite where black-and-white colobus and a variety of forest birds are resident. Another 3 km (2 miles) south, at the village of Kabata, Lake Kifuruka is a good place to see black-and-white colobus and the garish Ross's and great blue turaco, while its lily-covered surface is ideal habitat for African jacana and pygmy goose.

Also at Kabata, the homely up-market Ndali Lodge, on the rim of Lake Nyinambuga, offers panoramic views across the lakes towards the Ruwenzoris.

The opportunities for casual rambling in this region are without limit: five more crater lakes are visible from the 5-km (3-mile) road connecting Kabata to Kasenda, and another three lie alongside a back road – 2 hours on foot – connecting lakes Nkuruba and Nyabikere. ❑

QUEEN ELIZABETH NATIONAL PARK

The Queen Elizabeth National Park contains the country's best selection of large mammals and has more than 550 species of birds residing in its boundaries

Situated at the southern base of the Ruwenzoris Mountains near the town of Kasese, the **Queen Elizabeth National Park** ⑯ (QENP) protects 2,090 sq. km (815 sq. miles) of well-watered Rift Valley savanna, interspersed with patches of forest and several jewel-like crater lakes. Its dominant geographical feature is the 32-km (20-mile) long Kazinga Channel, which links the extensive Lake Edward on the Congolese border to the smaller, shallower Lake George on the park's eastern boundary. Gazetted in 1952 as the Kazinga National Park, QENP was renamed two years later to commemorate a visit by the Queen of England. The wildlife is now largely recovered from the heavy poaching of the 1970s and 1980s: Uganda kob, buffalo and hippo are abundant and a total of 200 lions was estimated in 2002, with the elephant population having risen from 150 to more than 1,000.

QENP is a park of several distinct sectors. The Kazinga Channel forms a natural barrier between the north and south, bridged only at Katunguru on the surfaced public road between Mbarara and Kasese. The bulk of QENP lies south of the channel and consists of three main areas of interest. These are the Maramagambo Forest immediately west of the Mbarara Road, the Chamburu (or Kyamburu) Gorge east of that road, and the remote Ishasha Plains, reached via a 60-km (35-mile) dirt road running southwest from the Mbarara Road 3 km (2 miles) south of Katunguru Bridge.

The more heavily touristed north of QENP is divided into three sectors, delimited by the Kasese road and the public feeder road running southwest from it towards Katwe. South of the Katwe road, a cover of flat, wooded savanna extends west from the Kasese road to the Mweya Peninsula at the confluence of the Kazinga Channel and Lake Edward. North of the Katwe road, the terrain is more mountainous and studded with crater lakes, while the Kasenyi Plains, which run east from the Kasese road towards Lake George, support relatively open grassland.

The Mweya Peninsula

The hilly **Mweya Peninsula**, which lies 6 km (4 miles) south of main entrance gate (on the Katwe Road 20 km/12 miles west of the turn-off from the Kasese road), is the site of the park headquarters, staff quarters, an up-market tourist lodge, a budget hostel and a campsite. The peninsula has a magnificent setting facing the

LEFT: a launch trip along the Kazinga Channel in the Queen Elizabeth National Park.

Map
on page
253

glacial peaks of the Ruwenzoris: elephant and buffalo often congregate on the opposite bank of the channel, and waterbuck, warthog, hippo and banded mongoose wander freely through the lodge gardens. At dusk, giant forest hogs sometimes emerge onto the airstrip, and shortly afterwards lions and hyenas perform their eerie nocturnal serenades. Avian highlights include the marabou storks that perch in the trees, and the scruffy tent-sized hamerkop nests in the wooded depression between the staff quarters and campsite.

Mweya is connected to Katunguru Entrance Gate (on the Kasese road, less than 1 km (1,100 yards) north of Katunguru Bridge) by a circuit of game-viewing tracks that pass through dense euphorbia-studded woodland where Defassa waterbuck, bushbuck, olive baboon and warthog are common. This small circuit is the only place in East Africa where the impressive giant forest hog is regularly seen in daylight. Elephants often cross the roads on their way to or from the water, melting into

the dense bush with surprising ease. At least one lion pride is resident in the area and spotted hyenas tend to be active around dusk and dawn. Shortly before sunset is the best time to take a slow drive along Leopard Track and around Campsite Two in search of the legendarily relaxed leopards that inhabit this patch of woodland.

Where to view game

The 2-hour **Kazinga Channel** launch trip leaves the jetty below Mweya at 3pm, 5pm, 9pm and 11pm daily. Hippos are everywhere, as are waterbirds – in particular pink-backed and great white pelicans and white-bellied cormorant. Hefty monitor lizards up to 2 metres (6 ft) long rest on the banks, as – with increasing frequency – do crocodiles, which became locally extinct during a bout of volcanic activity some 7,000 years ago, only to reappear in the early 1990s. The 3pm departure offers the best chance of seeing wildlife – in particular elephant and buffalo – at the water, but the light is better for photography after

5pm, and there's always the chance of lion, leopard or giant forest hog coming down to slake their thirst towards dusk.

The volcanically formed landscape north of the Katwe road is studded with deep, gaping calderas of which at least half a dozen support crater lakes of varying salinity. The most accessible of these, and one of the largest, Lake Nyamanuka is skirted by the Katwe road some 5 km (3 miles) from its junction with the Kasese road. **Lake Katwe** lies about 3 km (2 miles) west of main entrance gate and is separated from Lake Edward by the narrow belt of land on which stands the village of Katwe. This lake has been mined for coarse salt for centuries, and flamingos sometimes congregate in the shallows. Of interest more for scenery than wildlife, the rough 27-km (16-mile) Katwe Explosion Crater Track runs from opposite the main entrance gate to the Queen's Pavilion on the Kasese road, passing two more crater lakes as well as several dry calderas.

The **Kasenyi Plains** to the east of the Kasese road are the most reliable place to look for lions anywhere in Uganda. The drive from Mweya takes 45 minutes: follow the 6-km (4-mile) road to the main entrance gate, then turn right onto the Katwe road until after about 20 km (12 miles) you cross the Kasese road, where another dirt road runs west to the fishing village of Kasenyi on Lake George.

Approximately 5 km (3 miles) along the Kasenyi road, a series of rough tracks branches off from either side through an area of open savanna and clumped thickets that supports vast numbers of Uganda kob and buffalo as well as several lion prides. Lions are most active and visible for an hour or two after dusk, after which they usually retreat into the thickets. Listen out for the kobs' distinctive alarm calls. Common birds on the open plains include black-breasted snake eagle, white-headed vulture, grey crowned crane, red-throated spurfowl and yellow-throated longclaw.

Signposted from the Mbarara road 12 km (7 miles) south of the Katunguru Bridge, a 15-km (9-mile) dirt road leads southwest to

BELOW: Verreaux's eagle-owl often chooses to perch in an exposed position during the day.

Map on page 253

a pair of crater lakes – **Nyamasingire** and **Kasanduka** – in the heart of the Maramagambo Forest. Overlooked by a superb upmarket lodge and more low-key campsite, these lakes form the starting point for several guided day walks into the forest, which supports a rich avifauna as well as black-and-white colobus, olive baboon, and red-tailed, blue and L'Hoest's monkey. The most popular walk leads to a cave that hosts a large bat colony as well as a resident python. Boat trips on Lake Nyamasingire offer a good chance of seeing the elusive African finfoot. The forest's non-habituated chimpanzees are often heard calling from around the lodge, but are seldom seen.

The Chambura Gorge

If it's chimps you're after, a habituated community is confined to the forested **Chambura Gorge ⑰**, which cuts through the savanna 3 km (2 miles) east of the Mbarara road along a motorable track signposted 10 km (6 miles) south of Katunguru Bridge. The guided chimp-tracking excursions (maximum eight people) that descend into the gorge at 8am and 3pm daily carry a high success rate, especially in the morning. The black-and-white colobus is common, along with numerous forest birds – notably blue-breasted king-fisher and black bee-eater, the latter often perched openly near the rim.

The Chambura Gorge divides the QENP from the Chambura Wildlife Reserve, which protects a tract of acacia savanna notable for a nested crater lake that regularly hosts tens of thousands of lesser flamingos. To reach this lake, drive to Chambura village (on the Mbarara road a few minutes' south of the turn-off to Maramagambo), then follow the signposted turn-off to the east for 12 km (7 miles), passing another crater lake to your right about three-quarters of the way there.

The Ishasha Plains

Nudging up to the Congolese border south of Lake Edward, the Ishasha Plains can be visited en route between Mweya and Bwindi national parks. Until recently, most people paid a flying visit to Ishasha, due to a lack of accommodation other than basic

bandas and a campsite, but the opening of a luxury tented camp by Wild Frontiers in 2005 is likely to change all that. Ishasha is worthwhile both for its game viewing and its wilderness atmosphere. The lions of Ishasha, like their counterparts in Tanzania's Lake Manyara, habitually climb high into the acacia trees, a custom that probably developed to escape biting insects but is now ingrained.

In addition to its eccentric lion population – seen in arboreal action with increasing frequency over recent years – Ishasha supports healthy numbers of buffalo, elephant, topi and Uganda kob. The forest fringing the Ishasha River near the campsite harbours black-and-white colobus and a varied birdlife, including black bee-eater, double-toothed barbet, Ross's turaco and Cassin's flycatcher. Even if you simply bypass Ishasha en route between Mweya and Bwindi, it's worth stopping at the hippo pool on the south side of the road about 50 km (30 miles) past the junction with the Mbarara road. ❑

RIGHT: yellow-winged bats emerge before dark to hunt invertebrates.

BWINDI AND MGAHINGA NATIONAL PARKS

Bwindi is known for its mountain gorillas, its pristine rainforest and its diverse biological ecosystem, while Mgahinga is one of the smallest of Uganda's national parks

Bwindi National Park ⑱ covers 330 sq. km (128 sq. miles) of rainforest extending eastward from the Albertine Rift escarpment through the Kigezi Highlands of southwestern Uganda. Designated as a national park in 1991, the park spans altitudes of 1,100 metres (3,700 ft) to 2,400 metres (8,000 ft), a profoundly dramatic landscape of steep hills, narrow gorges, and transparent streams tumbling down a succession of waterfalls. The high rainfall, tropical climate, mixture of lowland and montane forests, and rich soils make this one of Africa's most biologically diverse ecosystems. The forest teems with wildlife, including 95 mammal, 350 bird and more than 200 butterfly species, but its star attraction is a population of roughly 320 mountain gorillas.

The focal point of tourist activities and accommodation in Bwindi is the northerly Buhoma entrance gate. This can reached directly from Kampala in a day, following the surfaced road towards Kabale to Ntungamo, 62 km (37 miles) past Mbarara, then turning right into a partially surfaced road that leads, after 45 km (27 miles), to Rukungiri. From Rukungiri, a series of rough dirt roads, passing through Kunungu, Burema and Butogota, arrive at Buhoma after about 75 km (45 miles). Tourists visiting Bwindi as part of a loop through western Uganda are likely to approach Buhoma along the dirt road that runs southwest from Katunguru Bridge (on the surfaced Kasese–Mbarara road through QENP) via the Ishasha sector of QENP, then through Kihihi, to connect with the Kampala route at Burema – a 5-hour drive or more, depending on road conditions.

Gorilla tracking

The most popular activity at Bwindi is gorilla tracking. Since late 2002, following a split in the ranks of the two habituated troops resident in the area, three different gorilla groups can be visited from Buhoma. Six tracking permits are issued per group daily, making a total of 18 permits, at a cost of US$275 per person. Permits must be bought in advance through the UWA headquarters in Kampala, and are often booked solid months in advance. Gorilla-tracking excursions depart from Buhoma at 8am, and although the success rate is practically 100 percent, it may take anything from 30 minutes to 5 hours to locate the gorillas.

It is for good reason Bwindi was formerly known as the Impenetrable Forest

LEFT: sitting in a discarded gorilla nest.

Map on page 253

Reserve. The hike often involves slithering up and down steep, slippery slopes covered with vicious nettles into valley floors matted with rotting vegetation and hanging lianas – robust shoes, thick trousers and long sleeves are in order.

No matter how tough the journey, any sense of fatigue will be alleviated by the spine-tingling first glimpse of a wild mountain gorilla. There is a primal thrill attached to standing deep in the heart of the rainforest, separated from the most magnificent of the great apes – a creature which shares more than 95 percent of its genes with humans – by nothing more than a few feet of lush undergrowth.

To avoid interfering with the gorillas' foraging and social interaction, visitors may spend no longer than one hour with them once they have been located. But during the walk back to Buhoma, and for years afterwards, there remains the haunting memory of seeing the liquid brown eyes of these gentle giants, possessed of immeasurable dignity, humanity and gravity.

The taxonomic status of Bwindi's gorillas has long been open to conjecture. They are generally referred to as mountain gorillas, a race otherwise confined to the Virunga Volcanoes, linked to Bwindi by a 25-km (15-mile) forested corridor until it was cleared for cultivation perhaps 500 years ago. Recent DNA testing, however, suggests that the Virunga and Bwindi gorillas are sufficiently divergent to be regarded as racially discrete. Whatever the case, this much is certain: the mountain gorilla has always been scarce by comparison to the two lowland gorilla races of west-central Africa, whose total population, even after heavy poaching over the past 50 years, is estimated at 40–50,000. By contrast, the combined number of gorillas in Bwindi and the Virungas amounts to fewer than 700.

Mountain gorillas live in family groups of females, their offspring, and sub-adult males, all led by a mature male silverback, named after the silvery-grey fur on its back and shoulder. A mature silverback is

exceedingly impressive, standing almost 2 metres (6 ft) tall and weighing up to 210 kg (460 lb). Gorillas have squat legs but long, muscular arms, thick trunks, and massive chests. Adult males have a ridge of bone at the top of their skulls that anchors their jaw muscles, giving them a bite of formidable power. Silverbacks have a legitimate need for such a capability. Each is the defender of his group and must be ever alert to rival males intent on stealing his mates.

Their extraordinary strength means that competing silverbacks would do great harm to each other if they ever engaged in total combat. Gorillas have consequently developed a broad repertoire of ritualised behaviour – chest drumming, foot stamping and mock charges – to obviate the need for actual fighting. They tear up vegetation and stuff it in their mouths or throw it at rivals; they howl, beat the ground, and generally raise a ruckus to express their profound displeasure with rivals. This extravagant behaviour once led to the popular misconception that gorillas are fierce and murderous beasts. Today we know that the opposite is true: gorillas are actually shy and retiring, and their aggressive displays are largely a ruse to avoid physical confrontation.

Family groups roam nomadically within a home range of 25–40 sq. km (10–15 sq. miles), feeding and resting as they move, but seldom covering more than 1–2 km (1 mile) in the course of a day's wandering. Their diet consists of a wide range of flora, including fruits, celery, bamboo, and nettles. In the evening, they construct nests by bending over branches and lining the concavities with grasses or leaves; they tend to foul their nests during the night and never sleep in the same place twice. The female mountain gorilla will not have her first baby before the age of 10. The gestation period is comparable to that of humans and she will give birth every three or four years at best. Nor is it particularly easy for mountain gorillas to conceive; the females are

BELOW: getting close to a mounta... gorilla.

Map
n page
253

fertile for only three or four days out of every month. Though infant gorillas develop more quickly than humans do, they are still virtually helpless when born, and remain heavily dependent on their mothers until they are three or four years old.

Other wildlife to see

Although gorillas form the main point of interest to most visitors, several other guided walks can be undertaken from Buhoma, ranging from 30 minutes to 8 hours in duration. An alluring list of rainforest mammals is resident along these trails, including chimpanzee, African golden cat, serval, giant forest hog, black-fronted duiker, yellow-backed duiker, Lord Derby's anomalure and tree pangolin. Hikers will soon realise, however, that in the shadowy forest of Bwindi, animals are more easily heard than seen – the only large terrestrial mammal likely to be encountered is the bushbuck. Arboreal primates are more visible. Black-and-white colobus, olive baboon and red-tailed, blue

and L'Hoest's monkeys are frequently observed on day walks, while a short nocturnal drive with a spotlight has been known to yield a glimpse of the potto, a large sloth-like primate related to the galagoes and the lemurs of Madagascar.

A more certain prospect is the clouds of gaudy butterflies that swarm around even the smallest of puddles, not to mention the forest's immense variety of birds, which includes all but one of the 24 Albertine Rift endemics recorded in Uganda.

Visitors with an ornithological bent should make contact with one of the park's specialist bird guides – as knowledgeable and enthusiastic as you could hope for – and might want to forsake the enclosed forest footpaths in favour of the short but dazzlingly productive stretch that leads uphill from Buhoma. Any shortlist of birds likely to be seen along this road will feel woefully inadequate, but the likes of bar-tailed trogon, black bee-eater, Elliot's woodpecker, red-throated alethe, icterine greenbul, montane masked apalis,

short-tailed warbler, strange weaver and white-collared oliveback should be sufficient to set any self-respecting bird-watcher's pulse racing.

Places to visit around Bwindi

With time to spare, a sturdy four-by-four and a pioneering spirit, it's worth visiting **Ruhija** in the southern part of the park. Ruhija was the informal base for gorilla tracking in the late 1980s, and the stone resthouse built for researchers during the colonial era now welcomes visitors. Set at a higher altitude than Buhoma, the Afro-montane forest around Ruhija harbours a markedly different species composition, while also offering commanding views across layers of extravagantly forested ridges to the distant outline of the Virungas. Using Ruhija as a base, visitors can follow the 3-hour **Mubwindi Swamp Trail**, which leads to a swamp at an altitude of roughly 2,070 metres (6,700 ft), a good area to look for elephant as well as several Albertine Rift endemics that are absent from Buhoma, notably African green broadbill and Grauer's swamp warbler.

In order to enlist the support of the local population in conserving Bwindi and its spectacular wildlife, a programme has been instituted that permits beekeeping and the sustainable harvest of wild plants within the forest. Local communities also benefit from tourism; villagers receive a percentage of the fees that visitors pay to enter the park. A rebel attack on Buhoma in 1999 claimed the lives of eight tourists and a park warden, forcing Bwindi to close for a month and resulting in a sharp drop in tourism over the following year. Security was beefed up after the attack, however, and subsequent Western government warnings against visiting Bwindi had all been withdrawn by 2002, leaving the park as popular as it ever was.

Places to visit around Kabale

From Buhoma, a 2- to 3-hour drive south along a dirt road through Kanungu and

BELOW: one of the many butterflies to be found in the forest.

Map
on page
253

Burema leads to **Kabale**, the largest town in the Kigezi Highlands, also connected to Kampala by a roughly 370-km (220-mile) surfaced road.

Of greater interest than Kabale itself is the serpentine **Lake Bunyonyi** ⑲, a flooded river valley that extends northwards from the Rwanda border for 25 km (15 miles) through the sheer contours of the lushly cultivated hills of Kigezi. Plenty of budget resorts line the lakeshore close to the fishing village of Rutinda (also known as Kyabahinga), 10 km (6 miles) from Kabale by road, while two isolated islands – both less than 15 minutes from Rutinda by boat – have more up-market lodges. The absence of bilharzia, crocodile and hippo means that swimming is safe in this beautiful spot. Birds are everywhere – indeed the name Bunyonyi translates as "place of little birds" – and (linked perhaps to the lack of crocs) there is surely no better place in Africa to observe spotted-necked otters bobbing and diving than in the bays around Rutinda.

Kabale is connected to the smaller and more westerly town of **Kisoro** by an 80-km (50-mile) dirt road, which skirts the northern tip of Lake Bunyonyi at Muko before running for several kilometres through the montane and bamboo forest of the Echuya Forest Reserve. Situated practically within spitting distance of the Congolese and Rwandan borders, Kisoro lies 3 km (2 miles) from the mountain-ringed Lake Mutanda in the imposing shadow of the Virunga Mountains.

Only 15 km (10 miles) from Kisoro, **Mgahinga National Park** ⑳ was gazetted in 1991 to protect the Ugandan slopes of Muhavura, Gahinga and Sabinyo mountains in the Virunga chain. It is the smallest national park in Uganda, extending over less than 35 sq. km (14 sq. miles), but its volcanic landscapes are breathtaking, and it harbours a wealth of large mammals (golden monkey, black-and-white colobus, leopard, elephant, giant forest hog, bush-pig, buffalo and black-fronted duiker) as well as 120 bird species of which 10 percent are Albertine Rift endemics.

No mountain gorillas reside permanently within Mgahinga, but several troops move freely between the park and its Rwandan and Congolese neighbours. One habituated group of nine individuals is reliably resident in Uganda from October to May, occasionally defecting to the DRC between June and September. The six daily gorilla-viewing permits are best booked in advance through the UWA headquarters in Kampala – the cost of US$220 will be refunded should the gorillas happen to be on a cross-border jaunt – but assuming availability, permits may also be bought a day or two ahead at the national park office in Kisoro.

Other guided activities in Mgahinga include hikes to the three volcanic peaks. The least demanding is the 6- to 7-hour round trip up the 3,475-metre (11,400-ft) Mt Gahinga; more challengingly is the 9- to 10-hour round hike ascent to the crater lake at the 4,127-metre (13,540-ft) peak of Mt Muhabura. The relatively flat 4-hour Sabinyo Gorge Trail is very rewarding for birdwatchers. All excursions leave at 8am from the park headquarters at the Ntebeko entrance gate. ❑

LAKE MBURO
NATIONAL PARK

*Despite its turbulent past Lake Mburo is well equipped to receive
visitors who can enjoy the beautiful lake and spot such
rarities as the African finfoot and shoebills*

Situated only 45 minutes' drive south of the surfaced Kampala–Mbarara road, along a dirt track branching from Sanga, **Lake Mburo National Park** ㉑ (LMNP) might have been custom-made to break up the arduous drive between Bwindi/Mgahinga and the capital. Yet this small savanna reserve is often neglected by safarigoers due to the absence of such glamorous plains species as elephant, rhinoceros and giraffe, and a paucity of large predators – aside from a fairly visible population of spotted hyena, a few characteristically secretive leopards and the odd vagrant lion. Get past the "big five" mentality, however, and LMNP is an underrated gem, harbouring several safari favourites that occur in no other comparably accessible Ugandan protected area. These include the handsome impala antelope for which Kampala is named, an abundance of Burchell's zebra, and herds of majestic eland – Africa's largest antelope – which roam seasonally between the hills and the plains. The park is also well equipped for visitors of all tastes and budgets, boasting one excellent up-market camp, an affordable national park rest camp, and an idyllic lakeshore campsite serviced by a great little restaurant

The centrepiece of LMNP is Lake Mburo itself, a lovely hippo-infested body

BELOW: hippo
can be spotted
by listening for
sighs as they
surface from
the water and
exhale.

Map on page 253

of water fringed by lush reed beds and enclosed by low, green mountains. According to folklore, the lake was formed overnight, when a formerly cultivated valley was submerged by a flash flood, and it is named after a farmer who drowned in the rising waters. Apocryphal, no doubt, but the legend of Mburo's violent birth does seem prescient to its somewhat torrid and bloody recent history *(see box below)*.

Game viewing

LMNP today bears few visible scars of its fractious past. The absence of elephants and resident lions – the latter hunted out in the 1970s – makes game walks reasonably safe, though the threat posed by hippos and buffalos means that they may be undertaken only in the company of an armed ranger.

Also highly enjoyable are motorboat excursions on Lake Mburo: hippo are everywhere, otters are seen occasionally, and the usual water-associated avian suspects are boosted by the localised African finfoot (most often seen swimming surreptitiously below overhanging branches) and Uganda's only protected population of papyrus yellow warbler.

Away from the water, the thick acacia savanna of LMNP is run through by a network of mostly well-maintained game-viewing tracks. Impala Track can be superb during the rainy season, when large numbers of impala, Burchell's zebra, Defassa waterbuck, warthog, topi and buffalo congregate in the open woodland around the junction with Warukiri Track.

During the dry season, the wildlife sticks closer to perennial water, for which reason Lakeside Track and Kigambira Loop – good habitat for bushbuck, bushpig and buffalo – are generally most productive. LMNP is the best site in Uganda for acacia-associated birds, and the checklist of 320 species includes the likes of barefaced go-away bird, southern ground hornbill, red-faced barbet and black-collared barbet at the northern extent of their range. ❑

GHT: a tawny gle soars.

THE HISTORY OF LAKE MBURO

The catalogue of misfortune started *circa* 1890, when Bahima cattle-herders were forced out of the Mburo area by a rinderpest epidemic, followed by tsetse-borne diseases in 1910. Declared a Controlled Hunting Area in 1936, Mburo acquired a reputation for man-eating lions – t is said that one male took more than 80 human lives.

n the 1950s, an ill-advised government strategy to starve he disease-carrying tsetse fly resulted in the depopulation of the plains of wildlife, although the tsetses survived.

n 1982, Lake Mburo was gazetted as a 642-sq.-km (256-sq.-mile) national park. The government promptly evicted thousands of Bahima and their cattle, an action that caused local antagonism towards the under-equipped angers. With the government's attention diverted by civil war in 1985–6, LMNP was almost entirely resettled and its nfrastructure was destroyed. Even after 1987, when 60 percent of the park's area was de-gazetted to accommodate squatters, tensions between local herders and the authorities ran high. Fortunately, they have dissipated since 1991, following the formation of a pioneering community conservation unit that decided – among other things – to divert a substantial portion of revenue raised by park entrance fees towards community projects.

EASTERN UGANDA

The star of eastern Uganda is the seldom-visited Kidepo Valley National Park which protects the country's only population of cheetah. Serious and non-serious hikers will enjoy the challenge of Mt Elgon

Map on page 253

Leafy **Mbale ㉒**, the country's third-largest town, is the gateway to eastern Uganda, situated 235 km (140 miles) from Kampala along a good surfaced road running through Jinja and Iganga. Mbale has a wide range of tourist facilities, but there's little to see there, for which reason most visitors head directly to one of the various lodgings on the lower slopes of Mt Elgon, which looms on the town's eastern horizon. The 4,321-metre (14,177-ft) Mt Elgon, which straddles the border with Kenya, is the eighth-highest in Africa, the relic of an extinct volcano that once stood taller than Kilimanjaro does today. The mountain is known locally as Masaba, Elgon being an Anglicisation of its Maasai name "El Kony", coined by Joseph Thomson, the first European visitor to the region.

Mt Elgon National Park

Elgon's tallest peaks lie on the Ugandan side of the border, encircling an 8-km (5-mile) wide caldera studded with crater lakes and hot springs, where they are protected within the 1,145-sq.-km (440-sq.-mile) **Mt Elgon National Park ㉓**, gazetted in 1993.

The park is ecologically similar to most other large East African large mountains: the evergreen forest and bamboo of the lower slopes gives way to heather and moorland at around 3,000 metres (10,000 ft), then Afro-Alpine vegetation dotted with giant lobelia and groundsel at higher elevations. Blue monkey and black-and-white colobus are common in the forest, which also harbours an isolated population of the striking long-bearded De Brazza's monkey. The bird checklist of 305 species includes the endangered bearded vulture (lammergeyer), together with several eastern montane species, most notably moorland francolin, elsewhere common only on Ethiopia's Bale Mountains.

Two bases are available for relaxed exploration of the Elgon footslopes. The pretty village of Sipi, overlooking the 100-metre (320-ft) high **Sipi Falls**, lies about 60 km (37 miles) from Mbale along the excellent surfaced road to the Suam border. Only 12 km (7 miles) from Sipi, the cosy log cabins at the Kapkwai Forest Exploration Centre, situated within the national park boundaries, form the hub for an excellent network of short day trails through the forest and bamboo zone.

For serious hikers, Elgon offers an experience comparable to Kilimanjaro or the Ruwenzoris, but at a fraction of the price and with a lower risk of altitude-related illness. The peaks can be explored over a four-day hike from one of three

FT: a young fassa terbuck in Kipepo ley tional Park. **GHT:** Sipi ls in the thills of Elgon.

trailheads, Budadiri, Kapkwata and Kap-kwai, all of which offer simple accommodation, though camping is necessary once on the trail. Hikes must be arranged at the national park office in Mbale – where camping gear can be hired – or at its equivalent at one of the trailheads. Bring plenty of warm clothing.

Pian-Upe Wildlife Reserve

Extending for 2,788 sq. km (1,075 sq. miles) across the semi-arid plains north of Mt Elgon, the little-known **Pian-Upe Wildlife Reserve** ㉔ is Uganda's second-largest protected area, a status it might soon relinquish should tentative plans to excise a section for an agricultural scheme and gazette the remainder as a national park ever materialise.

Scenically, the acacia savanna of Pian-Upe is dominated by the tortured black volcanic plugs of the 3,068-metre (10,066-ft) Mt Kadam, which rises in brooding isolation along the eastern boundary. The fauna, similar to that of the more northerly

Kidepo National Park, includes lion, leopard, cheetah, Burchell's zebra, buffalo, eland, roan antelope, greater kudu and patas monkey. Poaching was rife into the late 1990s, but an increased ranger presence has subsequently set wildlife populations on course to a slow recovery.

With further tourist development, Pian-Upe might yet realise its potential as one of Uganda's most exciting wildlife destinations, a more accessible alternative to the remote Kidepo National Park. Unfortunately, as things stand, game viewing is limited by the lack of any internal road network (aside from the main Mbale–Moroto road), though guided game walks are available, and there are plans to re-clear a disused vehicle track leading east from Maruajore to the game-rich Loporokocho Swamps. Access is straightforward – the Maruajore headquarters lie 90 km (55 miles) north of Mbale, alongside the reasonable dirt road to Moroto, and a few basic self-catering *bandas* opened there in 2002.

Pain-Upe forms the southern boundary of Karamoja – home to the Karimojong, whose obsessive love of cattle rivals that of the Maasai. Extending northward to the Sudanese border, Karamoja is the most overtly traditional part of Uganda, seldom visited by tourists due to its remoteness and ongoing security problems. Pian-Upe itself is reputedly safe, and the staff at the headquarters can arrange visits a Karimojong settlements bordering the reserve. But some risk is attached to travelling to Moroto, the principal town of Karamoja, which lies roughly 100 km (60 miles) north of Maruajore.

Security concerns relating to Moroto are amplified as you head further north into the arid heartland of Karamoja, where domestic and cross-border cattle-rustling is a way of life, and armed attacks on passing motor traffic occur with sufficient frequency to put off most visitors to Uganda. This is a shame, for the obvious reasons, and also because it has hindered tourist development of what is otherwise an exceptionally marketable and alluring wilderness destination: the magical Kidepo Valley National Park.

LEFT: patas monkey in the Pian-Upe Wildlife Reserve.

Kidepo Valley National Park

Map on page 253

Gazetted in 1962, **Kidepo Valley National Park ㉕** extends over 1,440 sq. km (560 sq. miles) of wild semi-arid country abutting the remote Sudanese border. High, freakish mountains, including the 2,750-metre (9,022-ft) Morungole and 2,797-metre (9,177-ft) Lotuke, demarcate the park's western, southern and eastern boundaries, while the Narus and Kidepo rivers course through the valleys.

The acacia grassland of Kidepo, with strong ecological affiliations to drier parts of Kenya and Tanzania, supports at least 20 large mammal species that go unrecorded in western Uganda. The widespread lion and leopard are supplemented by Uganda's only viable populations of cheetah, bat-eared fox, striped hyena and aardwolf. A remarkable 17 antelope species include several dry-country specialists: the magnificent greater kudu and Beisa oryx, along with Bright's gazelle, lesser kudu, roan antelope and Guenther's dik-dik. Also reasonably common are Jackson's hartebeest, topi, eland, bushbuck, Defassa waterbuck, elephant, Burchell's zebra, warthog, bushpig, buffalo and Rothschild's giraffe.

During the Idi Amin era, Kidepo was relatively undisturbed by poachers, due to the excellent work of game warden Paul Ssali, and also because of the former dictator's personal affection for this corner of eastern Uganda. During the early 1980s, however, the civil war transformed Kidepo into a free-for-all for cattle rustlers and poachers, but its very remoteness restricted the loss of wildlife.

Today, animal stocks cannot compare to, say, the Maasai Mara or Ngorongoro Crater, but there is plenty of game around – particularly during the dry season, concentrated along the river valleys – and the park is imbued with a sense of isolation and solitude rare in modern Africa.

Birdwatching

Birdwatching in the park is a sensational experience. Roughly 20 percent of the 480 bird species known from Kidepo are dry-country specialists with a restricted distribution within Uganda. These include the impressive ostrich, Kori bustard and secretary bird, the latter one of 56 raptors recorded within the park boundaries. The likes of carmine and little green bee-eater, Abyssinian roller, red-and-yellow and black-breasted barbet, yellow-billed and Jackson's hornbill, golden pipit, white-headed buffalo weaver and purple grenadier add welcome splashes of vivid colour to the somewhat monochrome and austere savanna.

Affordable access to Kidepo is a problem. The two-day drive from the capital traverses some very poor roads, and carries a risk of banditry that few would consider acceptable. The national park itself is secure, which means that chartering a flight from Entebbe is a viable – albeit wallet-draining – option. The only tourist lodge in Kidepo was privatised in 2003 and is scheduled to re-open as a luxury tented camp in early 2006. Assuming that this goes ahead as planned, cheaper packaged visits based around scheduled flights might well become available in the future. ❏

GHT:
Rothschild's giraffes can be seen in the Kidepo Valley National Park.

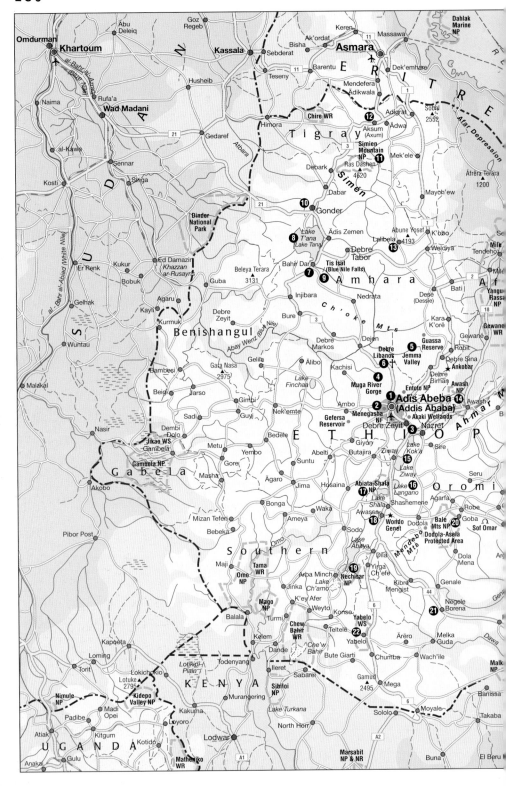

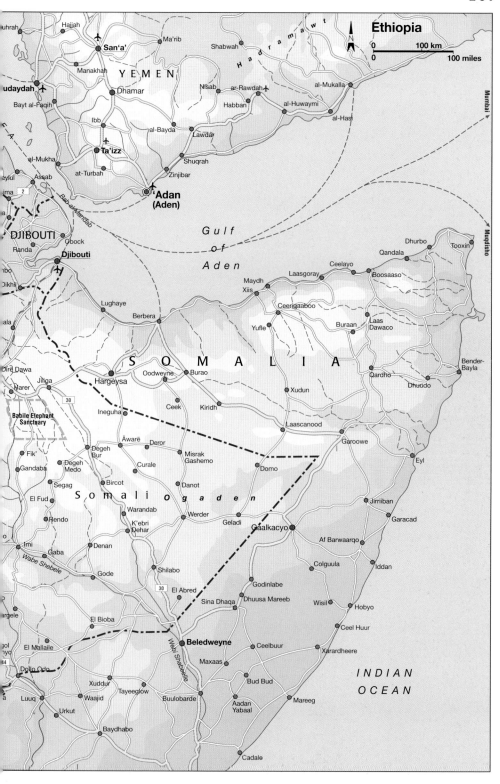

Ethiopia

uhrah
Hajjah
San'a'
Manakhah
Ma'rib
Shabwah
Hadramawt
al-Mukalla

YEMEN
udaydah
Dhamar
Nisab
ar-Rawdah
al-Huwaymi
Bayt al-Faqih
Habban
al-Has
Ibb
al-Bayda
Lawdar
Ta'izz
al-Mukha
Shuqrah
at-Turbah
Zinjibar
Assab
Adan
(Aden)
eylul
ima 2
a
Bab al-Mandab
DJIBOUTI
Randa
Obock
Djibouti
nbo
Dikhil
ala
Lughaye
Berbera
Dire Dawa
Jijiga
Hargeysa
Harer
30
Babile Elephant Sanctuary
Ineguha
Fik'
Äwarē
Deror
Degeh Bur
Degeh Medo
Curale
Gandaba
Segag
Bircot
El Fud
Somali
Rendo
Warandab
K'ebri Dehar
Imi
Denan
Gaba
Wabe Shebele
Gode
El Bioba
argele
El Mallaile
Dollo Odo
Xuddur
Luuq
Waajid
Tayeeglow
Urkut
Baydhabo

Gulf
of
Aden

Dhurbo
Tooxin
Qandala
Ceelayo
Boosaaso
Laasgoray
Maydh
Xiis
Ceerigaaboo
Yufle
Buraan
Laas Dawaco
Oodweyne
Burao
SOMALIA
Xudun
Ceek
Kiridh
Laascanood
Garoowe
Qardho
Dhuudo
Bender-Bayla
Eyl
Misrak Gashemo
Domo
Danot
ogaden
Jirriiban
Werder
Geladi
Gaalkacyo
Garacad
Af Barwaarqo
Colguula
Iddan
Shilabo
Godinlabe
30
El Abred
Sina Dhaqa
Dhuusa Mareeb
Wisil
Hobyo
Ceel Huur
Beledweyne
Ceelbuur
Xarardheere
Maxaas
Bud Bud
Buulobarde
Aadan Yabaal
Mareeg
Cadale

INDIAN
OCEAN

0 100 km
0 100 miles

Mumbai
Muqdisho

ETHIOPIA

*Popularly perceived to be a featureless desert, Ethiopia is in
fact the most geologically dramatic country in Africa*

Ethiopia is dominated by a vast, wrinkled and amply fertile
central plateau that rises in majestic isolation from the
low-lying badlands of the Somali and Kenya border regions.
These central Ethiopian highlands, which cover an area larger than
Great Britain, stand more than 2,000 metres (6,500 ft) above sea level
and include roughly 20 peaks topping the 4,000-metre (13,000-ft)
mark. Created by volcanic activity some 40 million years ago, the
highlands were subsequently divided into their present-day northwestern and southeastern components by the formation of the Great
Rift Valley, which sinks to a depth of 100 metres (330 ft) below sea
level in the far north.

The Ethiopian highlands have been cut off from similar high country for at least 20 million years, and many animals and plants have
evolved to cope with their unique conditions. Hence the very high
numbers of species – five large mammals and more than 30 birds
among them – that occur nowhere else but in Ethiopia (and in some
cases Eritrea, a sovereign state since May 1993). It is these endemics,
rather than the plains animals associated with more conventional
safari destinations, that attract nature lovers – in particular birdwatchers – to Ethiopia.

Wildlife conservation is not a high priority for the Ethiopian Government. Many of the national parks are difficult to reach and poorly
developed for tourism, and several have suffered badly from poaching. The spectacular Bale and Simien Mountain national parks, however, are both very accessible, and they harbour a good selection
of endemics. Other key wildlife areas that can be visited with reasonable ease include Awash, Abiata-Shala and Nechisar national
parks in the Rift Valley, and the indigenous forests at Wondo Genet
and Menegasha.

Ethiopia is a land of immense cultural and historical wealth. The
Ethiopian Orthodox Church, founded *circa* AD 350, is one of the
oldest denominations in the world, and certainly the most idiosyncratic, permeated by a stoically antiquated quality that is personi-
fied in more than 300 ancient rock-hewn churches, most still in active
use today. The country's Islamic community is almost as old, having
been founded during Mohammed's lifetime, while the far south supports a polyglot of animist pastoralist tribes whose traditional lifestyle
has survived into the 21st century with remarkably few concessions
to outside influences. Although this guide deals specifically with
wildlife, most visitors will seek to achieve an itinerary that balances
historical sightseeing with natural attractions, for which reason the
major wildlife areas – and several minor ones – are discussed in relation to associated historical and cultural attractions.   ❑

PRECEDING PAGES: the eastern edge of Ethiopia's Sanetti Plateau.
LEFT: the black-headed weaver, an enthusiastic builder of intricate woven nests.

Map
on pages
286–287

ADDIS ABABA AND ENVIRONS

*There are plenty of places to seek wildlife within easy reach of
Ethiopia's capital. If you are very short of time there's even
a national park that overlooks the city centre*

Founded by Emperor Menelik II in 1887, **Addis Ababa ❶**, the capital city of Ethiopia and normal port of entry to the country, has a moderate highland climate that reflects its setting at an altitude of 2,400 metres (7,800 ft) below the green Entoto Hills. Chaotic and sprawling, the city fails dismally to live up to the name bestowed on it by its founder – New Flower – and, a couple of excellent cultural and historical museums aside, it offers little in the way of compelling urban sightseeing. By contrast, the surrounding highland countryside has many worthwhile goals for short excursions during any sojourns into the city enforced by its role as the hub of the domestic road and flight network.

Overlooking the city centre, the 125-sq.-km (50-sq.-mile) **Entoto Natural Park**, established in 1995 by the Ethiopian Heritage Trust, can be explored either on foot or on horseback. The reserve was created with the aim of restoring some natural vegetation to the ecologically impoverished Entoto Hills, which are currently planted almost exclusively with the fast-growing eucalyptus tree, introduced to Ethiopia in 1894 to combat a chronic firewood shortage. Although the park supports small numbers of vervet monkey, common duiker, spotted hyena and even leopard, it is more notable for the expansive views from the peaks, and for the presence of a Ruppell's vulture breeding colony, the endangered bearded vulture, and a dozen endemic bird species.

Menegasha National Forest

Roughly 60 km (35 miles) west of Addis Ababa, the bizarrely underpublicised **Menegasha National Forest ❷**, set on the slopes of a 3,385-metre (11,100-ft) extinct volcano, is reached along a rough side road that branches south from the main road running west towards Ambo.

Menegasha is quite possibly the oldest conservation area in Africa, protected by imperial decree since the 15th-century reign of Emperor Zara Yakob. Black-and-white colobus and the striking jet-black Menelik's bushbuck are often seen in the indigenous juniper forest, along with the endemic Ethiopian oriole, yellow-fronted parrot, black-winged lovebird, Abyssinian woodpecker and Abyssinian catbird. Self-catering accommodation is available at the forest headquarters.

Like Menegasha, the Gefersa Reservoir, situated only 18 km (11 miles) from Addis Ababa along the road towards Ambo, is recommended to birdwatchers who are unable to cram the more remote Bale National Park or Wondo Genet into their

LEFT: a vervet monkey infant clings to its mother until it is four months old.
RIGHT: spotted hyena, in Entoto National Park.

itinerary. Gefersa is not the most sceni-cally memorable body of water, but it's a reliable site for water and grassland endemics such as blue-winged goose, wattled ibis and Abyssinian longclaw. It can be visited on its own as a 3-hour round trip from the capital, or in combi-nation with the Menegasha Forest as a full day or overnight excursion.

Continuing westwards, 125 km (75 miles) from Addis Ababa, the small town of **Ambo** is also known as Hagere Hiwot (Healthy Place) in reference to the hot springs that bubble into a swimming pool in the town centre. On the way to Ambo, the road bypasses Addis Alem (New World), founded and named by Emperor Menelik II in 1900 as an intended replace-ment capital for Addis Ababa. The Guder Falls, 13 km (8 miles) west of Ambo, aren't very spectacular, but the surround-ing forest harbours a troop of black-and-white colobus and plenty of birds. One hour's drive south of Ambo, the 3,386-metre (11,100-ft) Mt Wenchi is an mas-sive extinct volcano with a large crater lake and island monastery set in the Afro-Alpine vegetation around its peak.

Roughly 50 km (30 miles) southeast of Addis Ababa, transected by the surfaced road to Awash National Park and the Rift Valley lakes, the moderately sized town of **Debre Zeyit** ❸ stands at the heart of a field of pretty crater lakes. Of the five lakes that lie within easy walking distance of the town centre, Lake Hora is perhaps the most scenic, while the seasonally fluc-tuating Lake Chelekleka supports flocks of lesser flamingo, common crane and res-ident and migrant waterfowl. Debre Zeyit is a good day trip out of Addis Ababa with overnight accommodation available.

To the south of Debre Zeyit, Mt Zik-wala is topped by a 1,000-year-old mon-astery, which overlooks a beautiful sacred crater lake, encircled by indigenous for-est populated by black-and-white colobus and endemic birds. Another worthwhile site in this area, often hosting thousands of flamingos, cranes and waterfowl, the **BELOW:** flamingos flock to the Akaki Wetlands.

Map on pages 286–287

Akaki Wetlands lie immediately south of Akaki town, only 20 km (12 miles) from Addis Ababa along the Debre Zeyit road. Most tourists to Ethiopia concentrate on the historical sites of the north, but those whose main interest is natural history are likely to dedicate more time to the south, since it is generally better for wildlife and birds. There are, however, a few endemics – most notably the gelada baboon – whose range is more or less restricted to the north, and a few localities within day or overnight distance of Addis Ababa where some of these species might be seen.

Ankobar and surrounds

Perched on the Rift Valley escarpment northeast of Addis Ababa, at a breezy altitude of 3,000 metres (3, 281 ft), **Ankobar** is famed in ornithological circles as the locality of the Ankober serin, a nondescript but very localised endemic first recorded in 1979. The surrounding countryside supports large troops of gelada baboon, and grassland-associated endemic birds, as well as the scarce Somali chestnut-winged starling and bearded vulture. Ankobar is a good 3-hour drive from Addis Ababa – follow the surfaced road towards Dese (Dessie) for about 130 km (80 miles) to Debre Birhan (which has a few acceptable hotels), from where it's another 40 km (24 miles) on a fair dirt road.

From Ankobar, a 15-km (9-mile) road descends spectacularly to the Rift Valley floor and the small town of **Aliyu Amba**, only 3 km (2 miles) from a bridge across the Melka Jebdu River that's reputed to be the best site for observing the endemic yellow-throated serin. The Afro-Alpine moorland and grassland of the traditionally protected **Guassa Reserve** near Mehal Muda has a similar floral and faunal composition to Bale's Sanetti Plateau, including at least 30 Ethiopian wolves – the last viable breeding population of the race found northwest of the Rift Valley. Guassa is seldom visited, but it's reasonably accessible by bus or private vehicle, and very basic accommodation is available at Mehal Meda.

A straightforward goal for a day trip out of Addis Ababa – follow the Bahir Dar road north for about 40 km (25 miles) to Chancho, then turn left along a 20-km (12-mile) side road to Durba – is the magnificent **Muga River Gorge** ❹. This is the closest place to the capital where gelada baboons are resident, as well as being a good site for cliff-nesting raptors such as lammergeyer, black eagle and African harrier hawk. During September and October, the countryside erupts with wildflowers, and the waterfall that plunges into the gorge next to Durba is at its most voluminous.

From Chancho, take the Bahir Dar road north for 40 km (25 miles) and you reach Mukaturi. Here, a road on the right terminates at Alem Katema in the **Jemma Valley** ❺ – the only accessible site for the endemic Harwood's francolin. About 20 km (12 miles) north of Mukaturi, the historic monastery of **Debre Libanos** ❻ was the headquarters of the Ethiopian Orthodox Church prior to a massacre in 1937. A new church, built in the 1950s, is a bit bombastic, but the location is lovely, and the gelada baboon can be seen in the vicinity. ❏

Map on pages 286–287

NORTHERN ETHIOPIA AND THE SIMIEN MOUNTAINS

The four tourist centres on the "historical circuit" have much to offer birdwatchers, while the Simien Mountains National Park is superb for hiking and observing endemic mammals

Uniquely within East Africa, Ethiopia is not primarily known as a wildlife destination, but rather for a collection of cultural, historical and architectural sites that stands without peer in sub-Saharan Africa. Planning an itinerary through Ethiopia can place anybody whose interests extend to natural history in something of a quandary: the most important cultural sites lie to the north of Addis Ababa, while the major wildlife attractions are concentrated in the south, and it's impossible to do justice to both halves of this vast country in less than a month.

The easiest way to explore northern Ethiopia, and the only realistic option for those without the time or inclination to travel by bus along more than 3,000 km (1,800 miles) of rough highland roads, is by air. The four established tourist centres along the so-called historical circuit – Bahir Dar, Gonder, Axum and Lalibela – are linked to each other and to Addis Ababa by a reliable (albeit delay-prone) network of daily domestic flights. And although these four towns and their environs possess limited opportunities for wildlife-viewing by comparison to the south, they have much to offer birdwatchers, while the Simien Mountains National Park north of Gonder is a superb destination for hiking and for observing endemic mammals.

Lake Tana

A popular first stop in northern Ethiopia, **Bahir Dar ❼** is a large, modern town situated 560 km (340 miles) from Addis Ababa along a partially surfaced road via Debre Markos. Bahir Dar stands on the southern shore of the 3,670-sq.-km (1,430-sq.-mile) **Lake Tana ❽**, the country's largest body of water, dammed some 20 million years ago by a solidified lava flow. The grounds of Bahir Dar's lakeshore

hotels can provide excellent birdwatching, with an array of herons, egrets and pelicans supplemented by double-toothed and banded barbet, giant kingfisher, Bruce's green pigeon and white-crested turaco in the riparian woodland. It's also worth boating to one of the lake's 30 islands, many of which host atmospheric medieval monasteries, among them Ura Kidhane Mihret – less than an hour's ride from town – where a church covered in 16th-century murals is surrounded by lush forest teeming with monkeys and birds.

The Blue Nile flows out of Lake Tana immediately east of central Bahir Dar, below a bridge from where hippos and

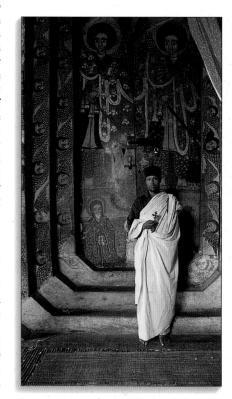

crocs are occasionally seen. Roughly 30 km (18 miles) downstream, the youthful river plunges over a 400-metre (1,300-ft) wide, 45-metre (150-ft) high cliff. Known locally as Tis Isat (smoking water), the **Blue Nile Falls ❾** was until recently one of the most impressive spectacles of its type anywhere in Africa. Sadly, however, it has been reduced to a mere trickle of late, following the opening of a hydroelectric plant through which 95 percent of the Nile's water is diverted. The road from Bahir Dar to the waterfall passes through cultivated fields where the black crowned crane and Abyssinian ground hornbill are often seen, while the footpath to the viewpoint in front of the waterfall crosses a forested gorge that harbours a similar range of woodland birds to the lakeshore hotel grounds.

About 60 km (35 miles) north of Lake Tana, **Gonder ❿**, founded in the 16th century as the capital of Emperor Fasilidas, is best known for the magnificent castles in the former royal compound and the inspirational murals adorning the church of Debre Birhan Selassie. About 30 km (18 miles) north of Gonder along the Axum road, Kosoye provides a great vantage point over the southern slopes of the Simien Mountains, particularly beautiful in September and October when the green hillside is covered in wildflowers. Kosoye can be a good place to see gelada baboon, black-and-white colobus and highland birds.

Simien Mountains National Park

The **Simien Mountains National Park ⓫**, was eulogised by the hardy traveller Rosita Forbes in the 1920s as "the most marvellous of all Abyssinian landscapes". Even in a country characterised by spectacular montane scenery, the Simiens are singularly awesome: a series of wild, jagged escarpments rising from impossibly deep river gorges to the 4,620-metre (15,200-ft) Ras Dashen, Africa's fourth-highest peak. Although primarily a scenic destination, the Simiens do harbour three large mammals endemic to Ethiopia. The Ethiopian wolf is very rare here, following a rabies epidemic

BELOW: Blue Nile Falls or Tis Isat (smoking water).

Map on pages 286–287

in the 1960s, and seldom encountered by visitors. The park is the last stronghold for the critically endangered Walia ibex, also rare – at most 600 individuals – but often seen on the cliffs by hikers. Far more certain is the magnificent golden-maned gelada baboon, with a local population estimated at more than 100,000, often congregating by the hundreds to graze on the highland meadows. The Simien Mountains are not a birdwatching destination to compare with Bale, with fewer than 100 species recorded, but several highland endemics are present, and there's no better place for close-up views of bearded vultures.

The gateway to the Simiens is the small town of Debark, which flanks the eastern park boundary on the Axum road 90 km (55 miles) north of Gonder. For those with limited time, a full-day or overnight driving excursion from Gonder, following an all-weather road from Debark 20 km (12 miles) east to Sankaber Hut, provides a good taste of the montane scenery and wildlife. Alternatively, inexpensive guided hikes or mule trekking excursions ranging from two to ten days can be arranged at the park headquarters in Debark. At least six days is required to ascend Ras Dashen, which lies just outside the eastern park boundary. Debark has a couple of small local hotels, and a bona-fide tourist lodge opened near the park entrance in 2005, but accommodation options along the trail boil down to pitching a tent at the rudimentary campsites, or bedding down alongside the goats and fleas in village huts.

Axum and Lalibela

North of Gonder, near the border with Eritrea, **Axum** ⓬ (Aksum) was founded 2,500 years ago as the capital of the Axumite Empire, contemporaneously regarded to be one of the four most powerful in the world. The modern town is dotted with ruined palaces and gigantic engraved stelae, and is the site of the country's oldest church, established *circa* AD 350, and said locally to be the resting place of the Biblical Ark of the Covenant. Although few large mammals survive around Axum, the leafy compound of this church – and those of other monasteries outside town – offer

refuge to a variety of colourful birds including the endemic black-winged lovebird and white-winged cliff chat.

The most compelling of Ethiopia's historical sites lies at an altitude of 2,630 metres (8,630 ft) within the small town of **Lalibela** ⓭, roughly 200 km (120 miles) east of Gonder as the crow flies. The centrepiece of Lalibela is a subterranean complex of 13 rock-hewn churches, carved out of solid rock some 800 years ago, and still in use today – regarded to be the unofficial eighth wonder of the ancient world. As with Axum, wildlife is rare around Lalibela, though the 8-km (5-mile) walk to Nakuta La'ab Monastery is rewarding to birdwatchers, with the endemic Ruppell's black chat, white-winged cliff chat and white-billed starling present alongside various highland raptors. The monastery of Mekina Medhane Alem, said to be 1,500 years old, lies on the slopes of the 4,193-metre (13,750-ft) Mt Abuna Yosef, a reliable site for gelada baboon and reputedly home to a relic population of Ethiopian wolf. ❑

RIGHT: Simien Mountains.

AWASH NATIONAL PARK

*The Awash River, which spills over an impressive waterfall to
run through an immense gorge, more than compensates
for any lack of wildlife in the Awash National Park*

S ituated in the Rift Valley 225 km (140 miles) southeast of Addis Ababa, the 750-sq.-km (290-sq.-mile) **Awash National Park ⓮** was gazetted in 1966 for its concentrations of arid grassland and acacia woodland fauna. Today, wildlife densities are relatively low due to poaching by local pastoralists. The surfaced road from Addis Ababa divides Awash National Park into two halves, with the limited tourist infrastructure centred in the smaller southern sector. Allow 3 hours to complete the 30-km (18-mile) southern game-viewing loop, split into three roughly equidistant legs connecting the main entrance gate, the park headquarters and museum in the southwest, and the splendidly located but

run-down Kereyou Lodge. The scenic highlights of this circuit are provided by the Awash River, which spills over an impressive waterfall near the park headquarters to run through an immense gorge, overlooked 10 km (6 miles) further downstream by the lodge.

From the surfaced Addis Ababa road, a track leads north to the base of Mt Fantalle, a dormant volcano that last erupted about 100 years ago, creating the primal black rockscapes around Lake Beseka outside the western park boundary. The stiff hike up Fantalle, best undertaken in the early morning, takes about 2 hours, offering tremendous views across the Rift Valley plains and into the 350-metre (1,150-ft) deep volcanic crater. The only other usable track in the northern sector runs for 30 km (18 miles) to the palm-fringed Filwoha Hot Springs, which gush from the ground at 35°C (95°F) to collect in deep, clear, blue pools – inviting but enervating if you take the plunge.

Watching the wildlife

The Beisa oryx is seen in open country along the main road or southern game-viewing loop, together with two Horn-of-Africa endemics: Soemmering's gazelle and Salt's dik-dik. Defassa waterbuck, warthog and vervet monkey are common in the riverine forest of the south, while klipspringer and the bushy-tailed Chanler's mountain reedbuck inhabit the slopes of Fantalle. The dense acacia bush north of the main road harbours greater and lesser kudu. Lion, spotted hyena and leopard are more often heard than seen. Awash lies at the territorial overlap of the olive baboon and localised silver-maned Hamadryas baboon: the former is most common in the south, the latter in the north, but mixed troops and hybrid individuals occur throughout. Grevy's zebra and the endemic Swayne's hartebeest are thought to be

LEFT: the black-bellied bustard is at home in Awash National Park

Map on pages 286–287

locally extinct. Awash's checklist of 450 species is most alluring to dedicated bird-watchers for the endemic yellow-throated serin and near-endemic sombre rock thrush – nowhere more easily seen than on the slopes of Fantalle – as well as the unde-scribed species of cliff swallow that breeds in the Awash Gorge. Savanna birds include the garish Abyssinian roller, the rare Arabian bustard, and massive kori bus-tard – sometimes used as a mobile perch by the northern carmine bee-eater.

Immediately east of the national park, Awash town offers a few cheap lodgings and views over the Awash Gorge to rival those from Kereyou Lodge. The main road continues east from Awash for 300 km (190 miles) to the walled city of Harer, the spir-itual heart of Ethiopia's Islamic community. The **Harer Elephant Sanctuary**, to the south, protects an endemic subspecies of elephant, the population of which now stands at around 150 individuals, after hav-ing plummeted to fewer than 100 in the 1990s. About 5 km (3 miles) east of Awash

town, the surfaced Assab road branches north from the road to Harer. Only 35 km (20 miles) north of this junction, a 10-km (6-mile) track runs west through the **Alleghedi Wildlife Sanctuary** to Bilen Lodge. Opened in 2001, the surrounding area around Bilen protects a similar range of birds and mammals to nearby Awash National Park. The lodge can arrange visits to the local Afar, semi-nomadic camel-herders who have occupied their present territory for 2,000 years. Another 110 km (65 miles) north along the Assab road, Gewane is the base for excursions into the vast **Yangudi Rassa National Park**, estab-lished in 1977 to protect the world's only surviving herd of African wild ass, the ancestor of the domestic donkey. Although the main road runs through this park for a full 50 km (30 miles), the odds of seeing wild asses are slim, unless you arrange to drive deeper into the park with a national park scout from Gewane – even then you'd be extraordinarily lucky to catch a glimpse of this critically endangered creature. ❑

BELOW: the spectacular Awash Falls.

THE SOUTHERN RIFT VALLEY

The Rift Valley floor south of Addis Ababa is the one part of
Ethiopia that truly conforms to popular expectations of East Africa
and includes two protected areas for very rare Swayne's hartebeest

Mostly lying at below 1,500 metres (5,000 ft), the Rift Valley floor south of the capital is far hotter than the highlands, and supports a cover of thick acacia woodland, becoming gradually more arid and scrub-like approaching the border with Kenya. Scenically, the area is dominated by a series of seven large lakes – similar to the better-known Rift Valley lakes in Kenya – of which four are protected within national parks.

The southern Rift displays greater faunal affinities to the East African savanna than it does to the Ethiopian highlands – indeed, this natural chasm forms a significant ecological barrier between the northwestern and southeastern highlands, reflected both in the divergent wildlife of

these two parts of Ethiopia, and their very different cultures. The nippiest access route to the southern Rift is via the surfaced road that runs east from Addis Ababa for about 75 km (45 miles) to Mojo, then south to Moyale via Ziway, Shashemene, Awassa, Dila and Yabelo. A more interesting route from the capital follows a dirt road south through Butajira to connect with the main surfaced road at Ziway, passing the Melka Kunture Prehistoric Site Museum, the country's most southerly intact rock-hewn church at Adadi Maryam, and a field of engraved medieval stelae at Tiya.

Four lakes

The small town of **Ziway**, roughly 160 km (100 miles) from Addis Ababa, is nothing

BELOW:
fishermen and
pelicans on
Lake Awassa.

Map
n pages
86–287

special, but 430-sq.-km (170-sq.-mile) **Lake Ziway** ⓑ (Ziway Hayk'), accessible from a causeway 1.5 km (1 mile) east of the town centre, is worth a look. The causeway is an excellent vantage point over a papyrus swamp that teems with birdlife, notably the uncommon black egret (called the umbrella bird for its habit of fishing with wings raised in a canopy), lesser jacana, lesser moorhen and various migrant waterfowls. Flotillas of pelicans are usually on the open water, and for a small fee, the jetty boatmen will take visitors out to look for hippos. The island monastery of Debre Tsion, reputedly founded by refugee priests from Axum in the 9th century AD as a sanctuary for the Ark of the Covenant, can also be visited by boat.

About 40 km (25 miles) south of Ziway, the main road runs between a cluster of three lakes, of which **Lake Langano** ⓰ (Langano Hayk') – its murky brown water reputedly safe for swimming – is the most developed for tourism. The three resorts on the western shore cater primarily for weekenders from the capital, but the upmarket Bishangari Lodge on the eastern shore is geared more towards ecotourism – black-and-white colobus and other primates are common here, and 250 bird species have been recorded.

Directly opposite the Bekele Mola Resort on Lake Langano stands the Dole entrance gate to **Abiata-Shala National Park** ⓱, which protects the two lakes for which it is named, as well as the isthmus that divides them, and a thin strip of land along the shores. **Lake Abiata** is a shallow alkaline pan, no deeper than 14 metres (45 ft) deep, surrounded by a flat floodplain that often becomes treacherously muddy when the water is low. **Lake Shala**, enclosed by green hills and foreboding black cliffs, and dotted with volcanically formed islands, plunges to a depth of 260 metres (850 ft), holding a greater volume of water than Ethiopia's other Rift Valley lakes combined.

Wildlife is scarce in Abiata-Shala, due to human encroachment, but Grant's gazelle, warthog and oribi are occasionally seen, and more than 400 bird species have been recorded, including a few ostrich kept in a

fenced enclosure near the main gate. Up to 300,000 greater and lesser flamingos regularly flock along the windward edge of Lake Abiata, to feed on algae concentrates. A great white pelican colony on an island on Lake Shala once hosted up to 13,000 pairs, making it the most important breeding site for the species, but numbers have dwindled in recent years following a change in the water level.

Of the tracks running through Abiata-Shala, the most worthwhile for wildlife and birds follows the shore of Abiata for 20 km (12 miles) between the Horakello and Dole entrance gates. Another track leads from Dole to the shore of Lake Shala, where hot steam, mud and water bubble to the earth's surface – relics of the volcanic activity that formed this amazing landscape. Revered locally for their medicinal properties, the hot springs (*filwoha*) near Shala have a sense of primeval mystery about them, especially in the cooler early mornings.

Several important routes through southern Ethiopia converge at the rapidly grow-

ing town of **Shashemene**, which lies about 50 km (30 miles) south of the main entrance to Abiata-Shala. The surfaced road from Addis Ababa to Moyale runs through the centre of Shashemene, while the dirt road to Dodola and Goba branches east 500 metres (550 yards) north of the town centre, and the surfaced road south-west to Arba Minch forks to the right opposite the central Mobil Garage.

Aside from strategic considerations, Shashemene really has very little going for it, and an overnight stay there would not be high on anybody's wish list.

More alluring is the hot-springs resort at **Wondo Genet**, 20 km (12 miles) south of town along a dirt road branching left next to the telecommunication centre. The lush indigenous forest at Wondo Genet supports troops of black-and-white colobus and olive baboon, and a plethora of forest birds including the raucous silvery-cheeked hornbill, exquisite Narina trogon, and endemic yellow-fronted parrot.

Back on the Moyale Road, 25 km (15 miles) south of Shashemene, **Awassa** ⑬, with its unusually neat city centre running down to the verdant shore of Lake Awassa, is a leading contender for the title of Ethiopia's most attractive town. The lakeshore hotels are shaded by tall fig trees, in which approachable troops of black-and-white colobus and grivet monkey frolic. The footpath running for about 1.5 km (1 mile) along the lakeshore offers superb birdwatching: pygmy goose, great white pelican and a host of other water-associated species on the lake, and blue-headed coucal, Bruce's green pigeon and most of the woodland-associated Ethiopian endemics in the fringing trees.

Another 90 km (56 miles) south of Awassa, **Dilla** is an important agricultural centre with a breezy location on the green eastern slopes of the Rift Escarpment. There's no specific wildlife viewing around Dilla, but some superb ancient rock engravings lie 6 km (4 miles) west of the town centre, and at least two major fields of medieval stelae are found within the forested hills to the southeast – the regional tourist office can arrange guides.

South of Dilla, the Moyale road descends into the arid badlands inhabited by traditional Borena pastoralists, after 210 km (125 miles) arriving at Yabelo *(see page 307)*. The border town of Moyale lies 200 km (124 miles) past Yabelo by road, passing through semi-desert thinly inhabited by gerenuk, Grant's gazelle and greater kudu, as well as many delightful birds – vulturine guinea-fowl, golden-bellied starling, golden pipit – associated with the arid north of Kenya.

Senkele Game Sanctuary

Along the road to Arba Minch, some 70 km (43 miles) from Shashemene, an 18-km (11-mile) dirt road branches south to **Senkele Game Sanctuary**. This small reserve was set up to protect a herd of Swayne's hartebeest, which once roamed the plains of the Horn of Africa in their thousands, but are now restricted to three localities in Ethiopia. Some 2,000 of these rich, chocolate-coloured hartebeest were once packed into the reserve, but poach-

LEFT: great cormorants vibrate their throats to keep cool.

Map
n pages
86–287

ing has reduced the number to about 800. Bohor reedbuck, oribi and many different birds are also present.

Nechisar National Park

The other main stronghold for the Swayne's hartebeest is **Nechisar National Park ⓳**, an underrated scenic jewel centred on the isthmus between Lakes Chamo and Abaya, and only 10 minutes' drive from the town of **Arba Minch** (Forty Springs).

Habitats in the park range from lush fig forest fed by groundwater springs immediately below Arba Minch, to the open Nechisar (white grass) Plains on the opposite side of the lakes. The impressive greater kudu is often seen on the isthmus, Guenther's dik-dik abound at every turn, and the northern shore of Lake Chamo is frequented by hundreds of monstrous crocodiles. On the open plains, Burchell's zebra, Grant's gazelle and large troops of olive baboon graze against a backdrop of jewelled lakes and the soaring mountains of the western highlands above Arba Minch. Birdwatchers can look out for the Nechisar nightjar, described in 1995 on the basis of a wing collected by a research expedition, but yet to be seen alive. The same expedition collected 15 formerly undescribed butterfly species, indicating that scientific knowledge of Nechisar is far from complete.

Arba Minch lies at the end of the tarmac, but a dirt road continues south, through Konso, to the remote and staunchly traditionalist south Omo region. Roughly 40 different tribes inhabit south Omo: a rich cultural mosaic whose components include body scarification, bull-jumping, stick-fighting, body painting, metal necklaces, wild-ochre hair braids, matted hair buns displayed proudly as the Mark of Cain, and grave statues that depict the leering deceased clasping a serpent-length penis in his hand. South Omo requires at least four days to explore properly, following a rough road circuit southwest from Konso through Turmi to Omorate, then north via Murelle to Jinka, the area's main town.

The wildlife in south Omo is not what it was 50 years ago, and few people visit the area for game-viewing alone. Neverthe-

less, along the roads connecting Turmi, Omorate and Murelle, you can expect to see bat-eared fox, Guenther's dik-dik, the bizarre stretch-necked gerenuk, Lelwel hartebeest and tiang (a Sudanese race of topi), as well as a host of colourful dry-country birds and raptors.

Between Murelle and Jinka, a rough track passes through the poached-out **Mago National Park** – bounded by the Mago and Omo rivers – which harbours small but viable populations of elephant, lion, buffalo, reticulated giraffe, Grevy's zebra and about 12 antelope species. The few travellers who make it to Mago invariably make an excursion to a Mursi encampment – the Mursi women wear large clay lip-plates in an incision between their mouth and lower lip.

Situated on the west side of the Omo River, **Omo National Park** protects a similar – and similarly depleted – large mammal fauna to Mago, but it has been all but inaccessible since the only bridge across the Omo washed away in 1998. ❑

BALE MOUNTAINS AND THE SOUTHEAST

The huge Bale Mountains National Park is the jewel of Ethiopia's protected areas and is the single largest home of the critically endangered Ethiopian wolf

The 2,200-sq.-km (850-sq.-mile) **Bale Mountains National Park ㉔** in the southeastern highlands is unquestionably the most compelling protected area in Ethiopia. True, it would be disingenuous to recommend Bale to first-time safarigoers ahead of the savanna reserves of Kenya or Tanzania. But with its rich assemblage of rare and endangered species – complemented by some fantastic mountain scenery – Bale will come as a genuine revelation to even the most experienced of African travellers.

The centrepiece of Bale, the 4,000-metre (13,000-ft) **Sanetti Plateau Ⓐ**, can be reached on foot or by donkey over a

couple of days from the park headquarters at **Dinsho Ⓑ**. More sedately, Sanetti is traversed by the highest all-weather road in Africa, less than one hour's drive from the substantial town of **Goba Ⓒ**. However you arrive there, the chill, thin air of the plateau can leave you gasping for breath. So, too, can the otherworldly beauty of its strange montane landscape: a pastel montage of lichen-covered rocks, tussocks of grey and white everlasting Helichrysum shrubs, small reflective tarns, clumped forests of shoulder-high heather, and the prehistoric-looking giant lobelia.

Sanetti Plateau

The plateau harbours few large mammals, though klipspringer and common duiker are resident, and golden jackal, leopard and the dark-maned Abyssinian lion are occasional vagrants. Smaller mammals, by contrast, are everywhere: the 2-kg (4½-pound) giant mole-rat and a variety of lesser fur-balls that dart manically between the manifold entrances to the subterranean labyrinths they inhabit. These burrowing rodents form the main diet of the critically endangered Ethiopian wolf, which – given its scarcity – is seen with remarkable ease from the main road, and is generally very relaxed around vehicles (but more nervous of pedestrians).

Sanetti's birdlife encapsulates Ethiopia's unique combination of ecological affinities: part Palaearctic, part Afro-tropical and part nowhere-else-on-earth. The only sub-Saharan breeding populations of the Palaearctic golden eagle and ruddy shelduck occur here, along with the most southerly breeding population of chough. Afro-montane species are represented by the magnificent auger buzzard, gem-like tacazze sunbird, localised chestnut-naped and montane francolins, and an isolated

LEFT: the Bal Mountains.

Maps:
Area 286
Park 305

northern breeding population of the endangered wattled crane. Easily seen endemics include the spot-throated plover, black-headed siskin and blue-winged goose – the latter more closely related to a South American fowl than any living Old World species. Then there is the peculiar Rouget's rail, an Ethiopian highland endemic which, despite belonging to a family noted for it secretiveness, struts through patches of rank vegetation with all the modesty of a model on a catwalk.

The national park headquarters and resthouse at Dinsho are surrounded by tall juniper forest permeated by the aroma of fallen hagenia leaves. Visitors can be confident of seeing reedbuck, warthog and the handsome Menelik's bushbuck within a few hundred metres of the resthouse. Resembling a shaggier and less distinctively striped version of the allied greater kudu, the mountain nyala is one of Africa's rarest large antelopes – total population estimated at fewer than 4,000 – but you'd hardly think so at Dinsho, where up to 100

individuals might be seen over a couple of hours walking. Dinsho is a good site for endemic forest birds, in particular the Abyssinian catbird, a secretive species that attracts attention with its melodious song. The Gaysay Valley – within easy day walking distance of Dinsho – harbours a small but regularly observed population of Ethiopian wolf.

Dodola-Asela Protected Area

Goba and Dinsho can be approached directly from Addis Ababa as a full-day drive via Nazret, Asela and Dodola, or from Shashemene in the Rift Valley, connecting with the above route a few kilometres before Dodola. Either way, Dodola is the site of the headquarters of the **Dodola-Asela Protected Area**, the most organised hiking destination in Ethiopia, established in 1999 with German funding and assistance. The five equipped mountain huts in the protected area are connected by a network of well-maintained hiking trails, passing through a similar combina-

RIGHT: Ethiopian wolf in the Bale Mountains National Park.

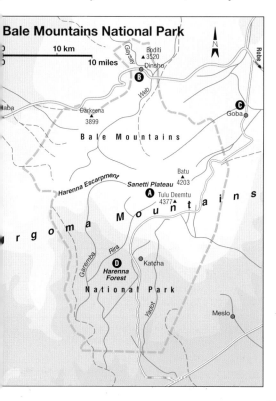

tion of forest and Afro-Alpine vegetation to Bale, and supporting a broadly similar fauna – though the Ethiopian wolf and mountain nyala are not so easily seen as in the national park.

Roughly 100 km (60 miles) east of Bale by road (via Robe and Goro), the **Sof Omar Caves** are named after a 12th-century Muslim leader who took refuge there, and they remain an important pilgrimage site for Muslim Ethiopians. From the entrance to the caves, a 2-km (1½-mile) walking trail follows the Web River underground into a series of vast limestone chambers studded with pillars up to 20 metres (60 ft) high. Sof Omar is one of two sites where the endemic Salvadori's serin is regularly seen, and both greater and lesser kudu might be seen along the approach roads.

Harenna Forest

The road across the Sanetti Plateau switchbacks down the southern escarpment into the third major habitat protected within the national park. This is the vast **Harenna**

Forest ❶, which has a more varied tree composition than the forest at Dinsho, and harbours black-and-white colobus, as well as bushpig, giant forest hog, bushbuck, leopard, lion, and possibly a relic pack of the endangered African hunting dog. Harenna is the main stronghold for the scarce bamboo-associated Bale monkey, which has a thick yellow-brown coat and prominent white beard, and is regarded by some authorities as a race of the widespread vervet, confined to southeastern Ethiopia's highland forests, and by others as a full species, Formative research in this relatively unexplored forest during the 1990s resulted in the discovery of several hitherto undescribed reptile, amphibian and small mammal species.

South of the Harenna Forest, a long, dusty road leads from Dola Mena though Genale, Negele Borena and Melka Guda, before veering east, through Arero, to Yabello on the surfaced Awassa–Moyale road. This route traverses an expanse of semi-arid bush country that is popular with

BELOW: giant lobelia can be found at high altitudes.

Maps:
rea 286
ark 305

ornithological tours for several sites associated with specific endemic or localised species. Serious birdwatchers should bank on requiring at least four and better seven days to cover this route, and they will need to adjust to the decidedly no-frills accommodation found in Dola Mena, Genale, Negele Borena, Arero and Yabelo.

The first key site along this route is **Genale**, where a belt of forest fringing the river is inhabited by the endemic Prince Ruspoli's turaco. This large and colourful frugivore was first collected in 1892, but the Italian explorer after whom it is named died without recording the location; only in the 1940s was another living specimen seen. The largest town in the region, **Negele Borena** ㉑, 15 km (9 miles) northwest of the junction of the Bogol Manyo and Yabelo roads, is where the endemic Sidamo short-toed lark can sometimes be located. For a chance of seeing the Degodi lark, an equally rare endemic, an overnight expedition 270 km (160 miles) southeast to the remote village of Bogol Manyo is required.

Yabelo Wildlife Sanctuary

Roughly 120 km (70 miles) south of Negele Borena, along the road towards **Yabelo**, the Dawa River Bridge near Melka Guda is the most accessible site for two Ethiopia-Somali endemics, the white-winged turtle dove and Juba weaver. About 60 km (35 miles) past this bridge, the forest around Arero is a good site for Prince Ruspoli's turaco and Salvadori's seedeater.

The drive between Arero and Yabelo bypasses the **Yabelo Wildlife Sanctuary** ㉒, an arid savanna reserve harbouring small populations of Swayne's hartebeest, Grant's gazelle, Grevy's zebra and greater and lesser kudu. The town of Yabelo lies at the core of the tiny territory occupied by the singular Streseman's bush crow – a colourful bird with no close genetic allies – and the more generic white-tailed swallow. Both are quite common in the wildlife reserve, but are just as likely to be observed from the surfaced Awassa–Moyale road for 50 km (30 miles) either side of Yabelo. ❑

GHT:
ot-breasted
owing, Bale
tional Park.

THE ETHIOPIAN WOLF

Listed as critically endangered, the Ethiopian wolf is the scarcest of the world's 37 canid species, and the rarest predator on the African mainland. Known also as the Simien fox or Ethiopian jackal, its genetic affinities were once the subject of controversy, but recent DNA testing revealed it to be more close to the European wolf than any African canid. Standing significantly taller than a jackal, the Ethiopian wolf is a handsome animal, distinguished by its rich chestnut coat and bold white throat and flank markings.

Unlike most mammalian predators, the Ethiopian wolf is predominantly diurnal, and a courser rather than a hunter, snacking on whatever rodents might cross its path. Only 100 years ago, the Ethiopian wolf was widespread throughout the Ethiopian highlands. Today, the wolf is mostly confined to uninhabited Afro-Alpine moorland, with roughly 10 isolated populations totalling no more than 600 individuals.

This decline is due to the infiltration of introduced diseases such as canine distemper and rabies, and also to interbreeding with domestic dogs. The largest single population – estimated at around 250 – is in Bale National Park, centred on the Sanetti Plateau and Web River Valley. Another 30–150 individuals live in the nearby Arsi Highlands, but the extent to which these populations interbreed is unknown.

RWANDA

Rwanda is an important destination for East African wildlife enthusiasts; its best-known attraction is gorilla tracking

Extending over 26,340 sq. km (10,290 sq. miles), Rwanda is a tiny country – about the same size as some of its neighbouring counties' larger national parks – yet it supports a population of roughly 8 million, making it the mostly densely inhabited nation in Africa. Much of the country, in particular Lake Kivu and the Virunga Volcanoes in the northwest, is spectacularly beautiful, comprised of fertile highlands that undulate from the Albertine Rift Escarpment down to the Lake Victoria Basin, spanning altitudes of 1,200–4,500 metres (3,960–14,760 ft).

A German, Von Goetzen, was the first European to reach Rwanda when in 1884 he crossed the Akagera River near the Rusumo Falls on the modern-day border with Tanzania. Here he found a feudal hierarchy in which Tutsi nobles dominated the more populous Hutu peasantry and the small numbers of Batwa hunter-gatherers who still subsisted in the country's forests. In 1899, Rwanda was made to recognise German sovereignty. This lasted until World War I, when Belgium took over Rwanda and neighbouring Burundi. Colonial ties were severed on 1 July, 1962, with the formation of the Republic of Rwanda.

In April 1994, long-standing tensions between Hutu and Tutsi culminated in a gruesome genocide that claimed an estimated one million lives in the space of three months and forced twice that number of people to flee to rudimentary refugee camps in Tanzania and other neighbouring states. The killing abated after the Rwanda Patriotic Front seized power in July 1994 to establish a broad-based government of national unity. Rwanda has subsequently enjoyed an increasing high level of stability. Practically all the refugees have been repatriated, and although the scars of the genocide will take decades to heal completely, visitors are made to feel very welcome today, and travel conditions are as safe as anywhere in Africa.

Rwanda has an excellent system of surfaced roads, some good hotels and lodges, and three very different national parks. The Parc des Volcans, famed for its mountain-gorilla tracking, re-opened in 1999, since when it has started to attract back a significant traffic of cross-border tourism from Uganda. The other two national parks are Akagera, which harbours a wide variety of savanna wildlife, and the lushly forested and richly diverse Nyungwe Forest, gazetted in 2001. ❑

PRECEDING PAGES: the deep-green valleys on the way to Ruhengeri are partially obscured by cloud cover.
LEFT: mountain gorilla.

PARC NATIONAL DES VOLCANS

One of Africa's oldest parks, the Parc National des Volcans was made
famous by Dian Fossey and her efforts to protect
its endangered mountain gorillas

The borders of Rwanda, Uganda and the Democratic Republic of Congo (DRC) converge at the 3,669-metre (11,930-ft) summit of Mt Sabinyo, the oldest of a magnificent chain of eight volcanoes – two of which remain active – known as the Virunga or Bufumbira Mountains. The Virungas' main claim to fame is their association with Dian Fossey and the endangered mountain gorillas that reside in the bamboo and evergreen forest on the slopes of the six inactive cones. But the chain of free-standing volcanoes is also one of the most dramatic sights in East Africa. Three of the mountains rise sharply from the surrounding hills to altitudes of above 4,000 metres (13,000 ft) and all but one top the 3,500-metre (11,483-ft) mark. The highest volcano, the 4,507-metre (14,786-ft) Mt Karisimbi, is tall enough to precipitate the frequent snow showers alluded to by its name, which means cowry (a white shell).

The Parc National des Volcans

The upper reaches of the Virungas are protected within a contiguous 435-sq.-km (180-sq.-mile) cross-border trio of reserves, of which the 125-sq.-km (50-sq.-mile) **Parc National des Volcans ❶** is the Rwandan component (the other two are Mgahinga National Park in Uganda and the DRC'S Parc National des Virungas). Rwanda's Parc des Volcans and its Congolese counterpart are Africa's oldest national parks, founded in 1925 when both countries were under Belgian rule, and named Parc National Albert after the Belgian king. The two parks have been separately administered since independence in 1962.

The foundation of the Parc National Albert was instigated by Carl Ethan Akeley, a renowned American museum collector who visited the Virungas in 1921 and was alarmed by the extent of gorilla hunting. The next notable gorilla conservationist, Walter Baumgartel, established the Travellers' Rest Hotel in Kisoro (on the Ugandan side of the volcanoes) as a base for tourists and researchers. It was from this legendary hostelry – still open today – that George Schaller conducted the pioneering 1960 study which did so much to dispel the prevailing perception of gorillas as mindlessly aggressive and violent creatures.

That gorillas, despite their fearsome appearance, are among the most peaceable of primates was confirmed by a more comprehensive behavioural study initiated by Dian Fossey in 1963. Mentored by the palaeontologist Dr Louis Leakey, who believed that studying great apes in the wild would cast light on the lifestyle and behaviour of our early hominid ancestors, Fossey set about habituating the gorillas in

LEFT: l'Hoest' monkey.

Map
on page
313

GHT:
a picking.

the Parc des Volcans, enabling her to monitor their behaviour at close quarters. The active and arguably vindictive role that Fossey played in apprehending and punishing gorilla poachers almost certainly lay behind her brutal – and still unsolved – murder in the park in 1985. Fossey's work, which gained popular acclaim through her book *Gorillas in the Mist* as well as several documentaries and feature films, continues posthumously through the Dian Fossey Gorilla Fund. As of 2002, visitors to the Parc des Volcans can visit Fossey's tomb, which is situated by the graves of some of her beloved gorillas at the research centre she established at Karisoke.

In 1979, Amy Vedder and Bill Webber initiated a pioneering project in which controlled tourist visits to the habituated gorillas of the Parc des Volcans were used to fund local environmental education and anti-poaching patrols. Initially controversial, gorilla tourism proved to be an unqualified success, and by the mid-1980s it was entrenched as Rwanda's third-highest

earner of foreign revenue. The cash flow generated by gorilla tourism revolutionised official and local perceptions of the great apes, leading to a sharp decrease in poaching – the 1989 census placed the gorilla population of the Virungas at 320, an increase of almost 30 percent since 1979.

Tourist activities within the Parc des Volcans were suspended after 1991, when civil war forced researchers and rangers to evacuate the park amid widespread concern for the future of the gorillas. But when the researchers returned in the late 1990s, it transpired that only four Rwandan gorillas could not be accounted for, two of which were old females that almost certainly succumbed to natural causes. Surprisingly, a census undertaken in 2001 revealed that the gorilla population of the Virungas stood at more than 355 individuals, the highest level since 1960.

The Parc des Volcans re-opened to tourism in 1999, since when its main attraction – as ever – has been gorilla tracking. Two different habituated gorilla troops stay

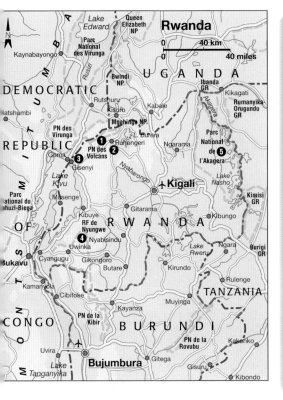

within tracking range on a permanent basis. The Susa Group, comprising of more than 30 individuals, is by far the largest gorilla group anywhere that can be visited by tourists – a uniquely exciting and chaotic experience, though the very steep ascent to the edge of the forest in which this group resides is not for the fainthearted. The smaller Sabinyo Group, by contrast, lives on a lightly forested saddle between Sabinyo and Gahinga, and can usually be reached without any heavy exertion. Two other habituated troops are also normally resident in the park, but they do occasionally cross the border into Uganda or the DRC. Eight permits (US$250 apiece) are issued daily for each group, which means that between 16 and 32 permits are available on any given day, depending on current gorilla movements.

The park also offers excursions to a habituated troop of the beautiful golden monkey, an endangered Albertine Rift endemic of which no more than a thousand individuals remain. The mountains' relic populations of elephant and buffalo are seldom observed, but evidence of their presence – steaming fresh elephant pats in particular – is often found along the trail. Other elusive highland forest species include the yellow-backed duiker and giant forest hog. For birdwatchers, a wide range of forest specialists includes at least 15 Albertine Rift endemics. Gorilla tracking tends to be a rather focused activity, for which reason any visitor who wishes to observe smaller mammals or birds might also want to hike along one of two trails to the volcanic peaks that re-opened to tourists in 2002.

Mt Visoke can be ascended as a roughly 7-hour round trip, passing through lush forest trails littered with mammal spoor and rustling with avian activity. At the summit, there are normally good views to the other volcanoes, most reliably nearby Karisimbi, and it's customary to take a brief dip in the small, chilly crater lake for which the mountain is named (Visoke means Watering Place). The hike to the peak of Karisimbi, the highest point in the

BELOW: eye to eye with a mountain gorilla.

Map on page 313

range, takes two days, and at the time of writing hikers must supply their own tent, sleeping bag, stove, food and other equipment. It can be very cold on Karisimbi, especially in September and October, when the peak is capped in snow.

Where gorilla trackers seldom ascend above the 3,000-metre (9,800-ft) contour, the hikes to the peaks offer an opportunity to experience the full range of vegetation zones associated with East Africa's highest mountains. The bamboo zone extends from 2,300 metres (7,500 ft) up to 2,600–3,000 metres (8,500–9,800 ft) depending on local conditions. Above the bamboo zone is an ancient forest of gnarled *Hagenia abyssinica* and *Hypericum lanceolatum* trees, draped with mosses, orchids, ferns and wispy strands of Unsea lichen (Old Man's Beard). At about 3,350 metres (11,000 ft), way higher than gorillas – or their human visitors – are likely to venture, the Alpine moorland zone hosts a fascinating array of Afro-Alpine plants, ranging from decorative fields of Helichrysum flowers to oth-

erworldly stands of giant senecios and lobelias growing up to 5 metres (15 ft) high.

The most convenient base for gorilla tracking and hikes in the Parc des Volcans (and the only realistic one for those without private transport) is **Ruhengeri ❷**, a substantial market town at the base of the Virungas. Ruhengeri has its fair share of basic budget hotels, but two more up-market options opened out of town in 2004: the Gorilla's Nest near the park headquarters and Virunga Lodge on the shores of nearby Lake Burera. Many tours also visit the gorillas as a day trip from Kisoro in Uganda (the departure time of 7.30am becomes 8.30am, since Rwanda is an hour ahead). With an early start you can visit the gorillas as a day trip from Kigali, the Rwandan capital, a 90-minute drive from Ruhengeri. A more attractive starting point – and worth visiting in its own right – is the port of **Gisenyi ❸** on the shores of Lake Kivu, which lies only 60 km (37 miles) west of Ruhengeri by surfaced road, and offers a good assortment of hotels. ❑

NYUNGWE FOREST AND AKAGERA NATIONAL PARKS

The Nyungwe Forest is a highly rated and important area of biodiversity while the Parc National de l'Akagera has the greatest diversity of large mammals in Rwanda

Gazetted in 2000, **Réserve Forestière de Nyungwe ❹** sprawls for almost 1,000 sq. km (360 sq. miles) across the mountainous southwest of Rwanda to protect what is the largest extant rainforest in East Africa. Nyungwe is also regarded as having one of the highest biodiversity levels in East Africa, partly as a function of its age. Some 10,000 years ago, when a change in rainfall patterns caused the forested Congo Basin to temporarily dry out, Nyungwe and the other highland forests of the Albertine Rift flourished, to provide refuge to innumerable forest life forms that might otherwise have become extinct. In the case of Nyungwe, biodiver-

sity through antiquity is enhanced by its exceptional altitude range, spanning 1,600 metres (5200 ft) to 2,950 metres (9,600 ft).

Infrequently visited by tourists, Nyungwe is nevertheless eminently accessible, situated only 3 hours' drive from Rwanda's capital city of Kigali. The forest is transected for a full 50 km (30 miles) by the nippy surfaced road that connects Kigali to Cyangugu Port via the sedate university town of Butare. The Uwinka reception centre/campsite stands adjacent to the surfaced road roughly 215 km (130 miles) from Kigali, while the agreeably low-key ORTPN rest house lies another 18 km (11 miles) towards Cyangugu.

Even as viewed from the road, Nyungwe is awesome. Forest-swathed mountains tumble like monstrous green waves towards the distant Burundi border, providing a primal contrast to the terraced cultivation and orderly tea plantations that otherwise characterise the countryside of Africa's most densely populated nation. Troops of vervet monkey and olive baboon stalk the road verges, as does the handsome white-bearded L'Hoest's monkey, a large and unusually terrestrial forest primate that has its main stronghold in Nyungwe. Another treat for unwary motorists is the improbably garish great blue turaco, flocks of which regularly flap across the road like psychedelic turkeys.

Where to watch the wildlife

To experience Nyungwe in full, take a guided walk along the network of trails that slither downhill from Uwinka reception centre to a lush riverine valley punctuated by several fern-fringed waterfalls. Along the way, you're bound to encounter the acknowledged star among Nyungwe's 13 primate species: the gracefully acrobatic Ruwenzori colobus, the only arbo-

LEFT: red-throated alethe, an Albertine Rift endemic.

Map
on page
313

real African primate known to move in troops of up to 400 individuals. Nyungwe's population of 500-plus chimpanzees generally retreats to inaccessible higher elevations for the dry season, but during the rains you'll almost certainly hear – and might well see – them along the forest trails.

First recorded in Nyungwe in 1989, the scarce owl-faced monkey is confined to bamboo thickets close to the Burundi border. This habitat is also the favoured stomping ground of the beautiful but vulnerable golden monkey, which – restricted to Nyungwe and the Virunga Mountains – has a global population of fewer than 1,000. Primates aside, Nyungwe affords sanctuary to such elusive forest specialists as golden cat, giant forest hog, giant forest squirrel, yellow-backed duiker and the endemic Lestrade's duiker. Buffalo, last recorded in 1976, are probably extinct here, but elephant may still survive in small numbers – a fresh corpse was discovered in 1999, cause of death unknown, but no spoor has been observed since.

GHT: walking
ail in the
✓ungwe
rest Reserve.

Inhabited by myriad butterfly and more than 100 orchid species, Nyungwe has much to offer specialists of all persuasions. Birdwatchers are particularly well catered for, with the very scarce Congo Bay Owl and 24 Albertine Rift endemics prominent on a checklist of 275 species. Behaviourally the most remarkable of these endemic is the red-throated alethe, a robin-like bird that habitually trails behind monkeys to pick off disturbed insects, and behaves with similar inhibition around people, hopping fearlessly between their legs in the forest undergrowth.

Walking through the forest interior can become frustrating, as one cryptic creature after another flits unidentifiably through the shadowy litter. For this reason, an excellent spot for initial investigation of Nyungwe's fauna is the small relic forest patch situated on the Gisakura Tea Estate, within walking distance of the ORTPN resthouse. Home to a troop of 40 Ruwenzori colobus as well as a solitary red-tailed monkey, this isolated stand of

THE VIRUNGA RANGE

Virunga is a geologically young range, formed over the past 2 million years along a fault line related to the same tectonic activities that created the Great Rift Valley. The ive volcanic cones situated partially within Rwanda and/or Uganda are all dormant or extinct, but mounts Nyiragongo and Nyamuragira, both of which lie entirely within the DRC, remain highly volatile. Nyamuragira is probably the most active volcano on the African mainland: it has erupted on 34 separate occasions since 1882 (most recently in July 2002), though only once did it cause any fatalities. Nyiragongo, though less regularly active than Nyamuragira, has been far more destructive. In 1977, a lava lake in the main crater drained in less than one hour, forming streams of molten lava that killed an estimated 2,000 people and terminated only 500 metres (1,640 ft) from Goma, a large port on the Congolese shore of Lake Kivu. Another eruption on 17 January 2002 killed at least 50 people and destroyed about one-quarter of Goma, forcing the town's 400,000 inhabitants to cross into Rwanda for temporary refuge. It is reassuring to know that, while kilometre-high plumes shooting out from these Congolese volcanoes sometimes illuminate the night sky at Ruhengeri or Kisoro, no active lava flow has come within miles of these towns in recorded history.

trees is enclosed within a steep ravine, allowing one to observe a fantastic variety of forest fringe creatures from the edge, without having one's neck cricked perpetually towards the high canopy.

Parc National de l'Akagera

The breezy, steeply contoured highlands of Rwanda give way in the far east to a relatively low-lying belt of open woodland, hemmed in by the meandering Akagera River along the border with Tanzania, and an associated labyrinth of lakes, swamps and channels. Since 1934, much of this sweltering and well-watered savanna region has been protected in **Parc National de l'Akagera ❺**, a safari destination which in its pre-civil war prime rivalled East Africa's finest for vast concentrations of plains grazers and attendant large predators. In 1994, however, Akagera was subjected to heavy subsistence poaching as hordes of terrified Rwandans fled across the border to the safety of Tanzania. Then, in the aftermath of the genocide,

many of the desperate returned refugees squatted within Akagera, leading to almost two-thirds of the park being formally de-gazetted in 1997.

The reduced national park, still a substantial 900 sq. km (347 sq. miles) in extent, remains somewhat ecologically compromised by human encroachment – the most common large mammal is almost certainly the domestic cow, and several of the lakes support illegal fishing camps.

Despite this, Akagera is a park of considerable merit. There is the tropical wetland scenery, its mesmerising wilderness character enhanced by the improbability of encountering another tourist vehicle. And while game densities are rather low – livestock aside, the only large mammal that could be described as common is the hippopotamus – they are still sufficient to hint at what Akagera must have been like in its heyday, and what, one hopes, it might eventually become again. Over the course of a day or two in Akagera, it is still possible to notch up 20 different mammal species. The

BELOW: Virunga Mountains at sunset.

Map on page 313

tangled woodland fringing the eight open lakes – easily explored along a serviceable track running north from the main entrance gate – supports small numbers of impala, bushbuck, waterbuck, warthog, buffalo and olive baboon, while the park's 60 surviving elephants are often encountered around Lake Hago. Giraffe, eland, zebra and oribi frequent the grassy Matumba Hills (reached by turning left from the main track at junction 23) while the northern woodland harbours large herds of topi and a relic population of roan antelope.

Black rhinoceros and African hunting dog are probably extinct within Akagera, but the ever-resilient leopard still survives in viable numbers, and lions – victimised by local livestock herders – are slowly re-colonising the park from neighbouring Tanzania. Night drives offer a good chance of encountering spotted hyena, white-tailed mongoose and other small predators, as well as the endearing bush-baby and elephant-shrew.

Prominent among 525 recorded bird species are the flocks of storks, ibises, pelicans, herons and egrets that haunt the lakes. The bizarre shoebill, regularly seen on boat excursions prior to 1994, is presumably still resident. Away from the water, characteristic East African savanna birds such as lilac-breasted roller, little bee-eater and Bateleur eagle are supplemented by several southern species – crested barbet, Souza's shrike and white-headed black chat – at the northern extent of their range. The range-restricted red-faced barbet is practically endemic to savanna habitats fringing the Kagera wetlands.

The state-owned Akagera Hotel, overlooking Lake Ihema, closed down in 1994 but re-opened in late 2003 as the privately managed up-market 58-room Akagera Game Lodge. A cheaper base for a non-camping trip into Akagera is **Kibungu**, a small town about an hour's drive from the park entrance, and 100 km (60 miles) from Kibale along a surfaced road. The two lakeshore campsites within the park would suit only fully self-sufficient visitors. ❏

BELOW: Lake Hago sunset.

INSIGHT GUIDES
Travel Tips

www.insightguides.com

☀ INSIGHT GUIDES

The World Leader in Visual Travel Guides & Maps

As travellers become ever more discriminating, Insight Guides is using the vast experience gained over three-and-a-half decades of guidebook publishing to create an even wider range of titles than before. For those who want the big picture, Insight Guides and Insight City Guides provide comprehensive coverage of a destination. Insight Pocket Guides supply personal recommendations for a short stay. Insight Compact Guides are attractively portable. Insight FlexiMaps are both easy to use and rugged. And specialist titles cover shopping, eating out, and museums and galleries.

CONTENTS

Getting Acquainted

The Place

Introduction

The three countries conventionally regarded to comprise East Africa, and which formed the (recently resurrected) East African community after independence in the early 1960s, are Kenya, Tanzania and Uganda. The slightly broader definition of East Africa used in this guide also embraces Rwanda and Ethiopia, the former best-known for its mountain gorillas, the latter of interest to wildlife enthusiasts for a wealth of mammal and bird species found nowhere else in the world.

Political Background

Kenya, Tanzania and Uganda are former British dependencies, though mainland Tanzania (known as Tanganyika in the colonial era) was a German colony prior to World War I, together with present-day Burundi and Rwanda, which fell under Belgian mandate between 1916 and the 1960s. Aside from a short-lived Italian occupation prior to World War II, Ethiopia has never been colonised, and it retained a strongly feudal political system until 1974, when its octogenarian Emperor Haile Selassie was deposed and killed in a military coup.

In one sense, all five countries experienced a similar pattern of political development in the latter part of the 20th century, with overt or *ipso facto* dictatorships giving way to more democratic systems of governance in the 1990s. Indeed, with the exception of Rwanda, which is headed in a similar direction at the time of writing, all the countries in the region now have official constitutions that restrict any given president or prime minister to two terms in office.

Examined in closer detail, the recent history of the five countries is wildly divergent. Tanzania has proved to be among the most enduringly stable of African countries, having negotiated the path to independence and subsequent move towards democracy with little bloodshed (excluding the 1964 revolution that rocked Zanzibar Island two months before the political union with mainland Tanganyika). Kenya, despite sporadic outbreaks of localised ethnic or political violence, has also essentially enjoyed political and economic stability throughout the post-independence era.

At the other extreme is Rwanda, where long-standing ethnic instability culminated in the brutal genocide of 1994, while Uganda and Ethiopia both experienced extended countrywide civil wars before their present governments took power, in 1986 and 1992 respectively. Today, the region is as politically stable as it has been at any point since independence, with only the far north of Uganda and to a lesser extent the Somali border areas of Kenya and Ethiopia experiencing regular conflict.

Geography & Climate

Kenya and Tanzania are bounded by the Indian Ocean to the east, while the so-called Albertine Rift – a western arm of the Great Rift Valley running through Lakes Albert, Edward, Kivu and Tanganyika – forms the eastern boundary of Uganda, Rwanda, Burundi and Tanzania. Ethiopia extends northwards from Kenya, where it is separated from the Indian Ocean by Somalia, Djibouti and Eritrea. The equator runs through Kenya and Uganda, passing close to the towns of Nanyuki, Kisumu, Entebbe and Kasese.

East Africa's major natural landmark is the Great Rift Valley, a vast chasm that runs south from the Red Sea through Ethiopia to split into discrete eastern and western arms that converge in southern Tanzania near the town of Mbeya. The East African Rift Valley is studded with a succession of at least 30 major lakes, including Lake Tanganyika (the longest and deepest in the world), Lake Nyasa-Malawi (the second longest) and Lake Turkana (the world's largest desert lake). Shared between Kenya, Tanzania and Uganda, Lake Victoria is the world's second-largest freshwater body, filling a shallow elevated depression that lies between the two major arms of the Great Rift.

East Africa's geographic diversity defies encapsulation: snow-capped peaks, translucent freshwater lakes, vast depopulated deserts, idyllic Indian Ocean beaches, salt pans tinged pink by the prolific growth of minute crustaceans, densely cultivated highland meadows, sweaty lowland jungles, breezy montane forests, surreal Afro-montane moorlands, coral reefs swirling with piscine psychedelia – and much else besides.

The predominant East African habitat, however, is savanna, a term that embraces everything from the moist, sparsely wooded

Highest Mountains

The five highest mountains in Africa all lie in East Africa. In order of rank, these are Kilimanjaro (Tanzania), Mt Kenya (Kenya), Ruwenzori (Uganda/Democratic Republic of Congo [DRC] border), Ras Dashen (Ethiopia) and Mt Meru (Tanzania). All but Ras Dashen are the product of volcanic activity or tectonic movement associated with the rifting process, as are the region's other impressive peaks: Mt Elgon (Uganda/Kenya border), the Virungas (Uganda, Rwanda and DRC border) and the Ngorongoro Crater (Tanzania), which probably stood higher than Kilimanjaro does today before its caldera collapsed.

grassland of the Serengeti/Mara ecosystem, through the dense brachystegia woodland characteristic of southern Tanzania, to the arid acacia scrub of northern Kenya – in effect any grassland or woodland habitat without a closed canopy.

Broadly speaking, the eastern part of the region is more arid than the west, with western Uganda in particular sharing closer affinities to the central African rainforest than to the rest of East Africa. Altitude plays an important role in moulding the East African landscape and climate, with higher elevations typically having a moister, cooler climate and more characteristically tropical appearance than lower-lying areas.

The most important exception to the above generalisations is the well-watered Indian Ocean coastline, though in several areas these lush beachfronts give way to dry scrub only a few kilometres inland. More detailed notes on local climates are included in the country-by-country coverage.

Planning the Trip

Visas & Passports

All countries in the region will refuse entry to anybody without a passport that remains valid for six months after the intended date of departure. Visitors may be required to produce vaccination certificates for yellow fever. Arriving by air at any East African country (but not overland), you are technically required to have a return ticket to your country of residence, but in practice this is not the potential stumbling block that it was a few years ago.

Most visitors to Kenya, Tanzania, Uganda, Ethiopia and/or Rwanda will require a separate visa for each of the countries they enter. All five countries permit visas to be bought upon arrival at any international airport or overland border. This can slightly protract immigration formalities, but it is generally a straightforward procedure and – unless you happen to live very close to an appropriate embassy or high commission – it is far less hassle than doing the paperwork in advance. That said, entrance formalities in Africa are notoriously prone to change, so do obtain current information from your nearest embassy or a reliable tour operator before pitching up without a visa.

The price of a single-entry visa varies from one country to the next, and may differ on the basis of nationality, but generally it costs between US$30 and US$50. Valid for up to three months on request, a single-entry visa to Kenya, Tanzania and Uganda will remain good so long as you travel within the borders of any of these three

countries, but not if you cross into Rwanda, Ethiopia or elsewhere.

A tax of between US$20 and US$40 is applicable upon departure by air from East Africa, depending on the country from which you are flying out of. This tax is normally included in the final airfare. If it is not, you will need to pay it in hard currency.

Customs Regulations

There is nothing out of the ordinary with regard to customs at entry points to East Africa. At the time of printing, duty-free limits for those over the age of 16 in all five countries are 1 litre of wine or spirits, 0.5 litre of perfume and 200 cigarettes, 50 cigars or 200 grams of tobacco.

Money Matters

The US dollar is the most widely recognised hard currency throughout East Africa. Up-market hotel rates, safari costs and national-park fees are generally quoted in US dollars, and in some countries they must be also paid in hard currency. Although other major international currencies such as the Euro, Pound Sterling, South African Rand and Japanese Yen are freely changeable at banks and bureaux des change (known locally as forex bureaux), the exchange rate is often proportionately inferior to the one for the US dollar and prices quoted in dollars often work out higher when paid in other international currencies. Put simply, it is not essential to bring your money in the form of US dollars cash or travellers' cheques, but it will simplify things.

Carry the bulk of your money in travellers' cheques, which will be refunded if they are stolen. It is also a good idea to bring some cash – say 25 percent of the total sum – in US dollars cash. Old US dollar banknotes (issued before 2000) may be refused in East Africa on the basis they could be forgeries. Bills of US$20 or below can be useful for ad-hoc payments, but since they often attract a very poor rate by comparison to higher denominations, take most of your money in US$50 and US$100 bills.

Exchanging Currency
Hard currency or travellers' cheques can be exchanged into local currency with ease at banks and forex bureaux in capital cities and at international airports. Private forex bureau are generally more efficient and offer better rates for US dollars cash than the banks, which in turn offer better rates than those up-market hotels that offer foreign-exchange facilities. Travellers' cheques attract a less-favourable rate than cash and are not widely accepted by private forex bureaux. Due to a recent spate of scams involving stolen travellers' cheques, many banks now insist on proof of purchase being provided before they will exchange them. In Uganda particularly, it is practically impossible to change travellers' cheques outside of the capital. Almost any town of substance throughout East Africa will have a bank or forex bureau where hard currency can be exchanged into local currency, two notable exceptions being Fort Portal in Uganda and Lalibela in Ethiopia.

There is no longer any black market worth talking about in most parts of East Africa. Anybody who approaches you on the street offering to exchange money is likely to be a con artist. The one instance in which it may be necessary to exchange money informally is when crossing overland borders where

no formal foreign-exchange facilities exist. Private money changers can be found at any such borders, but they offer poor rates and are not above creating confusion in the hope of ripping you off, so change no more than you need to get you through to the next main town – say US$20 – and ideally keep this separately from your main stash of cash.

Credit Cards
Major credit cards are of varying degrees of use in East Africa. They are widely accepted at smart restaurants and hotels in Nairobi and other tourist centres in Kenya, and to a lesser extent and often with a surcharge of 5 percent in Dar es Salaam, Arusha and Kampala. Only a handful of (generally very costly) hotels in Rwanda and Ethiopia accept credit cards, and again at a premium. Up to roughly US$200 in local currency can be drawn at select ATMs in Nairobi, Mombasa, Dar es Salaam, Arusha, Zanzibar and Kampala, but not in smaller towns, and nowhere in Kigali or Addis Ababa. Credit cards are of little use when paying for local services or goods such as budget accommodation, public transport, local restaurants, curios, foodstuffs and drinks.

On balance, it is wise to carry sufficient funds to see you through your trip in cash or travellers' cheques and to carry a credit card only as a fallback should you underestimate your money requirements or hit an emergency.

Health Precautions

Preparations
Since health risks are higher in Africa and medical care often inadequate, it is vital that your travel-insurance policy is comprehensive and includes emergency evacuation and repatriation. Have a dental check-up before you go and get a spare pair of prescription glasses if you wear them. If you are on medication, make sure you carry enough to last you, plus a prescription and letter from your doctor, to show to border officials who may suspect you of smuggling drugs.

Inoculations
Consult your doctor about inoculations at least two months before you leave. A yellow-fever inoculation is recommended if only because you may be required to produce a certificate upon arrival or face having a jab on the spot. Diphtheria and tetanus vaccinations are also a good idea. Boosters are required every ten years after a trio of injections while young. Typhoid is recommended for stays over two weeks.

A series of inoculations exist for hepatitis A and B. For hepatitis A, long-term protection (ten years) is available by an initial injection followed by a booster at 6–12 months. For short-term protection, an injection of gamma globulin (a ready-made antibody taken from blood donations) will protect you immediately for up to six months, depending on dosage.

Meningitis inoculations are recommended and will protect you against the major epidemic forms of the disease. Polio inoculations are usually strongly recommended.

Protection against tuberculosis is recommended for those living in the area for over three months, though the risk to travellers is low.

Rabies vaccinations are usually only given if you are likely to be in close contact with animals during your stay (for instance, working in a game farm or reserve). A full course of three injections takes several

National Park Fees

Something that may come as a surprise to some visitors is the high national-park fees in East Africa. These will usually be built into the cost of any organised safari, but independent travellers must pay them directly. The most costly countries are Tanzania and Kenya, where a fee of US$15–50 per 24 hours (US$100 for Gombe Stream) is levied. The

entrance fee for parks in Uganda varies from US$10–20 per day, but entrance fees for Ethiopian and Rwandan parks are negligible. In Tanzania and Kenya all park entrance fees must be paid in hard currency or travellers' cheques, as must gorilla tracking fees in Uganda and Rwanda. Elsewhere, local currency is fine.

weeks to administer. In the unlikely event that you are bitten by a mammal while in East Africa, it is important to get a rabies injection as soon as possible afterwards as a precautionary measure – the disease takes a while to incubate but is incurable once symptoms are displayed. The cholera vaccine is highly ineffective and no longer required (see Visas & Passports on page 323).

Malaria

Malaria is the most serious health risk in East Africa. Some risk of contracting malaria occurs anywhere within the region, but it is particularly high during the rainy season and in low-lying areas, and generally low at altitudes exceeding 1,800 metres (6,000 ft). The risk of catching malaria can be greatly minimised by the combination of anti-malarial prophylactics and taking precautions to avoid mosquito bites, so seek advice from a tropical institute before your departure.

If you decide to take anti-malarial tablets – and unless your travels are restricted to high montane areas, you'd be foolish not to – remember that mosquitoes in many areas are resistant to many of the proprietary brands of medication. The most commonly recommended prophylactics are: a cocktail of chloroquine and paludrine (which is about 60 percent effective); Larium (which gives many people nightmares); the antibiotic, doxycycline (which can cause photo-sensitivity in some people); and Malarone (which has few side effects and is effective, but is also hugely expensive and unsuitable for children).

No pills offer 100 percent protection, so it is wise to avoid getting bitten in the first place. While you can get bitten by other things, which will itch annoyingly, the malaria-carrying female anopheles mosquito is only active between dusk and dawn. At these times, avoid perfumes and aftershave; make liberal use of insect repellent containing DEET;

and wear light-coloured clothing that covers arms and legs, as well as thick socks and shoes (most bites occur on or below the ankle).

The best way to avoid being bitten at night is to sleep under a mosquito net, ideally one without any tears, and impregnated with permethrin. If netting is not available, ask the hotel staff to spray your room liberally with an appropriate insecticide about 30 minutes before you retire for the night, or – less effective but still useful – burn a mosquito coil overnight and/or sleep under a fan.

The most dangerous form of malaria often appears disguised as a heavy cold or flu, but usually without the associated bunged-up nasal symptoms. Symptoms are most normally first displayed within 10–14 days of an infected bite, sometimes considerably longer, which means that on a holiday of standard duration, the most dangerous period is not while you're on safari but the week or two after you return home. If you start displaying flu-like symptoms at any time within six months of your African trip, consult a doctor immediately, and be sure to tell them you have been exposed to malaria.

It is important not to panic unduly. Millions of people visit or live in Africa without getting malaria, and the risk is low if you take suitable precautions.

Contact the Malaria Reference Laboratory at the London School of Hygiene and Tropical Medicine for free advice about Malaria (tel: 0891-600 350) or, in the USA, the Centre for Disease Control (CDC) in Atlanta (tel: 404-332 4559).

Aids

Aids is a major problem in East Africa with up to a quarter of the sexually active population HIV Positive. Avoid high-risk activities such as unprotected sex. Make sure your first-aid kit includes syringes and avoid receiving blood transfusions unless it is a dire emergency and only after consulting your consulate or embassy.

● Ascend the mountain slowly, giving your system time to adjust. However, the treks on mounts Kilimanjaro, Kenya and Meru, especially budget ones, are geared for getting you up and down quickly.
● Take the longest route possible if this is your first high-altitude experience and **do not** hesitate to ask to go slower.
● Try sleeping lower than your maximum height that day. Not only does this give you a nice downhill trot at the end of the day, but lets your body adjust more easily.
● Drink lots of water and avoid heavy foods. Lighter foods will take less from your system. Avoid alcohol and sedatives, as these further reduce the blood's ability to absorb oxygen.

Hygiene

Many areas in East Africa are subject to regular epidemics of cholera and dysentery due to poor sanitation and hygiene. Be conscientious about washing your hands regularly with soap and water. The good hotels will ensure your water supply is safe. Elsewhere, use bottled, boiled or otherwise purified water for drinking and brushing your teeth. Avoid ice and take care with juices as their water sources may be suspect. Milk should be avoided as it is often unpasteurised. You may also be better off avoiding uncooked vegetables, salads, unpeeled fruit or frozen products unless properly prepared.

Altitude Sickness

This serious problem is only likely to be encountered by those who are trekking up mounts Kilimanjaro or Kenya and to a lesser extent the Ruwenzoris, Ras Dashen or Mt Meru. It is impossible to predict who will be affected and how severely – it takes little consideration of fitness. Mild altitude sickness is summed up

First Aid Kit

The following items should be
included in your first-aid kit:
strong mosquito repellent;
malaria prophylactics; sting relief
cream; antihystamine pills;
antiseptic wipes and spray;
several syringes; Imodium, for
diarrhoea etc; plasters for
blisters and cuts; condoms and
tampons (if required).

with headaches, lethargy, dizziness,
difficulty sleeping and loss of
appetite. Further ascent should be
avoided at this stage as the
sickness may become more severe
without notice and include
symptoms of breathlessness,
coughing that may produce frothy
pink sputum, vomiting and
unconsciousness. In this case
immediate descent is necessary or
it may lead to fatal pulmonary
oedema. The good news is that a
rapid descent to lower altitude will
cure the symptoms as rapidly as
they came on.

Automobile Accidents
Car crashes are a leading cause of
injury among travellers in East
Africa, so walk and drive
defensively, wear a seat belt and
avoid travelling at night.

Bilharzia
Avoid swimming in fresh water:
Even large lakes such as Lake
Malawi/Nyasa are known to harbour
Bilharzia parasites, which live in
snails that like reedy still water.
Fast-flowing, very cold or clear water
should be safe. If in doubt, rub
yourself dry thoroughly with a rough
towel and ask for a test on
returning home. There is a relatively
straightforward treatment to this
slow-moving disease if it is caught
in time.

Remember that fresh water may
also harbour crocodiles and hippos.

The Sun
The African sun is strong: sunblock
and a head covering are essential –
a wide-brimmed hat is ideal.

Equatorial sun is stronger than
European. If your skin is fair, use
sunscreen whenever you are going
to be out in the sun. Even if you
have dark skin, you are still at risk
if out all day – particularly if you are
going to be swimming or snorkelling
– the water reflects the sun's rays,
multiplying the effect, and the
coolness of the water is deceptive.
Remember, no matter how dark you
are, you can still burn.

Most first-time visitors
experience a degree of heat
exhaustion and dehydration that
can be avoided by drinking lots of
water and slightly increasing the
amount of salt in the diet.
Dehydration is more serious in
children, so monitor their intake of
liquids carefully.

Traveller's Diarrhoea
All too common, this traveller's
plague usually clears itself up within
a few days. If there is no sign of
improvement within 48 hours, it
could be a parasite or infection – go
and see a doctor.

The best way to avoid tummy
bugs is by being fastidious about
using purified or bottled water to
drink and brush your teeth. Watch
out for ice in drinks. If you are
felled, stop eating anything but dry
toast or biscuits (preferably salty),
but carry on drinking plenty of
water. Drinking ginger ale or other
tinned soft drinks is a good way to
inject calories, and help settle the
stomach. Avoid alcohol, coffee, tea
and any dairy products other than
yoghurt. Dehydration is the biggest
risk, particularly with chronic
diarrhoea and most dangerous with
children, who become dehydrated
more quickly than adults.
Rehydration requires salt and sugar
as well as liquid.

Sea Creatures
Sharks can be a hazard along the
coast. Make sure you know the
local situation before you go
swimming or diving. Although not
deadly, the jellyfish around Zanzibar
can give a nasty sting to
unsuspecting snorkellers and
swimmers. Keep an eye out when

gazing at the wonders of the deep.
Use beach shoes when wading off
the shore, not only to guard against
rough coral rock or shells, but in
case you step on a sea urchin. If
you get stung, bitten or cut by
anything in the shallows, try and
identify what caused it and seek
medical help.

Bugs and Beasties
Many snakes in Africa are
poisonous, though most will leave
you alone and are as anxious to
avoid you as you are to avoid them.
If walking in thick grasses or
undergrowth, wear sensible shoes
and thick socks, and always walk
heavily – most snakes will feel the
vibrations and get out of your way.
The black mamba is the only snake
that is aggressive enough to attack,
while the puff adder relies on
camouflage and is easy to step on
inadvertently. If you are bitten, keep
the affected part as immobile as
possible and seek immediate help.
Many of the huge spiders that freak
out visitors are completely
harmless – some are even
mosquito-munching friends.
However, it is best to keep a safe
distance, unless you are certain. Be
aware of children's curiosity
overcoming common sense. Check
the bed or the toilet seat before
sitting down, shake out your shoes
before putting them on, and never
put your hands on a rock or into a
crevice without checking it for
occupants first.

Tsetse flies can be a terrible
annoyance. Their appearance and
sharp painful bite are reminiscent
of a horsefly, they tend to swarm
and are attracted to the heat of a
car, the colours black and blue and
can even bite through denim.
Usually the pain from the bite
subsides within a minute or two,
though some people are mildly
allergic and have a more
sustained reaction, and the
occasional bite might swell up and
itch for several days.

Historically, the tsetse fly has
been responsible for spreading
plagues of trypanosomiasis (aka
sleeping sickness) in several parts

of East Africa, but this is no longer a serious concern in any part of the region likely to be visited by tourists. If infected by sleeping sickness, symptoms include swelling five days after the bite and a fever two or three weeks later. Treatment should be sought immediately at this stage, as it can be fatal.

Mosquitoes are to be avoided not just because of the itching bites, but because of the dangers of diseases such as malaria, which they spread *(see page 325)*.

Medical Contacts
In the UK, detailed health advice, tailored to individual needs, is available from the MASTA (Medical Advice for Travellers Abroad) dial-up travel service, tel: 0906-822 4100 (premium rate) or at www.medical online.com.au/medical/masta/. Alternatively, call the BA Travel Centres central number, tel: 01276-685040 for your nearest branch, log onto the NHS website, www.fitfortravel.scot.nhs.uk or check with your GP. The site www.who.int includes the World Health Organisation's recommendations for safe travel.

Two other important medical contacts are AMREF (African Medical and Research Foundation) and IAMAT. The former offers emergency regional evacuation by the Flying Doctors Society of Africa. A two-month membership costs about US$50. For further details contact the local office in Nairobi (tel: 0254-20-602495; fax 254-20-601594; email: flyingdocs@ amrefke.org) or in Dar es Salaam (tel: 051-116610/36731), or visit www.amref.org. The latter organisation, IAMAT, provides members with a list of approved doctors all over the world.

Local Medical Services
For minor complaints, there is no major concern attached to consulting local doctors or pharmacists, who generally speak good English and are skilled at diagnosing and curing locally common diseases and strains of

malaria. The standard blood test for malaria can be taken at any half-decent laboratory in East Africa, and involves a simple pinprick on the finger, but do make sure that the needle comes fresh from the packet or failing that sterilise it yourself.

If more serious medical attention is required, several factors might come into play. Hospitals in East Africa are generally understaffed and under-equipped, and thus best avoided by visitors except in a dire emergency. Realistically, however, there are circumstances in which immediate treatment might take priority over the existence of better medical facilities elsewhere. As a rule, there will be at least one good hospital or clinic in any large city, or any town that harbours a substantial population of expatriates or Asians, so if speedy treatment isn't critical then it would be worth delaying until you can get yourself to a good hospital in a major city, or you might even consider repatriation.

Nairobi probably has the best medical facilities in East Africa, but good facilities are also available in Dar es Salaam, Arusha, Kampala, Kigali and Addis Ababa. You can be confident that any resident expatriates, up-market hotel managers or registered safari operators in East Africa will be able to point you towards the nearest and best facility suitable to your circumstances. In smaller towns, the safest bet is probably a mission hospital, assuming that one exists. The Flying Doctor emergency number in Nairobi is 0254-20-315454/5 or (mobile) 0254-733-628422 or satellite phone 0873-762-315580.

Pharmacies

Pharmacies in the major towns of East Africa are generally well-stocked with western brand medicines. Medication in villages is limited. Be sure to check the expiry dates before purchasing medications. Keep receipts on hand for any purchases, as your travel insurance should reimburse you.

What to Bring
Clothing
If you are planning to spend most of the time on safari, you should bring a small, select wardrobe for all seasons – depending, of course, on where you intend to go. Light and casual for the coast and game-park safaris, and not necessarily the full professional hunter rig-out; muted colours, shirts, jeans and the like will do. For forest lodges, dress (almost) as for evening in a European ski lodge, or at least well wrapped up. Wherever you go, carry at least one light sweater or sweatshirt – many parts of the region cool down significantly after dark.

Clothing should be loose and comfortable, and made of natural fibres such as cotton, to help your skin breathe in the heat. Drip-dry clothing is recommended, and plenty of it. Soil is red and dusty just about everywhere, so clothes get grubby quickly. Don't bother bringing rainwear, even if the safari is timed for the rainy season. If necessary, a light waterproof can be picked up locally. Bring any specialist gear you may require (ie snorkelling, hiking, camping equipment) as local supplies are limited and below par.

Women will find cotton dresses cooler and more comfortable than trousers, particularly for daytime. If you prefer to wear trousers, make sure they are baggy enough to allow plenty of ventilation. The local *kanga* dresses or loose blouses are available in an infinite variety of designs and are good value. The *kikoi* – local wrap-around sarong – is also useful. An advantage of trousers over dresses is that they reduce the number of insect bites – most important after dark.

For footwear, comfort should take precedence over style. Shoes need to be sturdy and preferably ankle-protective as well, to provide a bit of protection against snakes and dead branches. However, to be seen on the Indian Ocean beaches with Gore-Tex ankle highs would be just plain silly. Even sandals are sacrilegious to some, who think putting anything between this sand and their toes is a sin. Take beach shoes for walking in the surf, where you can meet anything from rough coral to sea urchins. Though warm in the cities, closed shoes are recommended, as many areas are quite grungy and infections on blistered toes etc, inevitable.

On the coast, shorts are just about all right for visitors during the day, but the rule is to keep in mind the Muslim ethic for decency in dress. This, incidentally, precludes nude or topless bathing on the beach – although this is sometimes practised in flagrant breach of both the law and local sensibilities. A hat, sunscreen and sunglasses are crucial protection from the blazing midday sun.

Other Equipment

As all animals, even tall giraffes and two-ton elephants, can easily disappear behind a blade of grass, it would be absolutely pointless to venture out without a good pair of binoculars.

For mountain climbing, sturdy clothing and serious rain- and wind-proof cold-weather gear are essential. You will also need two adjustable climbing poles; a water pouch with a tube, carried in a daypack; high-energy snacks; a head-torch; and a medical pack with headache and diarrhoea tablets, plasters and re-hydration sachets.

Regardless of your ambitions as a photographer, you'll find an unlimited number of subjects to shoot, so come prepared with at least twice as much film as you think you'll need. In addition to your usual preferred film, bring a range of ISOs. Much of the time you will be shooting in bright sunlight so a slow film will be ideal. However, midday can produce harsh shadows: the narrow alleys in the old towns are always in deep shade; and you may spot that elusive leopard at dawn or dusk, so you also need some faster film. You may want to consider

taking out faster films – up to 1000 ASA – for artificially lit waterholes at night. Film costs more or less the same as it does in the UK and US, and is readily available in larger towns and tourist areas, but the quality varies widely and the expiry date should be checked. Finding more specialist film, such as slide film or Advantix may prove difficult. If you are using a digital camera make sure you take lots of rechargeable batteries and memory cards with you along with the appropriate plug converter.

Always ask permission before attempting to photograph people. In certain areas, for instance in Maasailand and most of Ethiopia, it is standard practice for people to ask for a small tip to be photographed. Some tourists find this request offensive or take it as a sign that the local people are overcommercialised – ironic, really, that anybody who earns sufficient money to afford a safari should level this accusation at an impoverished local hoping for a small tip – in which case they are advised to forget about photographing colourfully dressed ethnic people.

The most important piece of equipment is a high magnification lens, up to 300 mm, or bigger if possible. When you are out on safari, the animals seem close enough to touch, but photograph them with a wide-angle lenses and they look miles away.

Avoid photographing anything that may be considered strategic or of military importance such as bridges, police stations, etc. If in doubt ask.

Getting There

AIR

The most popular port of entry to East Africa is Nairobi's Jomo Kenyatta International Airport. There are also international flights from Europe to Mombasa, Addis Ababa, Kampala, Kigali, Kilimanjaro International Airport (between Moshi and Arusha) and Zanzibar. Travellers from North America

Air India
www.airindia.com
Air Tanzania
www.airtanzania.com
Air Zimbabwe
www.airzimbabwe.com
British Airways
www.british-airways.com
Egypt Air
www.egyptair.com.eg
Emirates Airlines
www.emirates.com
Ethiopian Airlines
www.flyethiopian.com
Gulf Air
www.gulfairco.com
Kenya Airways
www.kenya-airways.com
KLM
www.klm.com
Precision Air
www.precisionairtz.com
South African Airways
www.saa.co.za
Swissair
www.swissair.com
Yemen Airways
www.yemenia.com

usually route through Europe, South Africa or Asia. Further details of carriers are given under individual countries.

LAND

Anybody planning on travelling overland to East Africa from Europe via Egypt and Sudan or West Africa should make detailed research into the possibilities. However you travel, it's a hard trip, and conditions are prone to sudden change. Useful starting points are the overland truck companies that advertise in UK magazines such as *Time Out*, as well as Lonely Planet's *Africa On A Shoestring*, which – although perennially out-of-date as a result of its broad scope – is the only travel guide to include some information about every country on the continent. Crossing between the countries covered in this guide are contained in the country listings.

Tour Operators

A full list of international and local operators offering safaris to East Africa or countries therein would ramble over 100 pages or more. What follows is a broad-ranging list of recommended East African tour operators – locally and internationally based – offering conventional safari packages as well as customised itineraries trips and special-interest or off-the-beaten-track tours.

Abercrombie & Kent Ltd
Nairobi, Kenya
Tel: 020-334955
Fax: 020-215752
Tel: (US) 630-954-2944
or 800-554-7016
www.abercrombiekent.com
Excellent and long-standing specialist in quality luxury safaris within Kenya, Tanzania and to a lesser extent Uganda.

Afri Tours & Travel
Kampala, Uganda
Tel: 041-233596
Fax: 041-344855
Email: afritour@africaonline.co.ug
www.afritourstravel.com
This long-serving and reasonably priced safari operator and car-hire company offers quality general and specialist guided tours throughout Uganda.

Bushbuck Safaris
Arusha, Tanzania
Tel: 027-250 7779 or 254 4186
Fax: 027-254 8293/4860
Email: bushbuck@habari.co.tz
www.bushbuckltd.com
Reliable company specialising in up-market but not extortionately priced private northern Tanzania lodge safaris with a high standard of vehicles, drivers and guides.

CC Africa
Johannesburg, South Africa
Tel: +27-11-809 4300
Fax: +27-11-809 4400
Email: information@ccafrica.com / webenquiries@ccafrica.com
www.ccafrica.com
Owners of several of Tanzania's most exclusive lodges, including Mnemba Island in Zanzibar and the extra-ordinary Ngorongoro Crater Lodge, CC Africa operates superb lodges

and personalised fly or drive safaris.

Coastal Aviation
Dar es Salaam, Tanzania
Tel: 022-211 7959/60
Fax: 022-211 8647/7985
Mobile: 0741-324044 (emergency)
Email: safari@coastal.cc / aviation@coastal.cc
www.coastal.cc
Tanzania's Coastal Aviation offers flying safaris to the Selous Game Reserve, Ruaha, Ngorongoro and Serengeti. They also run scheduled flights to the likes of Rubondo Island and Mahale Mountains national parks.

Equestrian Safaris
Arusha, Tanzania
Tel: 0744-595517
Email: posthest@yahoo.com
www.safariridng.com
Remote horseback expeditions for experienced riders around Kilimanjaro and Lake Natron.

Ethiopian Rift Valley Safaris
Addis Ababa, Ethiopia
Tel: 011-552128/8591/1127
Fax: 011-550298
Email: ervs@ethionet.et
www.ethiopianriftvalleysafaris.com
This highly regarded operator specialises in up-market safaris to Ethiopia's South Omo and operates the only permanent lodge there.

Galaxy Express Travel
Addis Ababa, Ethiopia
Tel: 011-510355
Fax: 011-511236
Email: galaxyexpress@ethionet.et
www.galaxyexpressethiopia.com
Galaxy Express is perhaps the best-equipped tour operator in Ethiopia, with a large fleet of well-maintained vehicles, and branch offices in Gonder, Axum and Bahir Dar – a good first port of call for Ethiopian trips of all descriptions.

Gametrackers
Nairobi, Kenya
Tel: 020-338927
Fax: 020-330903
Email: game@africaonline.co.ke
www.gametrackers.com
In addition to the usual camping and lodge-based safaris in Kenya and Tanzania, Gametrackers runs exceptionally affordable overland truck safaris to the major game

reserves as well as to the remote and mysterious Lake Turkana.

Hoopoe Safaris
Arusha, Tanzania
Tel: 027-250 7011 or
(UK) +44-1923-255 462
Fax: 027-254 8226
Email: information@hoopoe.com / hoopoeuk@aol.com
www.hoopoe.com
Excellent private camping, lodge and walking safaris around northern Tanzania, including Hoopoe's own comfortable tented lodges near Tarangire, Manyara and Serengeti. Highly recommended for tailored safaris or anybody seeking a genuine bush experience in Tanzania.

Kigoma Hilltop Hotel
Kigoma, Tanzania
Tel: 028-280 4435/6/7
Fax: 028-280 4434
Email: kht@raha.com / info@kigoma.com
www.kigoma.com
Reasonably priced, well-organised chimp-tracking tours to Mahale Mountains and Gombe Stream (they also run lodges), using their private motorboat or – for those who prefer – the public ferry.

Kearsley Travel
Dar es Salaam, Tanzania
Tel: 022 211 502630
Fax: 022 211 5585
Email: info@kearsleys.com
www.kearsleys.com

Car Hire Companies

Avis
UK Central Booking:
Tel: 0870-606 0100
US Central Booking:
Tel: 1-800-230 4898
www.avis.com
Europcar (Inter Rent)
UK Central Booking:
Tel: 0113-2422 233
US Central Booking:
Tel: 1-877-940 6900
www.europcar.com
Hertz Rentals
UK Central Booking:
Tel: 0870-848 4848
US Central Booking:
Tel: 1-800-654 3131
www.hertz.com

Dynamic, straight-talking management with 50 years experience arranging up-market safaris throughout Tanzania, in particular the southern reserves of Selous and Ruaha.

Let's Go Travel Ltd
Nairobi, Kenya
Tel: 020-444 7151
Fax: 020-444 1030
Email: info@letsgosafari.com
www.letsgosafari.com
Highly regarded hotel booking agent and safari operator with years of experience catering for all budgets and interests. Mainly specialises in Kenya, it also has branch offices in Arusha and Kampala.

Marangu Hotel
Marangu, Tanzania
Tel: 055-275 6594
Tel/fax: 055-275 6591
Email: info@marangu.com
www.marangu.com
Decades of experience in arranging quality Kilimanjaro climbs from the base at Marangu. as well as other safaris in northern Tanzania.

Rainbow Tours
London, UK
Tel: 020 7226 1004
Fax: 020 7226 2621
Email: info@rainbowtours.co.uk
www.rainbowtours.co.uk
Specialist in Africa and the Indian Ocean, offering tailor-made safaris and other tours in Uganda, Ethiopia, Rwanda and Tanzania.

Roy Safaris
Arusha, Tanzania
Tel: 027-250 8010/2115
Fax: 027-254 8892
Email: roysafaris@intafrica.com
www.roysafaris.com
Dynamic and efficient company offering high-quality but reasonably priced budget and semi-luxury camping safaris and lodge safaris in northern Tanzania. Reliable Kilimanjaro and Mt Meru treks also arranged.

Safari Makers Ltd
Arusha, Tanzania
Tel: 027-254 4446
Email: safarimakers@habari.co.tz
www.safarimakers.com
Reliable, responsive and reasonably priced joint American-Tanzanian venture offering

personalised lodge and camping safaris throughout northern Tanzania, as well as cultural visits and mountain climbs.

Sunvil Africa
London, UK
Tel: 020-8232 9777
Fax: 020-8568 8330
Email: africa@sunvil.co.uk
www.sunvil.co.uk/africa
Respected Africa specialists with an expertly designed Tanzania programme concentrating on smaller, more remote parks and lodges – Selous, Ruaha, Mahale, Katavi, Udzungwa and Mikumi – and Zanzibar and Mafia archipelagos. Good value and hands-on knowledge.

Tribes
Suffolk, UK
Tel: 01728-685 971
Fax: 01728-685 973
Email: info@tribes.co.uk
www.tribes.co.uk
www.tribestravel.com (US)
Tribes, the award-winning Fair Trade travel company, offers tailor-made and small group holidays throughout East Africa, from classic driving safaris to walking safaris and mountain climbs.

Uganda Safari Company
Kampala, Uganda
Tel: 041-251182
Mobile: 077-489497
Fax: 041-344653
Email: info@safariuganda.com
www.safariuganda.com
Guided countrywide safaris and gorilla tracking tours specialising in the Semuliki Valley, where they operate the only permanent lodge. Likely to take over the only lodge in Kidepo National Park.

Village Ethiopia
Addis Ababa, Ethiopia
Tel: 011-523497, 508869
Fax: 011-510200
Email: village.ethiopia@ethionet.et
www.village-ethiopia.net
Reasonably priced and reliable company offering the usual Ethiopian historical packages, as well as visits to remote Awash and Afar regions and the rock-hewn churches of Tigray. Recommended for trekking, ornithological and other adventure or specialist tours.

Volcanoes Safaris
London (UK), Kampala (Uganda) and Kigali (Rwanda)
Tel: 0870-870 8480 (UK)
041-346464/5 (Uganda)
770-730 0960 (US)
250-76530, ext 2513 (Rwanda)
Fax: 0870 8708481 (UK)
041-341718 (Uganda)
250-76541 (Rwanda)
Email:
salesuk@volcanoessafaris.com (UK)
salesus@volcanoessafaris.com (US)
salesug@volcanoessafaris.com (Uganda)
www.volcanoessafaris.com
Highly regarded joint UK-Uganda company specialising in gorilla tracking out of its up-market tented camps at Bwindi, Mgahinga, Sipi Falls and near Ruhengeri in Rwanda, also arranging tours to other parts of Uganda and Rwanda.

Wild Frontiers
Johannesburg, South Africa
Tel: +27-11-702 2035
Fax: +27-11-468 1655
Email: wildfront@icon.co.za
www.wildfrontiers.com
Excellent, competitively priced Johannesburg-based tour operator with 15 years of experience arranging safaris to all corners of East Africa. It has its own well-equipped ground operation in Uganda and offers a good range of fixed-departure photographic, birdwatching, primate and other special-interest tours led by well-known experts in their fields.

Practical Tips

Media

RADIO AND TELEVISION

All five countries in the region have national broadcasting corporations running mediocre, mostly English-speaking, radio stations and television channels. In Uganda particularly, the last few years has seen the rise of several far better private radio stations. The South African satellite company DSTV beams 50 channels across East Africa and is widely available in smarter hotels and bars (but thankfully not game lodges) in all countries but Ethiopia. DSTV channels include CNN, Sky News. BBC News and innumerable sport channels that often attract crowds during major global and African sporting events.

NEWSPAPERS

The weekly *East African*, published in Kenya but also available in Tanzania, Uganda and Rwanda, provides exceptionally solid and balanced news coverage of these four countries. Good local dailies are published in English in Kenya *(The Standard, The Nation* and *Kenya Times)* and Uganda *(The Monitor* and *The New Vision)* and are widely available in major towns in Rwanda and Tanzania. The English-language dailies published in Tanzania and Ethiopia are lower in standard, a reflection of the fact that less English is spoken in these countries. Foreign papers and magazines are often available in capital cities and other urban tourist centres such as Arusha and Mombasa.

Post and Telecommunications

Postal service is generally reliable but slow. At best, airmail to Europe takes five days, but two weeks is just as likely. Poste-restante services are available in all major cities. Do not send valuable items via the post. Courier services (larger cities only) take 24–48 hours to reach Europe.

Most resort hotels and lodges will provide fax, telegram and internet services. Small shops often have fax, telephone and internet services, which are much cheaper and of equal reliability to the hotels. International calls are very expensive.

Internet and Email

Email has caught on rapidly in a region where all other forms of international communication are slow and/or unreliable and/or expensive. There are numerous cheap and reliable internet cafés in most larger towns in Tanzania and Kenya, as well as in Kampala and Jinja in Uganda, Kigali in Rwanda and Addis Ababa in Ethiopia. Similar but more expensive services are available in smarter hotels. Internet access is not generally available except in emergencies in game reserves, and it is non-existent in more remote and smaller towns throughout the region.

Women Travellers

Travelling as a lone woman is perfectly safe and often entertaining. East Africans are relatively conservative. You will be treated with respect, but the moment you are with a man, he will naturally be looked to as the decision-maker.

The coast of East Africa is predominantly Muslim, and elsewhere, although traditional dress may well be topless, locals know enough about Western culture to land you in difficulties if you do the same – or even wear anything too skimpy.

Be relatively formal in your dealings with men. Few African cultures have a concept of platonic friendship between the sexes and what may be regarded as normal in Europe may well be regarded as a serious come-on here.

If you do decide to indulge, remember that there is an extremely high incidence of HIV/Aids in the local populace and take suitable precautions.

Gay Travellers

East Africa is culturally conservative. Open displays of affection are frowned upon even in straight couples. It is safe to say that gay relationships are taboo. It is even against the law, carrying a 14-year prison sentence in Tanzania. However, for the discreet gay couple there should be no problem. Although it has no "scene" (straight or gay), Zanzibar is actually a popular gay destination. Don't be misled by the sight of East Africans of the same sex – male or female – walking around hand-in-hand, since this is an expression of friendship rather than sexuality.

Travelling with Children

Many Westerners are too timid to take their children to any developing country. This is a huge mistake. Not only will they have a great time, but it is a massive learning experience that can literally be life-changing – Zanzibar also has some of the world's best beaches.

Give children a project for the trip, such as a travel diary, to keep them interested and involved.

Most Africans are very child-friendly, will help you keep an eye on them, and having children with you can open doors of communication. And local children will immediately involve them in their games and activities.

All you need to take are some common-sense precautions.

Babies

Taking small babies into this environment may simply be more trouble than it's worth and they won't remember it anyway. They won't like the heat and you may find it difficult to get baby food and supplies once out of the major towns. It is unsafe to have babies on safari (most operators will not accept them). Their cries are said to resemble wounded animals and may attract predators.

Health
From the age of four or five onwards, things become far easier, but there are specific health considerations to watch out for.

Children are more susceptible to illness than adults. They also get dehydrated more quickly, so be sure to give them plenty to drink.

Be extra careful of children's delicate skin in the African sun. Large quantities of sunblock and a good hat are essential equipment.

There are lurking dangers not found back home. Make sure children wear shoes whenever they are out of the house, wash their hands frequently, do not scramble over rocks without checking where they put their hands, or start playing with any strange insects or wildlife they might meet before it is checked out by someone in the know. If they are scratched, take it seriously and use antiseptic, as bacteria can breed far faster in the heat. If they are bitten or stung, get expert advice immediately.

Food for Children
Food tends to be quite plain and frequently involves chips, so there shouldn't be any problems finding suitable food. Tourist hotels usually provide special children's menus (some also have kids' clubs). Bottled water and fizzy drinks are available everywhere.

Travelling
One of the biggest problems in travelling with children is simply the many long hours spent en route – even the charms of a Land Rover can pall quickly.

Take a supply of drinks, sucky sweets or chewing gum, and emergency food rations. A tape or

CD with headphones and a supply of music or talking books is a godsend, while for less bumpy journeys, travel games are also worth taking. Try not to schedule more than one long travelling day at a time.

Safaris with Children
Children on the whole do enjoy safaris. Most safari companies advise against bringing children under six years on safari, and some luxury lodges ban under-12s. It is considered that they will be bored, and cannot sustain the quiet concentration needed for game-viewing. Other lodges accept children but insist on the family having a private vehicle and not game-viewing with other guests. A very few enlightened operators are beginning to introduce special child-friendly safaris, with walks and game-viewing set up to appeal.

On trekking safaris, children need to be at least 14 to keep up with the rest of the group. Younger kids just don't have the stamina.

Travellers with Disabilities

Disabled travellers to East Africa have many practical difficulties and a frustrating lack of facilities, but find they are amazed at the help and understanding that they get from local people.

Facilities for the physically disabled are not good in East Africa. Even at the airport, everything is done manually – ie you are physically lifted on and off the plane. On the beaches there are no planks to help someone in a wheelchair to move. Wheelchair accessible hotels are few and far between.

Safaris can be a good holiday for physically disabled travellers, as you spend so long in vehicles. However, they do tend to be more expensive, firstly because you usually have to book it from abroad – and the budget companies don't tend to advertise internationally, and secondly because internal flights tend to be pricey. Many smaller lodges have scattered rooms in inaccessible places, but

the larger lodges, such as the Serena and Sopa chains, can usually manage to accommodate people in wheelchairs with advance warning.

For information before you travel
UK:
RADAR (Royal Association for Disability and Rehabilitation)
12 City Forum
250 City Road
London EC1V 8AF
Tel: 020-7250 3222
Fax: 020-7250 1212
USA:
SATH (Society for the Advancement of Travel for the Handicapped)
347 Fifth Ave
Ste 610
New York NY10016
Tel: 212-447 7284
Fax: 212-725 8253

Security and Crime

Generally, East Africa is not a dangerous region in which to travel. There is always a risk of theft in larger cities, particularly Nairobi and Addis Ababa, but also Dar es Salaam, Mombasa, Arusha and to a lesser extent Kampala and Kigali.

Crimes Against the Person
Rape and sexual assault are rare in a society that has fairly liberal access to sex. Should you be accosted, it's more likely that the villain is after your property than your body. Violent crime against tourists in not unknown, but nor is it common. In any threatening situation, the rule is don't panic or

Tipping

As far as tipping is concerned, the rules that you probably use at home should apply in East Africa. For instance, add 10 percent to a restaurant bill unless a service charge is included. The biggest tip will probably go to your tour driver if he or she has been helpful and responsive on the trip. As much as US$5–10 per person per day is expected on safari.

Official Advice

To check the situation in a country before you go, log onto www.fco.gov.uk for official UK Foreign Office advice. For the US State Dept. advice, go to www.travel.state.gov/travel_warnings.html.

make any sudden moves in attack or retreat. Keep quiet and do what you're told (within reason) – basically, apply common sense.

Theft

Expert pickpockets and confidence tricksters are the bigger problem, and convincing stories involving money can catch out even the most experienced traveller. The common-sense rules are to use taxis at night, wherever you are, and to avoid the sleazier bars and dance dives in large cities. Don't carry too much money or any valuables around, and avoid wearing expensive jewellery, particularly when visiting markets, bus stations and other busy places, but also when walking in town or on the beach. If you do carry a money-belt in towns (and its far safer to lock it away in your hotel), a belt that can be concealed under your clothing has obvious advantages over one that is visible to any passer-by.

If you travel by public transport, think twice before accepting any food or drink from fellow-passengers, however generous the offer may seem. It has been known for thieves to lace the "gift" with drugs, causing the unsuspecting recipient to fall asleep, and allowing the thief to make off with his or her possessions.

Make photocopies of all important documents including your passport, visas, travellers' cheques, insurance documents and vaccination certificates – this will ensure speedy replacement should they be stolen. Also leave a copy of everything at home, with someone you can contact if you get into difficulties.

Banditry

There are parts of East Africa – generally not regularly visited by tourists – where armed banditry is a genuine threat. The worst areas are the Somali border areas of Kenya and Ethiopia, where Somali *shifta* gangs regularly hold up vehicles and buses. The only road regularly used by tourists where this is a regular problem is between Malindi and Lamu on the Kenyan coast.

In Uganda, areas northeast of Soroti regularly experience bandit attacks, while the region northwest of Murchison Falls is the site of a localised civil war in which any passing tourist might find themselves a casualty. The most serious incident involving tourists in recent years was an attack on the tourist camps in Uganda's Bwindi National Park, in which nine tourists were killed. This is generally regarded as having been an isolated incident, perpetrated by exiles from Rwanda based in the DRC, and improved security measures have seen Bwindi removed from US and UK government lists of places that tourists should avoid.

Terrorism

The horrific bombings of the US High Commissions in Nairobi and Dar es Salaam and more recent hotel bombing in Mombasa might create the impression that East Africa is a hotbed of religious tension. Nothing could be further from the truth – this is one part of the world where Muslims and Christians have been living and working alongside each other amicably for centuries, and still do. Kenyans and Tanzanians of all creeds were shocked at what essentially amounted to their countries being used as a battleground in an international feud that has nothing to do with them.

Drugs

The soft smoke is called *bhang* locally. Like most plants in East Africa, it grows wild and abundantly. Needless to say, smoking or dealing

in cannabis is against the law, and don't even think about exporting it. Hard drugs are virtually ignored by the youngsters in Kenya. The only stuff in common use is a mild narcotic called *miraa* or *khat* (chat), which is grown extensively in Kenya's Meru and Embu districts and around Harer in Ethiopia. The leaves and sticks are chewed for mild stimulation, mostly by the northern Kenyan nomads and in Islamic parts of Ethiopia.

Etiquette

Greetings

In East Africa, greetings are very important, and not to be rushed. Africans often spend minutes holding hands after first greeting each other. It is considered bad manners to rush into a query abruptly without first observing the social niceties. As in Asia, people eat and shake hands with their right hand. Using the left is considered dirty as this is normally used for toilet purposes. Putting your feet up on a table or stool is considered rude. Physical displays of affection between sexes are frowned upon, as are displays of open anger and impatience. Realise that things often take longer in Africa and be philosophical and always polite if you want to get a favourable response from officials. Part of the African experience is to slow down to African time – you'll wonder what all the stress and rushing about are for when you get home.

Elderly people are shown a great deal of respect, particularly when being greeted.

Dress

Despite the nation's poverty, Tanzanians place a high premium on being clean and neatly presented. Tourists who dress scruffily will receive less respect than those who are well groomed. You can wear shorts in tourist areas, but they are considered childish. Business attire is recommended for meeting senior officials – always err on the side of dressing too conservatively.

Etiquette "Dont's"

Etiquette "Dont's"

- Don't show disrespect for authority, starting with the president. Don't try to take his picture, or that of any other leaders, and don't tear up his portrait on a banknote. Visitors have sometimes destroyed the last of their Kenyan cash at the airport before their departure – and have got into trouble for doing so.
- Don't photograph anyone without their consent, not even the tribesmen way out in the bush. A smile, waving your camera around and the offer of a few shillings is normally enough to get consent.
- Don't break the law, of course. For tourists, the main hazards are the Exchange Control Act (illegal deals with money), the traffic regulations, and the ordinances against prostitution, sexual offences and drug taking.

Remember that a large part of the coast is Islamic. In these and other areas, it is appropriate for women to wear discreet, long, loose-fitting clothes. Local women are often uncomfortable in the company of men. Modest clothes and bare feet are required for entry to mosques. Most mosques are not open to non-Muslims, so never enter unless specifically invited.

Bargaining

Haggling is expected and necessary in most shops and markets; bars and established shops have fixed prices. Obviously, it's a matter of choice how far you want to take it, but it's a good idea to check out a few asking prices before you start haggling – you can expect prices to come down significantly. The interaction need not be intimidating; it's a good opportunity to meet artists and other locals. This is a culture where things move slowly, and it is considered polite to take your time and make conversation.

Where to Stay

East Africa has a fine range of accommodation to suit most tastes and budgets. Tanzania, Kenya and increasingly Uganda are blessed with numerous fine city hotels, game lodges and beach resorts that conform to international standards. The region's best hotels are listed in this guide, but worth noting is that there is a vast selection of budget accommodation available too, with even the smallest town in Kenya, Tanzania, Ethiopia and Uganda likely to boast at least one – and perhaps dozens – of simple local guesthouses offering accommodation for well under US$5. This guide dwells mostly on game lodges, which fall into two broad categories. Older-style lodges tend to be large outmoded monoliths that cater mostly for package tours and are constructed along the lines of a city hotel, with minor concessions made to the wilderness location. More modern lodges tend to be smaller (5–20 double units) and more organic in feel, constructed from local stone, canvas or thatch in a manner that blends into the surrounding habitat. Although the latter style of lodge is generally costlier than its monolithic counterparts, and the immediacy of the surroundings may intimidate nervous first-timers to the African bush, it is generally far more aesthetically pleasing and offers a more holistic bush experience.

Accommodation for the wildlife reserves and other major tourist centres are included in the country-by-country coverage under the following price bands.

$$$$$	above US$275
$$$$	US$150–275
$$$	US$75–150
$$	US$20–75
$	below US$20

Where to Eat

Eating and Drinking

An excellent selection of international quality restaurants can be found in all of the region's capital cities – see country listings – as well as in larger towns such as Mombasa, Nakuru, Kisumu, Jinja, Arusha, Moshi and Mwanza. East Africa (aside from Ethiopia) has a large Indian population and smaller towns often boast at least one decent restaurant specialising in this cuisine. Wherever you travel, local restaurants – confusingly called *hoteli* in Swahili – serve greasy stews and grills served with maize porridge (*ugali*), cooked plantain (*matoke*) or potato chips.

The food on the coast is heavily influenced by Indian and Arabic cuisine – as one would expect from the Spice Islands – and often based on seafood cooked in coconut milk. Traditional Swahili or Indian restaurants may not serve alcohol.

Ethiopia's unique food (*see Ethiopian cuisine, pages 368–9*) – is difficult to miss when travelling in Ethiopia itself, and it can be sampled at some good Ethiopian restaurants in Dar es Salaam, Nairobi and Kampala.

Coconut Milk

A refreshing and nutritious alternative to the usual brand-name soft drinks is fresh coconut milk, sold by vendors on street corners – and drunk straight from the freshly decapitated nut – in Dar es Salaam, Mombasa and elsewhere along the coast.

In practice, most short-term visitors to East Africa will generally eat at their hotel or lodge. Whilst on safari, there is normally no other realistic option but to eat at the lodge, since rates are quoted as full-board, driving is forbidden after dark, and there are no independent restaurants in the game reserves.

Shopping

Sport

Local Beverages

Numerous locally brewed lager beers – including Kenya's famous Tusker – are available in 500ml to 330ml bottles throughout the region. Wine is imported, mostly from South Africa, and expensive by Kenyan standards, but not so much for European or American visitors. Local gins such as Konyagi and Waragi feel lethal, much like a train hitting your head, and that's before the hangover. A more tasty liqueur is Afrikoko, a chocolate and coconut blend that goes down nicely. Imported spirits are available at most places that regularly cater for foreigners.

Craft and Curios

The city and town centres usually have markets which sell curios such as African drums, jewellery, carvings and an endless supply of colourful *khanga* (wrap-around dresses) at very reasonable prices. Tinga Tinga paintings, batik prints and board games are also very popular in coastal Tanzania and Kenya, as is the embroidered *kofia* (traditional head covering) worn by most Swahili men. Also of interest is the elaborate jewellery and religious icons from Ethiopia, the pink and cream Kisii soapstone carvings from Kenya, and wonderful Makonde carvings from southern Tanzania. Another popular item with tourists is the *kiondo* basket, which is handwoven from sisal. Ethiopian rugs in brown-sandy tones are worth buying – except that they have been known to carry unhatched insect eggs. Safari drivers and other tourist guides are normally very helpful when it comes to recommending where to buy handicrafts, as well as ensuring that their clients aren't overcharged too blatantly.

Marine Activities

Scuba diving and snorkelling are particularly good around the islands of Zanzibar and Mafia and on reefs near mainland resorts such as Watamu, Kilifi and Pangani *(see page 247)*. There are also many secluded beaches around the islands, making for an idyllic setting in or out of the water. Diving can be arranged from the beach hotels or tour operators. Sharks can be a danger along Dar es Salaam coast, so check out the local conditions before booking. The best time for snorkelling is in the morning around 9–10am, and the visibility is better in summer.

Malindi, Watamu. Bagamoyo, Zanzibar and Mafia are all renowned for excellent deep-sea fishing. There are numerous resorts and operators here and in Dar es Salaam offering diving and fishing excursions. July to November is yellow-fin tuna and billfish season; December to March/April is best for broadbill, sailfish and spearfish. Most fish are caught, tagged, weighed and released these days.

Language

Basic Rules

Swahili is rapidly becoming the international language of East Africa and thereby one of the important languages of the world. Although a relatively easy language to pronounce, Swahili does require some effort for the first-time speaker. Every letter in the language gets pronounced, unless it is part of a group of consonants. If a letter is written twice it gets pronounced twice. Word stress almost always falls on the next-to-last syllable.

Vowels
a   as in "calm"
e   as in the "a" in "may"
i   as the "e" in "me"
o   as in "go"
u   as the "o" in "too"

Consonants
dh   as in "th" in "this"
th   as in "th" in "thing"
gh   like the "ch" of the Scottish "loch"
ng' as in the "ng" of "singer"
ng   as in the "ng" in "finger"
ny   as in the "ni" in "onion"
ch   as in "church"
g   as in "get"

Words & Phrases

Yes *Ndiyo/ Ndio*
No *A-a / Hapana*
OK *Sawa*
Please *Tafadhali*
Thank you *Asante / Nashukuru*
Sorry *Pole*
You're welcome *Karibu sana*
Excuse me *Hodi*
I don't speak (very much) Swahili *Sisemba/sisemi Kiswahili (sana)*

How do you say... in Swahili? *Unasemaje... kwa Kiswahili?*
Do you speak English? *Unasema Kiingereza*
Do you understand? *Unaelewa*
I don't understand *Sielewi*
I understand *Naelewa*
A little *Kidogo*
I don't know *Sijui*
Please write it down *Tafadhali niandike*
Wait a moment! *Subiri*
Slowly, please *Tafadhali sema pole pole*
Enough! *Kutosha!*
Good *Nzuri*
Fine *Salama*
Where is...? *...Iko Wapi?*
Where is the nearest...? *...Ya(/la) karibu liko(/iko) wapi?*
...toilet? *choo*
Good morning (literally, 'how's your morning been?') *Habari ya asubuhi*
Good afternoon *Habari za mchana*
Good evening *Habari za jioni*
Good night *Lala salama*
Goodbye *Kwa heri*
Kwaherini (more than one person) *Tutaonana* (see you later)
Later on *Baadaye*
May I come in? (to someone's house) *Hodi!*
Welcome! *Karibu!*
Reply: *Salama, nzuri/safi/njema*
Don't mention it *Rica ederim*
Pleased to meet you *Nimefurahi*
How are you? *Hujambo / Habari gani?*
Fine, thanks. And You? *Sijambo, wewe? / Nzuri, habari zako(/yako)?*
My name is... *Jina langu ni (naitwa)...*
I am (British/American/ Australian) *Natoka (Uingereza/ Marekani/ Australia)*
Leave me alone *Usinisumbue / Niache*
Go away! *Hebu! Toka!*
What time is it? *Saa ngapi?*
When? *Lini?*
Today *Leo*
Tomorrow *Kesho*
Yesterday *Jana*
Now *Sasa*
Later *Baadaye*
Tonight *Leo usiku*
Why? *Kwa nini*
Here *Hapa*

There *Pale*
Where can I find... *Wapi nawesa*
...a newspaper? *Gazeti?*
...a taxi? *Teksi?*
...a telephone? *Simu?*
Yes, there is *Ndiyo*
No, there isn't *Sivyo*

Days of the Week

Monday *Jumatatu*
Tuesday *Jumanne*
Wednesday *Jumatano*
Thursday *Alhamisi*
Friday *Ijumaa*
Saturday *Jumamosi*
Sunday *Jumapili*

Numbers

0	*sufuri/ziro*
1	*moja*
2	*mbili*
3	*tatu*
4	*nne*
5	*tano*
6	*sita*
7	*saba*
8	*nane*
9	*tisa*
10	*kumi*
11	*kumi na moja*
12	*kumi na mbili*
20	*ishirini*
21	*ishirini na moja*
22	*ishirini na mbili*
30	*thelathini*
40	*arobaini*
50	*hamsini*
60	*sitini*
70	*sabiini/sabini*
80	*themanini*
90	*tisiini//tisini*
100	*mia*
200	*Mia mbili*
1,000	*elfu (moja)*

Months

January *Januari*
February *Febuari*
March *Machi*
April *Aprili*
May *Mei*
June *Juni*
July *Julai*
August *Agosti*
September *Septemba*
October *Oktoba*

November Novemba
December Desemba

Health

Hospital Hospitali
Clinic Zahanati
First aid Huduma ya kwanza
Doctor Daktari
Dentist Daktari wa meno / Mganga wa meno
I am ill Naumwa
It hurts here Inaumwa hapa
I have a fever/headache Nina homa/kichwa kinamua
I am diabetic Nina dayabeti
I'm allergic to... Nina aleji ya...
I have asthma Nina ungonjwa wa pumu
I am pregnant Nina mimba
I was bitten by... Niliumwa na...

Directions

Near Karibu
Far Mbali
Left Kushoto
On the left/to the left Upande wa kushoto
Right Kulia
On the right/to the right Upande wa kulia
Straight on Moja kwa moja
City Mji
Village Kijiji
Forest Porini/mwitumi
Sea Bahari
Lake Ziwa
Farm Shamba
Church Kanisa
Mosque Misikiti
Post office Posta
North Kaskazini
South Kusini
East Mashariki
West Magharibi
Is it near/far? Iko karibu/mbali?
How far is...? Ni umbali gani?

Signs

Entrance Mlango/Mahali pa kuingia
Exit Kutoka
Emergency exit Mlango wa dharura
Open Wazi / Imefunguliwa
Closed Shamba / Imefungwa
Arrivals Wanaofika
Departures Wanaoondoka
Military zone Jeshi / Kijeshi

Emergencies

Help! Msaada (kusaidia) Saidia/Njoo/nisaidie
Fire! Moto!
Please call the police Mwite/muite polisi tafadhali
Are you all right? U mzima?
I'm ill naumwa
I'm lost nimepotea
(Get a) doctor (Umwite) daktari
Send for an ambulance Uite gari la hospitali
There has been an accident ajali/Pametokea ajali
He is (seriously) hurt Ameumia (vibaya)
I've been robbed! Nimeibiwa!
I'd like an interpreter Nataka mkalimani/mtafsiri

No smoking Usivute sigara
No entry Hairuhusiwi kuingia (**keep out:** Usiingie)
No photographs Naomba kupiga
Men Wanaume
Women Wanawake
WC Choo / Msalami
Arrival Kuwasili / Kufika
Departure Kuondoka
Information Maelezo

Road Signs

Beware/Caution Uwe / Mwangalifu
Danger Hatari
Slow polepole
Stop Simama
Go Endelea
Keep left Pita kushoto
Sharp turn Pindi la ghlafla
One way Mwiko kuingia
No through road Hakuna nija
Roadworks Njia inatengenezwa
No parking Hairuhusiwi kupak gari hapa

Travelling

Car Motokaa
Petrol/gas station Stesheni ya petroli / Kupata petroli
Petrol/gas Petroli
Give me (5) litres of petrol Nipe lita (tano) za petroli
Flat tyre/puncture Pancha / Kuna kitundu

My car has broken down Gari langu limeharibika / Motokaa yangu imeharibika
Bus station Stesheni ya basi / Kituocha mabasi
Bus stop Bas stendi / Pale inaposimama bas
Bus Basi / Bas
Train station Stesheni ya treni
Train Treni / Gari la moshi
Taxi Teksi / Taxi
Airport Uwanja wa ndege / Kiwanja cha ndege
Aeroplane Ndege
Port/harbour Bandari
Ferry Meli
Ticket Tikiti
Ticket office Wanapouza tikiti
Single ticket Kwenda tu
Return ticket Kwenda na kurudi
Timetable Orodha ya saa
What time does it leave? Tutaondoka saa ngapi?
Where do I go? Nifikeje?
How long does it take? Mpaka tufike itachukua muda gani?
How far is it? Ni umbali gani?
Which bus do I take for...? Niingie katika bas gani kwa kwenda...?
Please drive more slowly Endesha polepole
Stop! Simama!

Bank & Post Office

Bank Banki
Post office Posta
Credit card By name, eg. Visa, Mastercard, etc
What is the exchange rate on the dollar? Naweza kupata shilingi ngapi kwa dolla moja?
Stamps Stempu
Parcels Mizigo
Airmail Ndege

Shopping

How much (is this)? (Hii) bei gani / Ni ngapi?
I would like to buy... Nataka kununua...
Can I have? Nipatie...tafadhali?
No, I don't like it A-a, siipendi (/sipendi) hii
Do you have any...? Kuna...?
Price Bei
Cheap Rahisi
Expensive Ghali

Greetings

Courtesy is rated highly in Tanzania, and greetings should not be rushed. Always shake hands if possible and pay attention to how people greet each other. If you learn nothing else in Swahili, try to master some of the following:

Greetings (to an elder/authority figure): *Shikamoo...*
...elder *mzee*
...woman old enough to have children *mama*
...man old enough to have children *baba*
Reply: *Marahaba*
How are you...? *Hujambo...*
...Sir *bwana*
...Miss *bibi*
Reply: *Sijambo* (or *Jambo* if you want to convert to English)
Hello *Salama / Jambo* (*jambo* is mainly used for foreigners)
Reply: *Jambo* if want to speak English, or *Sijambo* if you want to try a little Swahili.

Old *Ya zamani*
New *Mpya*
Big *Kubwa*
Small *Ndogo*
How many? *Ngapi gani?*
Receipt *Risiti*
Good *Mzuri*
Bad *Mbaya*

Restaurants

Waiter/Waitress! *Bwana!/Bibi!*
Menu *Orodha ya chakula*
I didn't order this *Sikuagiza hii*
A little more of this *Ongeza kidogo*
Is the tip included? *Bakshishi imo ndani?*
I have had enough, thanks *nimetosheka, asante*
I'd like to pay *Nataka kulipa*
Keep the change *Chuk ua hizo zilobakia*
I'm vegetarian *Nakula vyakula vya mboga mboga*
I don't eat meat *Sili nyams*
I don't drink alcohol *Silewi(/sitimii) pombe*

Table Basics

Breakfast *Chakula cha asubuhi*
Table *Meza*
Cup *Kikombe*
Bottle (of) *Chupa (ya)*
Plate *Sahani*
Fork *Uma*
Knife *Kisu*
Spoon *kijiko* (teaspoon), *kijiko kikubwa* (large spoon)
Napkin *Kitambaa*
Salt *Chumvi*
Black pepper *Pilipili*
Soup *Supu*
Fish *Samaki*
Chicken *Kuku*
Meat *Nyama*
Eggs *Mayai*
Vegetarian food *Wasiokula nyama*
Vegetables *Mboga*
Vegetable dishes *Vyakula vya mboga*
Salads *Saladi*
Fruit *Matunda*
Bread *Mkate*
Drinks *Vinywaji*
Water *Maji*
Mineral water *Maji ya chupa*
Soft drink *Sharbeti/kinywaji baridi*
Beer *Biya*
Fruit juice *Maji ya matunda*
Wine (red/white) *Mvinyo / Divai (nyeupe/nyekundu)*
Local alcoholic beverages *Ulevi*
Hot ginger drink *Tangawizi*
Coffee (black/with milk) *Kahawa (na maziwa/nyeusi)*
Tea *Chai*

Further Reading

It is advisable to buy any books you want before you arrive in East Africa. There are good bookshops in Nairobi (next to the Stanley Hotel), Dar es Salaam (in The Slipway) and Kampala (in the Garden Plaza Mall), and adequate ones in Kigali and Addis Ababa, but they tend to be expensive. Some hotels also stock a limited selection of books in their curio shops, but elsewhere decent bookshops don't exist.

Field Guides

Birds of Kenya and Northern Tanzania by Dale A. Zimmerman, Donald A. Turner, David J. Pearson (Contributor) and Ian Willis (Illustrator). Princeton Univ Press, 1999. One of the best field guides to any African region in existence, this is an essential purchase for enthusiasts whose travels are restricted to Kenya and northern Tanzania but of limited use elsewhere.
Field Guide to the Birds of East Africa by Terry Stevenson and John Fanshawe. T. & A.D. Poyser, 2002. Excellent field guide with accurate and comprehensive coverage of Kenya, Tanzania, Uganda and Rwanda.
Birds of Africa South of the Sahara by Ian Sinclair and Peter Ryan. Struik, 2003. The only comprehensive field guide to the 2,105 bird species recorded in sub-Saharan Africa is surprisingly portable given its immense scope. A must-buy for the regular Africa visitor, it also provides the only comprehensive coverage available for Ethiopia.
The Safari Companion: A Guide to Watching African Mammals Including Hoofed Mammals, Carnivores, and Primates by Richard D. Estes. Chelsea Green Publishing Company, 1999. A comprehensive guide to watching and understanding the behaviour of Africa's mammals.

The Kingdon Field Guide to African Mammals by Jonathon Kingdon. Academic Press, 1997. The definitive guide to Africa's mammals, both great and small, packed with detailed information and lifelike illustrations – not cheap but without rival.
Field Guide to the Larger Mammals of Africa by Chris & Tilde Stuart. Struik Publishers, 1997. Relatively inexpensive and highly informative lightweight guide suitable for those with a less serious interest in mammals.
Field Guide to Common Trees and Shrubs of East Africa by Najma Dharani. Struik, 2002.

Wildlife

Mahale: A Photographic Encounter With Chimpanzees by Angelika Hofer, Michael A. Huffman, Gunter Ziesler, Jane Goodall. Stirling Publications, 2000. Photos from Tanzania's isolated Mahale Mountains.
Mara Serengeti: A Photographer's Paradise by Jonathan Scott, Angela Scott, Fountain Press, 2001. Breathtaking photographic study of the Serengeti and its inhabitants.
My Life with the Chimpanzees.
The Chimpanzees I Love: Saving Their World and Ours.
In the Shadow of Man.
Through a Window: My Thirty Years With the Chimpanzees of Gombe. Several titles by chimp queen, Jane Goodall, detailing her life and work with the Gombe Stream chimps.

Classic Field Guides

Field Guide to the Larger Mammals of Africa
Field Guide to the Birds of East Africa
Butterflies of East Africa
Field Guide to the Wild Flowers of East Africa
Reptiles and Amphibians of East Africa
Classic field guides, published by Collins and updated regularly, though the mammal and bird titles have been rendered obsolete by more recent publications.

Jane Goodall: Friend of the Chimps by Eileen Lucas, Millbrook Press, 1992. A touching biography of the ape protector.
The Beauty of the Maasai Mara by David Round-Turner. Camerapix, 1994. Pocket guide with colour photos provides a close-up look at Kenya's most popular wildlife theatre.
In the Lion's Den by Mitsuaki Iwago (Photographer). Chronicle Books, 1996. A photographic essay on the king of beasts.
Serengeti: Natural Order on the African Plain by Mitsuaki Iwago. Chronicle Books, 1996. A visual diary of life and death in the Serengeti.
The Serengeti's Great Migration by Carlo Mari (Photographer), Harvey Croze, Richard D. Estes. Abbeville Press Inc., 2000. One of Africa's greatest events depicted in wonderful detail.
Serengeti Shall Not Die by Bernard Grzimek. Fontana, 1969. Where it all started, the account of the struggle to preserve the Serengeti, by the man who made it happen.
Among the Elephants by Ian Douglas-Hamilton. Penguin, 1978. Compelling account of the elephants of Lake Manyara by the king of elephant research.
The Hunters and the Hunted by Karl and Katherine Ammann. Bodley Head, 1989. Incredible photographs tell the story of Kenya's predators and their prey.
The End of the Game by Peter Beard. Chronicle, 1988. Beard's dramatic photographs and story tell of the history – and questionable future – of African wildlife.
Run, Rhino, Run by E. & C.B. Bradley-Martin. Chatto & Windus, 1982. A detailed look at the rhinoceros and its plight. Many colour photographs.
The Orphans of Tsavo by Daphne Sheldrick. Collins, 1966. Famed conservationist Daphne Sheldrick tells the story of the ups and down of raising orphan elephants – and the equally fascinating trials and tribulations of Kenya's largest game park, Tsavo.
The Endemic Birds of Ethiopia and Eritrea by Jose Vivero. Shama,

2001. The most detailed and up-to-date coverage yet of the 30-plus bird species endemic to Ethiopia and Eritrea, making it an excellent supplement to a standard field guide.

Other Guides

Ethiopia: The Bradt Travel Guide by Philip Briggs. Bradt, 4th edition, 2005. 600-plus pages of comprehensive background coverage and practical information for visitors to Africa's most idiosyncratic and culturally absorbing nation.
Guide to Mt Kenya and Mt Kilimanjaro by Iain Allen (ed.). Mountain Club of Kenya, 1998. Useful introduction to hiking and climbing routes on East Africa's highest peaks.
The Dive Sites of Kenya and Tanzania by Anton Koornhof; New Holland, 1997. Excellent overview of the under-publicised attractions of East Africa's marine life.
Rwanda: The Bradt Travel Guide by Janice Booth and Philip Briggs. Bradt, 2nd edition, 2004. The first dedicated travel guide to the land of the mountain gorilla.
Uganda: The Bradt Travel Guide by Philip Briggs. Bradt, 4th edition, 2003. The most detailed guide to Uganda, thoroughly revised and expended for the current 4th edition.
Where to Watch Birds in Uganda by Jonathon Rossouw and Marco Sacchi. Uganda Tourist Board, 1998. Superb site guide to a dozen of Uganda's best birdwatching locations.

History, Culture & Background

Africa: A Biography of the Continent by John Reader. Vintage Books, 1999. A panoramic history of where it all began – and where it is today!
Africa Explored: Europeans in the Dark Continent by Christopher Hibbert. Cooper Square Publishers, 2002. The lives, journeys and impact of the 19th century European explorers.
African Ark by C. Beckworth, A. Fisher and G. Hancock. Harry N.

Abrams, 1990. Visually superlative and very expensive coffee table tome documenting the rich cultural heritage of Ethiopia, from South Omo to Tigray – one of the finest photographic books ever produced about Africa.

A History of Tanzania ed. N. Kimambo and A.J. Temu. Kapsel Educational, 1997. Tanzanian-written history of the country, with a refreshingly non-European angle. About the only general history to take serious notice of what was happening on the mainland before the Europeans arrived.

Empires of the Monsoon by Richard Hall. Collins, 1996. Ambitious, but thoroughly readable history of the countries and trade routes surrounding the Indian Ocean.

Lunatic Express by Charles Miller. Penguin, 2002. The story of the building of the railway from Mombasa to Uganda.

Origins Reconsidered by Richard Leakey and Roger Lewin. Abacus, 1993. Useful overview of man's evolution in East Africa.

Railway Across the Equator by Amin, Willetts and Matheson. Bodley Head, 1986. Great photography gives added depth to the story of the "Lunatic Line".

The Last of the Maasai by Amin, Duncan, Willetts and Eames. Bodley Head, 1987. An in-depth look at the Maasai people and customs, with many full-colour photographs.

Maasai by Beckwith, Carol and Ole Saitoti, Tepilit. Harry N. Abrams, 1980. Tells the Maasai story through the eyes of a Maasai tribesman.

The African Experience – Olduvai Gorge to the 21st Century by Roland Oliver. Phoenix Press, 2000.

The White Nile by Alan Moorehead. Haperperennial Library,. 2000. Ideal for those interested in European exploration of East Africa in the 19th century.

The Africans by David Lamb. Vintage Books, 1987. Part travelogue and part history of a continent at odds with itself. Written by former bureau chief for the *Los Angeles Times*.

No Man's Land: An Investigative Journey Through Kenya and Tanzania by George Monbiot. Green Books, 2003. Looking for justice in the area where conservation and land rights meet.

The Scramble for Africa by Thomas Pakenham. Abacus, 1994. Masterly unravelling of the complex politics and history involved in Europe's 19th-century land grab.

The Sign and the Seal by Graham Hancock. Heinemann, 1992. This quasi-historical account of the Ark of the Covenant's alleged arrival in Ethiopia is of dubious historical merit, but it does grab the imagination and provides a good introduction to Ethiopian history.

Layers of Time: A History of Ethiopia by Paul Henze. Hurst, 2000. The most approachable one-volume introductory history to Ethiopia in print, with an emphasis on modern history, but also a useful overview of ancient and medieval Ethiopia.

Uganda Ruwenzori: A Range of Images by David Pluth. Little Wolf Press, 1996. Compelling photography and readable text dedicated to the mysterious Mountains of the Moon.

Lives and Letters

African Voices, African Lives: Personal Narratives from a Swahili Village by Patricia Caplan. Routeledge, 1997. A story of three distinctive villagers, told through their words.

The Leakeys: Uncovering the Origins of Humankind by Margaret Poynter. Enslow Publishers, 2001. Biography of the first family of African prehistory.

Memoirs of an Arabian Princess by Emily Said-Ruete. Markus Wiener Publications, 1989. The autobiography of a princess from Zanzibar who elopes with a German to Europe. The author paints an intriguing historical portrait of Unguja in the days of the Sultans.

The Life of Frederick Courtney Selous by J.G. Millais. Gallery Publications, 2001. Biography of the first of the great white hunters.

Livingstone by Tim Jeal. Yale University Press, 2001. Authoritative biography of the greatest of the explorers.

Tanzania, Journey to Republic by Randal Sadleir. Radcliffe Press, 1999. This description of life as a District Commissioner in colonial Tanganyika is also a fascinating account of the road to independence.

Safari: A Chronicle of Adventure by Bartle Bull. Viking, 1988. The history of safaris, full of adventure and tales of daring, with many historical photographs.

Out of Africa by Isak Dinesen. New York. Random House, 1985. The famous autobiographic account of Isak Dinesen/Karen Blixen's life in Kenya, which inspired the Oscar-winning film of the same name.

Journey to the Jade Sea by John Hillaby. Paladin, 1974. The account of one man's adventurous 1,770-km (1,100-mile) walk to Lake Turkana, the "Jade Sea".

Flame Trees of Thika by Elspeth Huxley. Penguin, 1959. Also *Out in the Midday Sun* and *Mottled Lizard*. Elspeth Huxley's collection of wonderfully told tales about her childhood in East Africa.

I Dreamed of Africa by Kuki Gallman. Viking, 1991. A biographical account of one woman's love affair with Kenya.

Facing Mount Kenya by Jomo Kenyatta. Secker and Warburg, 1953. Autobiography of independent Kenya's iconic first president.

West With The Night by Beryl Markham. Penguin, 1942. Fascinating memoirs of a remarkable and adventurous woman who made Kenya her home.

My Kenya Days by Wilfred Thesiger. Flamingo, 1994. This British explorer is also the author of *Visions of the Nomad*.

White Mischief by James Fox; New York. Penguin, 1982. Fascinating account of the murder of Lord Erroll, which inspired the much inferior film of the same name.

Travel Writing

Africa Solo: A Journey Across the Sahara, Sahel and the Congo by Kevin Dertscher. Steerforth Press, 1998. A crisp, clean tale of solo travel in Africa.

Kilimanjaro: to the Roof of Africa by Audrey Salkeld. National Geographic, 2002. Accompanying coffee-table book to an Imax film on the mountain, with superb photography and an authoritative text.
Kilimanjaro Adventure by Hal Streckert, Kathy Wittert (Editor), Tom Tamoria (Illustrator). Mission Press, 1999. A climb to the roof of Africa.
Livingstone's Tribe: A Journey from Zanzibar to the Cape by Stephen Taylor. Flamingo, 2000. Former white South African journeys south from Zanzibar, looking at the people of Africa, black and white.
North of South: An African Journey by Shiva Naipaul. Penguin, 1997. Written in the 1970s, this humorous tale still holds water.
Sand Rivers by Peter Matthiessen. Bantam, 1982. A private safari in the Selous.
Tanzania: Portrait of a Nation by Paul Joynson-Hicks. Quiller, 1998. Beautiful photographs and well-written text.
A Tourist in Africa by Evelyn Waugh. Methuen, 1985. The comic novelist's journey through East Africa.
Going Solo by Roald Dahl. Puffin, 2001. Autobiographical account of working for Shell in 1930s Dar es Salaam before joining the RAF.
Ethiopian Journeys by Paul Henze. Shama Books, 2001. Reprint of a classic travel account of Ethiopia during the last years of the Imperial era.
Dark Star Safari: Overland from Cairo to Cape Town by Paul Theroux. Penguin Books 2003. Controversial travelogue documenting a continent-wide backpacking trip undertaken by the best-selling American novelist, praised by some for its honesty and damned by others for its cynicism, but unquestionably very readable and thought-provoking.

Fiction

Antonia Saw the Oryx First by Maria Thomas. Soho Press, Inc., 1993. A finely composed juxtaposition of two women: one black, one white.
An Ice Cream War by William Boyd. Penguin, 1983. Grimly comic novel

set during the World War I East Africa campaign.
Brazzaville Beach by William Boyd. Penguin, 1991, A young chimpanzee researcher struggling to come to terms with her life and surroundings.
The Snows of Kilimanjaro by Ernest Hemingway. Arrow, 1994. The master storyteller turns his attention, in part, to the African bush, where he spent many happy hours slaughtering its inhabitants.
Death in Zanzibar by M.M. Kaye. Penguin, 1984. Torrid romantic novel set in Arab Zanzibar.
Zanzibar Tales: Told by the Natives of East Africa by George Bateman. Gallery Publications, 2001. Collected Swahili folk tales, translated a century ago.

Other Insight Guides

The 200 Insight Guides have been joined by more than 100 Insight Pocket Guides, Insight Compact Guides, and a series of laminated Insight Guides Fleximaps.

Four Insight Guides are essential reading for any African safari:
Insight Guide: Kenya provides illuminating coverage of the country's superb wildlife reserves along with the magical Indian Ocean coastline and its rich variety of cultures.
Insight Guide: South Africa paints a complete portrait of what is currently one of the most exciting destinations in the world, with insightful reporting and superb and vibrant photography.
Insight Guide: Namibia is a comprehensive guide to this dramatic and beautiful country, which is being increasingly discovered by discerning travellers.
Insight Guide: Tanzania and Zanzibar gives a full run-down of all the essential attractions from bustling Dar es Salaam to the slopes of Kilimanjaro and details the great wildlife parks, prehistoric sites and spice plantations.

Kenya

The Place

Area: 582,644 sq. km (224,959 sq. miles) including 13,600 sq. km (5,250 sq. miles) of inland water.
Situation: Bisected by the equator north of Nairobi, Kenya is bordered by the Indian Ocean to the east, by Somalia, Ethiopia and Sudan to the north, by Uganda to the west and by Tanzania to the south.
Capital: Nairobi
Population: 32 million; Nairobi: 2 million.
Languages: Swahili and English are the official languages, and widely spoken throughout the country, but numerous other languages are spoken locally, notably Kikuyu around Nairobi and Luo around Lake Victoria.
Religion: Predominantly Christian in the interior and Muslim along the coast, with some Kenyans still practising traditional religions.
Currency: Kenya Shilling (Ksh), divided into 100 cents. At time of going to press, there were 136 Ksh to £1 sterling, 76 Ksh to US$1.
Electricity: 240 volts, three-pin plugs. US visitors should bring a small step-down voltage converter and an adaptor.
Weights and Measures: Metric.
Dialling Codes: 254 +2 (Nairobi) +11 (Mombasa).
Internet Domain: .ke
Time Zone: GMT+3. Daylight is almost a constant 12 hours with fast sunrises and sunsets at around 6.30am and 6.30pm.

Climate

With an altitude ranging from sea level to 5,199 metres (17,057 ft), the temperature, rainfall and humidity variations in Kenya are extreme. The coastal belt is hot and humid, while the central highlands around Nairobi have a fresh and invigorating climate rather like a Swiss summer, with Alpine weather conditions on the highest slopes of Mt Kenya. Falling between these extremes, the Rift Valley west of Nairobi is hot by day, cool by night, and relatively dry, giving way to semi-desert north of Mt Kenya, and true desert towards the Ethiopian border. The far west of the country has a warm but moister climate not dissimilar to that of neighbouring Uganda. The main rainy season runs from March to May, with the so-called short rains falling between October and November in eastern and central regions. The far west, around Lake Victoria, has similar wet and dry seasons, but they are less distinct than in the rest of Kenya.

Politics

The Kenya African National Union (KANU) held power from independence in 1961 until December 2002, led initially by the iconic "Mzee" Jomo Kenyatta, who died in 1978, and subsequently by the more divisive figure of President Daniel arap Moi. Kenya functioned as a one-party state until December 1992, when KANU and Moi were returned to power in the country's first democratic multi-party elections in 25 years, as they would be again in the second democratic election in December 1997. Political analysts generally regard Moi's successive electoral victories less as a reflection of any great popularity than of a certain amount of gerrymandering and a divided opposition, with 11 registered political parties in the 1997 election.

Under the present constitution, the president holds executive power assisted by a vice-president and cabinet chosen from the legislature, the national assembly. This body consists of 188 members elected by universal suffrage, 12 presidential nominees, the speaker and the attorney-general. The assembly's term is for five years unless dissolved by the president or its own majority "no confidence" vote. The constitution guarantees certain rights, including the freedom of speech, assembly and worship, but it also allows the president to detain without trial persons who have been deemed a threat to public security.

The present constitution also restricts any one person from serving more than two five-year presidential terms, which meant that in December 2002 Moi – to the surprise of many – relinquished his 24 year hold on KANU to make way for Uhuru Kenyatta, son of independent Kenya's first president. At the same time, the long-divided opposition finally coalesced into the ten-party National Rainbow Coalition (NARC), united primarily by its desire to end KANU's four decades in power. Led by former Mwai Kibaki, NARC won a comprehensive electoral victory, arguably the single most significant event in Kenyan politics since independence itself. It remains to be seen whether Kibaki will fulfil his electoral promises to eradicate the corruption that is endemic to Kenyan Government on practically every level. Sceptics point to the large number of former KANU politicians in the new government (indeed Kibaki himself once served as Moi's vice president) but nevertheless, at the time of writing, the mood in Kenya – and future outlook for the country – is as buoyant as it has been in decades.

Economy

Kenya is among the world's leading exporters of quality coffee, tea and pineapples. Other primary exports are horticultural produce, pyrethrum, sisal and other cash crops. Tourism is an important source of foreign exchange, with further substantial receipts from Kenya's position as the regional centre for communications, banking, insurance and general commerce.

Business Hours

Working hours in Kenya are something of a movable feast: shops and so on open any time from 8am to 5.30pm, with some general stores or Indian shops (dukas) staying open well into the evening and also most of the weekend. In Mombasa, shops and businesses may open as early as 7am, shutting for a long siesta any time from 12.30 to 4pm, and then opening up again until after dark. Normal banking hours are 9am to 3pm, Monday to Friday. Some banks open 9–11am on the first and last Saturday of each month. Banks at Nairobi's international airport run a 24-hour service.

Public Holidays

In addition to the variable Good Friday, Easter Monday, and Id al-Fitr, the following public holidays are taken.

1 January New Year's Day
1 May Labour Day
1 June Madaraka Day (anniversary of self-government)
10 October Moi Day (anniversary of President Moi's inauguration)★
20 October Kenyatta Day
12 December Jamhuri (Independence Day)
25 December Christmas Day
26 December Boxing Day
★It remains to be seen whether Moi Day will still be celebrated under the new government, and whether a new public holiday will be introduced to mark their electoral victory in 2002.

Tourist Information

For tourist information about Kenya before you leave home, contact the Kenya Tourist Board at the addresses below, or check the official website: www.magicalkenya.com
United Kingdom
25 Brooks Mews, London W1Y 1LF
Tel: 020-7355 3144
United States
424 Madison Avenue, New York, NY 10017
Tel: 212-486 1300

9150 Wilshire Boulevard #160, Beverly Hills, CA 90121
Tel: 310-274 6635
Once in Kenya, most private tour companies scattered around the urban centres are fairly liberal with information and there are plenty of publications available – in the form of maps, guides of varying quality, brochures, pamphlets and what's-on and going-out magazines, as well as *Travel News & Lifestyle East Africa*.

Embassies and High Commissions in Nairobi
Australia
Riverside Drive
Tel: 020-4445034–9
Austria
City House, Wabera Street
Tel: 020-228281–2
Canada
Comcraft House
Haile Selassie Avenue
Tel: 020-214804
France
Barclays Plaza, Loita Street
Tel: 020-339783–4
Germany
Williamson House, 4th Ngong Road
Tel: 020-712527–30
India
Jeevan Bharati Building
Harambee Avenue
Tel: 020-222566–7/334167
Italy
International House
Mama Ngina Street
Tel: 020-337356/337777/337320
UK
Upper Hill Road
Tel: 020-714699
USA
Mombasa Road
Tel: 020-537800

Getting There
BY AIR
Jomo Kenyatta International Airport, on the outskirts of Nairobi, is by far the busiest airport in East Africa, and the region's most popular point of entry. It is serviced by international flights by Kenya Airways, the national carrier, as well as a number of international airlines including British Airways, EpyptAlr, Emlrates, Ethloplan Airlines, KLM, Lufthansa and South African Airways. In addition, there are many direct charter flights to Mombasa, particularly from Europe, full of passengers travelling on all-in package holidays. There are no direct flights from North America or Australia; you'll generally have to change flights in Europe or South Africa.

BY SEA
Long gone are the days when a leisurely cruise to Mombasa was an everyday event. But short cruises are available on the Royal Star from Mombasa to Lamu or Zanzibar (book through African Safari Club in Mombasa, tel: 485906–8; www.ascag.net). It is also possible to take a dhow or catamaran from Mombasa to Zanzibar or Dar es Salaam in Tanzania.

BY ROAD
Overland entry into Kenya from the south and west is straightforward. Buses run from Dar es Salaam to Mombasa and Nairobi. A well-used and popular route is from Arusha or Moshi to Nairobi, which takes about five hours by bus or minibus, with a straightforward border crossing. There are regular bus services between Nairobi and Kampala in Uganda. Advice can be obtained by writing ahead to the Automobile Association of Kenya, PO Box 40087, Nairobi, tel: 820169/825296/723195.

Kenya Wildlife Services
Kenya's national parks and other reserves are mostly under the authority of the Kenya Wildlife Service, whose head office lies on Langata Road close to the entrance of Nairobi National Park. Contact details are:
Tel: 020 600800
Fax: 020 603792
Email: kws@kws.org
www.kws.org

Forms of Address
The masses in Kenya are known as the *wananchi* – the "people" – and the word carries a connotation of respect. Do not use "blacks" or "coloureds"; the terms are "Africans" or "Asians".
 In addressing an old man – anyone over 35 – call him *mzee* pronounced "mu-zay". It is a term of respect, meaning "old man" or "elder" and you can use it in shops, restaurants, anywhere. Call a mature woman (over 21) *mama* and a child *toto*. A word you will hear constantly is *wazungu*, meaning "white people" (*mzungu* in the singular). A waiter is addressed as "steward" or maybe *bwana*, which means "mister".

Getting Around
BY AIR
Kenya Airways runs scheduled services from Nairobi to Mombasa, Malindi, Lamu and Kisumu. Flamingo Airlines, a subsidiary of Kenya Airways, is the only airline in Kenya to offer online reservations (www.flamingoairlines.com; the earlier you book, the cheaper the ticket) and runs regular flights to Lamu, Malindi, Kisumu, Eldoret and Lokichoggio.
 Air Kenya operates regular flights between Nairobi, Malindi, Lamu, the Maasai Mara, Amboseli, Tsavo, Kiwayu and Samburu from Wilson Airport on Langata Road. Contact: PO Box 30357, Nairobi; tel: 020-605745/601727; fax: 020-602951; email: resvns@airkenya.com; www.airkenya.com. Mombasa Air Safari flies from Mombasa to Amboseli, Tsavo East and West, Taita Hills and the Maasai Mara, tel: 041-433061/5; fax 041 434264; email: airserve@mombasaairsafari.com; www.monbasaairsafari.com.

BY RAIL
Train travel is very good value and comfortable In both classes. The

main line runs from Mombasa on the coast, via Nairobi, to Kisumu in the west. Trains run from Nairobi to Mombasa on Monday, Tuesday, Thursday and Friday, and the other way on Tuesday, Wednesday, Friday and Sunday. The old-fashioned sleepers and dining car were once reminiscent of the old-world elegance of the original settlers. Sadly, today it's all a bit shabby and trains are slow, but its still a relaxing and enjoyable way to travel. Reserve your tickets well in advance from Nairobi or Mombasa station (tel: Nairobi 020-221211; Mombasa 041-312220).

BY BUS

Buses are the cheapest form of travel in Kenya, with a nationwide network wherever there are decent roads. The long-haul buses out of Nairobi and Mombasa are by no means excluded to visitors, but they are definitely rough and ready. One of the more reliable bus operators is Akamba Public Road Services, tel: 020-221779 or Mombasa 041-311559.

TAXIS

The only properly organised taxi service is a fleet of Mercedes, operated by the Kenatco Transport Company from the international airports and main urban hotels. You can usually take the driver's word for the set per-kilometre rate. Kenatco Nairobi, tel: 020-225123/ 230772; Mombasa 011-220304/ 227503.

Another fairly well-organised service in Nairobi is Jatco Taxis Ltd, tel: 4446096/575369.

Other than this, taxis are something of a free-for-all in Kenya. All are marked with yellow stripes but otherwise they are a decidedly motley collection of vehicles, in various stages of dilapidation, and none with meters. The fares are always negotiable, which presumes foreknowledge of reasonable rates.

At the airport, ask advice at one of the hotel or tour-operator booths and, in town, from your hotel porter.

OTHER VEHICLES

Matatus are private vehicles that offer a cheap service around the urban centres and between towns. They are crowded, sometimes dangerous, and not recommended to visitors. A number of luxury coaches, also privately operated, run between Nairobi and Mombasa.

DRIVING

It is perfectly possible for even first-time visitors, who do not want to be "packaged" by a tour firm, to simply hire a car and set off for a safari or to the coast. There is nothing particularly hazardous about driving around Kenya. Even so, try not to be too ambitious about the distances you want to travel in a day; pre-book your accommodation; and make sure you have sufficient maps, tools, food and water (for yourself and the car). Be sure also to fill your tank with petrol whenever you have the opportunity, since petrol stations are few and far between in some areas.

This isn't standard advice, however. Most locals will probably warn newcomers instead about the poor state of Kenya's bush roads, the kamikaze drivers, the chances of getting lost and so on. But you should not take such advice too seriously. Sensible drivers should be able to find their way around the country's main tourist circuits – Amboseli, Tsavo and so on – without too many problems. If you plan to do the 483-km (300-mile) drive from Nairobi to Mombasa, note that most of the road is in a bad state of repair, with disintegrating tarmac, huge holes and temporary bridges. (The exception is the stretch between Mtito Andei, Voi and Bachuma, which is a new, wide, fast road.) Allow plenty of time for your journey and be prepared to drive slowly.

In the more remote areas, such as north to Turkana, you need a four-wheel-drive vehicle and many more supplies, equipment and local experience, plus someone else driving in convoy.

Hertz, Avis and National operate in Nairobi and Mombasa, together with numerous other local entrepreneurs offering everything from Range Rovers to small saloons. In many cases, you will have the choice between the chauffeur-driven or self-drive.

Safari Notes

Caution and common sense must be exercised in both national parks and reserves. The Ministry of Tourism and Wildlife has compiled some rules and regulations and these are for the protection of the animals as well as the people. Many tourists from time to time forget that a reserve or park is not an open zoo with invisible bars. The rule is to stay in the car and if animals approach, close roofs, doors and windows.

● Touring the parks and reserves is restricted to daylight hours – roughly from 6am to 6pm. Before dusk, when the light turns a golden orange, is the time when the carnivores begin their hunt for dinner and the nocturnal animals come out of hiding. The best time for game viewing is in the early morning or late afternoon.

● Driving speeds in the parks and reserves are limited to 48 kph (30 mph), but driving slower is better as you'll be able to see more.

● Rangers are available as guides on game runs, and it's often a good idea to employ one since they know the area and the animals like the back of their hands.

● The Kenya Wildlife Service has introduced an electronic ticketing system for six of its most popular national parks: Nairobi, Amboseli, Tsavo East and West, Lake Nakuru and Aberdare. The smartcard, available from an office located at the entrance of Nairobi National Park, can be paid for in Kenya shillings or US dollars. There are three types of visitor cards: citizen, resident and non-resident. If you produce this card at the point of entry to one of the six parks, the entry fee will be deducted from the credit on your card.

Nairobi

WHERE TO STAY

Norfolk Hotel
Harry Thuku Road,
PO Box 40064, Nairobi
Tel: 020-216940
Fax: 020-216976
Email: sales@lonrhohotels.co.ke
www.lonrhohotels.com
The oldest hotel in Nairobi is a favourite of celebrities and other well-heeled visitors, with a historical atmosphere complemented by the fully modernised facilities. Situated on Harry Thuku Road a short walk from the city centre. **$$$$$**

Windsor Golf & Country Club
PO Box 45887, 00100 Nairobi
Tel: 020-862300
Fax: 020-860160
Email: windsor@imul.com
Only 15 minutes' drive from the centre of Nairobi, this attractive hotel is centred on an 18-hole championship golf course, but will also appeal to birdwatchers. **$$$$$**

Holiday Inn Mayfair Court Hotel
Parklands Road, Westlands,
PO Box 66807, Nairobi
Tel: 020-740920
Fax: 020-748823
Email: admin@holidayinn.co.ke
www.holiday-inn.com/nairobikenya
Good-value and historic hotel in the suburb of Westlands, set in attractive green grounds around a large swimming pool, and close to a couple of good shopping malls and a great many restaurants. **$$$$**

Nairobi Serena Hotel
Kenyatta Avenue,
PO Box 46302, Nairobi
Tel: 020-282 2000
Fax: 020-272 5184
Email: nairobi@serena.co.ke
www.serenahotels.com
Situated on the corner of Nyerere Road and Kenyatta Avenue, opposite City Park on the verge of the city centre, this is one of the few upmarket hotels in central Nairobi whose aesthetics seem

geared more to tourists than business travellers. Excellent food and service. **$$$$**

Stanley Hotel
PO Box 66807, Nairobi
Tel: 020-228830
Fax: 020-229388
Email: reservations@sarova.co.ke
www.sarovahotels.com
Another very comfortable and relatively reasonably priced Edwardian hotel, the Stanley is centrally located on the corner of Kimathi Street and Kenyatta Avenue. The Thorn Tree Café on the pavement remains one of Nairobi's most popular points of liaison. **$$$$**

Hotel Price Guide

$$$$$	above US$275
$$$$	US$150–275
$$$	US$75–150
$$	US$20–75
$	below US$20

Boulevard Hotel
PO Box 42831, 00100 Nairobi
Tel: 020-227567
Fax: 020-334071
Email:
hotel@hotelboulevardkenya.com
www.hotelboulevardkenya.com
This small but very comfortable garden hotel on Harry Thuku Road just beyond the plusher Norfolk Hotel is excellent value for money. **$$$**

Six-Eighty Hotel
PO Box 43436, 00100 Nairobi
Tel: 020-315680
Fax: 020-343875
Email: info@680-hotel.co.ke
www.680-hotel.co.ke
This centrally located and modern hotel is definitely on the bland side, but it's good value, and the first-floor veranda is one of the better places for a drink in the city centre. **$$**

Nairobi Park Services Campsite
Tel: 020-892261
Fax: 020-890325
Email: nps@swiftkenya.com
www.nairobipark,gq.nu
This out-of-town backpackers' haunt on the Magadi Road close to Nairobi National Park offers dormitory

accommodation, rooms and camping, while facilities include cheap internet access, a lively restaurant and bar with satellite television, and various day trips out of the capital. Their excellent airport shuttle service, inclusive of two nights' B&B accommodation and a guided day tour of local highlights, is a bargain and highly recommended to budget travellers wanting a secure first port of call in Kenya. **$**

WHERE TO EAT

Restaurants serving African, European and Asian cuisine can be found throughout Nairobi – the following are a few long-standing favourites but in general the food is of excellent quality and is reasonably priced.

Alan Bobbe's Bistro
Tel: 020-224945
Long-serving, high-quality and – by local standards – pricey French cuisine on Koinange Street.

Carnivore Restaurant
Langata Road
Tel: 020-575715
A Nairobi institution, this out-of-town restaurant on Langata Road near the entrance to Nairobi National Park is renowned for its all-you-can-eat buffets of barbecued game meat.

Daas Ethiopian Restaurant
Ralph Bunche Road
Tel: 020-712106
Excellent Ethiopian cuisine and dancing on Ralph Bunche Road, south of the city centre.

Dawat Restaurant
Shimmers Plaza, Westlands
Tel: 020-374 9337
One of Kenya's finest Indian restaurants, and unexpectedly reasonably priced, the Dawat is situated in Shimmers Plaza in Westlands.

Trattoria
Kaunda/Wabera Street
Tel: 020-340855
Central and reliably bustling Italian restaurant on the corner of Kaunda and Wabera streets – great pasta dishes, grills and pizza and memorable cakes and desserts.

Amboseli National Park

Tortilis Camp
Tel: 020-604053/4
Fax: 020-603066
Email: marketing@chelipeacock.co.ke
www.chelipeacock.com
This fabulous luxury tented camp is set in lush, green grounds on a hillside in the acacia woodland of the far southwest of the national park. The restaurant specialises in excellent Italian food and has a perfect view of Kilimanjaro. **$$$$$**

Amboseli Lodge
Tel/fax: 020-338888
Email: ksc@africaonline.co.ke
Situated in Ol Tukai, a village-like conglomeration of buildings set in a large acacia stand in the heart of the national park, Amboseli Lodge is an unpretentious old lodge offering comfortable accommodation and decent food, facing the imposing bulk of Kilimanjaro. **$$$$**

Amboseli Serena Lodge
Tel: 045-622361
Fax: 045-622430
Email: amboseli@serena.co.ke
www.serenahotels.com
Blandly luxurious lodge about 5 km (3 miles) south of Ol Tukai, set in flowering gardens overlooking a swamp where elephant regularly congregate. **$$$$**

Tsavo West National Park

Finch Hatton's Tented Camp
Tel: 020-553237/8
Fax: 020-553245
Email: finchhattons@iconnect.co.ke
www.finchhattons.com
Named after the Karen Blixen associate played by Robert Redford in the film *Out of Africa*, this immaculately luxurious tented camp is – as you might expect – in the exclusive old-style safari mould, set alongside a hippo pool fed by underground springs. **$$$$$**

Taita Hills & Salt Lick lodges
Tel: 013-30270/43
Fax: 013-30007
www.hilton.com
These two luxurious lodges lie in the private Taita Hills Wildlife Sanctuary, which protects a tract of dry savanna abutting Tsavo West, in the shadow of Taita Hills. Salt Lick Lodge in particular draws prodigious volumes of game to its waterhole in the dry season. **$$$$$**

Kilaguni Serena Lodge
PO Box 48690, Nairobi
Tel: 020-271 0511
Fax: 020-271 8100
Email: cro@serena.co.ke
www.serenahotels.com
This large and comfortable 1960s lodge overlooks a busy waterhole, with the Chyulu Hills and Kilimanjaro providing a dramatic backdrop. **$$$$**

Ngulia Lodge
Tel: 013-30091/30140
www.kenya-safari.co.ke
Another comfortable 1960s hotel, Ngulia Lodge has a great cliff-top location overlooking the expansive Yatta Plateau. **$$$**

Tsavo East National Park

Galdessa Camp
Tel: 020-712 3156
Fax: 020-712 2638
Email: webreservations@galdessa.com
www.galdessa.com
This intimate tented camp – only six units – offers superlative luxury tented accommodation and equally good food on the palm-fringed banks of the Galana River. It's let down slightly by the difficult game viewing in the surrounding dense scrub, through elephant regularly wander into camp and there's a good chance of spotting – perhaps even being charged by – black rhino on game drives. **$$$$$**

Voi Safari Lodge
Tel: 013-30019/30027
www.kenya-safari.co.ke
The tacky 1970s decor has past its sell-by date, but otherwise this hill-top lodge offers good, unfussy accommodation at a reasonable price, with agama lizards and rock hyrax all over the place, and a peerless view over endless plains where Tsavo's legendary elephants maintain an almost permanent presence and 1,000-strong buffalo herds regularly come to drink at the waterhole. **$$$**

Maasai Mara National Reserve

At least 20 permanent lodges and up-market tented camps are dotted in and around the Maasai Mara, which together with various temporary and permanent budget camp sites goes a long way to explaining why game drives tend to suffer from vehicle congestion by comparison to Tanzania's much larger and more sparsely developed Serengeti National Park on the southern border. The following selective list includes a spread of the better lodges in all price categories.

Governor's Camps
PO Box 48217, Nairobi
Tel: 020-273 4000
Fax: 020-273 4023
Email: info@governorscamp.com
www.governorscamp.com
The oldest lodge in the Maasai Mara is the original Governor's Camp, still a family-run operation, which consists of 35 comfortable en-suite standing tents strung along the riparian forest fringing the Mara River. The nearby plains are prime game-viewing territory – lion and cheetah are likely to be seen several times on a game drive – and benefit in terms of tourist traffic from being relatively inaccessible to camping safaris and most of the other lodges. Governor's also operates three more intimate and exclusive satellite camps nearby. Aimed at fly-in safarigoers, for which reason game drives are included in the rates. **$$$$$**

Kichwa Tembo Camp
Tel: +27-11-809 4300
Fax: +27-11-809 4400
Email: information@ccafrica.com
www.ccafrica.com
Excellent luxury tented camp set in an isolated and thus generally crowd-free part of the Mara, yet also offering very good game viewing, with leopards something of a local speciality. Game drives are included in the rates, making it an ideal lodge for fly-in safaris. **$$$$$**

Siana Intrepids Camp
Tel: 020-444 2115/6651
Fax: 020-444 6600
Email: sales@heritagehotels.co.ke

www.heritage-eastafrica.com
Top-notch luxury tented camp set outside the reserve in a good location for game drives as well as guided bush walks and night drives. **$$$$**

Keekorok Lodge (Maasai Mara)
Tel: 020-559529/533350
Fax: 020-650384
Email: sales@wildernesslodges.co.ke
www.wildernesslodges.co.ke
This long-serving and comfortable lodge, attractively located for game drives and balloon trips, is larger and more impersonal than the above, and caters mainly for drive-down packages. **$$$$**

Mara Serena Lodge
Tel: 020-271 0511
Fax: 020-271 8100
Email: cro@serenahotels.co.ke
www.serenahotels.com
Similar in style to Keekerok Lodge, but larger and more modern, this comfortable lodge conforms to Serena's usual high standards and caters mainly to drive-down safaris. **$$$$**

Fig Tree Camp
Tel: 02-218321/221439
Fax: 02-332170
Email: sales@madahotels.com
Long serving, comfortable and relatively moderately priced tented camp with an attractive riverine location near Talek Gate. Good game viewing in the vicinity. **$$$**

Aberdare National Park

Treetops Lodge
Tel: 020-445 2095–9
Fax: 020-445 2102
Email: adventure@aberdare safarihotels.com
www.aberdaresafarihotels.com
Treetops is one of three stilted tree hotels in the central highlands, all designed for overnight guests to watch nocturnal animals drink at a waterhole below. Set on the Aberdare footslopes just inside the national park boundary, Treetops trades strongly on its royal associations – the park was opened by Princess Elizabeth in 1952. The lush forest of those days has now been reduced to a few straggling trees, and although elephant, buffalo and even black rhinoceros

come past most nights, the game viewing doesn't compare to its competitors and the accommodation is unexpectedly rudimentary. **$$$$$**

The Ark
Tel: 02-216920/40
Fax: 02-216976
Email: sales@lonrhohotels.com
www.lonrhohotels.com
Similar in concept to Treetops, The Ark offers superior nocturnal game-viewing as well as a better chance of seeing forest birds and mammals. Elephant, buffalo, black rhinoceros, spotted hyena, genet, bushbuck and Defassa waterbuck come past most nights, and leopard, lion and giant forest hog pitch up regularly. There's a good photographic hide, and although the rooms are cramped, you're unlikely to spend too much time in them as the nocturnal procession keeps you glued to the viewing platform. **$$$$$**

Mountain Lodge
PO Box 48690, Nairobi
Tel: 020-271 0511
Fax: 020-271 8100
Email: cro@serenahotels.co.ke
www.serenahotels.com
The best yet most under-utilised of the central highlands' tree hotels, Mountain Lodge lies in a forest reserve on the southern boundary of Mt Kenya National Park, overlooking a marshy clearing encircled in tall gallery forest with views across to the mountains' glacial peaks. Black-and-white colobus and blue monkeys frolic on the wooden main building, and giant forest hog, bushpig, elephant, buffalo and black rhinoceros come past most nights.

Meru National Park

Elsa's Kopje
Tel: 020-604053/4
Fax: 020-603066
Email: marketing@chelipeacock.com
www.chelipeacock.com
A sure contender for the accolade of Kenya's most stunning lodge, Elsa's Kopje consists of six airy and spacious en-suite cottages built into the boulders atop a hill offering fantastic views across the

Hotel Price Guide

$$$$$	above US$275
$$$$	US$150–275
$$$	US$75–150
$$	US$20–75
$	below US$20

surrounding plains. World-class service, food and facilities – the swimming pool is a real gem. **$$$$$**

Samburu & Buffalo Springs National Reserves

Samburu Lodge
Tel: 020-559529/533350
Fax: 020-650384
Email: sales@wildernesslodges.co.ke
www.wildernesslodges.co.ke
Attractive and well-run package lodge of en-suite chalets strung along a prime location in lush riverine forest. Leopards, baited on a tree on the facing riverbank, come past most nights, while genets often wander through the dining area. **$$$$**

Samburu Intrepids Club
Tel: 020-444 6651
Fax: 020-444 6600
Email: sales@heritagehotels.co.ke
www.heritage-eastafrica.com
Excellent, well-priced, and relatively small tented camp consisting of 25 luxurious en-suite standing tents in the riverine woodland, with balconies overlooking the Ewaso Nyiro River. Personalised service, good food and a variety of interesting excursions offered, from camel-back safaris to hill-top sundowners. **$$$–$$$$**

Marsabit National Park

Marsabit Lodge
Tel: 069-2411
Fax: 069-2416
Email: info@marsabitlodge.com
www.marsabitlodge.com
This seldom-visited lodge's wonderful location on a forest-fringed crater lake – regularly visited by elephants – is doubly welcome after the long drive on rutted desert roads north from Isiolo. Accommodation is on the simple side, but is priced accordingly. **$$**

Hotel Price Guide

$$$$$	above US$275
$$$$	US$150–275
$$$	US$75–150
$$	US$20–75
$	below US$20

Rift Valley Lakes

Lake Naivasha Country Club (Lake Naivasha)
Tel: 020-650500/651991
Fax: 020-543810
Email: reservationsblockhotelske.com
www.blockhotelske.com
Sumptuous colonial-era hotel set in large wooded grounds with access to Crescent Island and its variety of ungulates and birds. Rated as one of the best birdwatching sites in Kenya, with up to 100 species recorded by experts before breakfast. **$$$$**

Sarova Lion Hill Lodge (Lake Nakuru)
PO Box 30680, Nairobi
Tel: 020-271 3333
Fax: 020-271 5566
www.sarovahotels.com
Pleasant chalet accommodation and friendly staff complement the wonderful views across the pink-fringed lake and its millions of flamingos. **$$$$**

Lake Baringo Club (Lake Baringo)
PO Box 40075, Nairobi
Tel: 020-650500/651991
Fax: 020-543810
Email: reservationsblockhotelske.com
www.blockhotelske.com
Well-established lodge offering comfortable chalet accommodation in lush lake-shore gardens that serve as the favoured nocturnal tramping grounds for the local hippos. Superb birdwatching, with good ornithological walks daily to nearby cliffs frequented by black eagle and several dry-country species at the southern extreme of their range. **$$$$**

Island Camp (Lake Baringo)
Tel: 020-444 7151/1705
Fax: 020-444 7270
Email: info@letsgosafari.com
www.letsgosafari.com

Set on a small private island in the lake, this luxurious tented lodge is an idyllic post- or mid-safari retreat, a great place to put up your feet for an afternoon, though the restricted area of the island might frustrate more active travellers. **$$$$$**

Shimba Hills National Reserve

Shimba Lodge
Tel: 020-445 2095–9
Fax: 020-445 2102
Email: adventure@aberdare safarihotels.com
www.aberdaresafarihotels.com
Underrated Treetops-style construction, only 30 minutes' drive from popular Diani Beach, overlooking a forest-fringed pool visited by elephant and small antelope. An unusual attraction are the red forest squirrels that clamber around the building by day, replaced after dark by several very habituated bushbabies. The sable antelope is common. Guided walks are available. **$$$$**

The Coast

Kenya's popular coastal resorts make the ideal place to rest after a safari. For a straight beach holiday, Diani and the other resorts of the Mombasa area are difficult to beat, while Watamu, further north, has the added attraction of superb marine life and several rare birds in the nearby Sokoke Forest. For a more authentic cultural experience, the fabulously time-warped and laidback old Swahili town of Lamu has changed little in appearance over the past 100 years. A few selected hotels follow:

Indian Ocean Beach Club (Diani Beach, south of Mombasa)
Tel: 040-320 3730/3550
Fax: 040-320 3557
Email: iobc@jacarandahotels.com
www.jacarandahotels.com
Top-of-the-range luxury beach resort set amid palms and baobabs in an isolated northern bay along what is otherwise Kenya's busiest stretch of white-sanded Indian Ocean waterfront. **$$$$**

Mombasa Serena Beach Hotel (Nyali Beach, north of Mombasa)
Tel: 041-548 5721/2/3
Fax: 041-548 7223
Email: mombasa@serena.co.ke
www.serenahotels.com
Sumptuous luxury hotel distinguished by its winning traditional Swahili architecture, great seafood and excellent range of facilities, including tennis, squash, diving and snorkelling. **$$$$$**

Hemingway's (Watamu)
Tel: 042-32624/327224
Fax: 042-32256
Email: reservations@hemingways.co.ke
www.hemingways.co.ke
The finest hotel in the resort village of Watamu, Hemingway's not unexpectedly caters well for game fishermen, but diving and

Private Ranches

Some of the best accommodation is on private farms and ranches. Usually these are near, but outside, national parks and reserves, so it's possible to go walking and take night drives (both forbidden in national parks). The farms and ranches below offer "homestays":

Ol Malo Laikipia
Wilderness Trails Lewa Downs, Isiolo
Kitich Camp Mathews Range
Patrick's Camp Solio
Rekero Maasai Mara

Lobolo Camp Turkana
Lokitela Farm Mt Elgon
Mundui Estate Lake Naivasha
Ol Kanjua (mobile camp) Amboseli
Sirata Siruwa South Kajiado
Tana Delta Camp North Malindi
Takaungu Kilifi
Accommodation at the above can be booked through:
Bush Homes of East Africa Ltd
Tel: 02-571647/49/61.
Fax: 02-571665.
www.bush-homes.co.ke.

The National Museum

Before you go on safari it is worth visiting Nairobi's National Museum of Kenya, where the displays of stuffed animals will help you to familiarise yourself with the creatures that you may see in the bush. The displays are live in the museum's snake park and aquarium. Books and leaflets on just about everything to do with Kenya's flora and fauna are also available. There are smaller national museums in Kisumu, Eldoret, Maralal, Meru, Lamu, Gede ruins (near Watamu) and Fort Jesus in Mombasa.

National Museum of Kenya
Museum Hill
Nairobi
Kenya
Tel: 020 374 2131
Fax: 020 374 1424
Opening Hours: 9.30am to 6pm
Mon–Sun
www.museums.or.ke.

snorkelling among the mushroom-shaped reefs is offered, and day trips to the nearby Sokoke Forest and Gedi Ruins are eminently worthwhile.

Peponi Hotel (Lamu)
Tel: 042-633421
Fax: 042-633029
Email: info@peponi-lamu.com
www.peponi-lamu.com
Set on the magnificent Shela Beach within walking distance of traditional Lamu town, this fabulous family-run lodge is an unabashedly hedonistic – and delightfully eccentric – variation on the standard bland beach resort. $$$$
Kipungani Lodge (Lamu)
PO Box 74888, Nairobi
Tel: 020-444 6651/4582
Fax: 020-444 6600
Email: sales@heritagehotels.co.ke
www.heritage-eastafrica.com
Exclusive and wonderfully isolated beach lodge made almost entirely of organic materials and set on a quiet mangrove-lined lagoon on the opposite side of Lamu Island to the town – the stuff of desert-island fantasies. $$$$

Tanzania

The Place

Area: Approximately 945,000 sq. km (365,000 sq. miles)
Situation: The United Republic of Tanzania, as it is officially known, lies between 290° and 410° longitude and 10° and 120° latitude. Bordered by the Indian Ocean to the east, Tanzania also shares borders with Kenya and Uganda (north), Rwanda, Burundi, and the Democratic Republic of Congo (east) and Zambia, Malawi and Mozambique (south).
Capital: Dodoma is the official capital and seat of parliament, but Dar es Salaam is the country's largest city and commercial hub.
Population: Approx. 38.5 million
Language: Swahili and English are the official languages. English is mainly spoken only in larger cities. Swahili is the lingua franca in Eastern Africa, but there are numerous other languages and dialects associated with Tanzania's 129 officially recognised tribes.
Religion: Tanzania's mainland population is evenly split between traditional beliefs, Islam and Christianity, with the addition of a small number of Hindus, Sikhs and Ismaelis. Zanzibar is predominately Muslim.
Currency: Tanzania shilling (TSh or TZs) divided into 100 cents, which are rarely used.
Electricity: 230 volts, 50Hz, square three-pin plugs (UK-style). Some three round pin plugs remain.
Weights and Measures: Metric, although some imperial measurements are still used.
International Dialling Code: +255
Internet Domain: .tz
Time Zone: GMT+3; EST+8. No daylight savings time.

Climate

Tanzania's varied geography creates drastic climatic differences within the country. The coast is hot and humid day and night, with maximum daily temperatures generally exceeding 30°C (86°F). The central plateau has hot days and cool nights, and is seldom humid. The hilly area between the coast and the northern highlands averages a pleasant 20°C (68°F) from January to September, while mountainous areas (including Kilimanjaro, the Usambara Mountains and the Northern and Southern highlands) register lows of 12°C (54°F) from May to August. Mt Kilimanjaro is snow-capped year-round, although climate changes are melting more ice each year.

The hottest months are from October to February and the main rainy season from mid March to late May. Heavy downpours during April and May are often accompanied by violent thunderstorms. There is also a short rainy season in November and December. The coolest months, June to September, are the most pleasant, particularly on the coast.

Government

Tanzania consists of the mainland (formerly Tanganyika) and the island of Zanzibar, which unified in 1964. From independence until 1985, Tanzania was ruled by Julius Nyerere, known across Africa as "Mwalimu" (the teacher), and one of Africa's most renowned statesmen. Nyerere believed strongly in socialism and self-reliance, and insisted on speaking Swahili, factors that helped Tanzania avoid tribalism in national politics.

Tanzania is a fledgling multi-party democracy. The president and most members of the unicameral national assembly are elected by direct popular vote to serve five-year terms. The national assembly is lead by the prime minister who is appointed by the president. Zanzibar elects a president and a house of representatives. The president of Zanzibar serves as vice president (along with the prime minister) of Tanzania. The Zanzibari House of Representatives has the right to appoint five members to the national assembly. Another 37 seats are reserved for women. The ruling party, led by President Benjamin Mkapa, is the CCM (Chama Cha Mapinduzi or the Party of the Revolution), the successor to Nyerere's TANU, which came to power on independence in 1961.

Economy

Tanzania is one of the poorest countries in the world and generated only $23.71 billion dollars (its GDP) in 2004. It owes over $7 billion to external donors and still receives nearly $1 billion per year in economic aid. Much of the income services the foreign debt, despite substantial debt relief. Its per capita GDP only provides $300 per person, a figure which includes the concentration of wealth in economic centres such as Dar es Salaam. Over 50 percent of the population live on less than US$1 a day. Luckily, many of these are subsistence farmers who can still scrape a living from the land.

Public Holidays

Good Friday and Easter Monday are taken as public holidays, as are the Muslim festivals Eid El Fitr, Eid El Haji and Maulid. Fixed date public holidays are as follows:
1 January New Year
12 January Zanzibar Revolution Day
5 February CCM Foundation Day
26 April Union Day
1 May Workers Day
7 July Saba Saba (Peasants' Day)
8 August Nane Nane (Farmers' Day)
10 September Prophet's birthday
9 December Independence Day
25 December Christmas Day
26 December Boxing Day

Agriculture is Tanzania's economic mainstay and employs 80 percent of the workforce. In addition to the spice crops of Zanzibar, plantations of sisal, coffee, tea, banana, cashews, cotton and sugar line the highways of Tanzania. Though it may seem the crops go on and on, the topography and climate only allow for cultivation in 4 percent of the land area. Industry is mainly limited to processing agricultural goods, although there are significant gold and tanzanite mines. The good news is that the economy is beginning to grow more quickly, especially in the tourism sector. Tourist dollars have increased tenfold over the past decade and the number of tourists over four times.

Business Hours

Business hours are becoming much more varied as more of Tanzania's economy becomes privatised. Here is a rough sample of the hours practised.
Offices: Mon–Fri 8am–noon, 2–5pm, Sat 8am–1pm, if open.
Government: Mon–Fri 8am–4pm.
Garages/Shops: Mon–Fri 8.30am–noon, 2–6pm, Sat 8.30am–12.30pm.
Banks: Mon–Fri 8.30am–4pm, Sat 8am–1pm.
Post Offices: Mon–Fri 8am–4.30pm, Sat 9am–noon.

Tourist Offices Abroad

In the USA, Australia and most other countries the Tanzania Tourist Board is represented by the local embassy or high commission. In the UK, it is represented by The Tanzania Trade Centre 80 Borough High Street, London SE1 1LL
Tel: 020-7407 0566
Fax: 020-7403 2003
Email: director@tanzatrade.co.uk
Also worth a look is the official site of the Tanzanian Tourist Board (www.tanzaniatouristboard.com), which contains a variety of useful information including foreign embassies and high commissions;

and Tanzania news, a classy news resource containing travel info and many links to other websites (www.tanzanianews.com).

Foreign Embassies & Consulates in Dar es Salaam
UK
78 Haile Selassie Road, Oyster Bay
Tel: 022-211 0101 or 266 6355
Email:
bhc.commercial@dar.mail.fco.gov.uk
USA
140 Msese Road, Kinondoni
Tel: 022-266 6010–5 or 266 8001
Fax: 022-266 6701
Email:
usembassy-dar1@cats-net.com
www.cats-net.com
Canada
38 Mirambo Street
(corner Garden Avenue)
Tel: 022-211 2831–5
Fax: 022-211 6897
Email: dslam@dfait-maeci.gc.ca
Australia
Australians needing assistance should contact the Canadian Embassy.
Ireland
1131 Msasani Road, Oyster Bay
Tel: 022-260 2355/6
Fax: 022-266 7852
Kenya
12th floor NIC Investment House corner Samora Avenue
/Mirambo Street
Tel: 022-270 1747
Fax: 022-211 3098
Rwanda
32 Ali Hassan Mwinyi Road, Upanga
Tel: 022-211 7631/5889
Fax: 022-211 5888
South Africa
Mwaya Road, Msasani
Tel: 022-260 1800
Fax: 022-260 1684
Uganda
25 Msasani Road, Oyster Bay
Tel: 022-266 6730/7009/7931
Fax: 022-266 7224

Getting There

BY AIR

There are international airports at Dar es Salaam, Kilimanjaro (between Moshi and Arusha) and

Zanzibar. Most international flights land at Dar es Salaam. Major carriers flying to Dar es Salaam from Europe include KLM (via Amsterdam and Nairobi), Ethiopian Airlines (via Addis Ababa), Swiss Air (via Zurich), SAA (from Johannesburg), Gulf Air (via Muscat) and British Airways (direct from London). Zanzibar is served by international flights from Gulf Air; Kenya Airlines (from Nairobi); Ethiopian Airlines and Air Tanzania. Kilimanjaro International Airport is also served by many airlines including Air Tanzania and Ethiopian, and KLM flies there directly from Europe.

BY SEA

Though a major shipping centre, the passenger trade in Zanzibar and Tanzania consists mainly of internal ferries. Ferries from Mombasa, Kenya connect to Stone Town, Dar es Salaam and Tanga. Some cruising companies have discovered the beauty of a cruise in these parts, including Hayes and Jarvis www.hayesandjarvis.co.uk Tel: 0870-898 9890 Luxury Indian Ocean cruises, including Zanzibar.

BY RAIL

The TAZARA rail line between Dar es Salaam and Kapiri Mposhi in Zambia is the only cross-border passenger train. The train departs from Dar es Salaam four days per week. The express train leaves on Tuesdays and Fridays and is the better option, taking just over 36 hours to reach Zambia, and passing through the Selous Reserve in daylight. The slow train leaves on Monday and Thursday. Delays are frequent on both services. Dar es Salaam booking office, tel: 022-286 5538.

On a far more luxurious note, Rovos Rail run an all-inclusive, annual rail tour originating in Cape Town and utilising the same track from Zambia to Dar es Salaam. See www.rovos.co.za for more details.

Park Rules

The national park rules laid down by Tanapa provide good guidelines to responsible safaris anywhere in Africa:

● Do not disturb any animals or birds.
● Do not cause any noise or create a disturbance likely to offend or annoy other visitors.
● Do not pick any flowers or cut or destroy any vegetation.
● Do not discard any litter, burning cigarettes or matches.
● Do not bring a pet into the park.
● Do not bring a firearm in the park.
● Do not feed the animals.
● Some parks require a guide before entering.
● Some parks do not accept children under seven (check before travelling).
● If walking in a park, stay strictly on the main trails.

BY BUS

Buses go from Dar south to Zambia and Malawi – and then to Zimbabwe and South Africa, north to Kenya (Nairobi and Mombasa) and east through Kenya to Uganda. Most long-distance buses leave Dar es Salaam from the Ubungo bus terminal, 5 km (3 miles) from the city centre on Morogoro Road – pickpockets are rife here. Several comfortable daily shuttle services connect Nairobi to Moshi and Arusha, typically leaving at 8am and 2pm and taking about 4 hours in either direction. The main termini for these shuttles – which can be booked through any local tour operator – are the New Stanley Hotel in Nairobi and the Mt Meru Novotel in Arusha, but most will collect or drop off passengers at the hotel of their choice.

National Parks

Tanzania National Parks (TANAPA) is a government organisation with headquarters in Arusha. It gazettes,

manages and protects the country's national parks. Contact details are:
Tel: 027-254 4082
Fax: 027-254 8216
Email: tanapa@yako.habari.co.tz
www.tanapa.com

Dar es Salaam and Environs

No longer the official capital of Tanzania, Dar es Salaam remains the country's largest city – with a population 10 times larger than its closest rival – and its economic, social and transport hub. Despite its Indian Ocean location, the city holds little appeal to tourists, for whom its main importance is as the site of the country's busiest international airport and the normal springboard for safaris to the southern reserves of Ruaha, Selous and Mikumi. Visitors who need to spend a night or two in Dar es Salaam might prefer to stay at a beach hotel along the lovely Indian Ocean coastline to its north and south.

There are two free listings magazines in Dar, the bi-monthly *Dar Es Salaam Guide* and the monthly *What's Happening in Dar es Salaam* (www.whatsondar.co.tz). Both are in English and give details of what's on as well as up-to-date addresses and telephone numbers. Available from most hotels.

Hotel Price Guide

$$$$$	above US$275
$$$$	US$150–275
$$$	US$75–150
$$	US$20–75
$	below US$20

WHERE TO STAY

Ras Kutani
Tel: 022-213 4802
Fax: 022-211 2794
Email: info@selous.com
www.selous.com
This exclusive hideaway consists of 12 luxurious cottages built from local material set on a stunning Indian Ocean beach and palm-fringed

lagoon. Service and food are superb. Sailing, fishing, island trips and riding. About 45 minutes by road south of Dar. **$$$$$**

Lazy Lagoon
Tel: 023-244 0194
Fax: 0741-327 706
Email: info@tanzaniasafaris.com
www.tanzaniasafaris.com
Isolated and beautiful luxury lodge on a sandy spit on the Mbegani Lagoon, about 60 km (40 miles) north of Dar es Salaam and 7 km (4 miles) south of the historic port of Bagamoyo. Ten attractively decorated thatched beach chalets, excellent seafood, a pool, fine beach and snorkelling on the nearby coral reef. **$$$$**

Sea Cliff Hotel
Tel: 022-260 0380/0444
Fax: 022-260 0476
Email: information@hotelseacliff.com
www.hotelseacliff.com
Plush 86-room business hotel in a stunning location on the Msasani Peninsula on the road out of Dar towards The Slipway. Good swimming pool with diving facilities but no sea swimming. Ten-pin bowling, fitness centre, casino, massage facilities, hair salon, three restaurants and a pastry shop. **$$$–$$$$**

Jangwani Seabreeze Lodge
Tel: 022-264 7215/7067
Fax: 022-264 7069
Email: info@jangwani.com
www.jangwani.com
Smart, efficient German hotel on Mbezi Beach, 35 km (20 miles) north of the city centre. Good food, excellent beach and pool, water-skiing, paragliding, boat trips and dive school. **$$$**

Q Bar & Guest House
Tel: 022-260 2150
Fax: 022-211 2667
Email: qbar@cats-net.com
Good budget hotel on Haile Selassie Road, with dormitory accommodation and en-suite rooms with TV, fridge and mosquito nets. The attached bar and restaurant is surprisingly good. Basic, comfortable and an easy stopover 18 km (10 miles) from the airport. **$–$$**

Kipepeo Beach Campsite
Tel: 022-212 2931
Fax: 022-211 9272

Email: info@kipepeocamp.com
www.kipepeocamp.com
Remote backpacker hangout on a stunning stretch of beach 7 km (4 miles) south of the city centre. Beach *bandas*, dormitory rooms and camping, with good, cheap food and a bar. **$**

Hotel Price Guide

$$$$$	above US$275
$$$$	US$150–275
$$$	US$75–150
$$	US$20–75
$	below US$20

WHERE TO EAT

All the hotels listed above serve good food. Among the better stand-alone restaurants in the city centre, all charging around US$5–10 for a main course, are the following:

Addis in Dar
Tel: 0741-266 299
Excellent and atmospheric Ethiopian restaurant on Regent Estate, highly rated by expatriates. Closed Sunday.

Baraza Bar & Grill
Tel: 022-213 2115
Part of the central Holiday Inn, this is one of the trendiest and best restaurants in Dar, serving excellent steaks, seafood and traditional Tanzanian dishes.

Sweet Eazy
Tel: 0745-754074
Situated in the Oyster Bay shopping centre, behind the hotel of the same name, this trendy restaurant and lounge bar has live music on Thursday and Saturday night. The kitchen is open from 11.30am to midnight daily, with happy hour from 5–7pm.

Karama Lodge
Tel: 027-250 0359
Email: info@karama-lodge.com
www.karama-lodge.com
Set about 5 km (3 miles) from central Arusha off the Old Moshi Road, this attractively rustic lodge consists of about 20 en-suite wooden chalets on a hill slope facing the (normally veiled) snows of

Kilimanjaro. The thickly wooded grounds offer much to birdwatchers, and the food is excellent, making it a useful suburban starting point for a longer safari.

The Slipway
Msasani Peninsula
Tel: 022-260 0893
This combination shopping mall and food hall has several good restaurants and cafés, including The Terrace (pasta, seafood and steak), the Mashua Waterfront (pizza and barbecue), Azuma (Japanese and Indonesian), The Pub (Continental) and Fairy Delights (ice cream and coffee), many with outdoor tables overlooking the sea. Excellent food and reasonably priced.

Arusha & Surrounds

Dodoma is Tanzania's official capital and Dar es Salaam its economic one, but the small but bustling town of Arusha – positioned below Mt Meru close to the border with Kenya – is the country's unofficial safari capital, the base for most visits to the country's peerless northern circuit of national parks. It is serviced by literally hundreds of tour operators, as well as a good selection of hotels and restaurants, a few of which are listed below. The tourist office on Boma Road is unusually well informed and helpful – and for those organising a budget safari on the spot, it maintains an invaluable list of blacklisted and registered operators. Attractions in the immediate vicinity of Arusha include the oft-neglected Arusha National Park and, of course, Mt Kilimanjaro, which lies about 80 km (50 miles) east of town by road, near to the towns of Moshi and Marangu.

WHERE TO STAY

Arusha Coffee Lodge
Tel: 027-250 0630–9
Fax: 027-250 8245
Email: info@elewona.com
www.elewona.com
Set in a coffee plantation near Arusha Airport, this is the newest of Arusha's luxury lodges, with 21

spacious colonial-style chalets. The furnishings and service are impeccable, the welcome warm and meals are taken at the superb Redds restaurant, part of the same complex. **$$$$**

Arusha Hotel
Tel: 027-250 7777/8870–3
Email: info@newarusha.com
www.newarusha.com
Dating to 1894 but thoroughly refurbished prior to re-opening in 2004, the former New Arusha Hotel is now the most luxurious place to stay in central Arusha, conveniently located opposite the Clock Tower. The stylish rooms with DSTV are complemented by an excellent Continental restaurant and a large swimming pool set in lushly wooded grounds. **$$$$**

Impala Hotel
Tel: 027-250 8448
Fax: 027-250 3326
Email: impala@cybernet.co.tz
www.impalahotel.com
Among the best hotels in central Arusha, the Impala is a mix of modern and jaded. The rooms are spacious with en-suite bathrooms. A new, well-designed swimming pool, some new rooms and bar area were added in 2000 – showing up the rather dilapidated appearance of other parts of the hotel. **$$–$$$**

Moivaro Coffee Plantation
Tel/fax: 027-255 3326
Email: reservations@moivaro.com
www.moivaro.com
Attractive and popular colonial-style hotel with thatched cottages scattered across brightly coloured gardens facing Mt Meru, 7 km (4 miles) from the town centre. Swimming pool, internet facilities and massage. **$$$**

Serena Mountain Village Lodge
PO Box 2551, Arusha
Tel: 027-255 3313
Fax: 027-255 4163
Email: mtvillage@serena.co.tz
www.serenahotels.com
Located 10 minutes from central Arusha and 40 minutes from Kilimanjaro Airport, in beautiful mature gardens overlooking the small crater lake of Duluti, with views to mounts Kilimanjaro and Meru. Spacious en-suite rooms in

creeper-clad *rondavels* thatched with banana stems. **$$$**

Hatari! (Arusha National Park)
Tel/fax: 027-255 3456
Email:
marlies@theafricanembassy.com
www.hatarilodge.com
Situated just outside Momella Gate, this owner-managed lodge is named after the film *Hatari!* (Danger!), which was shot in this part of Tanzania, and stands on property formerly owned by Hardy Kruger (one of the film's co-stars, along with John Wayne). The lodge consists of eight large double chalets that imaginatively blend a classic African bush feel with retro decor dating back to the era of *Hatari!* The food is excellent, the service highly personalised, and there are stirring views across to nearby Kilimanjaro and Meru. **$$$$$**

Keys Hotel (Moshi)
Tel: 027-275 2250/1875
Email: keys-hotel@africaonline.co.tz
www.keys-hotel.com
This friendly, family-run hotel lies on Ura Road, within walking distance of central Moshi, and is a good base for climbing Kilimanjaro. Spacious, airy en-suite rooms and *rondavels*, swimming pool and restaurant serving local and European cuisine. **$$**

Kilimanjaro Capricorn Hotel (Marangu)
Tel: 027-275 1309
Fax: 027-275 2442
Email: capricorn@africaonline.co.tz
www.capricornhotel.com
Located 3 km (1½ miles) from the Marangu Gate to Kilimanjaro National Park. A medium-sized hotel (48 double rooms) with friendly staff and well-furnished public areas and rooms. A peaceful setting in tropical gardens. International cuisine with local produce. **$$$**

Marangu Hotel (Marangu)
PO Box 40, Moshi
Tel: 027-275 6594/6361
Fax: 027-275 6591
Email: info@maranguhotel.com
www.maranguhotel.com
Located 7 km (4 miles) from the Marangu Gate to Kilimanjaro National Park. This family-run hotel was originally a farmhouse in a coffee plantation. Several comfortable guest

cottages in the grounds, all with en-suite facilities, and good meals with home-grown vegetables and freshly baked bread. Swimming pool. **$$$**

WHERE TO EAT

Café Bamboo Restaurant
Tel: 027-250 6451
Busy, centrally located café on Boma Road serving a good range of snacks, wholesome meals, coffee and cakes at reasonable prices.

Jambo's Coffee House, Makuti Bar and Restaurant
Mobile: 0744-305 430
Lively, popular and inexpensive coffee shop on Boma Street, with a cosy courtyard restaurant and bar providing welcome shade from the heat of the day. A good selection of food and fresh fruit juices.

Pizzarusha
Situated in the back streets behind the stadium, this is one of the nicest bites in Arusha. Very good-quality food, equally alluring prices, and friendly service in a cosy candlelit restaurant.

Spices & Herbs Ethiopian Restaurant
Moshi Road
A wonderful restaurant with delicious hot and spicy African cuisine, including Ethiopian and Continental specialities and an open-air barbecue.

Stiggy's Restaurant and Bar
Old Moshi Road, Arusha
A lively watering hole popular with the UN fraternity and local expats. A good range of food, from pizzas to an à la carte Thai menu. Stiggy's also has a satellite TV and pool table. **$$**

El Rancho
Tel: 027-55115
Situated in Moshi, off Lema Road, this Indian restaurant serves excellent vegetarian choices and international dishes. Closed Mondays.

Northern Safari Circuit

Tarangire National Park
Tarangire Treetops
Tel: 027-250 0630–9
Fax: 027-250 8245

Email: info@elewona.com
www.elewona.com
A delightful small lodge in the
Lolkisala Conservation Area,
immediately east of the National
Park. There are 20 (mostly) stilted
rooms with thatched roofs,
hardwood decking and canvas walls
which open right up to create an
open platform. Other facilities
include a bar, dining room and
plunge pool. Walks, mountain biking,
night drives, bush dinners and village
visits are available at an additional
cost. Hot water and power are
available in the mornings and
evenings. Elephants are frequent
visitors. Closed March to May. No
credit cards. A fee is paid to the
villagers for every bed night. **$$$$$**

Naitolia
Tel: 027-250 7011
Fax: 027-254 8226
Email: hoopoeuk@aol.com
www.hoopoe.com
A tiny camp run by East African
Safaris, with only three thatched
chalets and one treehouse, in the
Lolkisale Conservation Area, east
of Tarangire National Park. Each
chalet has an en-suite toilet and
bucket shower, but while
comfortable, this is probably best
suited to those with some bush
experience. Game drives, night
drives, walks, and village visits are
all included. A daily levy per visitor
is paid to the villagers. **$$$$$**

Oliver's Camp
Tel: 027-250 2799
Email: info@asilialodges.com
www.asilialodges.com
Small owner-managed luxury camp
in the southeast of the park, with
seven beautifully furnished tents
overlooking the swamps, an
excellent wildlife library,
knowledgeable guides and
permission to run walking tours
within the park. **$$$$$**

Swala Tented Camp
Tel: 027-250 9816/7
Fax: 027-250 8273/4112
E-mail:
tanzania@sanctuarylodges.com
www.sanctuarylodges.com
Overlooking a vast swamp in the far
southwest of the park, this small
and exclusive camp offers a

combination of superb food and
tented accommodation with a real
down-to-earth bush experience,
epitomised by the regular presence
of lion and elephant in camp. **$$$$$**

Tarangire Sopa Lodge
Tel: 027-250 0630
Fax: 027-250 8245
Email: info@sopalodges.com
www.sopalodges.com
Large but attractive hotel with 75
en-suite rooms (four with facilities
for disabled guests) in the central
area of the National Park. Buffet
lunches beside a magnificent
swimming pool set among rocks
and baobab trees. **$$$$**

Tarangire Safari Lodge
Tel: 027-254 4222
Mobile: 0742-401 199
Email: sss@habari.co.tz
With its fabulous clifftop view over
the Tarangire River, near the main
entrance gate, this popular and
reasonably priced lodge consists of
five small thatched chalets and 35
tents with thatched roof covers, all
en-suite. The communal areas
include a large bar and terrace,
pool and dining room. Solar power
is available from 6am–3pm, and
6pm–11pm. **$$$**

Lake Manyara National Park

Lake Manyara Tree Lodge
Tel: +27-11-809 4300
Fax: +27-11-809 4400
Email: information@ccafrica.com
www.ccafrica.com
Set deep in the southwestern part
of the national park, this idyllic
lodge consists of 10 simply but
beautifully furnished timber and
thatch rooms cradled in the boughs
of the mahogany forest. Open-air
living room, bar, dining room and
boma, and excellent game viewing.
Game drives and canoeing are
included in the price. Closed April to
May. **$$$$$**

Lake Manyara Serena Lodge
Tel: 027-250 4155/4058
Fax: 027-250 8282
Email: reservations@serena.co.tz
www.serena.co.tz
Much the best of the Serena
lodges, with 67 en-suite rooms in
thatched *rondavels* and a swimming
pool, on the edge of the Rift Valley

escarpment, looking down into the
park and across the lake. **$$$$$**

Lake Manyara Wildlife Resort
Tel: 027-253 9131 or 027-254 4595
Fax: 027-254 8633
Email: sales@hotelsandlodges-
tanzania.com
www.hotelsandlodges-tanzania.com
Built at the top of the escarpment
in 1970, this 100-room concrete
monolith sprawls along the cliff-top
for nearly half a kilometre. Pleasant
gardens and magnificent views
don't quite compensate for the tired
furnishing, poor food and
demoralised staff. Overpriced.
$$$$

Kirurumu Tented Camp
Tel: 027-250 7011
Fax: 027-254 8226
Email: information@hoopoe.com
www.kirurumu.com
Luxurious but relatively affordable
bush-style lodge, with 20 large,
well-furnished en-suite tents
scattered through the bush. The
location, at the top of the
escarpment, offers superb views and
spectacular sunsets. Well run
and friendly. **$$$$**

Twiga Campsite and Lodge
Tel: 025-253 9101
Mobile: 0744-288 430
Email: twigacampsite@hotmail.com
Situated in Mto wa Mbu, at the foot
of the escarpment near the park
gate, this is the best budget
accommodation in the Manyara
area, with basic en-suite double
rooms, a campsite and restaurant. **$**

Karatu

Gibbs Farm (Karatu)
Tel: 027-250 6702/8930
Fax: 027-250 8310
Email: ndutugibbs@habari.co.tz
www.gibbsfarm.net
This charming coffee farm near
Karatu is situated on the edge of
the Ngorongoro forest, and has 15
twin-roomed prettily furnished
cottages set in an idyllic garden.
Forest and bird walks, and excellent
Iraqw cultural tours. The food is
among the best in Tanzania. **$$$**

Plantation Lodge
Tel: 027-253 4364/5
Email: plantation@les-raisting.de
Slightly cheaper version of the

Gibbs Farm experience, staying in an attractive old thatched farmstead near Karatu, at the edge of the forest. **$$$**

Ngorongoro Safari Resort
Tel: 025-253 4287
Fax: 025-253 4288
Email: safariresort@yahoo.com
In the centre of Karatu, this hotel offers cheap, clean rooms in Tanzania's closest approximation of a motorway service station – garage, restaurant and internet café, plus a small well-kept campsite. A good compromise for the budget-conscious. **$$**

Hotel Price Guide

$$$$$	above US$275
$$$$	US$150–275
$$$	US$75–150
$$	US$20–75
$	below US$20

Ngorongoro Crater
Ngorongoro Crater Lodge
Tel: +27-11-809 4300
Fax: +27-11-809 4400
Email: information@ccafrica.com
www.ccafrica.com
A truly unique experience, this extraordinary hotel brings high camp baroque design to the African bush, all with spectacular views across the Crater. The sumptuous accommodation, which comes complete with chandeliers, raw silk, log fires, rose-strewn bubble baths and a personal butler, is divided into two camps with 12 suites each and a tree camp with six suites. Must be seen to be believed. **$$$$$**

Ngorongoro Serena Lodge
Tel: 027-250 4155/4058
Fax: 027-250 8282
Email: reservations@serena.co.tz
www.serena.co.tz
In a very 1970s version of eco-friendly unobtrusive design, this 75-room lodge is built long and low along the crater rim. It isn't visible from a distance, and once inside, the lack of charm isn't evident, leaving a comfortable chain-style hotel with superb views from all rooms. **$$$$$**

Ngorongoro Sopa Lodge
Tel: 027-250 0630
Fax: 027-250 8245
Email: info@sopalodges.com
www.sopalodges.com
The only lodge on the eastern rim, with its own access route to the crater floor, this has 100 attractive suites, a swimming pool, and superb views, with sunsets over the crater. **$$$$**

Serengeti National Park
Grumeti River Camp (Western Corridor)
Tel: +27-11-809 4300
Fax: +27-11-809 4400
Email: information@ccafrica.com
www.ccafrica.com
This wonderfully luxurious small bush camp has 10 tents protected by banana-leaf thatch, overlooking a hippo pool on a tributary of the Grumeti River, with year-round wildlife and front-row seats for the migration. The furnishings are stylish and comfortable, the service and food flawless, and wildlife from buffaloes to birds regularly visits. **$$$$$**

Kirawira Tented Camp (Western Corridor)
Tel: 027-250 4155/4058
Fax: 027-250 8282
Email: reservations@serena.co.tz
www.serena.co.tz
Unlike the other Serena properties, which are all large lodges, this luxury tented lodge deep in the Western Corridor, overlooking the Grumeti River, is pure Hollywood safari fantasy, with Edwardian decor and 25 spacious en-suite tents. Large swimming pool and fine food. **$$$$$**

Serengeti Stop Over (Western Corridor)
Tel: 027-253 7095
Email: serengetiso@yahoo.com
Presentable, friendly and clued-up budget lodge, alongside the main Mwanza road 1 km (⅔ mile) south of Ndaraka Gate. Ideally positioned for self-drive forays into the Serengeti, also offering day and overnight safaris for those without a vehicle. En-suite chalets **$$**. Camping **$**

Klein's Camp (northeast border)
Tel: +27-11-809 4300
Fax: +27-11-809 4400

Email: information@ccafrica.com
www.ccafrica.com
Set on a large private concession on the northeastern edge of the Serengeti, this delightful lodge has the best of all worlds, slap bang on the migration route, but with the possibility of driving off-road at night and game walks. There are 10 beautifully decorated twin-bedded en-suite cottages, a lounge, *boma* and pool. **$$$$$**

Loliondo Camp (northeast border)
Tel: 027-250 7011/7541
Fax: +255-27-254 8226
Email: info@kirurumu.com
www.kirurumu.com
A luxury tented camp in a remote private concession on the edge of the Serengeti, with no boundary fences and high game densities. Unparalleled opportunities for walking safaris and fly camping (sleeping under just a mosquito net). Loliondo provides conservation and development through sustainable ecotourism partnerships with the local Maasai community. Price fully inclusive of drinks and activities. **$$$$**

Migration Camp (Lobo Area)
Tel: 027-250 0630–9
Fax: 027-250 8245
Email: info@elewona.com
www.elewona.com
Perched on a rocky kopje overlooking the Grumeti River, in the park's northern sector, this exclusive camp has 16 luxurious en-suite tents, while the pool, library, dining room and viewing platforms are linked by wooden walkways. Friendly; good food. **$$$$$**

Ndutu Safari Lodge (southern plains)
Tel: 027-250 6702/8930
Fax: 027-250 8310
Email: info@ndutu.com
www.ndutu.com
This friendly, laid-back bush lodge is technically in the Ngorongoro Conservation Area, on the southern border of the Serengeti. It has 32 simply furnished double rooms, excellent food and friendly staff. The local genets arrive every evening to watch the diners. **$$$**

Serengeti Serena Lodge (southern plains)
Tel: 027-250 4155/4058
Fax: 027-250 8282
Email: reservations@serena.co.tz
www.serena.co.tz
This large hotel is built in the style of an African village, complete with 66 beehive-thatched *rondavels*. Its hill-top location offers wonderful views and an excellent base for exploring the central Serengeti, although the immediate area is too overgrown for really good game viewing. Pool. **$$$$**

Serengeti Sopa Lodge (southern plains)
Tel: 027-250 0630
Fax: 027-250 8245
Email: info@sopalodges.com
www.sopalodges.com
Located in the park's best game-viewing area between the Moru Kopje and the Seronera Valley, all 100 spacious en-suite rooms at this large, unwieldy lodge have a private balcony. The local game viewing is excellent and the food is good. Pool. **$$$$**

Sayari Camp
Tel: 027-250 2799
Email: info@asilialodges.com
www.asilialodges.com
Overlooking the Mara River, this isolated luxury tented camp, which opened in 2005, offers guests practically exclusive access to the plains that divide the Mara from the Kenya border, an area teeming with wildebeest, zebra, eland, topi and gazelle, and offering good sightings of predators, elephant, and – more occasionally – black rhino. **$$$$$**

Kusini Tented Camp
Tel: 027-250 9816/7
Fax: 027-250 8273/4112
E-mail:
tanzania@sanctuarylodges.com
www.sanctuarylodges.com
With a magnificent setting amongst the granite boulders that characterise the far south of the Serengeti, this exclusive tented camp offers good access to some remote game-viewing areas, and is especially rewarding from February to March when the migration takes up residence in the area. **$$$$$**

Other Game Reserves and National Parks

Saadani Game Reserve

Tent With a View
Tel: 022-211 0507
Fax: 022-215 1106
Email: tentview@cats-net.com
www.saadani.com
The only place to stay in Saadani Game Reserve, the only accessible place in Tanzania where the bush meets the beach. It has recently revamped its cluster of luxury beach *bandas* to a luxurious standard. **$$$$**

Hotel Price Guide

$$$$$	above US$275
$$$$	US$150–275
$$$	US$75–150
$$	US$20–75
$	below US$20

Rubondo Island National Park

Rubondo Island Camp
Tel: 027 254 4109
Fax: 027 254 8261
Email: flycat@habari.co.tz
www.flycat.com
Exclusive tented camp magnificently set on a secluded sandy beach punctuated by rocky outcrops and hemmed in by tall gallery forest. Tranquil, relaxed mood and good home cooking. Swimming pool and bar/restaurant built into a natural rock outcrop. Guided walks, boat trips, and game fishing available. **$$$$**

National Park Campsite & Bandas
Set on a forested beach 1 km (⅔ mile) north of Rubondo Island Camp. Booking (seldom required) by radio only. This campsite has basic *bandas* using common showers (**$**) and smart new self-contained chalets (**$$**). The staff shop sells basic foodstuffs, beers and sodas, and a cook is available, but it's best to bring food with you.

Gombe Stream National Park

Gombe Luxury Tented Camp
Tel: 028-280 4435–7
Fax: 028-280 4434
Email: kigomahilltop@hotmail.com

www.chimpanzeesafaris.com
This luxury tented camp, operated by the Kigoma Hilltop Hotel, opened in 2003. **$$$$**

Kasekela Rest Camp (Gombe Stream National Park)
The resthouse has two scruffy twin rooms with nets and a row of even smaller, scruffier rooms without nets. Very basic food can be arranged, but better to stock up in Kigoma. Bookings can be radioed from the Kigoma Hilltop Hotel but are rarely necessary. **$**

Mahale Mountain National Park

The Original Mahale Camp
Tel: 027-255 3819/20
Email: bookingsfp@fprim.com
Classic safari lodge, established in 1990, and set on a sandy private beach. Consists of six rustic but very comfortable double tents verging on the beach, not quite en-suite, but each with a private open-air long drop (toilet) and shower. The chic two-storey dining area is made entirely of organic material and canvas, and has a good reference library. Chimp tracking, snorkelling and other activities arranged. Very exclusive. Open May to November only. **$$$$$**

Nkungwe Camp
Tel: 028-280 4435–7
Fax: 028-280 4434
Email: kht@raha.com
www.kigoma.com
Established in 2001, this beautifully located retreat offers chimp tracking, snorkelling, swimming and other activities. En-suite standing tents have large double beds, flush toilet and shower. The dining and lounge area is a raised wooden construction on the beach. Open March to November only. **$$$$$**

Mango Tree Rest Camp (Mahale Mountain National Park)
Basic but clean en-suite chalets operated by the national park authorities. No food available. Bookings (seldom necessary) can be radioed from the Kigoma Hilltop Hotel or MV Liemba. **$**

Katavi National Park

Chada Katavi
Tel: 027-255 3819/20

Email: info@nomad.co.tz
www.nomad-tanzania.com
The oldest tourist lodge in this vast wilderness consists of six comfortable but uncluttered walk-in tents set among acacia trees overlooking the Chada Floodplain, a favoured haunt of elephant and lion. Not luxurious in any conventional sense, this – more, perhaps, than any other lodge in East Africa – offers an immediate and exclusive bush experience reminiscent of the days before package safaris, with superb food and chilled drinks on tap. Open May to November only. **$$$$$**

National Park Resthouse
P.O. Box 3134, Arusha.
Tel: 57-3471/6423/6426
Run by Arusha National Park and catering for national park officials but also tourists, this modern resthouse at the park headquarters in Sitalike has comfortable rooms, satellite television, basic meals and a bar. **$$**

Ruaha National Park
Mwagusi Safari Camp
Tel/fax: +44 (0)20-8846 9363
Email: tropicafrica.uk@virgin.net
www.ruaha.org
Personalised service, fine attention to detail, and a tangible empathy with the bush are hallmarks of this exclusive owner-managed tented camp, set in riparian woodland alongside the seasonal Mwagusi River. The walk-in tents – seriously spacious – are enclosed in wood, thatch and reed shelters leading to a vast private bathroom. Weather permitting, dinner is held in the riverbed, below the stars, surrounded by the sounds of the African night. Game viewing is excellent in the surrounding area and other vehicles are scarce. Exciting game walks are offered. **$$$$–$$$$$**

Ruaha River Lodge
Tel: 0744-237422 / 0741-237422
Fax: 0741-327706
Email: fox@tanzaniasafaris.info / fox@bushlink.co.tz
www.ruahariverlodge.com
UK Contact:
Tel: +44 (0)1452-862 288
Long-serving and highly regarded lodge situated on a rocky hillside

overlooking the Ruaha River 10 km (6 miles) from the entrance gate. Game viewing can be very good from the thatched bar and restaurant, as well as on the surrounding roads. The simply furnished stone cottages and standing tents are all en-suite. **$$$$–$$$$$**

Selous Game Reserve
Beho Beho Camp
Tel: 022-260 0352–4
Fax: 022-260 0347
Tel (UK): +44 (0)20-8750 5655
Email: reservations@behobeho.com
www.behobeho.com
This exclusive lodge is set some distance from the river on a hill overlooking a vast extent of open bush. The smart en-suite stone cottages have a fan, a good view, and fun outdoor showers. The dining area, shaded by a high *makuti* roof, is a winner. The remoteness from other lodges is apparent on game drives, when it's unusual to see another vehicle. **$$$$$**

Rufiji River Camp
Tel: 022-212 8662–3
Fax: 022-212 8661
Email: info@hippotours.com / hippo@twiga.com
www.hippotours.com
Popular and relatively affordable owner-managed lodge overlooking an action-packed stretch of the Rufiji River. The 20 en-suite tents have fans and are spaced comfortably apart. Informal and inclusive atmosphere enhanced by good Italian home-style cooking and an aura of flexibility. An excellent range of boat and foot safaris, as well as half-day game drives (encompassing three nearby lakes) and fly camping. **$$$$$**

Sable Mountain Lodge
Tel: 022-270 1497
Mobile: 0741-323 318
Email: tentview@cats-net.com
www.saadani.com
Midrange lodge 1 km (⅔ mile) outside of the western park boundary with eight en-suite double cottages scattered on a hillside overlooking a waterhole frequented by elephants and other large mammals. Guided walks, game drives, fly camping and river

trips. Budget visits using the Tazara Railway are a unique feature of this lodge. **$$$$**

Sand Rivers Selous
Tel: 027 255 3819/20
Email: info@nomad.co.tz
www.nomad-tanzania.com
The most luxurious of the Selous lodges, Sand Rivers consists of 16 airy and elegant en-suite stone cottages overlooking a wide bend in the Rufiji River, with an end-of-the-road, quiet location. Good game walks and fly camping, and boat trips through Stiegler's Gorge (leopard territory). Excellent Continental food, swimming pool. **$$$$$**

Selous Safari Camp
Tel: 022-213 4802
Fax: 022-211 2794
Email: info@selous.com
www.selous.com
UK Contact:
Tel: +44 (0)1367-253 810
Classic luxury bush camp consisting of 12 standing tents with fans and en-suite open-air showers spaced widely along the waterfront. Excellent food is eaten in a wonderful gas-lit stilted treehouse. Game drives, boat trips, guided walks and fly camping are all offered. **$$$$$**

Mikumi National Park
Fox's Safari Camp
Tel: 0744-237 422 / 0741-237 422
Fax: 0741-327 706
Email: fox@tanzaniasafaris.info / fox@bushlink.co.tz
www.ruahariverlodge.com
UK Contact:
Tel/fax: +44 (0)1452-862 288
Small, tranquil tented camp set on a rocky slope offering panoramic views over the Mkata floodplain and excellent game viewing. It's the only lodge in Mikumi sufficiently far from the Tanzam Highway that you don't hear the trucks. **$$$$$**

Vuma Hills Tented Camp
Tel: +871-76-203 1650
Email: 4vuma@bushmail.net
www.vuma.org
Owner-managed camp comprised of a dozen classy en-suite tents on stilted wood platforms with verandas offering great views over

the bushy hills south of the Tanzam Highway. Justifiably popular weekend retreat for Dar es Salaam residents. Quality Italian cuisine, swimming pool, game drives and guided walks available. **$$$$**

Mikumi Wildlife Camp (Mikumi National Park)
Tel: 022-260 0352–4
Fax: 022-260 0347
Email: obhotel@acaxnet.com
Affordable, under-utilised and good-value lodge consisting of 12 large en-suite stone chalets with private verandas spaced out in front of a waterhole that regularly attracts elephant, giraffe, zebra and other large mammals. Excellent location for game drives, night chorus of hyenas, lions and rumbling vehicles on the nearby Tanzam Highway. **$$$**

Genesis Motel
Tel: 023-262 0466
Fax: 023-262 0443
Modest hotel in Mikumi town, near the main park entrance, often used by budget tour groups and researchers. En-suite bungalows with satellite television, well-stocked bar and good restaurant, moderately interesting snake park attached. **$$**

Udzungwa Mountains National Park
Udzungwa Mountain View Hotel
Tel: 023-262 0466
Fax: 023-262 0443
Small no-frills hotel in Mang'ula, 1 km (⅔ mile) from the national park entrance gate, used by most tour groups visiting Udzungwa. There are a couple of cheaper lodgings nearby if it's full. **$$**

The Indian Ocean Islands

Not generally regarded to be wildlife destinations, the offshore islands of Mafia, Pemba and in particular Zanzibar are popular with tourists who wish to chill out after a dusty safari. For many, the main attraction is the beaches, for others Zanzibar's historic Stone Town, but the islands also offer superb diving and snorkelling as well as the

opportunity to see dolphins and marine turtles. The Jozani Forest on Zanzibar is home to habituated troops of endemic Kirk's red colobus monkey.

Chumbe Island Coral Park
(8 km/5 miles off the west coast of Zanzibar)
Tel/fax: 024-223 1040
UK fax: 0870-134 1284
Email: enquiries@chumbeisland.com
www.chumbeisland.com
An enchanted Robinson Crusoe island, with virgin forest surrounded by some of East Africa's finest coral reefs. There are only seven ingeniously eco-friendly wood and thatch cabins. Lighting and hot water are by solar power. Your rates pay for the maintenance and policing of Tanzania's first marine park and an active educational programme with local schools. Snorkelling and forest walks with trained rangers. Highly recommended. **$$$$$**

Serena Inn (Zanzibar Stone Town)
Tel: 024-223 1015
Fax: 0741-333 170
Email: zserena@zanzinet.com
www.serena.co.tz
Stone Town's only really smart hotel, the Serena has been sympathetically restored from two historic buildings on the Shangani waterfront. The rooms are thoughtfully furnished and come with all mod cons, air-conditioning and sea views. Two excellent restaurants, swimming pool, bar, business centre and shop. **$$$$**

Emerson & Green (Zanzibar Stone Town)
Tel: 024-223 0171
Fax: 024-223 1038
Email: emerson&green@zitec.org
www.emerson-green.com
This charming small hotel in a traditional Swahili house is furnished with antiques and every one of the 10 beautifully decorated rooms is different, some with balconies, sea- or roof-top views. The roof-top restaurant (booking required) is the main draw for tourists – dinner in the open air, seated on cushions, with a view over the minarets and church spires of Stone Town and

Hotel Price Guide

$$$$$	above US$275
$$$$	US$150–275
$$$	US$75–150
$$	US$20–75
$	below US$20

traditional music and dancing some nights. **$$$**

Tembo Inn (Zanzibar Stone Town)
Tel: 024-223 3005
Fax: 024-223 3777
Email: tembo@zitec.org
www.tembohotel.com
Once an Omani seafront mansion, this sophisticated and atmospheric hotel has a fine pool and restaurant, wonderful sea views and a central position – highly popular. **$$–$$$**.

St Monica's Hostel (Zanzibar Stone Town)
Tel: 024-223 5348
Fax: 024-223 6772
Email: cathedral@zanzinet.com
If you can ignore the ghostly presence of the so-called slave chambers in the basement, this hostel next to the Anglican cathedral is the best of the backpacker accommodation with cool, clean rooms, some en-suite, all with balconies and nets. **$**

Blue Bay Beach Resort (Zanzibar Island)
Tel: 024-224 0240–4
Fax: 024-224 0245
Email: reservations@bluebayzanzibar.com
www.bluebayzanzibar.com
Excellent large resort, on the northeast coast, with a grand Arab-style lobby and 88 double-storey thatched cottages with balconies. Tennis courts, fitness centre, business centre, shop, dive shop, watersports, various excursions, and a magnificent pool separated from the beach by picturesque coconut palms. **$$$$**

Ras Nungwi Beach Hotel (Zanzibar Island)
Tel: 024-223 3767/2512
Fax: 024-223 3098/9
Email: info@rasnungwi.com
www.rasnungwi.com
The largest resort hotel on the

north of the island, near Nungwi village, has friendly staff, excellent food and *makuti*-thatched coral rag cottages in lush gardens alongside a white sand beach. Snorkelling, diving, game-fishing, dhow cruises, water-skiing, windsurfing and kayaking. **$$$**
Fundu Lagoon (Pemba Island)
Tel/fax: 024-223 2926
Email: fundu@africaonline.co.tz
www.fundulagoon.com
Enchanting hideaway retreat consisting of 20 luxurious tents with verandas and beach access, connected by boardwalks through the coastal forest. Picture-perfect beach, fine restaurant, and water sports including snorkelling, sailing, fishing, skiing and kayaking. PADI dive school on site. **$$$$$**
Kinasi Lodge (Mafia Island)
Email: kinasi@mafiaisland.com
www.mafiaisland.com
This luxurious lodge caters mostly for divers and nature lovers, though the palm-studded gardens rising from the swimming pool and small beach are still the stuff of beach idyll fantasies, as are the 14 en-suite coral bungalows. Some of the best diving in Africa, plus snorkelling, windsurfing, game fishing, bird trail, mountain biking. Closed April and May. **$$$$$**
Chole Mjini Lodge (Mafia Island)
Email: 2chole@bushmail.net
www.intotanzania.com
Laudably idiosyncratic owner-managed lodge consisting of six treehouses set in a stand of baobabs rising from 19th century Swahili ruins. No electricity, no fan, no gift shop, but still perhaps the most aesthetically pleasing lodge on East Africa's coast. Diving, snorkelling, village visits. Community fee included in rates. First-class seafood. Not for everybody, but if you like the sound of it, you'll be smitten with the reality. **$$$$$**

Uganda

The Place

Area: 237,000 sq. km (91,000 sq. miles)
Situation: Uganda is bordered by Rwanda and Tanzania to the south, Kenya to the east, Sudan to the north and the DRC to the west. The equator runs right through southern Uganda, practically passing through Entebbe, the site of the international airport.
Capital: Kampala.
Population: Estimated at 27 million.
Language: English is the official language and is spoken by most reasonably educated Ugandans. Swahili, though not indigenous to Uganda, is widely understood but reluctantly used due to its association with the military. Among the country's 33 indigenous languages, Luganda is the closest to being the lingua franca of the relatively uneducated.
Religion: Predominantly Christian, though a significant proportion of Ugandans follow Islam, and certain tribes such as the Karimojong of the northeast still adhere to a traditional animist faith.
Currency: The Uganda Shilling currently trades at around Ush 1,800 to the US dollar.
Electricity: 240 volts at 50Hz.
Weights and Measures: Metric
International dialling code: 256 (Kampala: 41).
Internet Domain: .ug
Time Zone: GMT+3

Climate

The climate is enjoyable throughout the year. The hottest months are January and February when temperatures can reach over 30°C

(86°F). The coolest months are July and August. Higher areas, in the southwest, west and east, are colder, so a sweater for evenings is recommended. The highest town is Kabale. The forests and mountains experience a lot of rain. Rain falls throughout the year, especially during late afternoon and at night. The dry season starts in December and lasts until early March. The longer rains fall from March to May and in early September. Only northeast Karamoja has a comparatively dry climate.

Government & Economy

Uganda has had eight presidents since the country gained independence in 1962 and has been plagued by tribal and religious differences. Economic and political decline started with the takeover by Idi Amin in 1971. He was ousted by Tanzanian and liberation forces in 1979. A year later elections were held and officially won by former president Milton Obote. But according to many, they were rigged, and those dissatisfied with the results started a guerrilla war. In 1986 Yoweri Museveni, leader of the National Resistance Movement (NRM), brought a coalition government to power, and a process of democratisation followed.

Under Museveni, Uganda has largely recovered from the political turmoil of 1969-86 – indeed, its average annual growth rate of 10 percent per annum over the past two decades is probably the highest in Africa. This is reflected in the vastly improved road network, economic infrastructure and tourist amenities. The one exception to this relatively rosy picture is the far northwest, which remains highly unstable due to the insidious cross-border raids on civilian targets perpetrated by the Lord's Resistance Army.

Business Hours

Most shops open 8.30am–5.30pm. The small shops in the various suburbs remain open until about

Public Holidays

In addition to Good Friday and
Easter Monday, and the Muslim
Idd el Fitri (all generally March or
April), the following public
holidays are recognised:
1 January New Years Day
26 January NRM Government
Anniversary Day
8 March Women's Day
1 May Labour Day
3 June Martyr's Day
9 June Heroes Day
9 October Independence Day
25 December Christmas Day
26 December Boxing Day

11.30pm. On Sundays only these
shops are open. Banks open
8.30am to 2pm Monday to Friday.

Tourist Information

There are no tourist offices outside
of the country.
Uganda Tourist Board (UTB)
Impala House, Kimathi Street,
Kampala
Tel: 041-342196
Fax: 041-342188
Email: utb@mail1.starcom.co.ug
www.visituganda.com
The helpful UTB information office in
Kampala is a good source of
current travel information and
stocks a range of publications of
interest to tourists.
Uganda Wildlife Authority (UWA)
Kintu Road
Tel: 041-346287/8
Fax: 041-346291
Email: uwa@uwa.or.ug
www.uwa.or.ug
UWA is the authority in charge of all
national parks and wildlife reserves
in Uganda. All bookings for non-
private *banda* accommodation in
the parks should be made through
them. Although many tourists book
their gorilla-tracking permits for
Mgahinga and Bwindi national parks
through tour operators, the permits
can also bought directly from UWA.
The head office on Kintu Road
opens from 8am to 1pm and 2pm
to 5pm on weekdays and 9am to
1pm on Saturdays.

The Eye
Tel: 041-503013
Email: theeye@infocom.co.ug
This useful quarterly guide to
Kampala and Uganda, distributed
for free through most major hotels
and gift shops in the capital,
contains up-to-date listings of
hotels, restaurants, embassies,
cultural events and other services
of interest to tourists.

*Embassies & High
Commissions in Kampala*
Belgium
Ruwenzori House, Lumumba Avenue
Tel: 041-349559
Fax: 041-347212
Canada
IPS Building, Parliament Avenue
Tel: 041-258141
Fax: 041-234518
France
16 Lumumba Avenue
Tel: 041-342120
Fax: 041-349812
Germany
15 Philip Road
Tel: 041-256767/8
Fax: 041-343136
India
11 Kyandondo Road
Tel: 041-342994
Fax: 041-254943
Ireland
12 Acacia Avenue
Tel: 041-344344
Fax: 041-344353
South Africa
2B Nakasero Road
Tel: 041-343543
Fax: 041-348216
UK
10/12 Parliament Avenue
Tel: 078-312000
Fax: 078-312282
USA
Ggaba Road
Tel: 041-259791–3
Fax: 041-259794

Getting There

BY AIR

British Airways, Air France and
Lufthansa are the only European
carriers connecting Western Europe
with Uganda. Intra-African carriers

include Alliance Express (Rwanda),
Ethiopian Airlines, South African
Airways, Kenya Airways and Egypt Air.
Ethiopian Airlines is particularly worth
investigating for well-priced tickets
that effectively allow for a free
stopover of any reasonable duration
in Ethiopia. All flights land at Entebbe
International Airport about 40 km (25
miles) from Kampala. Special hire
taxis from Entebbe Airport to
Kampala are quite expensive at
around US$30 (negotiable). An
irregular bus service to town is
available and minibuses, referred to
as taxis, take people to the capital.

BY FERRY

The overnight ferry service
connecting the Lake Victoria ports of
Mwanza in Tanzania and Port Bell on
the outskirts of Kampala has been
suspended at the time of writing, but
may well resume at some point in the
near future. Most travellers heading
overland between Tanzania and
Uganda on public transport make
use of the thrice-weekly overnight

Cultural Attractions

The National Museum on Kitante
Road has an interesting selection
of historical and cultural exhibits,
notably a superb display of
traditional musical instruments.
Also worth a visit are the Kasubi
Tombs, off the Hoima Road,
where three of the most
important kings of Buganda are
buried in an enormous traditional
structure with a domed thatch
roof. The capital has two art
galleries. The Nummo Gallery
behind the Sheraton Hotel
exhibits contemporary art by
Ugandan artists, as does the
gallery near the Faculty of Fine
Arts at Makerere University. The
central National Theatre (tel: 041-
254567) has regular plays,
usually in Luganda but also often
in English, as well as musical
events and a cinema – big
banners in town announce
the programme.

ferry service between the Tanzania ports of Mwanza and Bukoba, the latter now connected to Kampala by a bus service timed to meet the ferries to and from Mwanza.

BY ROAD

Uganda can easily be reached by road from Kenya via the Busia or Malaba border post. Access by road is also possible via Rwanda or Tanzania. The borders with Sudan and the DRC have been closed for some years at the time of writing.

Getting Around

BY AIR

There are no scheduled domestic flights within Uganda as most of the major centres lie within half a day's driving distance of the capital. Charter flights are available with several local carriers and can be arranged through any reputable local tour operator. Unless you are very squeezed for time, the only tourist destination in Uganda that is most realistically visited by air – for security reasons as much as anything – is the remote Kidepo National Park in the northeast.

BY BUS

Bus services have improved greatly in recent years, with the battered old heaps and potholed roads of the late 1980s now almost entirely replaced by fast modern buses and good sealed roads. This has its advantages in terms of getting around quickly, but unfortunately the quality of bus driving is often dangerously reckless. One service that can be recommended is the Post Bus, which is run by the central GPO on Kampala Road in the capital. These buses are driven relatively sedately – but not ponderously – and leave from the main post office daily at 8am (except Sundays) for Kabale via Masaka and Mbarara, Fort Portal via Mubende, Gulu via Masindi, and Mbale via Jinja. Fares

are the same as commercial bus lines, and although tickets cannot be pre-booked, the buses are seldom full to capacity and you can be confident of obtaining a ticket if you're there by 7.30am.

Minibuses – locally called taxis – ply every conceivable route in Uganda with an aura of manic abandon that makes the buses look positively sober. Safety issues aside, minibuses are the fast way of getting around, and the simplest, because they leave as they fill up rather than at specific times. The old minibus park in Kampala generally services destinations to the east of the capital, while the nearby new minibus park services most destinations to the west. Fares are non-negotiable, but certain routes have acquired a reputation for overcharging foreigners, so ask another passenger rather than the conductor what the fare should be.

Taxis, or special hires as they're known locally, are widely available in Kampala, Entebbe, Jinja and other large towns. Fares are low by international standards but highly negotiable and should always be agreed in advance. It is possible to use special hires to reach some of the national parks, in particular Lake Mburo and QENP. Taxi drivers at Katunguru on the main Mbarara–Kasese road through QENP can offer affordable game drives on the Kasenyi Plains.

SELF-DRIVE

As with other countries in the region, few tourists to Uganda drive themselves around and most local companies – listed under tour operators below – are reluctant to rent out vehicles without a local driver. Car hire is very expensive, never less than US$100 per day, and to reach most parts of the country you will need a 4x4 vehicle. Please note that there are no breakdown services outside Kampala. If your car breaks down you will have to stop another passing car and go to the nearest village or town to get help. Motorists drive on the left.

Hotel Price Guide

$$$$$	above US$275
$$$$	US$150–275
$$$	US$75–150
$$	US$20–75
$	below US$20

Kampala & Entebbe

WHERE TO STAY

Nile Hotel International
Tel: 041-258080–9
Fax: 041-259130
Email: nileh@imul.com
This established landmark – associated with gruesome scenes of torture in the Amin era – is the finest hotel in the city centre, offering five-star accommodation and the full range of leisure and business facilities. $$$$ (en-suite rooms) or $$$$$ (suites)
Windsor Lake Victoria Hotel
Tel: 041-320644/5
Fax: 041-320404
Email: windsor@imul.com
Entebbe's top hostelry overlooks the golf course and is set some distance back from the lake. The specious en-suite rooms come with satellite television, and there's a good Indian restaurant and swimming pool area. $$$–$$$$
Ngamba Island Camp
Tel/fax: 041-321479
Mobile: 077-502155
Email: info@wildfrontiers.co.ug
www.wildfrontiers.com
This recently constructed luxury tented camp on Ngamba Island is an idyllic tropical refuge enlivened by chattering weaver colonies and the haunting pant-hoot call of the island's resident chimps. $$$$
Speke Resort & Country Club
Mobile: 078-227 111/438
Fax: 078-227110
Email: spekeresort@spekeresort.com
www.spekeresort.com
On the Lake Victoria shore at Munyonyo, 10 km (6 miles) south of central Kampala, this all-suite resort offers unbeatable value for money. The spacious tiled suites are stylishly decorated with wrought iron

furniture and come with satellite
television, a fan, a kitchen and
fridge, and a private balcony
overlooking a pretty marina and
forested island. Swimming pool,
horseriding and boat excursions;
good restaurant. **$$–$$$**
Fairway Hotel
Tel: 041-259571/4
Fax: 041-234160
Email: fairway@starcom.co.ug
www.fairwayhotel.com
This well-established and reasonably
priced 98-room hotel stands in pretty
gardens on the edge of the city
centre overlooking the golf course
near the Garden City complex. Free
airport shuttle, swimming pool and
gym, and airconditioning and satellite
television in all rooms. **$$$**
Blue Mango
Mobile: 077-500244
Fax: 041-541154
Email: bluemango@infocom.co.ug
Best known locally for its trendy
restaurant and sports bar, Blue
Mango also offers very comfortable
accommodation in a row of bright
en-suite double rooms (**$$**) and an
inexpensive dormitory (**$**).
Kampala Backpackers
Tel: 041-343059
Mobile: 077-430587
Email: backpackers@infocom.co.ug
www.traveluganda.com
Enduring Australian-owned
backpacker hostel in Natete, about 2
km (1½ miles) from the city centre,
set in green grounds that provide
sanctuary to vervet monkeys, ground
squirrels and a dazzling selection of
birds. Large campsite, en-suite
rooms and dormitories, lively bar and
restaurant, free internet access,
assistance with booking gorilla
permits and white-water rafting. **$**
Red Chilli Hideaway
Tel: 041-223903
Mobile: 077-502306/584054
Email: chilli@infocom.co.ug
www.redchillihideaway.com
Situated off the Old Port Bell Road,
this popular new budget hostel offers
a similar range of facilities and
services as the Backpackers and is
an excellent source of gritty travel
advice – the helpful British couple
who own and manage it also compile
the quarterly local guide *The Eye*. **$**

WHERE TO EAT

All the hotels listed above have
restaurants, with Blue Mango in
particular being a great place for a
meal and an evening out. A far cry
from the situation in the early 1990s,
Kampala also now boasts a fine
selection of stand-alone restaurants
catering for most tastes and budgets
– main courses typically in the
US$4–7 range at the better places –
and the list below is highly selective.

Garden City Shopping Mall
This spanking new shopping complex
on Yusef Lulu Road, adjacent to the
golf course, is as good a starting
point as any for an evening out, with
several good restaurants, a roof-top
bar, a bowling alley, the country's
best cinema complex, and a good
selection of shops (mostly closed in
the evening).
Fang Fang Restaurant
Communications House
Colville Street
Tel: 041-344806 / 340067
Kampala's most popular and central
Chinese restaurant has a varied
menu and consistently good service.
Le Chateau
Ggaba Road
Tel: 041-510404 / 077-898000
Ethnically decorated Belgian
restaurant serving fine Continental
cuisine – steaks, snails, guinea fowl,
imported mussels – situated about 3
km (2 miles) from the city centre.
Fasika Restaurant
Ggaba Road
Tel: 077-303716
This garden restaurant specialises
in tasty Ethiopian cuisine – it's a
good option for a night out, with the
legendary Al's Bar and Capital Pub
just up the road.
Haandi Restaurant
Commercial Plaza, Kampala Road
Tel: 041-346283/4
This classy north Indian restaurant
– with branches in Nairobi and
London – caters particularly well for
vegetarians.
Sam's Restaurant
Kampala Road
Tel: 041-251694
Top-notch Indian restaurant serving a
good range of Indian cuisine, grills

and – more adventurously – ostrich
and crocodile.
Ekitoobero
Kitante Road
Tel: 041-346834
For traditional Ugandan food in a
restaurant rather than from a stall,
this informal set-up – with a
massage parlour and beauticians out
the back – is fun and good value.

Around the Country

Near to Kampala
**Mpanga Community Campsite
(Mpanga Forest)**
Tel: 077-853290
Email: mpanga@avu.org
Simple but clean *banda*
accommodation (with netting) and
campsite in a forest clearing ideally
positioned for forest walks and
cultural visits. **$**
Gately on Nile (Jinja)
Tel: 043-122400
Mobile: 077-469638
Email: gately@utonline.co.ug
www.gately-on-nile.com
Homely, intimate and popular
Australian-managed restored colonial
retreat in large green gardens on
Kisinja Road, overlooking Lake
Victoria and bordering the town
centre. Good restaurant, email
service, satellite television lounge,
local travel advice, rafting bookings,
massage and reflexology. **$$$** with
some budget rooms **$–$$**
Jinja Nile Resort (Jinja)
Tel: 043-122190–2
Fax: 043-120402
Email: nileresort@source.co.ug
www.madahotels.com
Sumptuous international 100-room
resort with a great swimming pool
area on a forested stretch of the Nile
1 km (⅔ mile) from the Owen Falls
Dam on the road to Bujagali Falls.
The plush mini-suites have satellite
television, fans, netting and private
balcony. Good restaurants. **$$$**
Explorers Backpackers (Jinja)
Tel: 043-120236
Mobile: 077-422373
Fax: 043-121322
Email: rafting@starcom.co.ug
www.raftafrica.com
This well-run backpacker lodge, the
base for the white-water rafting

company Nile River Explorers (NRE), is the most popular budget option in Jinja, though many travellers prefer to stay at the same company's second lodge overlooking Bujagali Falls, the starting point for their rafting trips. Double rooms, dormitories and camping, and a lively bar with satellite television and good food. NRE can book gorilla permits for Uganda or Rwanda. **$**

Mabira Community Campsite (Mabira Forest)
Similar set-up to its counterpart in Mpanga Forest, with *bandas* and camping space available in a lovely forest clearing. **$**

Murchison Falls & Budongo Forest
Masindi Hotel (Masindi)
Tel: 0465-20023
Mobile: 077-420130
Fax: 0465-20501
Email: masindihotel@gmail.com
www.masindihotel.com
Built in 1923, this rambling hotel on the wooded town outskirts once hosted Ernest Hemingway and has reclaimed much of its character following renovations. Clean en-suite rooms with netting and hot water, camping permitted, decent if unimaginative food. **$$**

Busingiro & Kanyiyo Pabidi Tourist Sites (Budongo Forest)
Attractively rustic camps with self-catering *banda* accommodation and camping in a forest glade teeming with birds and monkeys, and offering twice-daily chimp-tracking excursions. Advance booking not possible. **$**

Paraa Safari Lodge (Murchison Falls NP)
Tel: 041-259390/4/5
Fax: 041-253399
Email: marasa@starcom.co.ug
www.paraalodge.com
This monolithic hotel, constructed in 1997 over the shell of a lodge gutted in 1988, is conveniently located on the north bank of the Nile opposite Paraa launch jetty. The luxurious en-suite rooms have a private balcony and walk-in mosquito netting and the food is good, with options for vegetarians. Two rooms cater for disabled guests. Good swimming pool area overlooking the Nile. **$$$$**

Nile Safari Camp (Murchison Falls NP)
Tel: 041-258273
Fax: 041-233992
Email: iou@africaonline.co.ug
www.innsofuganda.com
This small, intimate and utterly wonderful luxury tented camp lies immediately west of the park boundary in a lush stretch of riverine forest, where hippo, elephant and a variety of birds – including a pair of shoebills on a facing papyrus island – are regularly observed from the wooden deck and swimming pool. Campers welcomed. **$$$–$$$$**

Sambiya Lodge (Murchison Falls NP)
Tel: 041-233596
Tel/fax: 041-344855
Email: afritour@africaonline.co.ug
www.afritourstravel.com
This affordable but very comfortable lodge consists of 20 airy solar-powered en-suite cottages and a few more basic *bandas* sprawled along the forested Sambiya River. Conveniently located for chimp tracking at Kanyiyo Pabidi and visits to the top of the falls, but not so good for game drives. Swimming pool and good food. **$$–$$$**

Red Chilli Rest Camp (Murchison Falls NP)
Mobile: 077-709150/509150
Email: chilli@infocom.co.ug
www.redchillihideaway.com
Budget camp at Paraa, on the south bank of the Nile, frequented by warthog, bushbuck and a wide variety of birds. Basic huts, en-suite cottages, camping and decent food are available, as are game drives north of the river. Inexpensive minibus shuttle from Masindi (Monday and Saturday). **$**

Rabongo Camp (Murchison Falls NP)
Bookings through UWA

Rustic en-suite log cabins in the heart of Rabongo Forest in the remote southeast of MFNP, good for birds and primates (including chimpanzees). Camping permitted. **$**

Fort Portal & Environs
Ruwenzori View Guesthouse (Fort Portal)
Tel: 0483-22102/077-722102
Fax: 0483-22636
Email: ruwview@africaonline.co.ug
Run by an English-Dutch couple, this popular guesthouse lies on the outskirts of town in pretty grounds with a good view over rolling hills to the Ruwenzori peaks. The large en-suite rooms and expansive home-cooked dinners make a refreshing change from typical hotel fare. Exceptional value. **$$**

Ruwenzori Travellers Inn (Fort Portal)
Tel: 0483-22075
Also good value, this recently opened multi-storey hotel in the town centre has clean en-suite rooms with netting and hot water, as well as a decent restaurant and bar. **$**

Semliki Safari Lodge (Semuliki Wildlife Reserve)
Tel: 041-251182
Mobile: 077-489497
Fax: 041-344653
Email: info@safariuganda.com
www.safariuganda.com
Arguably the most aesthetically pleasing up-market bush camp in Uganda, Semliki Safari Lodge is distinguished by its organic decor, wonderful food and swimming pool area set in riverine forest teeming with birds and monkeys. Day and night drives, boat trips on Lake Albert, chimp tracking in the nearby forest and visits to Semuliki National Park. **$$$$$**

Mantana Tented Camp (Kibale Forest NP)
Tel: 041-321552
Mobile: 077-525736 / 401391
Fax: 041-320152
Email: mantana@kimbla-mantara.com
www.kimbla-mantana.com
Classic luxury tented camp consisting of eight secluded en-suite tents with solar lighting, eco-friendly toilet and private veranda, carved into a patch of primate- and bird-

infested secondary forest a short distance from the national park boundary. **$$$$**
Kanyanchu Tourist Camp (Kibale Forest NP)
Bookings through UWA
Kanyanchu is the main centre for chimp tracking and other tourist activities in Kibale Forest, with five stone *bandas* as well as a large campsite and a decent canteen. If the *bandas* are full, simple accommodation is 3–5 km (2–3 miles) south near Bigodi. **$**
Sebitoli Camp
Tel: 0483-22183
Mobile: 077-661752
Email: ktours@infcom.co.ug
Three double *bandas* and a campsite can be found at this new privately run camp in Kabale Forest, clearly signposted from the main Fort Portal-Kampala Road. **$**
Ndali Lodge (Lake Nyinambuga)
Mobile: 077-221309/487673
Email: ndali@ndalilodge.com
www.ndalilodge.com
Exclusive family-run lodge with a perfect location on the rim of Lake Nyamibuga. English country-house decor and a homely atmosphere with friendly staff. A good base for exploring Kibale Forest, about an hour distant, and a wonderful retreat in its own right. **$$$$**
CVK Resort (Lake Nyabikere)
Mobile: 077-792274/492274
Email: rosezaab@hotmail.com
www.traveluganda.co.uk/evk
Unpretentious en-suite rooms, adequate restaurant and spacious camp site overlooking a beautiful lake where monkeys and more than 100 bird species are regularly

observed. Conveniently located (about 20 minutes' drive) for chimp tracking in Kibale Forest. **$**
Lake Nkuruba Campsite (Lake Nkuruba)
Tel: 0483 22183
Fax: 0483-22636
Mobile: 077 661752
Email: info@infocom.co.ug
www.traveluganda.co.ug/lake-nkuruba
Simple *banda* accommodation, camping and local meals on the rim of a lovely forested crater lake protected within a community-run reserve. **$**

Queen Elizabeth National Park
Mweya Safari Lodge (Mweya Peninsula)
Tel: 041-259390/4/5
Fax: 041-253399
Email: marasa@starcom.co.ug
www.mweyalodge.com
Thoroughly renovated since it was privatised, this former government hotel is one of the smartest in the country, with excellent facilities topped off by a swimming pool and the splendid location above the Kazinga Channel. The luxury en-suite rooms (two rooms cater for disabled guests) have a private balcony and walk-in mosquito netting. The à la carte Continental and Indian cuisine includes plenty of choice for vegetarians. **$$$$**
Institute of Ecology Hostel (Mweya Peninsula)
Bookings through UWA
Situated about 500 metres (546 yards) from Mweya Lodge, this hostel consists of 10 adequate double rooms with nets, and

communal hot showers. The attached restaurant is dire, but you can eat well at the nearby Tembo Canteen & Bar or better still Mweya Lodge. **$**
Jacana Safari Camp (Maramagambo Forest)
Tel: 041-258273
Fax: 041-233992
Email: iou@africaonline.co.ug
www.innsofuganda.com
This small, intimate and beautiful lodge is comprised of luxury en-suite log cabins set along the shore of a forest-fringed crater lake in Maramagambo Forest. It's a great location for birds and monkeys, with boat trips and guided walks offered by the lodge, chimp tracking in the nearby Chambura Gorge, and the Kasenyi plains less than an hour away for game drives. **$$$–$$$$**
Ishasha Wilderness Tented Camp
Tel/fax: 041-321479
Mobile: 077-502155
Email: info@wildfrontiers.co.ug
www.wildfrontiers.com
This beautifully sited river-front camp, which opened in mid-2005, is the first tourist-class lodge to service the remote Ishasha sector of QENP, known for its tree-climbing lions (now seen with a high level of frequency) as well as the thrilling birds and primates resident in the riparian forest along the Ishasha River. **$$$$**
Ishasha Campsite
Bookings through UWA
The only budget accommodation in the Ishasha sector amounts to two basic self-catering double *bandas* using common showers and a little-used campsite on the banks of the Ishasha River. **$**

Tour Operators in Fort Portal and Kasese

Many travellers explore the national parks and other attractions around Fort Portal with Kabarole Tours, a very reasonably priced and helpful local tour company of 10 years standing, whose office lies on Moledina Street behind Don's Plaza. Tel: 0483-22183. Mobile: 077-661752. Email: ktours@infcom.co.ug.

The sole concessionaire for hikes within Ruwenzori National Park is Ruwenzori Mountain Service (RMS). Hikes with RMS can be arranged through any good tour operator, but independent travellers can set up a hike directly at their office next to the Snow View Forex Bureau in Kasese. Fax: 0483-44235. Mobile: 077-867357. Email: rms@Africaonline.co.ug

Bwindi & Mgahinga
Gorilla Forest Camp (Buhoma Entrance Gate, Bwindi NP)
Tel: 0254-2-6905 0002/0244
Fax: 0254-2-537173
Email: kenya@sanctuarylodges.com
www.sanctuarylodges.com
This compelling luxury tented camp, cut into a lush forest glade inside the park entrance, consists of eight secluded en-suite tents protected by thatch roof. The excellent food and drinks are served in an organically decorated open-sided common area.

Many birds and monkeys can be seen in the grounds. **$$$$$**

Volcanoes Bwindi Camp (Buhoma Entrance Gate, Bwindi NP)
Tel: 041-346464/5
Mobile: 075-741718
Fax: 041-341718
Email: sales@volcanoessafaris.com
www.volcanoessafaris.com
Attractively low-key tented camp overlooking the gallery forest on the park boundary. **$$$**

Gorilla Valley Lodge
Tel/fax: 041-321479
Mobile: 077-502155
Email: info@wildfrontiers.co.ug
www.wildfrontiers.com
One of only two lodges to lie within the park boundaries, as opposed to alongside the road leading to the park, this recently refurbished and renovated forest-fringed lodge offers reasonably priced semi-luxury accommodation to gorilla-trackers, as well as offering some great forest birdwatching in the grounds. **$$$**

Buhoma Community Bandas (Buhoma Entrance Gate, Bwindi NP)
Budget *banda* and dormitory accommodation at the park entrance with a decent canteen and bar. **$**

Ruhija Resthouse
Booking through UWA
This cosy stone cottage in the Ruhija Highlands offers unfussy, inexpensive self-catering accommodation. **$**

White Horse Regency Hotel (Kabale)
Tel: 0486-23336
Mobile: 077-444921/456412
Fax: 0486-23717
Pleasant former government hotel set in large grounds adjacent to the golf course: 35 carpeted rooms with satellite television and hot baths, bar with log fire and good restaurant. **$$**

Bushara Island Camp (Lake Bunyonyi)
Tel/fax: 0486-22447
Mobile: 077-464585
Email: busharaisland@africaonline.co.ug
www.acts.ca/lbdc
This superb community-run island resort, founded with the assistance of Canadian missionaries, is notable for its tranquil mood, tasteful organic architecture and good food. The en-suite standing tents are exceptional

value. Guided day trips to the Muko and Nyombe swamps available. **$$**

Lake Bunyonyi Overland Camp (Lake Bunyonyi)
Tel: 0486-23741/3
Mobile: 077-409510
Email: highland@imul.com
www.edirisa.org/overland
or www.bunyonyi.itgo.com
Popular overland camp on a papyrus-fringed bay frequented by otters. Facilities include a restaurant/bar with satellite TV, a small curio and grocery shop, and inexpensive kayak, canoe and mountain-bike hire. Standing tents and en-suite *bandas* available. **$**

Hotel Price Guide

$$$$$	above US$275
$$$$	US$150–275
$$$	US$75–150
$$	US$20–75
$	below US$20

Mgahinga Safari Lodge (Lake Mutanda)
Tel: 041-266917/267430
Mobile: 077-419238
Fax: 041-255288
Email: travel@africaonline.co.ug
This confusingly named camp is set on the shore of Lake Mutanda some 14 km (9 miles) from Kisoro in the opposite direction to Mgahinga National Park. Six en-suite tented chalets are on raised platforms with views over the lake to the Virungas. Motorboat rides available. **$$$**

Kisoro Tourist Hotel (Kisoro)
Tel: 0486-30155
This unpretentious new multi-storey hotel in central Kisoro is competently managed and the airy en-suite rooms have tiled floors, satellite television, hot showers and private balconies. A good restaurant is attached. **$$**

Travellers Rest Inn (Kisoro)
Mobile: 077-445805
Email: postmaster@gorillatours.com
Local landmark that once hosted such eminent gorilla experts as George Schaller and Dian Fossey. Renovated in 2002, the comfortable en-suite accommodation is similar to the more functional Kisoro Tourist Hotel. **$$**

Mt Gahinga Rest Camp (Mgahinga National Park)
Tel: 041-346464/5
Mobile: 075-741718
Fax: 041-341718
Email: sales@volcanoessafaris.com
www.volcanoessafaris.com
Situated a few hundred metres from the entrance gate, Mt Gahinga Lodge consists of a huddle of spacious en-suite stone cottages and a cosy restaurant/bar warmed by log fire on the chilly highland evenings. **$$$**

Lake Mburo National Park
Mantana Tented Camp
Tel/fax: 041-321552
Mobile: 077-525736 / 401391
Fax: 041-320152
Email: mantana@kimbla-mantana.com
www.kimbla-mantana.com
This up-market bush camp consists of eight fully furnished en-suite tents strung along a wooded ridge with great views across to the lake. The open-sided dining tent serves good breakfasts, three-course lunches and five-course dinners. **$$$$**

Rwonyo Rest Camp
Bookings through UWA
Basic but comfortable rest camp offering a choice of huts, standing tents or camping, all using communal hot showers. A good lake-shore canteen stands in the main campsite 1 km (⅔ mile) away. Firewood is available for self-caterers. Plenty of wildlife wanders through the camp. **$**

Eastern Uganda
Mbale Resort Hotel (Mbale)
Tel: 045-33920/34485
Fax: 045-33922
Email: sales@mbaleresort.com
This very smart but modestly priced resort lies in a leafy spot 2 km (1½ miles) east of the town centre. The en-suite rooms have netting, satellite television and hot water. Facilities include a large pool, a gym and a restaurant serving good grills. **$$**

Mt Elgon View Hotel (Mbale)
Mobile: 077-445562
The best hotel in the town centre, close to the taxi park, restaurants, bars, and internet access. Clean en-suite accommodation; great Indian restaurant on the ground floor. **$**

Sipi Falls Resort (Sipi Falls)
Tel: 041-346464/5
Mobile: 075-741718
Fax: 041-341718
Email: sales@volcanoessafaris.com
www.volcanoessafaris.com
Built around a colonial governor's
residence overlooking Sipi Falls, this
is the best lodge in eastern Uganda,
offering en-suite accommodation in
bamboo-and-thatch *bandas* with
netting and hot showers. **$$$**
**Kapkwai Cottages and Rest Camp
(Mt Elgon Exploration Centre)**
Tel: 045-33170
Fax: 045-33332
Email: uwaface@imul.com
Excellent and under-utilised rest
camp inside the park entrance gate
at Kapkwai, with four immaculate
en-suite log cabins, five en-suite
standing tents, a campsite, a good
canteen, and good walking
opportunities. **$–$$**
**UWA Bandas (Pian Upe Wildlife
Reserve)**
Booking details as for Kapkwai
Four basic self-catering *bandas*
opened at the reserve headquarters
in 2002. No meals available. **$**

Hotel Price Guide

$$$$$ above US$275
$$$$ US$150–275
$$$ US$75–150
$$ US$20–75
$ below US$20

**Apoka Rest Camp (Kidepo
National Park)**
Bookings through UWA
Only 500 metres (546 yards) from
the lodge, this little-used rest camp
consists of several self-catering en-
suite *bandas* with solar lighting.
Bring all food with you. **$**
**Kidepo Safari Lodge (Kidepo
National Park)**
Tel: 041-251182
Mobile: 077-489497
Fax: 041-344653
Email: info@safariuganda.com
www.safariuganda.com
The Semliki Safari Lodge
organisation is opening a luxury
tented camp in Kidepo in 2006.
Expect prices in the **$$$$$** range.

Ethiopia

The Place

Area: 1,043,000 sq. km (395,000
sq. miles)
Situation: The landlocked Federal
Republic of Ethiopia (formerly
Abyssinia) lies on the horn of Africa,
north of the equator, where it is
bordered to the south by Kenya, on
the east by Somalia and Djibouti,
on the north by Eritrea and on the
west by the Sudan.
Capital: Addis Ababa.
Population: Estimated at 74.2
million, the vast majority
concentrated in the central
highlands.
Language: At least 70 languages
are spoken, representing most of
Africa's major linguistic groups,
including one – Omotic of south
Omo – unique to Ethiopia. The
lingua franca and until recently
Ethiopia's only official language,
Amharic or Amharigna, is a Semetic
tongue indigenous the Lake Tana
area. Other major languages are
Tigrigna (also Semetic, spoken in
the northern province of Tigray) and
Oromigna (the Cushitic language of
the southern Oromo, who comprise
40 percent of the national
population). The Semetic languages
of Ethiopia are transcribed in a
unique script containing more than
200 characters, which derives from
Ge'ez, the language and script of
ancient Axum and the modern
Ethiopian Orthodox Church. English
is an official language, used for
secondary education and widely
spoken within the tourist industry.
Religion: The main religion of the
north is the Ethiopian Orthodox
Church, a unique and archaic
denomination founded *circa* AD 350
in Axum and often but inaccurately

referred to by outsiders as the
Coptic Church, with which it bears
strong historical affiliations.
Ethiopian Christianity retains several
customs associated with Judaism
(male circumcision shortly after
birth), others that were abolished by
Rome after the two churches split in
the 5th century (dancing and
drumming during Mass) and others
that are unique (a church is
sanctified only when it contains a
replica of the Ark of the Covenant,
called a tabot). Islam is widely
followed in the east, where the
walled city of Harer is regarded to be
the fourth most holy city in the world.
Southern Ethiopia is dominated by
more recently introduced Protestant
denominations, while many of the
pastoralist peoples of the Rift Valley
and south Omo region adhere to
traditional animist religions.
Currency: The Ethiopian birr has
been one of Africa's most stable
currencies, trading at roughly birr 9
to the US dollar – welcome respite
from the decimal shifts entailed in
currency conversions elsewhere in
East Africa.
Electricity: 220 Volts at 50 Hz.
Weights and Measures: Metric
International dialling code: 251
(Addis Ababa: 11).
Internet Domain: .et
Time Zone: GMT+3. With
characteristic perversity, Ethiopia
retained the Julian calendar when
the rest of the Christian world
adopted the Gregorian calendar in
1582. Divided into 12 30-day
months and one five-day month (six
days in a Leap Year), the Julian
calendar falls seven years and eight
months behind the rest of the
world, with New Year's Day on 11
September (12 September in a
Leap Year). In other words, in 2005
it will be 1997 in Ethiopia until 10
September and 1998 thereafter. It
remains to be seen whether
Ethiopia will experience a delayed
bout of millennial hysteria in 2007.

Climate

The climate varies locally
depending largely on altitude. The
central highlands enjoy a temperate

climate and extremes of heat or cold are unusual except at above 3,000 metres (9,843 ft). The lower-lying Rift Valley is far warmer, while the northern Rift and other very low-lying areas experience blistering daytime temperatures but cool down significantly at night. The central, western and southern highlands and the Rift Valley south from Awash to Awassa are reliably well watered, though most of the rain falls between May/June and September/October. The drier northern highlands generally receive an adequate level of precipitation during the same months, but this highly populated region is prone to periodic rainfall failures, the cause of the devastating local droughts and famines with which Ethiopia is commonly associated. The Somali and Kenya border regions and northern Rift Valley have arid climates and are very thinly populated by pastoralists.

Government

Ethiopia is the only African country not to have experienced sustained colonialism, though it was occupied by Italy from 1936–41. Prior to 1974, Ethiopia was a feudal empire, ruled from 1930 onwards by His Imperial Majesty Haile Selassie, the last in a lineage of 237 Solomonic rulers who somewhat tenuously claimed descent from the progeny of an illicit union between King Solomon of Israel and the Queen of Sheba.

Haile Selassie was killed in a 1974 coup led by Mengistu Haile Maryam, who established a "provisional" military Marxist dictatorship known as the Dergue. The Mengistu era – marked by a brutal intolerance of dissidence and a protracted civil war – ended in 1991 when the Dergue was deposed by the Ethiopian Peoples' Revolutionary Democratic Front (EPRDF) and Eritrean Peoples Liberation Front (EPLF). In December 1994, a new federal constitution was enacted, dividing the country into eight semi-autonomous regions and three city-

states delineated along ethno-linguistic lines. Prime Minister Meles Zenawi and President Nagasso Gidada were elected in the first democratic election in Ethiopia's history, held during May 1995. A second democratic election held in May 2000 returned the same pairing to power. An election in May 2005 witnessed a mass retraction of support for Zenawi, whose party won with 327 of 547 seats, as opposed to all but 12 five years earlier. The opposition took all 23 seats in Addis Ababa, the country's most sophisticated voting block.

Economy

Ethiopia is one of the world's poorest and least-developed nations, with a per-capita income of roughly US$120 per annum and an adult literacy rate of only 42 percent. Most Ethiopians are subsistence farmers, who grow various crops, most importantly *tef* (an endemic grain used to make the local staple of *injera*) on the fertile Ethiopian highlands. Coffee accounts for 60 percent of Ethiopia's exports. Several large rivers run through the country, including the Blue Nile, Wabe Shebele, Awash and Omo, but their potential for irrigation projects is largely untapped. So too are the country's rich mineral deposits, which include gold and iron ore. Manufacture is limited to processing agricultural produce. One reason for this lack of development is that the country's financial resources were drained by civil war during the Mengistu era and more recently by a war with Eritrea.

Business Hours

Shops and offices are generally open from 8am to 5pm on weekdays, with a lunch break between 1pm and 2pm.

Public Holidays

Many public holidays, most notably Meskel, are also religious festivals, which generally involve colourful celebrations and processions, so it is

worth trying to get to one of the main religious sites – Lalibela, Gonder or Axum – for the occasion. In addition to the set dates below, the movable Islamic celebrations of Ramadan and Moulid and Ethiopian Good Friday and Easter are observed as public holidays.

7 January Christmas
19 January Epiphany
2 March Adwa Day
6 April Patriots' Victory Day
1 May Labour Day
28 May Downfall of the Dergue
11 September New Year
27 September Meskel

Tourist Information

The Ethiopia Tourist Commission (ETC) headquarters on Meskel Square sometimes stocks informative free booklets on Lalibela and Simien and Bale national parks.

Foreign Embassies in Addis Ababa

Austria
Tel: 011-712144
Fax: 011-712140
Belgium
Tel: 011-611813
Fax: 011-613636
Canada (also assists Australians)
Tel: 011-713022
Fax: 011-710333
France
Tel: 011-550066
Fax: 011-511180
Germany
Tel: 011-550433
Fax: 011-551311
Holland
Tel: 011-711100
Fax: 011-711577
Ireland
Tel: 011-710835
Israel
Tel: 011-610999
Fax: 011-610608
Italy
Tel: 011-553044
Fax; 011-550218
Sweden
Tel: 011-516699
Fax: 011-515830
Switzerland
Tel: 011-710577
Fax: 011-712805

UK
Tel: 011-612354
Fax: 011-610588
USA
Tel: 011-551002
Fax: 011-551166

Getting There

BY AIR

Addis Ababa is sometimes known as the "diplomatic capital of Africa" due to the presence of both the Organisation of African Unity (OAU) and the UN Economic Commission for Africa (ECA). As a result, the city is well-served by international air routes, particularly by the national carrier Ethiopian Airlines, one of the best airlines on the African continent. Bole International Airport is only 6 km (4 miles) from Addis city centre, and receives flights direct from Europe (including London, Frankfurt, Rome, Moscow, Berlin, Athens), Asia (including Jeddah, Abu Dhabi, Mumbai, Beijing) and many African cities (including Nairobi, Entebbe, Dar es Salaam, Johannesburg, Harare, Djibouti, Lusaka, Khartoum, Cairo and many West African cities). Additional airlines serving Addis Ababa include Kenya Airways, Lufthansa, Aeroflot, Alitalia, Air Djibouti and Yemenia.

BY ROAD

It is possible to drive to Ethiopia from Kenya via the Moyale border post. The sealed road north of Moyale is very good, but the rutted road south of the border is diabolical. Bandit attacks in northern Kenya are possibly not the risk they were a few years ago, but seek local advice and if necessary travel in convoy.

Getting Around

BY AIR

Ethiopian Airlines operates a good network of domestic flights, very affordable when bought in conjunction with an international flight with the same airline. The only

realistic way of exploring northern Ethiopia in a limited time frame is by using the daily flights that link Addis Ababa, Bahir Dar, Gonder, Axum, Lalibela and Mekele. Although these flights are reasonably reliable, departure times are often brought forward or delayed at short notice, for which reason it's not a good idea to book flights on successive days. The south is more normally explored by road, but there are flights from Addis Ababa to Dire Dawa (for Harer), Goba (for Bale National Park), Arba Minch (for Nechisar National Park) and Jinka (for south Omo).

BY TRAIN

The only rail service in Ethiopia connects Addis Ababa to Dire Dawa (60 km/40 miles from Harer) via Awash. One train daily undertakes this 20-hour journey in either direction, in theory leaving Addis Ababa at 2pm daily and Dire Dawa at 11am, though delays are commonplace and tickets can be bought only on the day of departure. Creature comforts are minimal, especially now that the first-class service is suspended, and theft is a genuine problem. Tickets cost around US$8.

On Foot & Horseback

One of the joys of Ethiopia is to travel on foot or horseback in the mountainous areas along routes still rarely travelled and uncrowded, where you could not take a vehicle if you wanted to. Horses and mules are still an important form of transport in rural areas and can be hired by the day for an agreed price.

BY BUS

Local buses or minibuses cover practically every conceivable route in Ethiopia, but the state of the vehicles generally matches that of the roads – not a compliment – and generally they cover no more than 30 kph (19 mph) on dirt roads and perhaps 50

kph (30 mph) on surfaced roads. This means that visiting all the main sites on the northern circuit by bus requires at least two weeks, ideally longer. Long-haul buses in Ethiopia typically depart at around 5–6am, and offer few concessions to comfort, not least because of the quaint local custom of bolting closed all windows for the duration of the trip, no matter how hot or stuffy it becomes.

TAXIS

Taxis can easily be located in Addis Ababa and other major towns and tourist centres. Ethiopian taxis are generally not metered and while fares are inexpensive by Western standards, they should always be negotiated in advance – ideally before you enter the vehicle.

SELF-DRIVE

Few tourists drive themselves around the country, and are advised not to – at least not unless they're qualified mechanics with experience of navigating appalling roads populated by the world's most suicidal pedestrians and livestock. It is safer to travel with a local driver, and most tour operators and car-rental companies will insist on this. Ethiopians theoretically drive on the right-hand side of the road – though they'll as happily weave along the centre, or stick to the left, depending on how the mood takes them.

Ethiopian Cuisine

Ethiopia has a cuisine every bit as unique as its wildlife and religion. An endemic grass called tef is the staple carbohydrate, made into a large thin circular pancake called injera, and eaten with a wide variety of sauces and stews, generically known as wat. These sauces vary from mild (alicha) to fiery red (kai) and might be made with vegetables (atkilt), meat (siga), lentils (shiro), chicken (doro) or eggs (inkolala). An unexpected feature of

Ethiopia, something you'll seldom see elsewhere in East Africa, is the pastry shops that proliferate in the cities and can usually be found in even the smallest towns. These generally serve superb espresso-style coffee (the coffee plant was first cultivated in Ethiopia) as well as fruit juices, fresh bread and a selection of yummy pastries. At most pastry shops a filling and satisfying breakfast is unlikely to set you back more than one US dollar.

Craft Shopping

Ethiopia is a souvenir hunter's dream. Beautiful white cotton shamma cloth can be bought in the form of shawls, bags, wraps and blankets, as can ancient (and more recent) silverware, beads, the famous Ethiopian crosses, bracelets and earrings; more expensive and usually modern gold articles; modern paintings on parchment; old church relics; parchment books; colourful Harer basketry; Ethiopian herbs and spices; delicious Ethiopian coffee; and horse artefacts such as the colourful saddle cloths. All these are available in tourist shops near Addis Ababa's main post office on Churchill Road, in hotel curio shops and, of course, at the capital's famed *mercato* – reputed to be Africa's biggest market. If you buy old Ethiopian jewellery or artefacts, it is wise to have them approved for export by the National Museums of Ethiopia, which avoids the possibility of customs officials confiscating them as protected antiquities. No need to worry about obviously new items.

Addis Ababa

WHERE TO STAY

There must be a thousand hotels dotted around the capital, the vast majority of them unmitigated dumps that charge little more than US$1 for a basic room. The following is a selection of the more popular and commodious hotels that grace the city.

Addis Ababa Sheraton
Tel: 011-171717
Fax: 011-172727
Email: reservationsaddisababa@luxurycollection.com
Ethiopia's one truly world-class hotel, the incongruously lavish Sheraton lies on Taitu Street in the city centre. Immaculate rooms and service are complemented by several excellent restaurants, a swimming pool, a piano bar, an up-market nightclub and several shops, banks and travel agents. Credit cards accepted. **$$$$$**
Addis Ababa Hilton
Tel: 011-518400

Hotel Price Guide

$$$$$	above US$275
$$$$	US$150–275
$$$	US$75–150
$$	US$20–75
$	below US$20

Fax: 011-510064
Email: hilton.addis@ethionet.et
Set in large landscaped grounds near the UN Headquarters, the Hilton isn't in the same league as the Sheraton, but international standard facilities include television, a thermal swimming pool, tennis courts, jacuzzi, sauna, several good restaurants and full business services. **$$$$**
Ghion Hotel
Tel: 011-513222
Fax: 011-515381
Email: ghion@ethionet.et
Set in the heart of the city in wonderful green gardens, this flagship for the synonymous government hotel chain feels a bit tatty at the asking price. Facilities include a thermal swimming pool, several restaurants, a nightclub and casino, in-room television, secretarial services and tennis courts. **$$$**
Queen of Sheba Hotel
Tel: 011-615400/188282
Fax: 011-613174
Email: QueenShebaHotel@ethionet.et
Situated on Asmara Road, 1 km (⅔ mile) from the city centre, this new hotel offers an appealing combination of traditional decor,

good international facilities and efficient service, all at very reasonable rates. All rooms are en-suite with a large bedroom, lounge, satellite television and fridge. Visa cards accepted. **$$**
Crown Hotel
Tel: 011-341444
Fax: 011-341428
Situated 10 km (6 miles) from the city centre on the Debre Zeyit road, the Crown Hotel is popular with tour groups for its good-value en-suite rooms and scintillating traditional restaurant and dancing. **$$**
National Hotel
Tel: 011-515166/513768
Fax: 011-512417
Centrally located on Meskel Square, this is an attractive compromise between comfort, location and cost. The large en-suite rooms have satellite television and hot water, and hotel residents have free access to the swimming pool at the affiliated Ghion Hotel next door. **$–$$**
Iteque Taita Hotel
Tel: 011-560787
Founded in the early 20th century by the princess for which it is named, the Taitu oozes period character and the en-suite rooms are as individualistic a budget deal as you'll find in East Africa. Pretty good traditional restaurant too. **$**
Wutma Hotel
Tel: 011-562878
This popular hotel, conveniently located on Muniyem Street off the Piazza, is an established budget hangout and thus a good place to catch up on current information with other travelllers. The double en-suite rooms are small but clean and have hot running water. If it's full, the Baro Hotel directly opposite is similar in price and standard. **$**

WHERE TO EAT

Addis Ababa is well equipped with restaurants to suit most tastes and budgets, and the following selection should be viewed as no more than a starting point. Booking is not necessary. Smarter restaurants typically work out at around US$4–5 for a main course, while those geared more to the local market shouldn't cost more than US$2.

Blue Top Restaurant
Popular restaurant near Siddist Kilo with an extensive menu of sandwiches, burgers, salads, pasta dishes and grills – a good lunchtime stop en route to or from the National Museum.

Castelli's Restaurant
Established by its Italian owners on the *piazza* more than 50 years ago, Addis Ababa's oldest (and arguably best) restaurant specialises in pasta dishes, grills and seafood.

Karamara Restaurant
Excellent traditional restaurant on Bole Road, noted for its hypnotic traditional music and dancing, and popular with tourists without being overtly touristy.

La Parisienne
Great breakfast stop on Bole Road, serving delicious cakes, croissants, other snacks and coffee.

Old Milk House
Situated on Tito Road around the corner from the Hilton Hotel, this hangout is popular with expatriates and trendy locals and serves pizzas and other international cuisine either indoors or al fresco.

Miru Pastries
Centrally located on Churchill Avenue, the fabulous fare served by this pastry shop wouldn't look or taste out of place in a European capital.

Sangam Restaurant
Addis Ababa's best Indian restaurant is on Bole Road, near the airport.

Shoa Restaurant
Situated a short distance from the city centre along Asmara Road, the Shoa serves excellent traditional food, with live music and dancing at weekends.

Top View Restaurant
Set on the Intoto footslopes near the British High Commission, and more notable perhaps for the grandstand view towards the city centre than the adequate Italian cuisine.

Around the Country

Near Addis Ababa
Menegasha Forestry Resthouse (Menegasha State Forest)
Tel: 011-154975

Rustic self-catering en-suite cottages and dormitories in the heart of the closest indigenous forest to Addis Ababa. **$**

Ambo Ethiopia Hotel (Ambo)
Tel: 011-362002/7
Email: amboethhotel.ethionet.et
Faded but not uncomfortable former government hotel opposite the hot springs and swimming pool. **$**

Hotel Price Guide

$$$$$	above US$275
$$$$	US$150–275
$$$	US$75–150
$$	US$20–75
$	below US$20

Hora Ras Hotel (Debre Zeyit)
Set on the rim of Lake Hora, this formerly run-down government hotel was privatised in 1999 and closed for renovation and – with the same owner as the Addis Ababa Sheraton – it is likely to eventually be vastly improved in standard when it re-opens. Expect prices in the **$$$** range.

Ethiopian Airforce Officers' Club (Debre Zeyit)
Tel:011-338035
Currently the best lodging in Debre Zeyit, with good en-suite rooms, an acceptable restaurant, and satellite television. **$$**

Adaklu Hotel (Debre Birhan)
Tel: 011-811115
This above-par local guesthouse is favoured by ornithological tours visiting nearby Ankober. Basic but clean en-suite rooms with hot water; commendable local food. **$**

Ankober Lodge (Ankober)
Tel: 011-510433 / 091-653643
Fax: 011-515506
Email: ankoberlodge@yahoo.com
This new tourist lodge with a commanding and historic location on Ankober Hill offers comfortable accommodation in traditionally styled rooms, while the restaurant, rebuilt in the style of the great hall of Emperor Menelik, serves a variety of European and national dishes. **$$**

Northern Ethiopia
In addition to the places listed below, good hotels exist in the

northern towns of Gorgora, Adigrat, Mekele and Dese. A plethora of cheaper guesthouses can be found in all major towns, and even the smallest urban centres in northern Ethiopia can be relied upon to have at least one basic local lodging.

Tana Hotel (Bahir Dar)
Tel: 011-110634
Fax: 011-111920
Part of the government Ghion chain, this relatively smart hotel has a fabulous lakeshore location 1 km (⅔ mile) from the town centre. Comfortable en-suite rooms with hot water, good Western food and local dishes prepared by request. **$$**

Papyrus Hotel (Bahir Dar)
Tel: 058-201500
Fax: 058-205047
Modern multi-storey hotel in the town centre, lacks for lake frontage, but the large swimming pool and very comfortable rooms compensate. Good food. **$$**

Goha Hotel (Gonder)
Tel: 011-110634
Fax: 011-111920
Part of the government Ghion chain, set on a tall hill overlooking the town centre, offering comfortable en-suite accommodation and good food. **$$**

Fogera Hotel (Gonder)
Tel: 058-110405
Former government hotel housed in Italian Occupation-era villa close to the town centre. Acceptable en-suite chalets and popular restaurant. **$$**

Simien Park Hotel (Debark)
Tel: 058-113481
The better of two basic lodges in Debark, the normal base for Simien hikes. All rooms use communal showers. Local food available. **$**

Simien Lodge
Tel: 011-189398
or (Europe) +33 476643078
Email: simiens@simiens.com
www.simiens.com
Filling a niche for genuine international accommodation in the Simien Mountains, this eco-friendly new lodge opened in late 2005 at Buyit Ras, between Debark and Sankaber. It combines traditional tukul-style exteriors with appropriate high-altitude features such as solar heating and hot water. The

surrounding area is populated by habituated geladas, and the lodge will organise foot and horse treks in the mountains. **$$$$** (plus dormitory accommodation **$** per person).
Yeha Hotel (Axum)
Tel: 034-750605
Axum's representative of the government Ghion chain stands in leafy grounds on a low hill above the historical stelae field. **$$**
Ramhai Hotel (Axum)
Tel: 034-751501
Fax: 034-751849
Stylish but soulless new multi-storey hotel, centrally located with comfy en-suite rooms and a decent restaurant serving local and Western dishes. **$$**
Roha Hotel (Lalibela)
Tel: 033-360156
Situated 2 km (1½ miles) from the town centre and offering views across the surrounding mountains, the local unit in the government Ghion chain is the smartest option in Lalibela, with en-suite rooms and a decent restaurant. **$$**
Lasta Hotel (Lalibela)
Tel: 033-360047
Email: jghondts@ethionet.et
Small new hotel, also 2 km (1½ miles) from the town centre, with immense views, helpful management, comfortable en-suite rooms and good traditional food. **$–$$**

Awash National Park and Eastern Ethiopia
Kereyou Lodge (Awash National Park)
Tel: 011-517287
The only lodge in Awash National Park is a cluster of 20 unventilated and run-down caravans baking in the direct sunlight. Good place to stop in for a drink, though, if only for the view over Awash Gorge. **$$**
Buffet D'Aouache Hotel (Awash town)
Tel: 022-240008
Appealingly time-warped French-run hotel, whitewashed and draped with creepers, only 30 minutes' drive from the national park entrance gate. Excellent food, and en-suite accommodation including the Head of State Room (about US$10), where Emperor Haile Selassie and Charles de Gaulle stayed. **$**

Bilen Lodge (near Awash National Park)
Tel: 011-523497 / 515166 ext 220
Fax: 011-551276
Email: village.ethiopia@telecom.net.et
www.village-ethiopia.com
The closest thing to an East African-style luxury tented camp in Ethiopia, this eco-friendly lodge overlooks Bilen Hot Springs on the Awash River 50 km (30 miles) north of Awash town. Plenty of game and birdlife in the vicinity. 15 en-suite chalets mimicking local Afar huts. **$$$**
Agip Hotel (Gewane)
The best base for driving into Yangudi Rassa National Park is the basic local hotel behind the Agip Garage in Gewane. **$**
Harer Ras Hotel (Harer)
Tel: 025-660027
This ageing, uninspiring government hotel is the most up-market address in town with reasonable en-suite rooms and food. **$$**
Belayneh Hotel (Harer)
Tel: 025-662030
This justifiably popular multi-storey hotel on the periphery of the walled town centre has comfortable en-suite rooms with hot water and the best food in town. **$$**

Southern Rift Valley
In addition to the hotels listed below, basic guesthouse accommodation can be found in Mojo, Tiya, Dilla, Yabello, Moyale, Sodo and most other small towns in southern Ethiopia. Accommodation in south Omo is sparsely distributed and, with the exception of Murelle Lodge (listed below), somewhat basic. There are acceptable guesthouses in Konso and Jinka and scruffier ones in Key Afer, Turmi, Dimeka and Omorate. Attractive campsites can be found near Turmi and in Mago National Park.
Fikado Asore Hotel (Butajira)
Tel: 046-150142
This central modern high-rise block is the most comfortable place to break up the drive from Addis Ababa to Ziway via Butajira. Large en-suite doubles with satellite television and hot water, and good local dishes. **$**
Tourist Hotel (Ziway)
Tel: 046-410267

Comfortable en-suite rooms with hot water; superb fish, fresh from the lake. **$**
Wabe Shebele Hotel (Lake Langano)
Tel: 011-517287
The best resort on the west shore of the lake, this government hotel has adequate chalet accommodation and a restaurant. **$$**
Bishangari Camp (Lake Langano)
Tel: (UK) 01273-623790
Lovely tented ecotourism camp set in a private game sanctuary on the east side of the lake. **$$$**
South Rift Valley Hotel (Shashemene)
Tel: 046-101458
This popular mid-range hotel is by far the best in Shashemene, offering en-suite accommodation with hot water in compact green grounds. **$$**
Wondo Genet Wabe Shebele Hotel (Wondo Genet)
Tel: 011-517287
Large, comfortable government hotel near the forest and hot springs at Wondo Genet. En-suite accommodation, good food, and camping permitted. **$–$$**
Hotel Pinna (Awassa)
Tel: 046-201231
Excellent if somewhat bland central hotel whose large modern rooms all have netting, hot shower and satellite television. **$–$$**
Awassa Wabe Shebele Hotel #2 (Awassa)
Tel: 046-215397
This popular hotel's slightly grungy rooms are amply compensated for by lakeshore gardens that double as a fine bird and monkey sanctuary. The nearby Wabe Shebele #1 is a bit smarter but lacks the wildlife. **$**
Bekele Mola Hotel (Arba Minch)
Tel: 046-810046
Set on a cliff top overlooking Nechisar National Park, this stalwart hotel has accommodation in en-suite chalets and a good restaurant. Camping permitted. A smarter-looking hotel is being built. **$**
Evangadi Lodge and Campsite (south Omo)
Tel: 011-632595
Email: reservations@evangadilodge.com

www.evangadilodge.com.
Owned and managed by Greenland
Tours, this newly opened tented
camp skirts the normally dry Little
Kaske River, about 1 km (⅔ mile)
out of Turmi along the Konso Road.
Accommodation is in furnished
rooms or fixed, shaded tents; plus
campsite with separate facilities.
$$

Hotel Price Guide

$$$$$	above US$275
$$$$	US$150–275
$$$	US$75–150
$$	US$20–75
$	below US$20

Murelle Lodge (South Omo)
Tel: 011-55 2128/8591/1127
Fax: 011-55 0298
Email: ervs@telecom.net.et
www.ethiopianriftvalleysafaris.com
Operated by Ethiopian Rift Valley
Safaris (ERVS), this former hunting
lodge consists of 10 airy cottages
set in the riverine forest fringing the
Omo River south of Mago National
Park. It's generally visited as part of
a fly-in or drive-down package to
south Omo with ERVS. An excellent
campsite (**$**) is attached. **$$$$**

**Bale Mountains and the
Southeast**
In addition to the accommodation
listed below, basic guesthouses are
available at Dola Mena, Genale,
Negele Borena and Arero along the
route from the Harenna Forest to
Yabello.
Wabe Shebele Hotel (Goba)
Tel: 011-517287
This government hotel on the
outskirts of Goba is the most
comfortable near Bale – mediocre
en-suite rooms and restaurant. **$**
National Park Resthouse (Dinsho)
Set in the juniper forest at the park
headquarters, this cosily rustic self-
catering rest house has a few
double rooms, dormitories,
communal hot showers and a
lounge lit by log fire at night.
Camping permitted. **$**

Rwanda

The Place

Area: 26,340 sq. km (10,290 sq.
miles)
Situation: Rwanda is a landlocked
country 120 km (72 miles) south of
the equator, bordering Uganda to the
north, the Democratic Republic of
Congo to the west, Burundi to the
south and Tanzania to the east.
Capital: Kigali
Population: 8.5 million. The
population density of almost 300
people per square kilometre is the
highest in Africa.
Language: In addition to the local
Kinyarwanda tongue, French and
English are recognised as official
languages. Swahili is also widely
spoken.
Religion: Most of the population is
Catholic, with Islam and various
Protestant denominations adhered
to by minorities.
Currency: The Rwanda franc (Rfr)
trades at roughly Rfr 520 to the US
dollar.
Electricity: 230/240 volts at 50Hz.
Weights and Measures: Metric.
Dialling Code: No domestic dialling
codes exist. Dialling from outside
the country, the international code
of 250 should prefix the local
phone number.
Internet Domain: .rw
Time Zone: GMT+2 (an hour behind
the other countries covered in this
guide).

Climate

Despite its equatorial location,
most of Rwanda lies at medium to
high altitude and has an equable
temperate to warm climate, often
becoming quite nippy at night,
though the lower-lying Tanzania

border region can be very hot. The
main rainy season typically runs from
late February into early June, while
the so-called short rains generally
fall over October and November. The
country is at its most scenic during
and shortly after the rains, but this
is the worst time to track gorillas.

Government

The Rwanda Patriotic Front (RPF),
which seized power in July 1994,
established a broad based
transitional Government of National
Unity (GNU) under President Pasteur
Bizimungu, who was succeeded by
Paul Kagame in March 2000. The
signing of a new constitution in
June 2003 marked the end of the
period of transitional government.
Two months later, Paul Kagame was
returned to power for a seven year
term with 95 percent of the vote in
the country's first Presidential
election, which took place in a
peaceful, almost celebratory
atmosphere.

Economy

The genocide of 1994 shattered the
country's economic infrastructure,
and although remarkable progress
has been made over subsequent
years, most Rwandans are
subsistence farmers with a basic per
capita income of below US$215 in
rural areas. The main exports are
coffee and tea. There is no
manufacturing or mining industry of
note. Prior to the genocide, gorilla
tourism was the country's third most
important source of foreign revenue.

Business Hours

Banks, shops and offices are open
from 8am to 5pm on weekdays,
with a lunch break taken between
noon and 2pm. Banks are open
from 8am to noon on Saturdays.

Public Holidays

Good Friday and Easter Monday,
which fall on variable dates, are
recognised in Rwanda. Other public
holidays are as follows:

1 January New Year's Day
28 January Democracy Day
7 April Genocide Memorial Day
1 May Labour Day
1 July Independence Day
4 July National Liberation Day
1 August Harvest Festival
15 August Assumption Day
8 September Culture Day
25 September Republic Day
1 October Heroes Day
1 November All Saints' Day
25 December Christmas Day
26 December Boxing Day

Tourist Offices

There is no Rwandan tourist office outside of the country. The Office Rwandaise du Tourisme et des Parcs Nationaux (more commonly referred to as ORTPN) has tourist offices in central Kigali and Ruhengeri, as well as at Kanombe International Airport. Gorilla-tracking permits for the Parc National des Volcans must be booked through the Kigali office of ORTPN on Boulevard de la Révolution, or through one of the domestic tour operators listed below. Contact details for ORTPN are as follows:
Tel: 576514 or 573396
Fax: 576515
Email:
webmaster@rwandatourism.com
www.rwandatourism.com

***Embassies & High
Commissions in Kigali***
Several Western countries have no diplomatic representation in Kigali. For Austria, Australia and the Netherlands, the embassy in Nairobi is responsible for Rwanda. For Denmark, India, South Africa and Ireland, that role falls with the embassy in Kampala.
Belgium
Rue de Nyarugenge
Tel: 575551; fax: 573995
Canada
1534 Rue Akagera
Tel: 573210
Fax: 572719
France
Avenue Paul IV
Tel: 575206
Fax: 576957

Germany
8 Rue de Bugarama
Tel: 575141
Fax: 577267
UK
Boulevard de l'Umuganda
Tel: 84098
Fax: 82044
USA
55 Boulevard de Revolution
Tel: 505601-3
Fax: 570319

Getting There

BY AIR

Jointly owned by South African Airways (SAA) and the government of Rwanda, Alliance Express is effectively the national carrier, offering a similar standard of service to SAA. It flies directly to Kanombe International Airport 10 km (6 miles) outside Kigali from Entebbe, Johannesburg, Nairobi and Bujumbura. In partnership with SAA, it also flies there from the USA via Johannesburg and from London via Entebbe. Tel: 72928 or 77777. Email: aer@aer.com.rw; www.aer.com.rw. Other intra-African flights are with Kenya Airways, Ethiopian Airlines, Air Tanzania and Air Burundi.

OVERLAND

The most common overland ports of entry are Katuna and Cyanika on the Uganda border, which respectively lie about 20 km (12 miles) south of Kabale and 10 km (6 miles) south of Kisoro. Several buses daily connect Kampala (the capital of Uganda) to Kigali via Katuna – the road is surfaced in its entirety – and a fair amount of local transport runs between Kabale, Katuna and Kigali. It's also no problem to find public transport along the 37 km (22 miles) of partially surfaced road between Kisoro and Ruhengeri via Cyanika, the latter being the normal base for gorilla tracking in the Parc des Volcans. A fair proportion of tourists to Uganda nip across the Cyanika border to track gorillas in Rwanda,

and this is easily arranged with any reputable tour operator in Kampala.
Although the borders with Burundi and the DRC are technically open, both are dead ends in travel terms at the time of writing. The only border post with Tanzania is at Rusumo Falls, to the south of Akagera National Park. Although the road between Kigali and Rusumo is surfaced and in excellent condition, roads on the other side of the border are in poor condition, particularly after the rains, and you'd be looking at two days or longer of rough driving or even rougher public transport before you get to Mwanza or Kigoma, the most important towns and travel hubs in northwestern Tanzania.

Getting Around

BY AIR

There are no domestic flights in Rwanda, nor is there any great need for them when most of the country's tourist attractions lie within 2–4 hours drive along a good surfaced road from the capital.

BY BUS

The main form of public transport in Rwanda is the minibus (often referred to as taxis) that dart manically through the hilly countryside between all major centres and towns. Minibuses are quick, inexpensive, and leave throughout the day on all major routes.

SELF-DRIVE

Very few tourists drive themselves around Rwanda – most tour operators prefer to supply a vehicle with driver – but those who do should be alert to the fact that Rwandans, unlike their easterly neighbours, drive on the right-hand side of the road. Most roads in Rwanda are sealed and in a good state of repair, which together with the hilly terrain can make for some hair-raising encounters with oncoming drivers who possess no inhibition about overtaking on blind corners. Another potential hazard comes from sows and other livestock, and to a lesser extent pedestrians, wandering blithely onto the roads.

Around the Country

Kigali
Rwanda's hilly and centrally located capital city retains a somewhat provincial atmosphere by comparison to its sprawling counterparts in neighbouring countries. All international flights to Rwanda land at Kanombe International Airport, 10 km (6 miles) from central Kigali, and the city boasts the country's best selection of hotels, restaurants, tour operators, internet cafés and other tourist facilities. Most of Rwanda's main tourist attractions lie within 2–4 hours drive of Kigali, and – with an early start – the city can be used as a base for a day trip to the gorillas of the Parc des Volcans.

WHERE TO STAY

Hotel des Mille Collines
Tel: 576530/3
Fax: 576541
Email: millecollines@millecollines.net
www.millecollines.net
Kigali's flagship hotel, though somewhat overpriced and lacking in character, consists of 113 comfortable rooms and suites on the fringe of the city centre. Facilities include a shady swimming pool area, good restaurant, satellite television in all rooms, and internet access, and credit cards are accepted. **$$$$** (rooms) or **$$$$$** (suites).
Hotel InterContinental Kigali
Tel: 597100
Fax: 597101
Email: adminich@rwanda1.com
www.intercontinental.com
This smart new hotel on Boulevard de Revolution, 15 minutes walk from the city centre, is easily the best in Kigali, lacking in atmosphere perhaps, but with all the facilities you would expect of a five-star international hotel. **$$$$–$$$$$**

Hotel Chez Lando
Tel: 82050/84394
Fax: 84380
Email: lando@rwanda1.com
This popular and long-serving hotel consists of 30 well-equipped chalets set in expansive green gardens between the city centre and the airport. A good restaurant serves local and continental dishes, and the attached nightclub is very popular at weekends. **$$**
Hotel Okapi
Tel: 576765
Fax: 574413
Email: okapi@rwanda1.com
The Okapi is a modern, centrally located hotel offering comfortable accommodation and good facilities. **$$**

Hotel Price Guide

$$$$$	above US$275
$$$$	US$150–275
$$$	US$75–150
$$	US$20–75
$	below US$20

Hotel Gloria
Tel: 571957
Above-par budget hotel with en-suite rooms and a useful central location close to the bus station and several restaurants. **$**

WHERE TO EAT

La Baguette
Tucked away on Rue l'Epargne a block downhill from the central market, this Flemish *pâtisserie* is Kigali's top breakfast spot – excellent coffee, baguettes and other snacks – but also good for lunch or dinner. The attached supermarket is the best in the country.
Flamingo Restaurant
Excellent Chinese cuisine on Avenue de Kiyovu about 1 km (⅔ mile) east of the Milles Collines Hotel.
City Centre Restaurant
Situated next door to the Hotel Gloria, this relaxed first-floor restaurant serves decent and reasonably priced French cuisine.

Parc Des Volcans, Ruhengeri & Gisenyi
The basic huts that once serviced the Parc des Volcans were destroyed during the civil war of the early 1990s and have not been rebuilt. The closest accommodation to the national park is in Kinigi, but a more popular base for gorilla tracking is Ruhengeri, particularly convenient for those without private transport since all gorilla tracking excursions depart from the ORTPN office in its municipal buildings on Avenue du 5 Juillet. A more attractive base for motorised travellers is the Lake Kivu port of Gisenyi, 60 km (35 miles) from Ruhengeri on a good surfaced road. Even more convenient is the Volcanoes Safaris' tented camp constructed on Lake Burera.
Kinigi Tourist Village
Tel: 546984
www.rwanda-gorillas.com
Book through Kiboko Tours:
Tel: 520118/19
Tel/Fax: 501741
Email: kiboko@rwanda1.com
Situated 13 km (8 miles) from Ruhengeri near the base of Mt Sabinyo, the Tourist Village (run by the Association of Solidarity between Rwandan Women, ASOFERWA) looks attractive enough, with its pretty rural setting, Alpine facades and comfortable lounge and dining areas. The rooms are disappointing – poorly ventilated and blighted with dodgy plumbing and shoddy carpentry – although there are some VIP suites and development is ongoing. **$$**
Hotel Muhabura (Ruhengeri)
Tel/fax: 546296
Ruhengeri's smartest lodging is a rather run down but pleasant colonial-era hotel set in compact suburban grounds on Avenue du 5 Juillet. The large en-suite rooms and suites have running hot water. The attached restaurant is the best in town. Good value. **$–$$**
Home d'Accueil Moderne (Ruhengeri)
Tel: 546525
Fax: 546904
This popular budget hotel lies opposite the central market on Avenue du 5 Juillet, a couple of

hundred metres from the main minibus stand. The clean, bright rooms with nets and en-suite hot shower are excellent value, as are the attached restaurant and bar. **$**

Volcanoes Tented Camp (Lake Burera)
Tel: 576530 ext 2513
Mobile: 085-36908
Fax: 576541
Email: salesrw@volcanoessafaris.com
www.volcanoessafaris.com
Opened in late 2003, this up-market tented camp on the shores of Lake Burera, 20 km (12 miles) from Ruhengeri off the Cyanika Road, conforms to the high standards set by Volcanoes' three lodges in Uganda. **$$$**

Hotel Izubu Meridien (Gisenyi)
Tel/fax: 083-227772
Set in lovely wooded gardens on Lake Kivu, this large but under-utilised hotel approaches international standards – good restaurant and well-maintained, clean, carpeted rooms with satellite television, telephone, fridge, private balcony and hot bath. Great value. **$$**

Palm Beach Hotel (Gisenyi)
Mobile: 085-00407
The Art Deco facade, stylish decor and light airy atmosphere combine to create a distinctly European feel, at odds with the tropical lake-shore setting. The largest rooms are en-suite with a private balcony and bath. The restaurant is the best in town. **$–$$**

Hotel Regina (Gisenyi)
Tel: 085-02226
The last word in faded tropical languor, this old colonial hotel comes complete with antiquated furnishings, wooden floor and a wide shady veranda set in an overgrown garden overlooking the lake. Not exactly luxurious, the spacious en-suite doubles are good value, and the pervasive aura of lethargy is perversely addictive. Good food. **$**

Nyungwe National Park, Butare and Cyangugu
Nyungwe National Park is serviced only by basic accommodation and a campsite. Better accommodation is available in the attractively sprawling

port of Cyangugu, which lies on the southern Lake Kivu shore 55 km (33 miles) from the national park boundary. Coming to Nyungwe from Kigali, it is also worth stopping en route at Butare, which houses the country's main university as well as a national museum whose historical and cultural displays rank with the finest in East Africa. In the vicinity of Butare, the royal palace at Nyanza was the traditional seat of the Rwanda monarchy in pre-colonial times, while the former Murambi Technical School is the site of a chilling genocide memorial in which 18,000 skeletons of genocide victims have been left in-situ.

Hotel Ibis (Butare)
Tel/fax: 530335
This stalwart hotel on the main street through Butare offers comfortable, albeit unremarkable, accommodation in en-suite rooms with hot water and television. There's a good veranda bar and restaurant. The Hotel Faucon, a couple of doors down, is the best bet if the Ibis is full. **$$**

Uwinka Campsite (Nyungwe National Park)
Set on a 2,300-metre (7550-ft) high ridge close to the main Butare-Cyangugu road, this wonderful campsite is regularly visited by L'Hoest's and silver monkeys, and a variety of forest birds. It is also the trailhead for guided walks into the forest. Drinks and firewood available, but bring your own food – and sufficient warm clothing. **$**

ORTPN Resthouse (Nyungwe National Park)
Bookings through the ORTPN office in Kigali
Situated 2 km (1½ miles) from the national park boundary near the Gisakura Tea Estate, this government-run guesthouse is less than luxurious and has a somewhat erratic water supply, but the rooms are clean and comfortable and it has a very homely atmosphere. Plenty of good walking opportunities in the vicinity. **$**

Hotel du Lac Kivu (Cyangugu)
Mobile: 085-27709
The comfortable French-run Hotel du Lac Kivu is the most up-market

in southwestern Rwanda, its smartness exaggerated somewhat by a location amid a row of semi-dilapidated buildings near the DRC border post. The open-air bar/restaurant exudes tropical riverfront ambience, and serves good food too. The en-suite rooms all have a hot shower and balcony, while suites also have television – and an extra room bereft of furnishing. **$$**

Peace Guesthouse (Cyangugu)
Tel: 085-22727
The aptly named Peace Guesthouse, built by the Anglican Church in 1998, is clean and friendly and has an attractive rustic setting overlooking the lake. Cottages, en-suite rooms and rooms using communal hot showers are available, as are decent meals. **$–$$**

Akagera National Park
Umbrella Pine Guesthouse
Tel: 66269 / 72567
Situated in Kibungo, an hour's drive from the main entrance gate to Akagera National Park, this cosy local guesthouse consists of a dozen clean but rather gloomy rooms enclosing a green central courtyard bar and unexpectedly good restaurant. **$**

Akagera Game Lodge
Tel: 567805
Email: agl@rwanda1.com
This 58-room lodge in Akagera National Park was forced to close down after the genocide in 1994 but it re-opened under private management at the end of 2003. Though somewhat monolithic in style, it offers comfortable accommodation and good facilities, from satellite television to a swimming pool and tennis court, as well as game drives and walks in the park itself. **$$$**

National Park Campsites
At least four designated campsites lie within the park. The most attractive is on the edge of the forest-fringed, hippo-infested Lake Shakani, but the sites at lakes Ihema and Hago and on the Matumba Hills all hold some appeal. Provided you've paid the nominal entrance fee, there is no charge for camping.

ART & PHOTO CREDITS

INSIGHT GUIDE
East African Wildlife
Cartographic Editor Zoë Goodwin
Production Linton Donaldson
Cover Design
Klaus Geisler, Tanvir Virdee

Index

Numbers in italics refer to photographs

Countries are identified against listings, where appropriate, with the following: Ethiopia (E); Kenya (K); Rwanda (R); Tanzania (T); Uganda (U)